# Islam and Democracy in the Middle East

A *Journal of Democracy* Book

•

Published under the auspices of
the International Forum for Democratic Studies

# Islam and Democracy in the Middle East

*Edited by Larry Diamond, Marc F. Plattner, and Daniel Brumberg*

The Johns Hopkins University Press

Baltimore and London

9 8 7 6 5 4 3 2 1

Chapters in this volume appeared in the following issues of the *Journal of Democracy:* chapters 21–23, April 1996; chapter 12, January 1998; chapter 20, July 1999; chapters 1–3, July 2000; chapters 13–15, October 2000; chapter 30, April 2002; chapters 28–29, July 2002; chapters 4–10, October 2002; chapters 11, 16–17, January 2003; chapters 18–19, 24–27, April 2003. For all reproduction rights, please contact the Johns Hopkins University Press.

The Johns Hopkins University Press
2715 North Charles Street
Baltimore, Maryland 21218-4363
www.press.jhu.edu

**Library of Congress Cataloging-in-Publication Data**

Islam and democracy in the Middle East / edited by Larry Diamond, Marc F. Plattner, and Daniel Brumberg.
    p. cm. — (A journal of democracy book)
Includes bibliographical references and index.
    ISBN 0-8018-7847-0 — ISBN 0-8018-7848-9 (pbk.)
    1. Middle East—Politics and government. 2. Islam and politics—Middle East. 3. Democracy—Middle East. I. Diamond, Larry Jay. II. Plattner, Marc F., 1945- III. Brumberg, Daniel. IV. Series.

    JQ1758.A58I85 2003
    320.956—dc21
                                                                    2003010508

A catalog record for this book is available from the British Library.

# CONTENTS

# ACKNOWLEDGMENTS

For the *Journal of Democracy,* and we hope perhaps for the wider field of democratic studies, *Islam and Democracy in the Middle East* represents a milestone in several respects. It is the fifteenth book we have published with Johns Hopkins University Press, and it marks the tenth anniversary of the publication of our first *Journal of Democracy* anthology, *The Global Resurgence of Democracy* (which has since appeared in a second edition). More importantly, it reflects both the growing concern within Middle East studies to explain the region's rather distinctive resistance to democratic change, and the recognition within comparative democratic studies of the urgent need to integrate the Middle East into our theoretical and analytical frameworks. Finally, it is the product of our conviction as editors (dating from well before September 11) that the political implications of Islam, and of trends in Islamic thinking and organization, require more careful and nuanced analytic scrutiny.

We are very pleased to be joined as coeditors of this volume by Daniel Brumberg, Associate Professor of Government at Georgetown University and a Visiting Scholar at the Carnegie Endowment for International Peace. As one of the most active members of the *Journal*'s Editorial Board, Dan has played a key role in helping to shape its treatment of the Middle East. He also made a very substantial contribution to the organization of this book, and coauthored its introduction with Larry Diamond. Marc Plattner took the lead in recruiting for the *Journal* most of the essays included here; during the past academic year, however, he was engaged in a writing project at the European University Institute in Florence, and thus played a somewhat more limited role in the preparation of this volume. Two other members of the *Journal*'s Editorial Board, Abdou Filali-Ansary and Shaul Bakhash, both represented here by essays of their own, have also been most generous in offering us advice on the region.

Some of the essays in this volume originated in two meetings that our studies program at the National Endowment for Democracy, the

International Forum for Democratic Studies, sponsored jointly with the Woodrow Wilson International Center for Scholars. The first meeting, on 13 June 2000, produced the three essays by Haleh Esfandiari, Ladan Boroumand, and Daniel Brumberg clustered under the title "Is Iran Democratizing?" The second meeting, on 25 September 2002, asked a group of distinguished Muslim speakers and commentators to identify and reflect upon the key distinguishing tenets, and the influence and prospects, of the broad tendency within current Islamic thought that is often described as "liberal" or "reformist" or "modernizing." That discussion generated the essays by Abdou Filali-Ansary ("The Sources of Enlightened Muslim Thought"), Abdelwahab El-Affendi, Radwan A. Masmoudi, and Laith Kubba appearing in the final section of this book. We are most grateful to Haleh Esfandiari, the Consulting Director of the Middle East Project at the Wilson Center, for her advice and cooperation in helping to organize and host these two meetings.

Like our previous *Journal of Democracy* collections, this book owes much to the work of an outstanding *Journal* editorial staff. Executive Editor Phil Costopoulos and Associate Editor John Gould were deeply involved in editing the more recent contributions, and we also want to thank for their contributions to the editing and production Associate Editor Zerxes Spencer, Assistant Editor Anja Håvedal, and several former members of our editorial staff: Jordan Branch, Mark Eckert, Mahindan Kanakaratnam, Kristin Helz, Miriam Kramer, and Annette Theuring. We owe a special debt to our Managing Editor, Stephanie Lewis, who supervised the production of this book—and of seven preceding *Journal of Democracy* books—with tireless skill, professionalism, imagination, patience, and good humor. We would also like to thank Craig Brown of The Last Word Indexing, who prepared the index for this volume efficiently and meticulously.

Since we began publishing in 1990, the *Journal of Democracy* has benefited from the annual financial support of the Lynde and Harry Bradley Foundation, and the enthusiastic backing of our parent organization, the National Endowment for Democracy. We are pleased to have an opportunity, once again, to thank the Bradley Foundation, the NED Board of Directors, and our friend and colleague, NED President Carl Gershman, for these many years of faithful partnership. In that same spirit, we thank once again as well the Executive Editor of Johns Hopkins University Press, Henry Tom, with whom we have worked closely on all fifteen of these books, and who was especially encouraging of our idea to produce this volume on Islam and democracy in the Middle East.

—Marc F. Plattner and Larry Diamond

# INTRODUCTION

### Daniel Brumberg and Larry Diamond

This book addresses one of the major puzzles in comparative democratic studies today. Why is the Middle East the only region of the world to have been largely untouched by the third wave of global democratization? Since 1974, the absolute number of democracies in the world has nearly tripled, while the percentage of the world's states that are democratic has doubled. Democracy has expanded significantly in every other major region of the world. In Eastern Europe and the former Soviet Union, the number of democracies has gone from none (before the downfall of communism) to 19, or 70 percent of the 27 states. In Latin America and the Caribbean, 30 of the 33 states are democracies. In 1974, less than two-fifths of those states were democracies; now nine-tenths are. In Asia (excluding the Pacific Island states), the number of democracies has increased from 5 in 1974 to 12 in 2002 (or about half of the 25 states). Even in Sub-Saharan Africa, which came late to the third wave, the number of democracies has increased from 3 to 19, about two-fifths of the 48 states.

Only in the Middle East and North Africa (what we will hereafter simply call the Middle East) has democracy failed to expand in the past three decades. In fact, in 1974, the whole region had but a trio of democracies—Israel, Turkey, and Lebanon. Today, only the first pair remains, and in Turkey, the persistence of democracy has been punctuated and constrained by repeated military interventions. Overall, the 19 states of the Middle East also have by far the lowest average levels of freedom. On the 7-point combined Freedom House scale of political rights and civil liberties, with 1 being most free and 7 the least free, the states of the Middle East have an average score today of 5.53. Not only is this the least free region of the world—by more than a full point on the Freedom House scale, as compared to the next most repressive region—but it is also the only region where the average level of freedom has *declined* since 1974 (see Table 1 on the following page). Moreover, if we examine only the 16 predominantly Arab states of the region (excluding Israel, Turkey, and Iran), the picture is even more uniformly

TABLE 1—DEMOCRACY AND FREEDOM BY REGION, 2002

| REGION | NUMBER OF COUNTRIES | NUMBER OF DEMOCRACIES (% OF TOTAL)* | NUMBER (%) OF LIBERAL DEMOCRACIES FH SCORE < 2.5 | AVERAGE FREEDOM SCORE FOR REGION | |
|---|---|---|---|---|---|
| | | | | 1974 | 2002 |
| Western Europe & Anglophone states | 28 | 28 (100%) | 28 (100%) | 1.58 | 1.04 |
| Latin America & Caribbean | 33 | 30 (91%) | 17 (52%) | 3.81 | 2.49 |
| Eastern Europe & Former Soviet Union | 27 | 19 (70%) | 4 (15%) | 6.50 | 3.39 |
| Asia (E, SE, and S) | 25 | 12 (48%) | 4 (16%) | 4.84 | 4.38 |
| Pacific Island | 12 | 11 (91%) | 8 (67%) | 2.75 | 2.00 |
| Africa (Sub-Sahara) | 48 | 19 (40%) | 5 (10%) | 5.51 | 4.33 |
| Middle East– North Africa | 19 | 2 (11%) | 1 (5%) | 5.15 | 5.53 |
| Total | 192 | 121 (63%) | 73 (38%) | 4.39 | 3.38 |
| Arab Countries | 16 | 0 | 0 | 5.59 | 5.81 |
| Predominantly Muslim Countries | 43 | 7** | 0 | 5.29 | 5.33 |

*Source:* Adrian Karatnycky, "The 2002 Freedom House Survey: Liberty's Advances in a Troubled World," *Journal of Democracy* 14 (January 2003): 100–13.
* The current number of democracies as classified by Freedom House.
** Counted among this group are Bangladesh, Mali, Niger, Senegal, Indonesia, Turkey, and Albania.

authoritarian. Among the 16 Arab states, there are no democracies, and the average level of freedom in 2002 was 5.81, compared to an average of 3.16 for the other 176 states of the world. This gap (2.65 points on the 7-point scale) has doubled since 1972 (when it was 1.34). Table 2 on page xii presents the current Freedom House rankings for all 18 Muslim-majority Middle Eastern states.

Although it is frequently asserted that Islam is incompatible with democracy, the presence of large Muslim majorities in most Middle Eastern states is not, statistically, a persuasive explanation. There appear to be 43 countries in the world where the populace is predominantly Muslim.[1] Of these, 27 are outside the Arab world, and seven among them (or about a quarter) are democracies (see Table 1 above). While this proportion is the lowest of any region of the world, it is not trivial. Moreover, as Alfred Stepan has recently noted, when one examines the level of democracy in the non-Arab Muslim world in relation to level of economic development, one finds an unusual number of "great electoral overachievers," that is, political systems that have at least a minimal electoral democracy, or what Stepan calls an "electorally competitive regime," despite falling below the level of economic development that is usually thought necessary to sustain democracy. Further, Stepan shows, non-Arab Muslim countries have witnessed considerable electoral competition over the last three decades, while the Arab world—with the sole exception of Lebanon for a few years before civil war broke out in the mid-1970s—has seen none.[2] As several of the essays in the concluding section of this book argue, there are strong substantive reasons as well to question the assumption that Islam as a religion presents a formidable obstacle to democracy.

So if Islam is not the problem, then what is? What can account for the dismal levels of democracy and freedom in the Middle East?

## Who Fears Democracy, and Why?

Autocrats do not willingly commit political suicide. In the Middle East, particularly, autocracies have repeatedly outlived predictions of their demise. This is an imposing fact, and our contributors face it squarely. Rather than speculate about the absence of substantive democratization, they highlight the roots, the nature, and most of all the perdurability of autocracy in the Arab world and Iran. This is not to underestimate the struggles of the region's democrats, which also receive space in these pages. Nor does it support the too-pat idea that Islam is a stumbling block to democracy. As the essays on Turkey and Iran suggest, and as the concluding section reminds us, political leaders have shaped Islamic norms and symbols to advance both autocracy and democracy. Still, as Guillermo O'Donnell once wrote, reality *is* compelling. So far, the durability of autocrats is *the* story of the Middle East. We can only hope that one day a happier tale will be told.

Half of our story is about rulers whose grip on economic as well as political power gives them reason to fear democracy, since political reform could strip them of their booty. The other half tells of weak oppositions that are financially and institutionally dependent on the state and, worse yet, profoundly divided by religious and ideological cleavages. These fragmented oppositions can sometimes unite to assail this or that controversial policy, be it peace with Israel or privatization of state-run industries. But saying no is not the same as saying yes. In much of the Middle East both rulers and oppositions lack the means or incentive to negotiate a political accommodation or "pact" that would ease their exit from a deeply rooted legacy of autocratic rule.

This sad outcome is the work of political, socioeconomic, cultural, and ideological forces whose roots go back decades. Mohamed Talbi's opening essay discusses two of these factors: the creation of repressive security establishments, and the control that they and their allies exert over economic resources. The tenacity with which Arab security establishments hang on to power reflects the circumstances of their birth. As Talbi notes, many an Arab ruler has climbed to the top by shoving aside or even murdering his rivals or his predecessor. Having made so many enemies, a Qadhafi or an Assad can hardly envision a safe surrender of the throne to forces outside his control. Paradoxically, the

**TABLE 2—MUSLIM-MAJORITY MIDDLE EAST STATES**

| COUNTRY | FH RANKING (PR, CL) | REGIME TYPE |
|---|---|---|
| Algeria | 6, 5 | Partial Autocracy |
| Bahrain | 5, 5 | Partial Autocracy |
| Egypt | 6, 6 | Partial Autocracy |
| Iran | 6, 6 | Partial Autocracy |
| Iraq | 7, 7 | Collapsed Full Autocracy |
| Jordan | 6, 5 | Partial Autocracy |
| Kuwait | 4, 5 | Partial Autocracy |
| Lebanon | 6, 5 | Partial Autocracy |
| Libya | 7, 7 | Full Autocracy |
| Morocco | 5, 5 | Partial Autocracy |
| Oman | 6, 5 | Partial Autocracy |
| Qatar | 6, 6 | Partial Autocracy |
| Saudi Arabia | 7, 7 | Full Autocracy |
| Syria | 7, 7 | Full Autocracy |
| Tunisia | 6, 5 | Full Autocracy |
| Turkey | 4, 4 | Illiberal Democracy |
| United Arab Emirates | 6, 5 | Partial Autocracy |
| Yemen | 6, 5 | Partial Autocracy |

longer such rulers survive, the more ruthless and potent this circular reasoning looms. A vast security apparatus may silence opponents. But its "success" only raises the cost of relinquishing power. That is why figures such as the late Moroccan king and the late Syrian president (as well as the current Egyptian president) have made such efforts to pass their rule on to their respective sons. But one thing that Middle Eastern rulers will not do is expose their rule to the uncertainties of real democracy. In other regions burdened by a lack of democracy—Latin America springs to mind—transitional "pacts" negotiated with the opposition have given autocrats such as Chile's Augusto Pinochet a kind of "insurance policy" to help ease their exit from power. Nothing like this has ever happened in the Middle East. Instead, most rulers have devoted themselves to sustaining the original "ruling bargain" by which the state provides jobs, subsidies, and a modicum of social order in return for political quiescence.

State control over economic resources—particularly (though not exclusively) oil rents—has made this autocratic social pact possible. As William Quandt, Michael Herb, and Jean-François Seznec remind us, the oil rents that flow to state elites have fused political and economic power in ways that magnify the risks of reform. State control of the economy allows rulers to fund huge patronage systems that turn workers, professionals, intellectuals, and businesspeople into dependents. While in recent years some of these client groups have pushed for democracy, the porous boundaries between business and the state powerfully promote an unhealthy collusion between commerce and autocracy.

The hobbling of forces that might otherwise play a democratizing role also has a cultural dimension, which includes but goes far beyond the question of Islam. As the contributors to this volume show us, rulers and their opponents have invoked, shaped, reinterpreted, or distorted a myriad of religious, tribal, or ethnic symbols to defend or challenge autocracy. While it may be going too far to claim, as Talbi does, that "Arab dictators have succeeded in hypnotizing their people," even an upbeat analyst such as Laith Kubba acknowledges that dictators' ability to provide jobs, welfare, and political stability has given them "broad appeal." To further close off the path to change, rulers have deliberately "depoliticized" their societies, severing people from everyday politics and encouraging apathy. While Maghraoui traces the contours of this strategy in Morocco, depoliticization remains one of the most pernicious cultural and ideological legacies of autocracy throughout the Middle East. Culturally, its patrimonial nature encourages excessive deference to hierarchical authority while harnessing symbols and traditions rooted in rural Islamic structures. Ideologically, it pushes totalitarian ideologies with decidedly *Western* roots.

Rulers have paid a high price for "normalizing" these patrimonial visions of authority. The state's dissemination of religiously inspired statist ideologies has crowded out secular, ethnic, or liberal Islamic alternatives, thus reinforcing the influence of illiberal Islamists. This is not merely because they have access to the mosque and other religious institutions. As Maghraoui notes, Islamists have made significant strides because they advance a moralistic and thus highly *apolitical* notion of authority that echoes the patrimonial ethos of the state itself. Islamist slogans such as "Islam is the solution" reproduce a legacy of depoliticization whose long-term costs are most visible in the absence of a vibrant political society throughout the Arab world.

Yet, the persistence of autocracy cannot be reduced to Islam or to its manipulation by rulers and opposition. Instead, the more fundamental *cultural* impediment to democracy lies in the failure of both Middle Eastern rulers and oppositions to forge a democratic solution to the question of national identity. As Brumberg observes, and as our case studies of Yemen, Kuwait, Morocco, and even Egypt suggest, autocracies have tolerated, sustained, and even abetted religious, tribal, ethnic, and ideological cleavages rather than resolve them democratically. This pattern is hardly unique to the Middle East. As students of "divided societies" have observed, in giving one or more ethno-religious groups the power to marginalize opposing groups (absent strong constitutional guarantees and a culture of constitutionalism), democratic elections generate risks for minority groups. These risks of democracy are especially great for minority groups that have long monopolized power by authoritarian means, and the more abusive their rule has been, the greater the risk they will suffer retribution under democracy. Nowhere has this fear been more palpable than in Syria and Iraq, where all the talk of "Arab nationalism" has barely disguised the brutal sway of an ethnic or religious minority. Over time, the very endurance of such minority-based regimes makes it more likely that even the slightest political opening will invite revenge from those who have been violently shut out. This grim logic partly accounts for the ruthlessness of Saddam Hussein's regime and the rather hasty abortion of the *glasnost* presided over by Syria's Bashar Assad.

## Liberalized Autocracy: Weakening or Growing Stronger?

While ethnoreligious divisions and their manipulation have hindered democratization, they have not excluded political reform. The leaders of Egypt, Morocco, Algeria, Jordan, and Yemen have all initiated political openings despite the persistence of profound disagreements between Islamists and secularists in the first three countries, between Bedouin tribes and Palestinians in Jordan, and between tribes representing North and South in Yemen. Indeed, the striking thing about the Middle East, and the Arab world in particular, is that despite the mix of socioeconomic, political, cultural, and ideological forces that have encouraged rulers to hold on to power, many have *promoted* a measure of political liberalization while maintaining the essential instruments of autocracy. Why is this so? What do such hybrid regimes mean for the region's future?

Many of our contributors implicitly or explicitly tackle these important questions by analyzing the roots, nature, and most of all the consequences of "liberalized autocracy" in the Arab world. In contrast to the "full autocracies" of Libya, Tunisia, Syria, and Saudi Arabia, which do not abide the slightest expression of dissent or pluralism, liberalized autocracies not only tolerate but *depend on* a limited, state-managed pluralism of ideas and organization as a strategy for legitimation and hence survival. Often adopted in response to economic crises (and in particular austerity programs mandated by the International Monetary Fund), limited liberalization and greater political participation are methods by which Arab rulers hope to offset the pain of economic reforms.

The trick, of course, is to ensure that such political openings never get out of hand. As our case studies show, Arab leaders look to liberalization as a way to divide the opposition even while letting it blow off steam. The proliferation of civil society groups, a somewhat open press, and access to the Internet and satellite television can create a feeling of virtual democracy without opening the doors to dramatic reforms. State-monitored political parties and even state-managed elections can also serve these purposes, so long as the key "ministries of sovereignty" remain under regime control. Liberalization without popular sovereignty or political accountability is thus the essence of liberalized autocracy—a form of hybrid regime that produces "elections without democracy."[3]

Is this good or bad? The answer depends at least in part on whether one sees liberalized autocracy as opening a possible path toward democracy—whatever the rulers intended—or as a self-contained system whose features hinder a transition from liberalization to democracy.

Our contributors are hardly of one mind on these crucial questions. Daniel Brumberg, for example, seems ambivalent about both the costs and benefits of liberalized autocracy. On the one hand, he argues that it can mitigate ethnoreligious and ideological conflict by providing secular, Islamist, and ethnic groups space in civil society, parliaments, and even cabinets. Such state-mandated power sharing can promote a greater measure of peaceful coexistence than might otherwise obtain in a truly competitive election, particularly one with a majoritarian, "winner-take-all" character. On the other hand, Brumberg argues that by design or default, liberalized autocracy eventually abets the influence of Islamists, thus setting the stage for a zero-sum regime-opposition conflict that raises the cost of further political reforms. For this reason he sees it as a "trap" that can ensnare regimes by encouraging even the most modern of new leaders, such as the kings of Jordan and Morocco, to skirt the challenges of substantive democratization.

William B. Quandt and Michael Herb each gives liberalized autocracy a mixed review as well. Quandt believes that Algeria's 1997 political opening has helped Berbers, Islamists, and secularists to achieve an "uneasy peace." Yet he also recognizes that state-controlled elections "have done little either to legitimize governance or to challenge the positions of those in power." Similarly, while Herb affirms that Kuwait's parliament has indeed given opposition forces real influence, he speaks volumes with his account of how easily royal factions played on Islamist-secularist splits to deflect opposition demands for an unprecedented vote of confidence. While "partial democratization," notes Herb, has allowed Islamists to advance a "good deal of illiberal policy," it has also institutionalized divisions that stymie them. Thus while affirming a "serious disconnect between democracy and liberalism in the Gulf," Herb implies that this gap has been bridged by a hybrid system that ensures that "elections matter"—but not *too* much.

Little ambivalence is on display in Jillian Schwedler's study of Yemen, Russell Lucas's analysis of Jordan, Jason Brownlee's account of Egypt, or Abdeslam Maghraoui's essay on Morocco. The first three weave an unhappy tale that begins on a positive note with a political opening that gives Islamists, Arab nationalists, secular democrats, tribal formations, or ethnic groups space to speak out and occasionally cooperate. With their command of the mosques and occasional support from elements of the regime, Islamists invariably make greater electoral gains than secularists. Fearing that Islamists are getting too powerful, regimes respond by revising constitutions, rewriting electoral rules, tightening press and association laws, or even by postponing elections, as has been the case in Jordan. As for Morocco, while Maghraoui's story ends just prior to the 2002 elections, the fact that the Islamist Justice and Development Party came in third—an unprecedented victory for any Islamist party in Morocco—suggests that the ruling establishment may one day face similar pressures to back away from political reform.

This "deliberalization" process has been especially marked in states that are vulnerable to regional and global pressures for market reform, or with pro-Western foreign policies unacceptable to key portions of the population. The monarch in Jordan has been unlucky on both scores. As Lucas observes, political liberalization sparked opposition to structural adjustment while also giving voice "to opposition critics who could not reconcile themselves to peace with Israel." In the wake of the U.S.-led war in Iraq,[4] and absent dramatic progress toward a resolution of the Palestinian-Israeli conflict, this unfortunate convergence of domestic and regional politics could spur new bouts of deliberalization, even in such recently liberalized autocracies as Bahrain and Qatar. Still, both ruling and opposition elites are likely to see the advantages of reviving forms of political accommodation that provide for some state-managed participation and pluralism even while falling short of democracy.

Indeed, it is possible that one or two full autocracies may move toward liberalized autocracy. Jean-François Seznec's analysis of Saudi Arabia, for example, suggests that despite the regime's dependence on the clerical establishment and its conservative Wahhabi-Islamic ideology, the practice of negotiation and consultation among the 15,000 or so princes of the ruling House of Saud may set the stage for a modest loosening. Finally, as some contributors argue, if Western and especially U.S. support is crucial to some liberalized autocracies, there will likely be more outside pressure for economic and political liberalization. That said, given the weakness of parliaments, the fecklessness of opposition parties, the coopted and constrained character of civil society, the subordination of judges to the executive, the state's domination of economic resources, and the challenge of illiberal Islamism, a transition from liberalized autocracy to competitive democracy still seems a long way off.

## Iran

There are many possible kinds of transitions. To get a sense of the variety, consider Iran and Turkey—two large countries of almost 70 million people each on the edge of the Middle East. The former teeters between a return to full autocracy and a chaotic move into the "gray zone" of liberalized autocracy, while the latter appears to be exiting decades of constrained and partial democracy into a more freely competitive regime. Moreover, in both countries the struggle over Islam is playing a central role in redefining the political game. While the futures of Turkey and especially Iran remain uncertain, their stories illustrate what happens when large numbers of people, some in the name of Islam, seize upon unexpected historical conjunctures to cast a ballot for democratizing change.

In Iran, as Shaul Bakhash points out, the would-be reformist President Mohammad Khatami was first elected almost by happenstance in May 1997, but then he and his reformist allies in the Majlis (parliament) won decidedly nonaccidental victories in the 2000 legislative and 2001 presidential voting. On both occasions, the wins were byproducts of at least two features of the Islamic Republic itself.

First, Khatami's victory stemmed partly from what Brumberg calls the multidimensional or "dissonant" nature of Iran's formal political system, with its strange mixture of democratic and clerical-authoritarian notions of rule. Factional tensions in the Majlis between the clericalist right and the Islamic-reformist left were serious, but the system endured because generally speaking the losers of any one fight could expect to survive politically. As Bakhash notes, with the emergence during the 1996 Majlis elections of the "Servants of Construction," a centrist group led by then-President Hashemi Rafsanjani, the "*potential* for meaningful politics" suddenly surfaced. For by backing Khatami, an important member of the clerical left, Rafsanjani opened the door to an alliance between this key wing of the ruling establishment and millions of young people in a youth-skewed population. Thus as Ladan and Roya Boroumand write in their otherwise gloomy analysis of the 2000 elections, if by the turn of the century the Iranian electorate had in fact become "an important player," this was the unintended consequence of a regime that had long ago "introduced a subversive element within a closed ideological system."

That the opposition turned this system against the clerical establishment also had something to do with the profound ideological and social changes that the Islamic Republic engendered. Some of these outcomes were hardly blessed by the clerics. By attempting to impose Islamic edicts on a new generation of young people, the clerics not only produced, in Ramin Jahanbegloo's words, a "younger generation (that) is today almost completely 'de-Islamicized,'" they also encouraged intellectuals (such as Abdul Karim Soroush) who had once championed the Islamic Revolution to rethink its very ideological foundations by holding, for instance, that Muslim piety will actually benefit from more distance between mosque and state. With its high levels of literate citizen engagement and its openly squabbling political factions, Iran presents a picture far different from that of the largely depoliticized Arab world. Keen to take on the system, young Iranians displayed a striking capacity for collective action during the 2000 elections, as Haleh Esfandiari's describes firsthand.

Three years later, much of this enthusiasm has waned under clerical-authoritarian assault. The contributions of Ladan and Roya Boroumand

and Mehrangiz Kar trace this distressing story of repression and persecution. All three remind us that the effort to silence reformists within and outside the Majlis was, and continues to be, sanctioned by the many articles in the Constitution that give ultimate power to the clerics and their Supreme Leader. Thus the very "dissonance" which at first promoted political reform has also served to contain it.

Where then is Iran going: back to full autocracy, haltingly toward liberalized autocracy, or to genuine democracy? Our contributors differ. The Boroumands see the Islamic Republic as a "unique" form of modern theocracy whose foundations rest on an ideological vision of the "people as the faithful." Enshrined in the Constitution and enforced by the Supreme Leader, this theocratic notion of community can neither abide pluralistic democracy nor long tolerate state-managed political liberalization. Thus they conclude that political reform in the Islamic Republic is inherently unstable. It will either provoke a final bout of repression and thus a return to full autocracy, or it will unwittingly open the doors to the eventual victory of democracy—or as they put it, the principle of "the people as individuals." Brumberg disagrees, arguing that Iran's evolving political system is not unique, and that its multidimensional roots might eventually support a relatively stable, if messy, blend of autocracy and political liberalization. By contrast, Jahanbegloo and Kar believe, like the Boroumands, that the contradictions that animate the Islamic Republic will probably prove its undoing.

## Turkey

While Iran may or may not be moving toward a form of liberalized autocracy, Turkey seems to be in the midst of going from a hybrid regime that blended elements of democracy, autocracy, and pluralism to one that is more liberal *and* democratic. This as-yet incomplete transformation was heralded by the resounding success of the Islamic-oriented Justice and Development Party (AKP) in the November 2002 elections. This landmark vote has prompted speculation not only about the capacity of Islamists to advance pluralistic democracy, but also about the relevance of the Turkish example for the Arab world.

Our two chapters on Turkey highlight the distinctive nature of the Turkish story. Among the historical events or trends that helped make the AKP's win possible were these: the debate over membership in the European Union that heated up after Turkey was passed over in 1997; the 1999 earthquake, which as Soli Özel puts it, "shattered" the "reified idea of an omnicompetent, paternalistic *devlet baba* (daddy state)"; the economic crises of November 2000 and February 2002, which increased the EU pressure on Turkey to undertake deeper economic and political reform; and finally, the abysmal turnout in the 2002 elections, which let the AKP sweep the board. Combined with the 10 percent threshold, this unprecedentedly low participation rate helped the AKP win nearly two-thirds of the seats with just over a third of the vote! Thus the November 2002 election was hardly a victory for political Islam. Exit polling suggests that every other AKP voter was casting a protest ballot against the traditional parties.

The deeper socioeconomic and political conditions that set the stage for the AKP's victory were also peculiar to Turkey. Among the most striking features of the Turkish case is the close and mostly *positive* connection between the perceived failures of a state-managed economic reform program and the rise of a new coalition of democratic forces outside the inherited party system. The corruption and inflation associated with economic reform alienated both the pro-globalization, export-oriented business community and the myriad of globalization skeptics represented by small businessmen, unskilled workers, and white-collar government employees. As our two essays clearly show, AKP's great feat was to craft a religious-cultural message that attracted support from both groups despite their divergent interests. This communitarian or "third way" message is not new; Islamists have long emphasized shared religious identity over class. What makes the AKP distinct is that while it is an avowedly *non-Islamist* party that favors the EU path, the AKP's popularity depends on a certain Islamist vision of politics. Is the AKP genuinely committed to liberal democracy? Our contributors offer a *qualified* yes. The AKP's support for democracy, they argue, is rooted in a long and often stormy process of political learning through which its leaders came to repudiate, in Özel's words, the "bolder—indeed at times bigoted—claims about the role of religion in politics" advanced by the AKP's Islamist predecessors.

Of course, one of the most critical factors that sets Turkey apart from the region is a state devoted to protecting secularism. While Turkey's rulers have not always consistently defended this ideal, the military's role means that the price of entry into (and survival in) the system for any party is repudiating the very idea of an Islamic state. No Arab state has an equivalent legal mechanism, nor does any have a political history that has produced such widespread and continued support for secularism as a principle of state. In addition, Turkey differs from all Arab countries in having an established tradition of truly competitive multiparty politics, which makes Islamists only one of several serious players.

Our contributors suggest that great uncertainties face the AKP. Some are economic: As Özel asks, how long can a party that represents "both many net winners and many net losers from Turkey's integration into the global economy" sustain this alliance? The other challenge is ideological. As E. Fuat Keyman and Ziya Öniş ask, how long can the AKP's hardcore supporters skirt the question of secularism by ignoring controversial issues such as the wearing of headscarves by Muslim women in public institutions? These and many other factors—not least, the fallout from the war in Iraq—may eventually fracture a party whose rise, as Özel puts it, "may have been too rapid for its own good." In as much as it "remains a coalition of forces rather than a coherent political apparatus," it will take much more than the goodwill of its leaders to turn the AKP into the Muslim equivalent of Europe's Christian Democrats.

## Secularism and Islamism

The rise of democratic Islamist forces in Turkey and Iran has generated hopes for a liberal-democratic alternative to the illiberal Islamism that has dominated much of the Middle East. Moreover, the efforts of new Islamic groups such as Turkey's AKP and Iran's leading reformist party, the Islamic Participation Front, have compelled scholars and policy makers to ask if Islamists can embrace the principle of separating, or at least distancing, mosque and state. In short, is some form of secularism compatible with and necessary for Islamist participation in a democratic political order? While many chapters in this book touch on these questions, the third section faces them most directly. Some contributors focus on the conceptual challenges of interpreting Islamic ideas in ways that support a more liberal agenda, while others emphasize the role of changing social, economic, and political conditions. While these are hardly antagonistic approaches, those who focus on the challenge of reinterpreting Islam envision a prolonged intellectual and political struggle to overcome what they believe is a deeply rooted illiberal Islamic vision of community.

To overcome this, liberal Muslim thinkers distinguish between what they see as the spiritual message of Islam and its translation over time into "historically contingent" institutions and ideologies. For example, Abdou Filali-Ansary boldly argues that Islamic values and norms are not intrinsically hostile to secularization. If the latter means a distancing of state and mosque that *protects* piety, then Islam is compatible with this notion, since nothing in its spiritual precepts or early history mandates—or even accepts—the idea of a clerical establishment with a sacred mandate to impose a single vision of *the* truth on state and society. The idea that Islam calls for a marriage of mosque and state is, he argues, a relatively recent development. The result of a tenacious misunderstanding by which nineteenth-century Islamic reformists conflated the separation of religion and politics with state-enforced atheism, this confusion has led both Muslims and non-Muslims to think of Islam as the "religion . . . most hostile to secularization and to modernity in general." With this in mind, Filali-Ansary suggests conceptual, political, and legal strategies that will help Muslims correct this stubborn misapprehension.

Ladan and Roya Boroumand advance a similar argument in their effort to trace the recent historical forces that have given rise to Islamic radicalism in Shi'ite Iran and the Sunni Arab Islamic world as well. Radical Islam, they argue, is not only of recent vintage, but much of its ideological content is inspired by or directly borrowed from Marxist-Leninist or fascist notions of political leadership and community. Thus while Islamists despise the West, some have "imported and then dressed up in Islamic-sounding verbiage some of the most dubious ideas that ever came out of the modern West," not least of which is the very notion of a totalitarian ideology. Given this imposing legacy, the only way forward is for Muslims to rediscover their "own cultural heritage" by "exposing the antimony between what the Islamists say and what Islam actually teaches."

Yet, the reader will surely ask, who has the right and moreover the power to say what Islam "actually" teaches, especially if so many lessons have already been taught? Undoing the consequences of history is no simple task, whether that history is two centuries old, as Filali-Ansary suggests, or just a few decades young, as the Boroumands argue. Since the boundary between what Islam is as a religion and what it becomes as history (or ideology) is in fact not so clear, what may count most is the capacity of one religious vision of politics to take hold in the public mind and thus obscure other alternatives, including liberal Islam. This is surely one of the key lessons suggested by Bernard Lewis's contribution to these pages. Regardless of whether one agrees with Filali-Ansary's assertion that Lewis sometimes conflates "religion" and "historical civilization," one cannot easily dismiss Lewis's claim that for centuries the "idea of freedom . . . remained alien" to Islamic societies. Indeed, the central quest of liberal Islam is to reclaim for Islamic civilization (or Islam) the very idea of individual freedom.

Radwan Masmoudi's "The Silenced Majority" takes up this challenge by arguing that Islamic practices such as *shura* (consultation) and values such as *adl* (justice) are in effect the pillars of *both* Islam and Islamic liberalism. In contrast to this well-established modernist approach, Filali-Ansary insists on a form of historicism that rejects the proposition that Islam's sacred principles carry within them any specific political message. Given what he deems the "inaccessibility of absolute truth," he rejects the idea of Islam as an archetype of truth that can serve as a blueprint for social and political order. Thus he is not keen to embrace historically bounded concepts such as Reformationism or even Islamic liberalism. Instead, he speaks of "enlightened Muslim thought," a term that points to a way of thinking rather than a form of politics. This form of thought has a postmodern feel but a long intellectual pedigree, going back to Ali Abderraziq, an early twentieth-century Egyptian reformer whose argument in favor of separating Islam and politics shook the Islamic world. And while Filali-Ansary recognizes the potential pitfalls of his "critical" approach—whose relativist spirit might be seen by some Muslims as hostile to religion itself—he nevertheless believes that "enlightened Muslim thought" provides the only conceptually safe harbor for individual freedom, the value he most cherishes. For Filali-Ansary, commitment to freedom of belief, rather than any "assertions of collective identity," ultimately distinguishes the true from the false liberal Muslim or "reformationist." This is why, in his "Muslims and Democracy," he considers Iran's Abdulkarim Soroush to be one of enlightenment Islam's leading spokesmen, while he dismisses Tunisia's Rachid al-Ghannouchi as a "counter-Reformationist" whose ultimate goal is to subordinate the individual to the collective power and authority of the Islamic community.

The reconceptualization of Islam that enlightened (or liberal) Islamic thinkers call for will probably not be achieved for years or even decades. A conceptually complex project, it has frequently been undermined by rapid social, economic, and political changes that have weakened its social base. Indeed, as Abdelwahab El-Affendi notes, liberalism and democracy are potentially antagonistic projects, a point amply illustrated by the election of illiberal Islamists in Algeria, Egypt, Kuwait, and Morocco. Masmoudi agrees. He and his Muslim liberal colleagues, he writes, "are caught between a rock and a hard place," in that they are equally opposed to the quasi-secular autocracies that rule the Arab world and to the illiberal Islamists who are the first to benefit from the former's hesitant political openings.

Are there political and institutional solutions to this familiar dilemma? Given what he sees as the "hotly contested" nature of the term "liberal," and even more so, the distinct possibility that a push for a genuine reformation of Islam will produce more rather than less political stability, El-Affendi appears to favor a pragmatic coalition strategy that brings together a myriad of Islamist parties and trends, including those that "prefer to postpone or bypass the thorny issues implied by a commitment to both liberalism and Islam." Similarly, rather than exclude illiberal Islamists from the political arena, Vicki Langohr thinks that Arab leaders should promote a policy of "gradual democratization" by which new secular or non-Islamist parties gain effective entrance to the political system. While the participation of such parties would not be sure to make Islamists drop their illiberal agendas and ideologies, it might eventually contain the latter's influence, making reform less risky and hence more likely. All this assumes, of course, that those in power will be willing to undertake the kinds of reforms that most Arab leaders have thus far skirted. Brumberg makes a similar point in his "Islamists and the Politics of Consensus." Yet he also argues that absent a legacy of relative political pluralism or "dissonance," even the best-intentioned reformers will find it hard to manufacture political competition, or to move beyond the state-managed power-sharing arrangements that are typical of liberalized autocracies such as Jordan, Algeria, Morocco, and Kuwait.

## Will Anything Really Change?

The war in Iraq took place as this book was going to press. It is difficult to comprehend from this vantage point how the collapse of Saddam Hussein's regime —and the postwar reconstruction of Iraq—will affect the overall political climate in the Middle East and the prospects for *sustained* political liberalization and democratization in the region. Certainly, a successful political reconstruction of Iraq along relatively democratic lines could encourage democratic reform elsewhere in the region. Yet it is all too easy to imagine ways in which failure to establish a democratic and genuinely independent Iraq could broadly impair democratic prospects in the Middle East.

Even if political reconstruction in Iraq manages (against long odds) to overcome the challenges of religious, ethnic, and factional divisions, and to avoid a destabilizing popular reaction against the transitional process itself, a huge regional challenge will need to be confronted. The future of democracy in the Middle East will remain bleak absent a permanent, peaceful, and mutually negotiated two-state solution to the Palestinian-Israeli conflict. Over the past several decades, this conflict has generated a heavy fog over Arab politics. Arab governments have used it relentlessly to legitimate their rule—by stressing the authenticity of their commitment to something larger than themselves—and have relied on it more and more as the older forms of nationalism and pan-Arabism have lost their luster. The conflict siphons off much energy and passion that Arab intellectuals and political activists might otherwise devote to political failings closer to home. The discussion of the true shortcomings that hamper Arab development—so eloquently expressed in the 2002 *Arab Human Development Report*[5]—has been distorted and deflected by this intense symbolic struggle over Arab identity and dignity. Until this fog lifts—so that the peoples of the Arab world can see and debate more clearly the real obstacles to national progress, and so that radical Islamists lose one of their most powerful rallying cries—genuine and lasting democratization will be unlikely in the region.

Democratization in the Arab world will also require serious thinking about the modes, phases, and sequences through which political liberalization and democratization might ultimately occur in different kinds of states. As the many essays in this volume remind us, while rapid democratization might sometimes invite radical forces and thus lead to more rather than less autocracy, a process of political "reform" intended mainly to sustain autocracy is hardly promising. The key challenge facing the Arab world is not political liberalization per se, but rather how to transform liberalization into a vehicle for genuine and lasting democratization.

Such a transformation will require innovative thinking. A demand-side approach that makes civil society organizations the sole or chief vehicle of change must be supplemented by a supply-side approach that harnesses a wide variety of state, or state-linked, institutions to the drive for genuine political reform. Courts must be given genuine independence. Constitutions must be redrafted not only to protect basic human rights, but also to give parliaments real authority to speak, legislate, and monitor executive power on the voters' behalf. And political parties must benefit from laws and constitutions that give them the means and the right to speak on behalf of different constituencies and interests. With such an infusion of ideological and institutional pluralism into the still-hobbled civil and political societies of the Arab world, regimes and oppositions that had previously faced off in a zero-sum confrontation could find new ways to compromise and thus redefine the very goals of political liberalization.

Timing and sequencing could prove crucial. As the essays in this volume show, Arab political systems today have a highly distorted political landscape. In the "liberalized" autocracies, many of the parties and interest associations that dominate politics today are in effect arms of the ruling apparat. The main alternatives are often illiberal Islamist organizations and political parties. Thus, moderate, pluralistic, questioning, and tolerant political forces (whether secular or Islamist) are caught between the rock of the patrimonial state and the hard place of illiberal Islamism. A quick political opening, moreover, could make things worse by forcing moderate forces to compete unprepared. A program of political liberalization that *actually* intended to achieve democratization would provide breathing space for these tendencies. It would lift virtually all restrictions on the press, on intellectual life, and on peaceful associations of citizens. And it would set up independent institutions of "horizontal accountability"—not only courts but electoral commissions, audit offices, anticorruption agencies, and central banks—that would constrain the power of government and so lower the stakes in controlling power. These reforms could then generate the climate for more meaningful, free and fair electoral competition, which might be phased in (at successively higher levels of political authority) over some period of years. Needless to say, such a process of gradual democratic transformation would take considerably longer in a closed autocracy like Saudi Arabia, with no history of organized civil and political pluralism, than it would in Morocco or Jordan. But every Arab state could develop a strategy and make a start—if there was the *will* for truly democratic reform.

Yet it is precisely this will that is lacking. The Middle East faces a paradox that is hardly unique to the region: Real, lasting, and peaceful democratic change requires the state to implement far-reaching reforms. But for this to occur, the state must also reform itself. Overcoming this paradox will require a push from both within and without. From within, democratization requires political leaders with the vision and political skill to challenge those in power who want to retain liberalization (if at all) simply as a handy tactic for autocrats. From without, democratization will require the West—and especially the United States—to take a new stand. Having talked about the need for democracy in the Arab world, the present and future U.S. administrations must address the heart of the matter, which remains the nature of the Arab state in all its political, social, and ideological manifestations.

While this collection of essays highlights the endurance of Middle East autocracies, we remain hopeful that such a combination of change from within and pressure from without will eventually open a path to real democratization. State-managed liberalization may be a trap, but because the severity of that trap differs from regime to regime, some states are better positioned to adopt the kinds of reforms that we have outlined above. Smaller countries that are not hamstrung by economic crisis, and that are just beginning to travel the path of liberalization, may be better positioned to turn liberalization into a force for real change. To date, the signals from new liberalizers such as Bahrain and Qatar have been mixed. They have opened up politics somewhat, and Bahrain has even held parliamentary elections. But Bahrain's ban on political parties and its constitutional reinforcement of monarchical authority are not encouraging. Experience suggests that the longer a country goes down the path of liberalized autocracy (with its frequent detours and cul-de-sacs), the harder it becomes to chart a new path to real democracy.

That said, some of the more experienced liberalized autocracies that boast some legacy of competitive party politics, and which are led by innovative leaders who can see beyond the logic of day-to-day survival, might also make some progress. Among these Morocco may be the leading candidate. It must tackle profound economic problems and then ensure that its Islamists face strong-enough competition from non-Islamist parties to keep the Islamists within the bounds of pluralistic politics. Kuwait is also a candidate to move beyond liberalized autocracy. The royal family must stop playing secularists off against Islamists, must allow the creation of formal political parties, and must promote constitutional changes that would give parliament real authority. But given the sharp divisions between parliament's Islamist and secularist factions, and in particular the repeated and often successful efforts of the former to pass various illiberal laws, Kuwait's leaders lack the incentive to redefine the rules of the game.

What of full autocracies? While there are far more impediments to change in these regimes than in liberalized autocracies, the term "full autocracy" covers a range of regimes, some of whose leaders and oppositions may eventually see the advantages of moving from full to liberalized autocracy. For example, while the Al-Saud family's dependence on the conservative clerical establishment surely limits its capacity for reform, it has also generated unhappiness with Wahhabi ideology within some modern sectors of society. This discontent might eventually be tapped through the Shura Council to create a constituency for reform that can counterbalance the Wahhabi clerics. Turning to the Maghreb, it is not inconceivable that Tunisia's leaders will one day see the logic of state-managed liberalization. The country's relative economic success has created a middle-class constituency that President Ben Ali has counted on to back his version of bureaucratic authoritarianism. But this very constituency might one day press him or his successor (as it did the authoritarian leaders of South Korea and Taiwan) to initiate a political opening.

History does not provide fertile ground for optimism about the democratic prospect in the Middle East. Barring fundamental change from within and without, new political reforms seem likely only to repeat the cycle of repression and liberalization, or in some cases, to enlarge the ranks of liberalized autocracies in the Arab world. But virtually every region in the world that has witnessed substantial democratization had, at some prior point, a history that projected a dim future for freedom. Cultures can and do change. Powerful events, social and economic forces, and skillful, determined leaders can reshape history. Autocracies have survived in the Middle East, but have failed at governance and failed to gain popular legitimacy. The people of the region are ready for systemic political change. This readiness at least opens the possibility that, with the right type of strategy, leadership, and international engagement, political change in the Middle East might finally open a path to democracy.

## NOTES

1. Freedom House lists 47 such states, but it is not clear that Nigeria, Sierra Leone, Eritrea, and Burkina Faso are Muslim-majority states.

2. Alfred Stepan with Graeme B. Robertson, "An 'Arab' More Than 'Muslim' Electoral Gap" *Journal of Democracy* 14 (July 2003).

3. For an exploration of the concept of hybrid regimes and the dynamics of "elections without democracy," see the articles by Larry Diamond, Andreas Schedler, Steven Levitsky, and Lucan A. Way, and Nicolas van de Walle, in the *Journal of Democracy* 13 (April 2002): 21–80.

4. As noted later in this intro, this book went to press just at the time Saddam was overthrown, and most references to Iraq refer to the Ba'athist regime.

5. United Nations Development Programme, *Arab Human Development Report 2002* (New York: UNDP, 2002).

# I

# Democratization in the Arab World

# 1

# A RECORD OF FAILURE

## Mohamed Talbi

*Mohamed Talbi is a Tunisian historian who has authored a number of books and articles on the history of the Maghreb. His publications in-clude* Iyal Allah *(God's family), published in French translation in 1996 as* Plaidoyer pour un Islam moderne. *This essay originally appeared in the July 2000 issue of the* Journal of Democracy *and was translated from the French by Zerxes Spencer.*

Everywhere today, democracy is proving contagious. It may be spread-ing faster in some regions than in others, but it is spreading. Even in Serbia and even in China. Everywhere except in the Arab world. This calls for reflection and at least an attempt at explanation. If the criterion of a democracy is the turnover of political power by peaceful means, that is, by elections considered free, fair, perfectly transparent, and in-disputably and irrefutably incontestable—in a word, honest—then not a single Arab country is democratic today. Lebanon, which paid a heavy price for its civil war (1976–91), is a special case. It is still too early to draw any conclusions from the apparently free elections that took place in Kuwait in June 1999 (especially if one considers previous failures), and the Algerian elections of 1999 were disappointing.

A leader who gains power by taking the life of his predecessor, and in doing so runs the risk of having his own life taken, lets go of power only when he in turn is eliminated. He stops short of no crime in order to cling to power (and to life) for as long as possible. This is the classic scenario in Arab countries today, not of alternation in power but of suc-cession through violent death or, in the best of cases, death by natural causes. It is that simple. Gamal Abdel Nasser of Egypt, who had de-posed King Farouk I in 1952, escaped several assassination attempts and ended up dying in his bed in 1970, adored by his people. His suc-cessor, Anwar Sadat (1970–81), was not so lucky. If Hosni Mubarak, who succeeded Sadat, is still alive, it is not for want of zeal on the part of his adversaries. On 26 June 1995, they barely missed killing him at the airport in Addis Ababa, where he was on his way to attend a summit of the Organization of African Unity. At the end of August 1999, he escaped a third amateur assassination attempt, this time by knifepoint, at Port Said in Egypt. By resorting to repression and tight security—very tight if necessary, with two or more police officers stationed every 100 meters along the route to public appearances and with metal detectors set up at the entrance to meeting places—and by resorting to crimes as well, one who deposes or kills in order to take power may be fortunate enough to die of natural causes. Luck also plays its part. That was the case with the late King Hassan II of Morocco who, on two occasions, miraculously survived well-planned assassination attempts—the first on 10 July 1971, when 200 people lost their lives at the Skhirat Palace near Rabat, and the second the following year, when his royal Boeing aircraft, fired upon and seriously damaged in an attack by six Moroccan soldiers, succeeded in landing without loss of human life.

The seizure of power, particularly by assassination, inevitably creates a vicious circle that leaves no room for any other alternative, much less for alternation of power. The system is not angelic and it is not run by choir boys. Moreover, it is old—very old—in the Arab world. It is a tradition. In the history of the Arab-Muslim world, "Oriental despotism" (the term is Montesquieu's) has always had its own ruthless and bloody logic. One might respond that this same model can be found throughout human history. Yes, of course, but with this difference: Wherever democracy has taken root, the battlefield has been displaced as the arena for gaining power. The clash of arms has given way to the verdict of the ballot box. One might reply that the Arab world is not lacking in ballot boxes. I would agree. I would even add that they are not only numerous but also very well stuffed. And that is precisely where the difference lies.

In some parts of the Arab world, democracy simply doesn't exist—because, in the eyes of Islamic radicalism, it is incompatible with Islam: "There is no power other than God's." This is clear and unambiguous. Saudi Arabia's constitution is the Koran. Elsewhere in the Arab world, democracy is indeed in the constitution.[1] In such cases, things are much less clear and very ambiguous. For there is a huge gap between theory and practice. In virtually all Arab states, democracy in practice is no more than a theatrical production. We are actors in a democratic play, with all the stage settings and all the Western words that the play demands, including the suspense that surrounds the counting of the votes. Western newspapers speak of fairs and carnivals, and they are not wrong. As a matter of fact, elections in the Arab world are nothing but a bad joke, a farce, an immense masquerade, after which the stuffing of the ballot boxes begins behind closed doors. All the Arab democracies are characterized by surreal and absurd vote totals for the ruler, whoever he may be. Except in really exceptional cases, like the recent elections in Algeria, the passing grade always lies above 99 percent.

These percentages are not, as one might believe, the result of naiveté, and still less of political blunders. They are carefully calculated. As in all fascist states based on sham elections, these deliberately absurd and intentionally ridiculous percentages serve a specific purpose. In the first place, the regimes are able to discredit and dishonor the intelligentsia by making them swallow these sham results and even publicly affirm them. Thus the backbones of the intellectuals are softened beyond all limits. They are neutralized, rendered servile, and if need be, compromised by being induced to partake of the dubious but irresistible benefits of power.

All the Arab countries have seen, to varying degrees, huge fortunes amassed in the shadows of power. Ibn Khaldun (1332–1406) had already made this observation. Corruption and dictatorship go hand in hand. Not that corruption is always necessary, by the way. All it takes is to offer promotions, the highest-ranking and best-paid positions, foreign diplomatic posts, cars, honors, awards, even taxi licenses, to the most deserving and unconditionally devoted—all the privileges that can be withheld or withdrawn from the rest for their lack of zeal and then redistributed. All the Arab authors of *Nasihat al-Muluk* (Counsel for kings) insisted on the perpetual need for the king to have something to give, to withdraw, or, if need be, to confiscate, in order to keep a tight rein on his world.

## The Freedom To Shut Up

Invited by Robert Badinter to attend the commemorative ceremonies of the fiftieth anniversary of the Universal Declaration of Human Rights on 7–10 December 1998, I was able to bear witness to the bad publicity Tunisia was getting in the area of human rights. Morocco, which had made serious efforts in this field, was among the states represented by its prime minister, who had the honor of delivering an address from the podium. Representatives from Tunisia were very few, as the state had confiscated the passports of its most credible human rights activists. Assigned to prominent (and empty) seats, they were conspicuous by their absence. Tunisia could not have made a worse decision. The result? The two states singled out for their grave human rights abuses were Algeria and Tunisia.

Returning to Tunis, I witnessed quite a change in tone and setting. The event was celebrated with great caution. The High Committee for Human Rights and Basic Liberties, a governmental body of which I am a member, chose as its venue for the celebration a small room in a hotel and did not spend much on publicity. Most of the committee members did not bother to attend. Before a small crowd of no more than 20 people, the opening speaker traced the history of human rights, going very far back into the past. The next speech, a highly abstract sociophilosophical presentation, was delivered by a well-known sociologist and respected academic who had always (alongside his teaching job) held senior administrative positions in Tunisia or served as a Tunisian delegate to international bodies. There were only mid-level officials in the room. A young academic who also served in some cultural post within the ruling party seized the opportunity to distinguish himself. "What you are saying is all very well," he said, putting his foot in it, "but tell us what happened to human rights in Tunisia after the 'blessed turn'?" (This expression is used to refer to the deposing of President Habib Bourguiba in 1987 by his prime minister Zine el-Abidine Ben Ali, who succeeded him as president.) There was no way to sidestep the issue. The speaker was forced to extol the virtues of the government. With an appropriately solemn tone of voice, he declared: "In all its history, Tunisia has never enjoyed so much liberty and respect for human rights." Thus was said what had to be said. End of discussion. The meeting could have come to an end there and then, and it did. As we left, the young academic turned to me and said: "You're the one who taught us to be critical!" There are moments when one regrets having been a teacher. I do not know what followed. I never went back.

Dishonored, discredited, and compromised, Tunisia's intelligentsia has been domesticated and, at the slightest divergence of opinion, disposed of. Brains are thus weakened, emptied of all principles, of all thought, of all desire for thought. Bodies are stripped of their bones to the point where human beings are reduced to invertebrates crawling before their master. As for intellectuals who remain defiant, they are, in the best of cases, left with but one freedom: the freedom to shut up. In the name of "encouraging" culture, the state has set up several governmental organs, all of which, operating under different designations, play the role of a Holy Office for Mental Purity. All that is heard, seen, read, and written within the country is tightly controlled and filtered.

I can offer some examples from my own relatively privileged experience as a writer and academic. My two books published by Cérès (Tunis), *Iyal Allah* (God's family) and *Umat al-Wasat* (The median community), were first banned and then, after the intervention of the publisher (who had directed Ben Ali's first presidential campaign), were finally granted publication. The first book brought me three pages of invective in *Al-Sahafa,* where I had already been labeled a fundamentalist (the most serious accusation in Tunisia), an opportunist, and finally, a traitor. I was immediately relieved of my duties as president of the National Cultural Committee. The author of the pages in question then found himself entrusted with the duties of director of publications and copyright registration in the Ministry of the Interior. Nothing enters the country or gets published without his authorization. I had to approach him on 30 March 1999 to obtain clearance from Customs to release Tariq Ramadan's book, *Aux sources du renouveau musulman* in Tunisia. It was not the first time. Nothing escaped the vigilance of the department that he directed—he has since been transferred—not even erudite university theses. One such thesis, on the topic of *ridda* (apostasy) in Islam (not exactly a dangerous subject for the state), was defended under my chairmanship and awarded highest honors but was never allowed to be published in Tunisia. It appeared in abridged form and under a different title in Morocco. My ten-year-old request to publish, in collaboration with university colleagues, a journal called *Al-Maqasid,* aimed at contributing to a renewal of Muslim thought, has remained unanswered.

On 24 February 1999, I received an invitation from the Tunis-based ALESCO, the Arab UNESCO, to contribute to an encyclopedia of Arab and Muslim men of learning. At the bottom of the registration form were the words: "To secure your participation, is it necessary to gain prior permission from your government, or from any other authority? If so, to what department and at what address must the request be directed?" It is as if a French academic, invited by UNESCO to write a biographical entry on Du Bellay, Ronsard, or Thomas More for the *Encyclopædia Universalis,* first had to obtain authorization from Jacques Chirac, Lionel Jospin, or another authority, who could only be the minister of the interior. In their eagerness to hunt down all free thought, Arab countries fear no ridicule whatsoever. They have undeniably become masters in this field, who can proclaim, without feigned indignation, that they really have "no lessons to learn from anyone." I returned the form with this simple note: "Thank you for your offer. I find in it an eloquent indication of the extent of a researcher's freedom in the Arab world." Arab countries do not allow freedom of thought. How can they allow true democracy, which respects human dignity and human rights? Where necessary, their surveillance spares neither the telephone nor the mail, neither the fax nor the Internet. That is the sad truth to which we must resign ourselves.

## Information Is the Enemy

As for what comes from abroad, the censors do their best within the limits of technology. And Arab countries are all experts in this field. We would be more than willing to share the optimism of David Gardner, who writes in the *Financial Times:* "The Arab powers will lose their battle against the Internet, for the ways of evading censorship are evolving very rapidly."[2] For the moment, however, it is censorship that is winning and that brings in money, for it is in good hands and it pays well. Today, it is Saudi Arabia—the property of the Al-Saoud family—that has "the most ambitious plan in the region to block the flow of undesirable information," notes Human Rights Watch. Saudi Arabia also relies upon limiting the number of its Internet subscribers, who constitute less than one percent of the population. Other countries are even stricter. Iraq and Libya are simply not connected to the World Wide Web. Syria, which had been connected, subsequently blocked access to it. Bahrain, whose economy relies on communications, has recourse to standard methods of surveillance. That is the case with Tunisia as well. Yet we are assured that the methods of evading censorship are evolving faster than the technology of controlling information. This is a race that the leaders of the Arab world will make every effort to win. For them, information is the enemy.

The leaders of the Arab countries cannot take freedom of information lightly. Democracy is ruinous. Nelson Mandela is poor, and the poet Leopold Senghor lives in the clouds. The presidency of South Africa and of Senegal, respectively, have left them with nothing for their old age. What improvidence! While democrats fail to get rich because democracy requires working under the bright light of day, dictators amass huge fortunes because their system allows them to work under cover of darkness. Thus the choice of all the Arab leaders. The historical model will no doubt remain that of President Mobutu of Zaire (1960–61 and 1965–96), which makes him worth recalling. Mobutu was a master of the field who knew how to strike a fine balance between his personal fortune, discreetly concealed in the West, and the foreign debt of his country. He had seized power in a putsch and he was ousted from power in a putsch by Laurent Désiré Kabila. While Mobutu may not have carried his treasures with him to heaven—or rather, to hell—he nonetheless remains to his fellow dictators an exemplar of foresight and know-how, thanks to his infallible system of control over information and all forms of expression of which democracy is capable and culpable.

In Iraq, we find a deadlier version of the same scenario. It would not be good for Iraqis, dying today of sickness and hunger after seeing hundreds of thousands die on the battlefields, to find out that the personal fortune of their president, Saddam Hussein, in power since 1979, amounts to $6 billion, all in unfrozen foreign assets, as far as we can tell. This news would surely be of little consolation to them. It might even trouble them greatly. Hence the absolute imperative of controlling information. Too bad! The advantages of the Internet to the economy are sacrificed, despite the knowledge that this adds to the misery of an already sufficiently miserable people. On all fronts, democracy runs counter to the ruler's own interests. Thus it must be burned at the altar of the cult of the leader and served up as offerings, for which the ruler has a voracious appetite and without which his anger would rival that of the gods. He also has his own hell to punish the ungrateful. The Orient has its traditions.

In May 1999, *Forbes* magazine published a list of the ten wealthiest heads of state in the world. It included the Sultan of Brunei (1st), Queen Beatrix of the Netherlands (7th), and Queen Elizabeth II (10th). The remaining seven largest fortunes were owned by Arab rulers, all of whom govern poor countries. The list is presented, without further comment, in the Table on the facing page.

With the drop in the price of oil—which no longer exercises the same constraints on the world economy thanks to the discovery of new oil deposits and new sources of energy—Saudi Arabia is beginning to face financial difficulties and even to go into debt. Yet its king continues to

## TABLE—THE WORLD'S WEALTHIEST HEADS-OF-STATE

| RANK | NAME | COUNTRY | FORTUNE (in billions of $) | IN POWER SINCE |
|------|------|---------|---------------------------|----------------|
| 1 | SULTAN HASSANAL BOLKIAH | Brunei | 30.0 | 1967 |
| 2 | KING FAHD | Saudi Arabia | 28.0 | 1982 |
| 3 | SHEIKH ZAYED IBN SULTAN | Abu Dhabi | 20.0 | 1966 |
| 4 | PRINCE JABER | Kuwait | 17.0 | 1977 |
| 5 | SHEIKH MAKHTOUM | Dubai | 12.0 | 1990 |
| 6 | SADDAM HUSSSEIN | Iraq | 6.0 | 1979 |
| 7 | QUEEN BEATRIX | The Netherlands | 5.2 | 1980 |
| 8 | PRINCE HAMAD | Qatar | 5.0 | 1995 |
| 9 | PRESIDENT HAFIZ AL-ASSAD | Syria | 2.0 | 1971 |
| 10 | QUEEN ELIZABETH II | United Kingdom | 0.45* | 1952 |

Source: Forbes, May 1999.
* This figure is higher ($16 billion) when the Royal Collection, with the crown jewels, is included.

live with the same ostentation as in *One Thousand and One Nights*. The French magazine *Jeune Afrique* describes what a stir his arrival last year caused at his Marbella Palace in Spain, which he had not visited in 12 years: "Two hundred tons of luggage, 25 Rolls Royces and other luxury vehicles, 400 servants, cabinet ministers (including the minister of health—the king is 78 years old and diabetic), the renting of 250 suites and deluxe rooms in the hotels of the Coast. . . . The people in his entourage spend lots of money: 120,000 French francs per day in the large department stores alone, which are opened at night especially for them."[3] What? A proper fairy tale in the true Oriental tradition, one that does not fall short of the legendary munificence of Harun al-Rashid . . . but with infinitely less power and historical weight.

## Corruption and the Rule of Law

In an interview reported in the French weekly *Le Point,* Jean-Michel Foulquier reminds us that "corruption gave rise to Islamism in Arabia and in Algeria."[4] We too often forget this! One need only add: not just in Arabia and Algeria. It is true, however, that Saudi Arabia remains an unsurpassable model. Whereas France devotes 4 percent of its GDP to the military, Saudi Arabia devotes 30 percent. Why? Is the country so threatened? Its neighbors and Israel are nothing but alibis. All events prove it. No, the secret lies elsewhere. Arms purchases are lucrative for "the royal family, which receives, for every contract, 30–40 percent in commissions." Too bad if the "number of combat planes already greatly exceeds the number of qualified pilots available"![5] For combat, there are the Americans, who, as everyone knows, do not work for nothing— which of course increases the bill. But the royal family must feed itself, and it must feed its 6,000 princes. This is not *baqshish* (bribery) or small-scale corruption. It is not a petty theft that deserves, as a just and heavenly punishment, the amputation of the hand. This is High Art, for which the jesuitism of the well-paid Grand *Faqihs* (Guardians) of the Kingdom will find proper *fatwas* that render all dissidence punishable under Holy Law.

All Arab dictators maintain that the law—whether it be Islamic law *(shari'a)* or civil law—is on their side. They all claim to adhere to the "rule of law." If that is what they want to say, fine. But one must know what law and what justice? After all the observations that we have made, it may at first seem surprising to note the absence of protests and the chorus of praise that accompany each electoral exercise and its obvi- ously absurd results. To understand, one must have read George Orwell's famous novels *Animal Farm* and especially *Nineteen Eighty-Four*. The English novelist's predictions were mistaken only in terms of geogra- phy. Big Brother is indeed governing in the Arab "democracies," which, according to the irrefutable slogan, have "no lessons to learn from any- one." A very sophisticated police force, well staffed with law-enforcement officers, ensures that order reigns. A vigilant justice system pursues and severely punishes acts of defamation and anything else that may disrupt public order. And in the absence of convincing evidence to the contrary— evidence that is, moreover, impossible to furnish—all protests are acts of defamation inherently prone to disrupting public order. The punishments provided by law can greatly exceed ten years of incarceration in condi- tions that, according to countless corroborating testimonies, would make anyone shudder. To protest under such conditions, one must be a candi- date for martyrdom. And I have not even mentioned the parallel processes that provide a still more powerful and effective deterrent: disappearance, abduction, torture to the point of death, the destruction of goods, and all kinds of troubles that render daily life unlivable.

Today, the Arab world has captured the sad prize, previously held by Latin America, for cruel treatment of all kinds. One has merely to consult the publications of the specialized international organizations—Amnesty International, Human Rights Watch, Actualité-International, Reporters Sans Frontières, and the United Nations—to see how scathing they all are regarding the Arab countries. There is also a whole body of literature available to those seeking more information. Some examples include: Jean-Michel Foulquier (France's former ambassador to Riyadh), *Arabie Saoudite, La Dictature protégée*; Gilles Perrault, *Notre ami le roi* (Hassan II of Morocco); Ahmad Manaï, *Le Jardin secret du général Ben Ali* (the president of Tunisia); and Pierre Guingam, *Hafez El Asad et le parti Baât en Syrie*. There is also the journal *Conscience et liberté*. Yet who could ever calculate and tally all the deaths in the prisons of Syria? Who could ever count the victims of Iraq's "campaign to cleanse prisons" by murder or the victims of its war waged with chemical weapons against the Kurds in 1988? The Algerian Movement of Free Officers (MAOL), founded in 1997, maintains that, from 1992 to 1998, the Algerian civil war claimed 173,000 lives, including 25,000 to 26,000 members of the security forces. On 18 August 1999, the MAOL urged the families of the disappeared to file a lawsuit against those responsible for the tragedy, starting with the generals.[6]

## Applauding the Leader

When one considers the great lengths to which Arab leaders go to quash the spirit of freedom of their people, the latter's apparent lack of protest no longer seems so surprising and becomes easier to understand and explain. Today, the Arab countries are the world leader in the industry of repression, ranging from disinformation to the use of poison gas. Operated with perfect know-how and with an energy that leaves no room for scruples, it turns the masses into puppets, a development that is unique to Arab countries and is visible on television to all observers. It is more than just lethargy: Arab dictators have succeeded in hypnotizing their people.

Everyone applauds the leader. There is not even any need to press a button anymore. Worshipping one's leader has become a conditioned reflex, reminiscent of Pavlov's dog: The leader's appearance always triggers thunderous applause. The most zealous vow to sacrifice their blood for him and shriek their undying loyalty until their voices are hoarse and their bodies exhausted. It is not uncommon to see some of them contorting themselves as if in an enraptured dance. It is a gripping spectacle, greatly enjoyed by the leader, whose passage through the crowds has the effect of a huge collective brainwashing. Bourguiba had become a master of this art. Now we are better able to understand how the system works and endures. We also understand why the leader of an "Arab democracy," who has invariably assumed power through a putsch—deposing or taking the life of his predecessor—or by rigging the system, does not become a criticizable swine until his successor has, in turn, eliminated him. *Ut fata trahunt!* As fate determines! Some may think that is a reference to the "fatalism" of Islam, but the proverb is Latin.

Has anything actually changed for the Arab masses since they gained their independence? They are told that they are now citizens. *Muwatinun la Ra'aya* (Citizens, not subjects) was the title of a book that caused quite a stir in the Arab world in the middle of the twentieth century. But the Arabs have never been citizens. They have had neither the time nor the opportunity. Subjected to corrupt, perverted, and crumbling powers, they became colonized natives, and they now find themselves subjects again, even if they are pompously called citizens to create an illusion of modernity. They are still led by the *Asa al ta'a* (the stick of obedience), about which Ibn Khaldun wrote such illuminating accounts that they scarcely seem to have aged a day. Today, the *Asa al ta'a* has taken the form of more effective tools in the hands of the police, but that is where modernity stops. With the stick, and with all the many other kinds of tools that modern technology offers, the so-called citizens of the Arab world are driven down uncertain, hazardous paths not of their own choosing, paths that draw them into disastrous wars (Israel or Iran), inter-Arab conflicts (Saudi Arabia–Yemen–Egypt, Iraq-Kuwait, Algeria-Morocco-Mauritania-Polisario), or civil wars (North Yemen–South Yemen, the Lebanese-Syrian imbroglio, Sudan, Algeria). The crowning moment, disastrous for all the Arabs, was the Gulf War—that masterpiece of stupidity triggered by Saddam Hussein, who was nonetheless a "good dictator," greatly prized by the United States for services rendered against Iranian Islamism. His pigheadedness until almost the very end was so absurd that it is hard not to think that he had been manipulated by the CIA, as many believe.

As for economic development, what can one say? There is famine in Sudan, that potentially rich breadbasket that could feed the entire Arab world and beyond. Overall, Arab countries depend on the rest of the world for their food. Their wealth lies abroad, largely frozen in property holdings. They export workers and import unemployment. Those Arabs with money invest it first and foremost in the West, and sparingly in the Arab world, for the latter is considered altogether less stable and less profitable. Arab dictators embrace each other heartily and distrust each other even more heartily. When circumstances change, the leaders are often unpredictable, which makes their commitments hollow and often without result. The consequences for development are fatal.

Nevertheless, the balance sheet is not altogether negative. None of the Arab countries are bankrupt, and there are some successes. The differences one encounters from one country to the next are sometimes enormous. Yet there remains a yawning gulf between what could have been done by people exercising democratic control over their lives and what has in fact been done by alienating, degrading, corrupt, and corrupting dictatorships. There is nothing in the initially far richer Arab countries to remind one of South Korea—a country that, at a critical juncture in the middle of the twentieth century, chose democracy and knew how to achieve it. It would be difficult, I believe, to dispute this assessment. Yet the Arab peoples, having been thoroughly subjugated, continue frantically to applaud.

## NOTES

1. See *Dustur,* in *L'Encyclopédie de l'Islam II,* 655–94; Abdefattah Amor, *Constitution et religion dans les Etats musulmans;* "L'Etat musulman, Conscience et liberté" in *Conscience et liberté I* 54 (1997): 55–69; "La Nature de l'Etat: L'Organisation de l'Etat," in *Conscience et liberté II* 55 (1998): 122–41; "La Législation et la politique de l'Etat" in *Conscience et liberté III* 56 (1998): 15–30.

2. David Gardner, *Financial Times,* repr. in *Jeune Afrique* (Paris), 20–26 July 1999, 30.

3. *Jeune Afrique* (Paris), 17–30 August 1999, 87.

4. Jean-Michel Foulquier, *Le Point* (Paris), 4 February 1995, 34.

5. Alain Gresh, *Le Monde diplomatique* (Paris), August 1995, 9.

6. *Le Monde,* 20 August 1999, 34.

# 2

# ILLUSIONS OF CHANGE

*Emmanuel Sivan*

**Emmanuel Sivan** *is professor of history at the Hebrew University in Jerusalem. He is the author of numerous works, including* Radical Islam *(1990) and* Mythes politiques arabes *(1995), and the editor of* War and Remembrance in the Twentieth Century *(1999). This essay originally appeared in the July 2000 issue of the* Journal of Democracy.

Many observers regarded 1999 as a year of progress for democracy in the Arab world. Yemen, Egypt, and Tunisia all held presidential elections in what was deemed a relatively free atmosphere. In September, Algeria held a referendum on a "Civil Concord" that sought to end a seven-year civil war by offering amnesty to Islamist rebels who would lay down their arms. Combined with the recent changing of the guard in Jordan and Morocco, where young monarchs succeeded the two most veteran Arab rulers, these events were widely viewed as a significant move toward more pluralistic and participatory politics.

But are we actually witnessing meaningful political change? There is reason for doubt. Hosni Mubarak has been elected for the fourth time, Tunisia's Zine el-Abidine Ben Ali for the third time, and Yemen's Ali Abdallah Salih for the second time—after 18, 12, and five years of rule, respectively. Mubarak ran unopposed, while Saleh faced just one token candidate from within his own party (the candidacies of leaders of the opposition parties were not approved by the Electoral Committee). In Tunisia, the two contenders allowed to run came from minor opposition parties and got barely 0.6 percent of the vote. This compelled the presidential palace, which had promised that the opposition would get one-fifth of the seats in the parliamentary elections, to resort to changing the size of electoral districts in order to give the opposition its "due share" of the parliamentary vote. In Algeria, all six opposition candidates planning to run in the April 1999 elections against the army's candidate, Abdelaziz Bouteflika, quit the race in protest against the government's strong-arm tactics against their activists. In the run-up to the September referendum, no advertisements opposed to granting amnesty to the rebels were allowed on government-controlled radio and television, and there was virtually no public debate on the merits of the proposal. If all this does not constitute a return to the old rule of *thalath tis'a* (99.9 percent), it comes very close.

No less significant, perhaps, was the low turnout for these elections, estimated by seasoned observers at one-third of registered voters in Egypt and two-fifths in Tunisia. Election fraud, long a common occurrence in the Middle East, was less blatant, but still alive and well. As for the broad declarations from the official press about new "winds of liberty," a June 1999 study by the Jordanian Institute of Strategic Studies showed that 71 percent of those questioned said they are still afraid of speaking out on public affairs, and just 16 percent said they have no fear of criticizing the government.

Voter apathy is also related to suspicion of the official media. Those who can afford it prefer Arab-language satellite television, which is considerably freer (especially al-Jazeera broadcasting out of Qatar), Radio Monte Carlo, and (in North Africa) French television on cable or via satellite. The two new kings, Abdallah II of Jordan and Mohammed VI of Morocco, have somewhat relaxed the restrictions on the press laid down by their fathers in recent years as part of the fight against radical Islam. Yet this so-called Arab *glasnost'* does not go very far. In Jordan, the editors of two opposition dailies were arrested for publishing reports that female nurses in Aqaba had been sexually harassed in public by the prime minister's son. The Department of Human Rights, which had just been created in the prime minister's office, was, of course, unable to intervene. In Egypt, where press laws are still heavily skewed in favor of those in authority, the editor and two journalists of the pro-Islamist daily *Al-Sha'ab* got stiff prison sentences for slandering the deputy prime minister with allegations that he had personally profited from "commerce with the Zionists." Protests by the Journalists' Syndicate were of no avail. In a similar case in Yemen, journalists were condemned to flogging, and the editor of the independent Algerian daily *El Watan* is under investigation for accusing a former general of masterminding the assassination of journalists three years ago.

Underlying all this is what Palestinian human rights activist Ayyad al-Sarraj calls the "essential lack of confidence of the masses in those in power."[1] A Moroccan commentator explains the situation in the following fashion:

Whenever I read Arab commentators who try to persuade our citizens that the function of the police is to defend and not to beat them, I am reminded of the following anecdote: A patient goes to a psychiatrist complaining that he [the patient] is a grain of wheat, and thus when he sees a hen he is filled with fear that she will eat him up. After a long and costly course of therapy, the man is finally cured, and he no longer thinks of himself as a grain of wheat. When taking leave of the doctor, he says: "I know that I'm cured, thank God; I know I'm a human being, not a grain of wheat. But tell me, doctor, does the hen know that?" Thus when I hear the declarations about the police as the citizens' servant, etc., I'm reminded of dozens of cases of extralegal executions, of thousands of cases of humiliation and torture, of tens of thousand cases of political arrest. And I ask myself: Do the police [that is, the hen in our story] know that we are human beings?[2]

These words were written five months before the death of Hassan II. The writer may be more hopeful now under Mohammed VI. Moroccan interior minister Driss Basri, whose reign of terror had lasted for 20 years, was deposed by the new king in November 1999. Treatment of dissidents has been relaxed to some extent and promises of further liberalization have been made. Whether the latter will be kept, however, remains to be seen. It is also unclear whether the king intends to rule as a constitutional monarch or an enlightened autocrat. Like his father, he maintains direct control over the so-called sovereignty ministries (interior, foreign affairs, defense, justice, and religion). Needless to say, Basri's replacement, Ahmad Midawi, is an appointee of the king; so are the two men who replaced Basri's top aides in the other domain he had controlled, the Information Ministry, and the army chief of staff, the regime's third most important figure, who was kept in his post. Prime Minister Abderrahmane Youssoufi is an opposition-party leader who won a plurality in the 1997 elections and was consequently appointed by Hassan II (the first time that such "alternation" had taken place in Morocco). Yet Youssoufi's room to maneuver remains limited to social and economic affairs.

In Egypt, too, the "sovereignty portfolios" did not change hands when a new prime minister, Atef Ubeid, was appointed in the wake of Mubarak's reelection. Ubeid did change the holders of 11 ministries, but almost all of these were economic ministries. The two key personalities of the regime—military-intelligence chief Omar Suleiman and defense minister Marshal Tantawi—remained in their posts. Ubeid himself is hardly a new figure; he has served as a minister in all but one of the governments during the Mubarak presidency. Old-timers make up two-thirds of the Ubeid government (including two who had served under Sadat). As the French say, *plus ça change, plus c'est la même chose*.

In fact, this is true of the entire top political class in Egypt. Party leaders, whether of the governing National Democratic Party or of the opposition, are virtually all in their sixties and seventies and have been around ever since Sadat made "forums" (and later political parties) legal a quarter-century ago. Even the Muslim Brotherhood, the only real (though illegal) mass party, is led by septuagenarians, former inmates of Nasser's jails and detention camps.

Party activity continues to consist mostly of issuing a weekly or monthly publication and some action within professional associations; only rarely (except during electoral campaigns) do parties conduct meetings and rallies, let alone other grassroots activities. There are probably no more than two thousand party activists in all of Egypt. (This does not include the Muslim Brotherhood, which has vibrant local branches.) In their internal governance, these parties, all of which put democratization high on their agenda, are run in an authoritarian fashion, as are the majority of professional syndicates and other nongovernmental organizations (NGOs). This is yet another sign, after decades of military-populist and monarchical regimes, of the "absence of democratic political culture" that George Tarabishi and Hussein Ahmad Amin, two of the best Arab political thinkers, decry so strongly.[3]

The lethargy of the parties matches that of the electorate. Parties have no way to influence decision making or even the public debate. Egypt's National Democratic Party, for instance, had no say in the makeup of the Ubeid cabinet. Only rarely, as in the 1997 debate about the tenancy rights of peasants, does the opposition succeed in putting its concerns on the government's agenda. The opposition was weakened by the shift in the 1990s from a party-list system to a constituency-based system for parliamentary elections, which resulted in the opposition's share of the seats declining from 20 to 3 percent. This was part of a policy of "turning the screws" (or "deliberalization") by a regime that saw itself as under siege by a resurgence of Islamist violence. A similar approach was followed in Morocco and Jordan, which, like Egypt, were shaken by the rise of the Islamic Salvation Front (FIS) in Algeria in 1990–91.

## The Historical Context

This deliberalization of the early-to-mid-1990s provides the context in which today's supposed "winds of change" should be evaluated. Are we witnessing the reversal of a trend and a return to the relative liberalization of the 1980s, with greater freedom of the press, assembly, and association, improved transparency, and an opening up of the political process to allow for the partial inclusion of forces hitherto disbarred from it, such as radical Islam?

That earlier liberalization was partly a response to the economic crisis resulting from the decline of oil prices, which hit both oil-producing countries and other Arab states dependent upon remittances from the Gulf, subsidies from oil-rich emirates, and revenues from Gulf tourists or from oil tankers (passing through the Suez Canal). This crisis was exacerbated by high fertility rates.

After years of interventionist attempts to transform society under populist-military (Nasserist or Ba'athist) regimes, Arab states now had to retreat from many fields, abandoning them to NGOs and market initiatives. Governments also had to marshal public support for IMF-imposed austerity plans and thus had an interest in eliciting somewhat greater political participation. By so doing, they could also curry favor with Western donors, who saw the combination of economic and political liberalization as a panacea. In a reversal of virtually four decades of interventionism, civil society was given room to operate, some legal restrictions on freedom of association, assembly, and the press were lifted or loosened, and elections were less closely "engineered." Responsibility for parts of the education, welfare, and health sectors were moved from the state to charitable organizations or left to the emerging private sector.

It is a matter of debate whether the regimes actually believed in the combination of economic and political liberalization, even at the very beginning. In any case, by the early 1990s, while they remained largely committed to economic liberalization (that is, dismantling the statist structures of the command economy), Arab states came to entertain serious doubts as to the wisdom of combining it with political liberalization. For the void left by the retreating welfare state was mostly filled by Islamist associations funded by remittances from migrant workers and private Gulf foundations. For these associations, helping the poor was not just a charitable task but an act of *Da'wa* (spreading the Word), designed to Islamize society from below and thus to set the public agenda on issues ranging from the status of women to school curricula. Their ultimate goal was to gain control of the political process through the growing number of Islamist mayors and legislators. In Algeria in 1991, the Islamic associations, under the umbrella of the FIS, were on the verge of winning a plurality in parliament.

In response to this growing danger to their monopoly of power, the regimes made an about-face. In Algeria, the government cancelled the second round of parliamentary elections and decreed a state of emergency. In Tunisia, the country that first launched "deliberalization," the almost-senile Habib Bourguiba, judged to be too weak in his response to the Islamists' mounting challenge, was deposed from the presidency in 1987 by the security establishment. His interior minister, Zine al-Abidine Ben Ali, a tough former police officer, was appointed president. Ben Ali curtailed basic liberties and outlawed Islamist associations—even those not affiliated with the violence-prone radicals who, too impatient to wait for the *Da'wa* process to mature, had attempted to seize power, either directly or by trying to destabilize the country through acts of terrorism. Five years later, Egypt, Jordan, Morocco, and Kuwait followed on the same track, though (unlike Algeria and Tunisia) without replacing their heads of state. In Iraq,

Syria, Libya, Saudi Arabia, and other Gulf states, there had never been any political liberalization to speak of, and hence there was no need for an about-face.

Where a real about-face did take place, it was directed not only against Islamists directly implicated in violent action but also against those who were at least ostensibly committed to advancing their radical agenda by nonviolent means—and even against many Islamists who were quite moderate indeed. "Preventive measures" involved the wholesale curtailing of civil liberties (though one must note that, generally speaking, there was no return to the horrors of the 1950s and 1960s). These measures also hit leftists, pan-Arabists, human rights associations, and other non-Islamic opposition forces; their publications were censored, their NGOs were severely controlled (financially and otherwise), and their activists were harassed in their personal and professional lives.

Among the relatively liberalized states we discuss here, it was Tunisia that spearheaded the turn toward greater regimentation and went farthest along that road at the same time as it pursued economic liberalization (privatization, export-oriented industries, tourism, and the like) with unequaled perseverance. The result conformed to the Pinochet model: economic takeoff combined with political repression. Under Zine al-Abidine Ben Ali, Tunisia achieved export-led growth (4.5 percent annually through the 1990s), foreign investments attracted by the country's political stability and educated manpower, a rising standard of living (per-capita income of $2,200—double that of Egypt), an expanding middle class (more than three-quarters of Tunisian households own their own apartments), and the virtual elimination of poverty (unlike Egypt and Jordan, where 52 and 24 percent of the people, respectively, live on less than two dollars a day). These material benefits came at the expense of the closing of the political system—blatantly manipulated elections, a muzzled press, censored books, and the persecution of opposition and human rights activists.

If Tunisians, especially middle-class Tunisians, accept this state of affairs, it is in part due to what is sometimes called *khobzisme* (from *khubz*, the Arabic word for bread)—that is, satisfaction with one's material lot. Yet this acceptance is also motivated by fear of the sort of civil war going on in Algeria, where radical Islam has become indelibly associated with unbridled atrocities. The government plays on this theme, of course, but just watching the evening news on French and Italian television via satellite is enough to drive home the message.

Egypt, Jordan, Morocco, and Kuwait followed suit, though they never went to the same extreme as Tunisia on either of the two tracks. They gave absolute priority to economic liberalization (where substantial results have indeed been realized, at least in Egypt and Morocco) and retreated from political liberalization.

## Mixed Signals

The agenda for the coming years in these countries once again privileges economic liberalization. In Egypt, Atef Ubeid's government, which has recruited fresh technocratic talent, is intent on pushing forward with so-called "megaprojects" in the south (Aswan, Toshka), north, and northeast (Port Said, Sinai, Gulf of Suez). These are designed not only to spur economic growth but also to stop the rural and provincial exodus to Cairo. Nurturing high-tech and biotech industries is likewise high on Ubeid's agenda, though here the specifics are less clear. Morocco's new king pays special attention to the underdeveloped east and northeast (the proverbial Dar al-Siba, or Land of Revolt), while his Jordanian counterpart tries to woo foreign investors and renegotiate his country's foreign debt with Europe and the United States.

On the political front, the signals are mixed. In Algeria, although the referendum victory was a big psychological coup, Bouteflika took eight months to form a new government and has not taken any meaningful measures toward opening up the political process or integrating some of the former rebels into the army. The Algerian press—which, paradoxically, has become one of the freest in the Arab world over the last decade—shows signs of growing impatience and disappointment.

Although Algeria is an exceptional case because of its civil war, Bouteflika's problems indicate where some of the roots of the current Arab predicament may lie. Opposition from within the army hierarchy to both the makeup of the government and the measures taken with respect to the rebels and the former FIS seems to be blocking the decision-making process—which, as always, is shrouded in secrecy. The pivotal role of the military and the intelligence services in the power structure (as in other Arab countries) is not just a legacy of the postindependence state; it is also due to the menace of radical Islam, which, despite severe setbacks in recent years, remains a potential threat. Although Mohammed VI has been able (presumably with the army's consent) to depose Basri, he is still dependent upon Basri's successor and upon the military hierarchy, especially since the Islamists have recently made a big show of force in the form of mass demonstrations against a bill designed to modernize the status of women. Abdallah II has not deposed General Samih al-Beteihi, the head of the intelligence services and the regime's number-two man, who was the new king's best ally during the succession process.

In other words, none of the new rulers—that "new generation" on whom so many hopes are pinned in the Arab and world press—is yet master of his own domain (at least to the extent that the Egyptian, Yemeni, and Tunisian presidents are, and even the latter depend upon the military and security services). This holds true even for the oldest and most experienced of the new lot, Bouteflika, who has to maneuver between the hard-liners and the more conciliatory elements in the army. Mohammed VI and Abdallah II have hardly any political experience (though the latter has considerable military experience), as their fathers had never given them a share in governing. They have never been tested in the heat of political crisis. As for the new ideas they may have picked up from their studies abroad (the new Moroccan monarch studied political science at the University of Grenoble, while King Abdallah was educated at Deerfield Academy in Massachusetts and at Britain's Royal Military Academy at Sandhurst), their impact remains to be seen.

These doubts are even more applicable to Bashar al-Assad of Syria and Qusai Hussein of Iraq. Both of them were reared under exceedingly illiberal regimes, which their fathers are about to transform from populist-military to "hereditary" republics. Qusai never left Iraq for a substantial period. Bashar did a residency in ophthalmology at a London hospital, but how much of British political culture did he really absorb? Two other sons being groomed to succeed their fathers—the sons of Libya's Muammar Qadhafi and Yemen's Ali Abdullah Saleh—are also unlikely to be agents of democratic change.

## Fear and Magnanimity

By early 2000, the diagnosis of *"plus ça change . . ."* seemed to be confirmed on a daily basis: Twenty of the Muslim Brotherhood's leading activists within professional syndicates were arrested at a meeting in Cairo and brought before a military tribunal for activity prejudicial to the security of the state. Riot police prevented syndicates controlled by Jordan's Muslim Brotherhood from holding a Friday noon prayer beseeching Allah for rain and asking Him not to punish the country for the elites' moral turpitude. In Tunisia, police spread disinformation alleging that human rights activists were receiving money from foreign governments and NGOs and engaging in sexual perversion. In other words, civil society is in a state of siege.

How can this be? The political situation would seem ripe for exactly the opposite course, namely, political liberalization—not so much because of the accession of a "new generation" of rulers as because the war against Islamist insurgency and terrorism is being won. The threat of violence has been contained, if not yet eradicated.

In Tunisia, the war was won about a decade ago. In Egypt, a new wave of terrorism reached its pinnacle with the assassination attempt against Mubarak in 1995 and the Luxor massacre of 1997, which had a devastating impact on tourism, but this wave seems to have been beaten back over the last year or so. One of the two most important Egyptian terrorist groups, the Jama'a Islamiyya declared a unilateral cease-fire, and the other, the Jihad organization, was smashed by antiterrorist squads in its stronghold in Upper Egypt; dozens of Jihad activists who took refuge abroad (and attacked Egyptian legations there) were delivered to the Egyptian authorities from all over the globe, from Pakistan and Uruguay, South Africa and Albania. Yemen's Islamist terrorists, who collaborated with the Aden separatist forces and were particularly active in the kidnapping of foreign tourists, have been decimated. The bloodiest of all these struggles, the Algerian civil war, is still going on, but the army seemed to have won the fight by late 1998. The Islamic Salvation Army (AIS), the armed wing of the FIS, has laid down its arms. A good part of the more extreme Armed Islamic Group (GIA) has done the same, though many of its die-hard members still roam the countryside. It is in this atmosphere of relative calm and stability that presidential elections took place in Algeria in April 1999, and an amnesty law was promulgated by parliament in July and endorsed by referendum in September. The incorporation of former AIS members into the Algerian army, another sign of national reconciliation, is currently being negotiated.

Will the state show magnamity in victory? This is the crucial question, not so much with regard to former Islamist terrorists, but with regard to those radical Islamists who have not been implicated in violence in their efforts to establish an Islamic state based on Islamic law. These groupings suffered from the heavy-handed preemptive tactics used by the state during the struggle against their violent counterparts—not just in countries where the armed struggle was waged but also in neighboring countries (Jordan, Kuwait, Morocco) intent on stopping the contagion from spreading.

In this historical context, magnanimity may be considered not so much a moral virtue as a political one. Some opening of the political process or partial inclusion that would cover nonviolent Islamists as well as those former extremists who are now ready to play by the rules would seem to be in order. Giving excluded groups and social strata a share, however modest, in the system would arguably be a long-term investment in stabilizing the polity. Given the importance of radical Islamic movements, the question of whether, and to what degree, they might be included in the political process is crucial for the fate of democratization. As long as these movements are legally banned (as in Egypt, Tunisia, and Algeria) or are legal but restricted (as in Yemen and Jordan), there can be no question of a meaningful democratic process, whatever these regimes may promise.

Yet magnanimity does not seem to be what the regimes have in mind. The legacy of vengefulness and suspicion, especially among the top security establishment, left by the years of violence is partially to blame.

It encourages them to be wary even of those opportunistic Islamists who reject violence but share the extremists' agenda: Wolves in sheep's clothing, they could try to infiltrate the state apparatus and key social sectors, gradually transforming the state from within. Once they gain power, it is feared, they will never relinquish it; their devotion to democratic principles can be expressed by the aphorism: "One man, one vote, one time." (The Islamist regime in Sudan is a case in point.) The security apparatus sees pluralism as a Trojan horse. If the price for preempting radical Islam is the further reduction of the public sphere, so be it. They want a strong state, but have little patience for politics.

These suspicions explain, for instance, why the Egyptian state cracked down on Muslim syndicalists, despite a court order that struck down government measures sequestering professional syndicates controlled by the Brotherhood (that is, taking them over and controlling their properties) and required them to hold new elections. The crackdown may have also served as a preemptive strike to deprive the Brotherhood of 20 of its most dynamic young candidates in the upcoming parliamentary elections.

## Suspicions About the Islamists

The authorities are not alone in their distrust of radical Muslims. Suspicion is also prevalent among various opposition groups, especially the liberals, who are an important force in the new middle class. They have reason to be suspicious. In the 1970s, the Islamists adopted the rhetoric of democracy in a rather cavalier fashion, without giving much thought to its implications or trying to follow it into their own behavior. The advantage of adopting democratic slogans was obvious: It would get the Islamists out of the legal limbo they had been pushed into by formerly populist regimes that were now beginning to declare their own commitment to pluralism, multipartism, human rights, and the like. In any event, violence was not an attractive option for militants just coming out of Nasser's jails. They had learned their lesson (a lesson many of the younger extremists would have to learn the hard way several decades later).

In the 1970s, the radical Islamists adopted a line premised on an argument common to Muslim apologetic thought earlier in the century—namely, that democracy is analogous to the *shura,* the duty of the ruler to consult with his subjects. In fact, however, *shura* actually refers to consultation with Muslim jurists, not with representatives of the electorate. And even this medieval concept was honored more in the breach than in the observance.[4] Issues like the freedom to express thoughts that run counter to Islamic orthodoxy, let alone atheism or agnosticism, were (and still are) rarely tackled head-on; at best, they were swept under the rug by ambiguous formulas such as "all in accordance with Islamic law." The same formulas are employed with regard to thorny issues like equality for women or for non-Muslims in the future state governed by the *shari'a*.[5]

Purists—or extremists, if you will—in the Islamist camp tend to take the position that democracy is a Western import, suffused with the poison of modernity, that should be rejected out of hand. Such purists are common among the violence-prone associations *(jama'at)*, as well as among firebrand preachers and thinkers. Thus the blind sheikh Umar Abd al-Rahman recently issued a *fatwa* (or legal ruling) from his American jail cell declaring the establishment of political parties of any kind, including Islamic ones, to be illegal. According to the *fatwa*, in Islam there can only be "one party, that of Allah." The notion of free competition in the marketplace of ideas or in the electoral arena is absurd, claimed the sheikh. The embarrassed Muslim Brotherhood hastened to wash their hands of this *fatwa*, which, as might have been expected, was embraced by the clandestine Jihad organization.

These extremists accuse the more moderate Islamists of vacillation, opportunism, and inconsistency, accusations that ring true in the ears of suspicious government officials and anxious liberals. This does not necessarily mean, however, that the concept of *shura* cannot be developed to incorporate the notions of individual rights, alternation of power, and limited government, notions alien but perhaps not contradictory to the medieval outlook of *shari'a*. After all, thinkers like John Courtney Murray half a century ago used certain medieval concepts (such as *subsidium,* or subsidiarity) to justify the acceptance of liberal democracy by Roman Catholics.

Yet no such elaboration of the concept of *shura* was made. Difficulties were not addressed; they were simply glossed over. There were very few voices like that of Munir Shafiq—an independent radical writer of Palestinian origin, who, as early as 1992, called for unqualified acceptance of the notions of human rights and alternation of power, for the introduction of democratic norms within Islamic movements themselves, and for an effort to make *shari'a* laws, which had always been a product of their time and place, conform to these liberal principles.

Shafiq called upon the movement to face reality: The resurgence of Islam, he argued, requires a free civil society, which is possible only under democracy. One could even say that the very survival of the Islamic way of life—threatened with decline, if not extinction, under the current despotic regimes—depends upon it. Ideas and precedents may be found in the Islamic tradition, particularly from the age of the Companions of the Prophet, to justify many components of democracy. Shafiq warned that without a bona fide acceptance of liberal democracy on the part of Islamists, they would find it impossible either to persuade the authorities to open the gates of pluralistic politics to them or to forge viable alliances with other opposition forces in the fight to extend the public sphere.[6]

Yet Shafiq's arguments had no palpable impact. Throughout the 1990s, even nonviolent Islamists continued to demonstrate distinctly antidemocratic proclivities. In the three Egyptian *causes célèbres*—the assassination of secularist thinker Faraj Foda, the attempted assassination of Nobel Prize–winning novelist Najib Mahfouz, and the court action against the scholar Nasir Hamid Abu Zayd, who was accused of apostasy—the Muslim Brotherhood and those close to them took ambiguous positions. Without actually justifying the violence employed in the first two cases, they more or less hinted that Foda and Mahfouz had brought it upon themselves by attracting the rage of young zealots. In the last case, they openly backed the sheikhs who had charged Abu Zayd with taking an excessively critical look at the history of early Islamic law, and they cheered the verdict, which annulled his marriage—a woman cannot stay married to an apostate—thus effectively driving him into exile.

These were not the only instances. Despite its heterogeneity and its nebulous structure, Egypt's Islamist movement united behind the press campaigns against other "apostates"—modernist Islamic scholars Hasan Hanafi, Sayyid al-Kimni, and Khalil Abd al-Karim. In Jordan and Kuwait, Islamists tried to ban "irreligious" (insufficiently orthodox) books from book fairs. Islamist members of the Kuwaiti parliament presented bills calling for harsher punishments for "sacrilegious" writings. Recently, some Kuwaiti Islamic radicals launched criminal proceedings for blasphemy against the liberal thinker Ahmad al-Baghdadi, who had written an article critical of the Prophet Mohammad's failure to propagate the faith during the early years of his mission. The court sentenced him to one month in jail.[7] Buoyed by their success, they proceeded to lodge similar complaints against two female poets. Their Sunni counterparts in Lebanon had a court case brought against a popular singer, Marcel Khalifa, a Christian, for committing blasphemy by singing a poem by the Palestinian Muhammad Darwish that includes a Koranic verse.

The Khalifa case, together with the Islamists' fight to build a mosque near the Church of the Annunciation in Nazareth, raised anew the matter of Islamist attitudes toward non-Muslims. Here the Muslim Brotherhood has been rather circumspect, condemning acts of violence recently committed against Copts in Upper Egypt. Yet their new Supreme Guide, Mustafa Mashhur, caused quite an uproar when he maintained that in a future Islamic state the Copts should have, as in the Caliphate of yore, the status of protected but second-class subjects whose access to positions of authority would be limited, and who would have to pay a special tax.

Only a few voices within the Brotherhood were raised in criticism of

Mashhur, but respected jurist Muhammad Salim al-'Awa was prominent among them. 'Awa also used his enormous erudition in Islamic jurisprudence to condemn the accusations of blasphemy brought against Abu Zayd and Khalifa as "irrelevant and smacking of ignorance," and to argue that there is no point in this day and age in calling (as the Islamists do) for the application of certain punishments laid down in the Koran (such as stoning for adultery or chopping off thieves' hands).[8] Few within the "mainstream" of radical Islam seemed to listen to 'Awa (or, for that matter, to Shafiq), or to dwell upon the dilemma that these two thinkers posed—that there can be no effective *Da'wa* without democracy. The dilemma is all the more acute now that efforts to spread the Word through violent means have so dismally failed.

No wonder the Arab liberals consider the Islamists to be, at best, proponents of "illiberal democracy," if not totalitarians in disguise. This impression—which the authorities share—was reinforced by the unpleasant experience of many liberals and other oppositionists in collaborating with radical Islamists in parliamentary alliances (in Egypt in 1984–87 or in the Jordanian and Kuwaiti parliaments in the early 1990s). In all these cases, the Islamists endeavored to monopolize power. Working with them within professional syndicates of doctors, lawyers, engineers, journalists, and the like, they saw the Brotherhood's strong-arm tactics at their worst, combining authoritarianism with a cavalier attitude toward the finances of these associations. Hence liberals are reluctant to fight to legalize the Brotherhood either as a political party or as a social-action NGO (as in Jordan, Morocco, and Kuwait), or even just to take them out of illegality into some semilegal limbo (as in Egypt, Algeria, and Tunisia). As a consequence, the opposition is greatly weakened in its fight to open up the political system.

## Overcoming the Past

An exception to this overall picture is Algeria, where the lesson many opposition parties have drawn from the abrogation of the 1991–92 elections and the subsequent civil war is that some parts of the chastened FIS should be allowed, under strict conditions, to enter the political game. The problem, however, is to identify which factions of the FIS are actually fit and ready for such a partial inclusion (probably the ones led by Abassi Madani and Rabah Kabir, respectively, and perhaps also the Jazara faction, which had been led, until his recent assassination, by Abdelkader Hashani).

Arab rulers are definitely not going to be more liberal than the liberals, especially since their long violent struggle against the Islamists has left them with bitter memories and a craving for vengeance. The worse the memories, the weaker the tendency toward magnanimity. Thus Bouteflika, despite his popular mandate and his skill at political maneuvering, will have difficulty overcoming the past.

The initiative for breaking with the past can come either from the top or from below—from the rulers or the ruled—but it requires the cooperation of both. If there is some movement in this direction, it owes nothing to the "winds of change" referred to in the beginning of this essay, but rather comes from a series of recent steps that put the ideas of Shafiq and 'Awa into organized action.

The most interesting of these initiatives was launched three years ago by a group of Muslim Brotherhood militants in their late thirties, most of whom had risen through the student associations in Upper Egypt and had even spent some time in jail in the early 1980s. They announced the establishment of a political party called Al-Wasat (the center), led by Abul Ula Madi, which represents a generational revolt against the septuagenarian leadership of the Brotherhood, even though it swore fealty to that movement. The turn toward violence, Al-Wasat argued, had been disastrous; political, social, and educational action had become increasingly shackled. The only way out of the impasse would be to accept, unambiguously and without preconditions, all the principles of liberal politics: individual rights, basic freedoms, limited government, competitive politics, alternation, and transparency. (The party did not, however, accept the legitimacy of agnostic or atheistic opinion.) Even partial, cumulative reforms are more conducive to an "Islamic solution" than is the current impasse. The stagnation of the movement harms the cause of Islam and accelerates its decline as a viable social force. There can be no Islamic solution without the people.[9]

The leadership of the Brotherhood rejected this challenge and expelled the founders of Al-Wasat. The Madi group has persisted, even though it has not yet received a party license from the authorities. Still, in what may signal a change of heart, the state did grant them some legal standing in April 2000. The Ministry of Social Affairs gave a group consisting mostly of Al-Wasat founders the license to establish an NGO called the Egypt Society for Culture and Dialogue, whose aim is to "support the culture of dialogue in a society in which violence prevails."

The beginnings of a debate about pluralism can also be detected in the Al-Nahda (renaissance) movement, Tunisia's equivalent of the Muslim Brotherhood. A much more heated discussion along these lines is going on among the factions of the former FIS in Algeria with regard to the Civil Concord Act.

Yet these rumblings in the Islamist movements are, for the moment, just that—rumblings. They have no effect on the impasse in which these movements find themselves, since they are incapable either of taking power by force or of transforming their attitude toward democracy so as to be able to bring about the reform of state and society. Given the weakness of the non-Islamist opposition and the absence of any real commitment to political liberalization on the part of the regimes, this impasse is bound to continue, and perhaps even to get worse.

## NOTES

1. *Al-Quds al-Arabi* (Paris), 20 February 1999.

2. *Al-Sharq al-Awsat* (London), 15 June 1999.

3. George Tarabishi, *Fi Thaqafat al-Dimuqratiyya* (Beirut: Dar al-Tali'a, 1998); Hussein Ahmad Amin, "Al-shabab wa-l-kilab," *Al-Dustur* (Nicosia-Cairo), 12 and 19 March 1997.

4. See, for example, Muhammad 'Imara, *Al-Islam wa-Huquq al-Insan* (Cairo: Dar al-Shuruq, 1991); Rashid Ghannushi, *Al-Hurriyat al-Ama'a fi-l-Islam* (Beirut: Markaz Dirasat al-Wahda al-Arabiyya, 1992); 'Abdalla Muhammad Ahmad, *Al-Harakat al-Islamiyya fi Misr wa-Qadaya al-Tahawwul al-Dimuqrati* (Cairo: Madbuli, 1995).

5. See Khalil 'Abd al-Karim, *Al-Islam bayna-l-Dawla al-Diniyya wa-l-Dawla al-Madaniyya* (Cairo: Dar Sina, 1997).

6. Munir Shafiq, *Al-Nizam al-Alami al-Jadid* (Beirut: Dar al-Nashir, 1992): 130–137.

7. See Ahmad al-Baghdadi, "Al-Insan al-Muslim wa-'asr al-'Awlama," in 'Abd al-hamid Charfi, ed., *Al-Muslim fi-Ta'rikh* (Casablanca: Al-Muasasa al-Arabiyya li-l-Nashr, 1999), 9–21.

8. 'Awa's articles in *Al-Sha'ab* (Cairo), 14 July 1995; *Al-Wafd* (Cairo), 17 April 1997; and *Al-Hayat* (London), 18 October 1999.

9. Abul Ula Madi, *Jama'at al-'Unf al-Misriyya al-Murtabita bi-l-Islam* (Cairo: Dar Sina, 1997); interview with *Al-Hayat* (London), 25 December 1996.

# 3

# THE AWAKENING OF CIVIL SOCIETY

*Laith Kubba*

**Laith Kubba** *is senior program officer for the Middle East at the National Endowment for Democracy. The holder of a bachelor's degree from the University of Baghdad and a Ph.D. from the University of Wales, he was the director of the international program of the Al-Khoei Foundation in London and the founder of the Islam 21 project. He has been an active participant in a number of Iraqi democratic organizations and has served on the boards of such regional institutions as the Arab Organization for Human Rights and the International Forum for Islamic Dialogue. This essay originally appeared in the July 2000 issue of the* Journal of Democracy.

Despite variations in their political histories, culture, and wealth, Arab countries have had remarkably similar political experiences. As Mohamed Talbi and Emmanuel Sivan recount, they have been—and largely continue to be—ruled by authoritarian governments that pay mere lip service to constitutions, violate civil and human rights, resist political liberalization, and remain unaccountable to their people. Heads of states, even if they hold elections, are never voted out of office; despite the dismal performance of corrupt and unpopular governments, rulers retain power for many years, often for life. They govern with virtually no checks and balances, take strategic decisions without referendums, dismiss ministers at will, and often pocket public assets.

Surprisingly, however, these regimes are stable. They succeed in providing essential public services, and they seem able to adapt to a changing political environment without facing serious challenges from within. The resilience, stability, and continuity of these despotic regimes raise serious questions about the prospects of democracy in the Arab world. How long can these regimes last? Is democracy viable in Arab countries? Is it compatible with Arab political culture? Do Arabs have a preference for despotism? In exploring these questions, both Mohamed Talbi and Emmanuel Sivan focus on the nature and the politics of the contemporary Arab state and reach conclusions that are quite pessimistic. While not disputing their analyses of the Arab state, I believe that, by ignoring civil society, they miss an important aspect of the larger picture, one that provides much greater ground for optimism about democratic prospects in the Arab world. A new era is emerging in Arab politics today, one in which the state will increasingly be forced to retreat before a vibrant civil society.

## Disillusionment and Dictatorship

Democracy in Arab countries has its roots in the evolution of the modern state at the turn of the last century. The Arabs rose up against the Ottoman Empire and were granted independence, with the help of European colonialists, who worked with tribal chiefs and elites to lay the foundations of modern states with democratic institutions. In these new states, Arabs experimented with democracy for the first time in their history. For more than three decades, Egypt, Syria, and Iraq had functioning democracies in which deputies were elected, government officials were held accountable to laws and rules, the judiciary was independent, the press was free, and the people enjoyed equality before the law and basic civil and human rights.

At that time, active citizenship and participatory political systems were still alien concepts to tribal, agricultural Arab societies. Civil society and democratic traditions evolved slowly, with little participation by the majority, whose attitudes remained those of passive subjects rather than active citizens. The influence of civil society and of the middle class on governments was far less significant than that of tribal chiefs, religious leaders, and military officers.

Governments followed constitutional and legal procedures, but they did not address the needs of the people. Although the political process was open to all citizens, the high illiteracy rate and the slow pace of social and economic development excluded most people from the benefits of democracy, which remained an urban phenomenon that primarily served the elites and left rural people behind. Delivery of public services was uneven, and the economy grew too slowly to bridge the gap between the rich, who supported the system, and the poor majority, who remained outside it. The frustration of the majority was given expression by political activists who advocated radical alternatives to the slow pace of democracy. Political parties, which were vocal, active, and visible on university campuses and in major cities, called upon the army to overthrow constitutional governments and to carry out speedy reforms.

The post–World War II political climate gave further reasons for military officers to move against their governments. The establishment of the state of Israel incited nationalism and political radicalism, and the competing superpowers encouraged officers to stage military coups.

Arab democracies, still in their infancy, were too weak and lacking in public support to withstand military intervention. Generals, supported by political parties, abolished parliaments with no public protest. Patriarchal Arab societies, accustomed to strong chiefs, had little appreciation for the slow processes and competing authorities of democratic rule. Popularly supported military coups in Egypt, Iraq, and Syria were followed by similar attempts in most other Arab countries. Even countries that survived military takeovers, such as Morocco and Jordan, suspended social and political liberties, and authoritarian rule became entrenched. Repression and excessive state power came to characterize Arab politics. The state was controlled by force and conspiracy rather than by votes and legal procedures.

In Egypt, Gamal Abdel Nasser, who seized power following a 1952 military coup, controlled the state, which, in turn, controlled the people through propaganda, a state-sponsored political party, a state-controlled People's Assembly, the secret police, and so on. Nasser's popularity throughout the Arab world inspired other army generals to follow his example. In Iraq and Syria, the ruling Ba'ath party succeeded in controlling both state and society by introducing the party and tribal kinship to state power. In these countries, power is firmly in the hands of an intertwined alliance of army generals, tribes, and elites. The level of authoritarianism and repression is determined by the level of challenges that governments face: The greater the challenges, the more repressive the regime becomes.

For nearly five decades, Arab states have controlled public life in all its dimensions—political, social, and economic. Rulers regard any opposition to the state as a threat to national security and ruthlessly suppress it. Security forces have rounded up, tortured, and killed thousands of opposition activists of all sorts, including nationalists, Islamists, and leftists. Not all of the victims were terrorists or power seekers; in fact, many were apolitical. Yet all were perceived as threats because of their real or potential dissent or opposition to state policies. Government repression was made easier by the silence and apathy of the majority. Yet fear of state retaliation was not the only reason why people condoned authoritarian regimes. Arab dictators also adeptly exploited the psychology of their people to their own advantage.

First, people preferred strong leaders able to act swiftly and promptly to address their needs, to provide stability and security, and to assume responsibility for social and economic development. Second, popular disillusionment with political change led to apathy and cynicism. Initially, people cheered armies that led republican revolts against monarchies and promised change for the better, but life got worse and the promises were not fulfilled. Military governments proved unable to run their economies efficiently or to realize their societies' political aspirations. The popular political parties who worked with army factions to broaden political participation ended up creating repressive police states with no political representation. Often, the opposition was also undemocratic and simply aimed at replacing the ruler without changing the rules and policies of authoritarian governments. Third, people seemed to value national security and political stability more than civil and political liberties and feared that demanding reform would undermine stability without necessarily leading to better government. Dictatorship had broad appeal because it seemed at least to guarantee stability, security, and continuity.

## Transition and Reform

Recently, however, Arab countries have been undergoing a transition that threatens to erode dictatorships which have lasted for many decades. Although the region remains stable, there is a widespread anticipation of change and a growing public discourse on issues previously considered taboo. Violations of human and civil rights are being publicized, as are the demands of minorities, debates on reform, and promises from leaders to implement transparency and anticorruption measures. The transition is evident every day in the news and in the lively discourse in the Arab media, especially in the London-based newspapers *Al-Hayat, Al-Sharq Al-Awsaat, Al-Quds, Azzaman,* and *Al-Arab.* It is also evident in the remarkable popularity of open debates on the Qatar-based al-Jazeera satellite TV channel, which has encouraged other Arab satellite channels to run similar debates. The impact of the al-Jazeera debates is so widely felt by Arab governments that they sometimes have registered formal protests and threatened Qatar with a diplomatic boycott.

Despite the slow pace of change, laws in many Arab countries that restrict nongovernmental organizations (NGOs), the closure of associations and newspapers, continuing human rights violations, and the enactment of emergency laws, civil-society activity and demands for liberal reforms are on the increase. Thousands of private organizations have survived government attempts to thwart their activities and reduce their influence. Civil-society groups are breaking new ground and finding loopholes in current legislation that enable them to operate and develop despite the restrictions. Local groups have linked up with regional and international networks, produced and distributed a wide range of publications, promoted human rights, called for a free and open press, disseminated democratic values, and advocated women's rights. The mushrooming NGO movement is pressing governments to be accountable, to adhere to the rule of law, and to abide by broad principles of good government.

Some observers attach little value to these early signs of reform and misinterpret the current tension between state and society as evidence of a slide back toward dictatorship. Yet although power remains concentrated in unelected and unaccountable governments, the growth of civil society and the promise of the state to undertake reforms are both developments that advance the democratic cause. Although the same despots still remain in power, the global and domestic landscape has changed dramatically, forcing the state to retreat in favor of civil society. This transition to greater political and economic liberalism and less state control in Arab society cannot be attributed to one factor or to simple causes.

Over the past few decades, progress has been made on the social and educational fronts, with the achievement of high literacy and education rates, gains for women in terms of equal opportunities and political participation, and the modernizing of public administration. Incremental gains in education, urbanization, and industrialization have changed the structures of conservative tribal societies. Today, Arab societies are fundamentally different from what they were a century ago. They now have a critical mass of highly educated people with considerable experience in advocacy and organizing as well as the ability and willingness to express their ideas openly.

Moreover, Arab states are losing one of the most effective instruments of authoritarian rule: control over the flow of information. All Arab states have ministries of information charged with controlling the flow of information into their respective countries and ensuring the steady flow of state propaganda, but these ministries have been unable to withstand the inexorable impact of mass communication technologies. In all the countries of the region except Iraq, people now enjoy a horizontal flow of news and views and are no longer limited to the top-down flow of state propaganda.

The ability to communicate freely with the outside world is having a variety of effects on the views of the people, reinforcing some and changing others. The high-speed flow of information and the constant exposure to different cultures and belief systems is reshaping the opinion, values, concepts, and perceptions of citizens in formerly closed societies. By looking at old problems through new prisms, people will have a better chance of finding the right solutions and will benefit from the experience of their fellows in other parts of the globe.

In addition, Arab governments are under international pressure to relax their strict controls over their respective societies. The World Bank, the European Union, the United States, and other international actors often make foreign aid, trade, and investment in Arab countries contingent upon the implementation of market reforms, which, in turn, requires a more open economic system grounded in a sound legislative framework and free access to information. In the long term, social and economic reforms cannot be separated from political liberalization. In response to these pressures, some states (notably, Morocco, Egypt, Jordan, and Lebanon) have become more free and begun to offer real opportunities for change, although others (such as Libya, Iraq, and Saudi Arabia) are largely immune to international pressures and remain closed societies. Governments in Tunisia and Palestine are becoming more authoritarian, but those in Yemen and Algeria are seeking reconciliation with their societies and attempting reforms.

Governments are also under increasing domestic pressure to respond to demands for transparency, accountability, participation, women's rights, and respect for human and civil rights. The national and regional agendas of Arab countries are shifting from political to economic concerns, from centralized to local reforms, and from radical to pragmatic approaches. The resumption of the Arab-Israeli peace process and its anticipated success will shift the focus of public debate in the Middle East from national and regional security concerns to domestic issues, giving new salience to popular demands for political reforms, human rights, and open societies.

It is in the interest of the new generation of Arab rulers to heed the public call for reform. Some of them have declared as national priorities strengthening the private sector, fighting government corruption, trimming the public-sector bureaucracy, solidifying the judiciary as an independent institution, and strengthening civil society. While it remains to be determined whether these rulers will be able to carry out reforms and resist the influence of the old guard, initial developments are encouraging. The new rulers in Morocco, Jordan, and Bahrain, who hold a political perspective different from that of their predecessors, have responded positively to public demands by releasing political prisoners, promising wider representation, and focusing on political and economic reforms.

## Opportunities and Challenges

This new phase of political reform and transition faces serious challenges. Arab regimes, enjoying full power with no accountability, are not eager to have civil society as their partners (or competitors), and they are fighting back to protect their security, stability, and sovereignty. Rulers appeal to fears of instability and to the need for speedy economic reforms in a bid to win domestic and international support. They exaggerate the threat of political Islam to civil liberties and regional stability in order to justify harsh measures against the opposition. Groups that believe that Islam should have a greater role in public life are popular and visible in all Arab countries; they owe their popularity less to public sympathy for their own program than to public resentment of corrupt Arab regimes. The official press gives maximum publicity to radical and violent groups, portraying political Islam as a bogeyman that justifies undemocratic measures and the exclusion of all Islamic groups from social and political participation. This only hardens Islamic groups and radicalizes their political approaches. Jordan and Morocco are the only two countries that have included Islamists in the political process and have allowed them free speech.

Although most governments fear the loss of control and see civil-society organizations and prodemocracy groups as threats that must be curtailed, they also understand that there is a need for reform. They are aware of the changes in the global environment that will force their hand on the economy and make it impossible for them to control the flow of information. Thus they cannot remove all opportunities for civil-society groups to operate. Currently, only a narrow margin of freedom is permitted for privately owned media organizations, independent trade-union movements, and public-policy forums, but even this restricted space offers real opportunities for democratic development. Moreover, many Arab countries periodically hold both local and national elections, which, despite all their limitations, represent an official commitment to the democratic process and provide a potential opening for democratic forces.

Democratization in the Arab world also must contend with the abuse of religion. Islam continues to be one of the major political forces in the Middle East, and it is often put forward as a simple solution for all political problems. The century-old debate about its proper role in public life has been further complicated by controversy over which interpretation of Islam should predominate and how its authority should be exercised; different versions of Islamic rule have been adopted in Iran, Sudan, and Saudi Arabia. Efforts to promote liberal and pluralistic democracy in the region must consider how to deal with those whose Islamic faith has become rooted in radical politics. The original texts that define Islam provide general principles on governance and the penal code but do not provide laws for modern societies and states. Moreover, political Islam is not monolithic; there is no consensus among Muslims on how to apply Islamic texts to modern political life. Even if Islamic coalitions gain power and people vote to live under the *shari'a,* they still have to assign the legislative, executive, and judicial functions to independent public institutions. Reformers in the Middle East are fully aware of the magnitude of the task that lies ahead. Even though the nascent efforts of liberal Islamists are being challenged, both within their societies and by outsiders who assert that democratization is a destabilizing force in this strategically important region, liberal interpretations of Islam are slowly but surely gaining in popularity.

It would be foolish to underestimate the formidable obstacles to democratization in the Arab world. As we enter the twenty-first century, however, it is equally important not to overlook the forces favorable to democratic progress being unleashed by socioeconomic development, the communications revolution, and the growing vitality of Arab civil society.

# 4

# THE TRAP OF
# LIBERALIZED AUTOCRACY

*Daniel Brumberg*

***Daniel Brumberg*** *is associate professor of government at Georgetown University and a visiting scholar during the 2002–2003 academic year at the Carnegie Endowment for International Peace in Washington, D.C. This essay originally appeared in the October 2002 issue of the* Journal of Democracy.

Over the past two decades, the Middle East has witnessed a transition away from—and then back toward—authoritarianism. This dynamic began with tactical political openings whose goal was to sustain rather than transform autocracies. Enticed by the prospect of change, an amalgam of political forces—Islamists, leftists, secular liberals, NGO activists, women's organizations, and others—sought to imbue the political process with new meanings and opportunities, hoping that the "inherently unstable" equilibrium of *dictablandas* would give way to a new equilibrium of competitive democracy.[1]

It is now clear, both within and far beyond the Middle East, that liberalized autocracy has proven far more durable than once imagined.[2] The trademark mixture of guided pluralism, controlled elections, and selective repression in Egypt, Jordan, Morocco, Algeria, and Kuwait is not just a "survival strategy" adopted by authoritarian regimes, but rather a *type* of political system whose institutions, rules, and logic defy any linear model of democratization.[3] And while several of the authors who write about the Middle East in this collection of essays argue that political liberalization is moving forward, Jillian Schwedler's essay on Yemen, Jason Brownlee's piece on Egypt, and Russell Lucas's analysis of Jordan, suggest that in fact *deliberalization* may be underway.

Perhaps these states will join the ranks of Bashar al-Assad's Syria, where the door was opened a crack and then quickly closed, and countries such as Tunisia and Saudi Arabia, where the rulers have never risked even the most controlled liberalization. Certainly, the outrageous August 2002 decision of Egypt's Supreme Court to uphold the conviction of Saad Eddin Ibrahim and his young colleagues appears to support the notion that Middle East regimes are becoming less rather than more autocratic.[4] Yet what we are witnessing is probably *not* a return to full authoritarianism, but rather the latest turn in a protracted cycle in which rulers widen or narrow the boundaries of participation and expression in response to what they see as the social, economic, political, and geostrategic challenges facing their regimes. Such political eclecticism has benefits that Arab rulers are unlikely to forgo. Indeed, over the next few years Bahrain and Qatar may expand the ranks of Arab regimes dwelling in the "gray zone" of liberalized autocracy.[5]

In the Arab world, a set of interdependent institutional, economic, ideological, social, and geostrategic factors has created an adaptable ecology of repression, control, and partial openness. The weblike quality of this political ecosystem both helps partial autocracies to survive and makes their rulers unwilling to give up *final* control over any strand of the whole. But there is more to the story than wily rulers and impersonal "factors," for the governments of Algeria, Morocco, Jordan, Kuwait, and even Egypt receive a degree of acquiescence and sometimes even support from both secular and some Islamist opposition groups. Such *ententes* can take the form of arrangements that give oppositionists a voice in parliament or even the cabinet, and may also involve a process of "Islamization" by which the state cedes some ideological and institutional control to Islamists.

This ironic outcome reminds us that while liberalized autocracies can achieve a measure of stability, over time their very survival exacts greater and greater costs. Because they have failed to create a robust *political* society in which non-Islamists can secure the kind of organized popular support that Islamists command, these hybrid regimes have created circumstances under which free elections could well make illiberal Islamists the dominant opposition voice, leaving democrats (whether secularist or Islamist) caught between ruling autocrats and Islamist would-be autocrats. Hence the great dilemma in which substantive democratization and genuine pluralism become at once more urgently needed and more gravely risky.

While the solution to this dilemma may lie in gradualism, any reforms worthy of the name must address the weakness or even absence of political society in the Arab world. This will mean promoting independent judiciaries; effective political parties; competitive, internationally observed elections; and legislatures that represent majorities rather than rubber-stamp the edicts of rulers. Such changes will demand bold initiatives from Arab rulers, new thinking from mainstream Islamists, and a readiness from the United States to support a policy of democratic gradualism whose purpose is to help liberalized autocracies carefully move beyond the politics of mere survival.

While it is true that the Arab world boasts no democracies, some of its autocracies are decidedly less complete than others. To understand this variation, and to grasp why some partial autocracies are better than others at sustaining survival strategies, we must ask how the rulers perceive the threats they face, and we must look at the institutional, social, political, and ideological conditions that tend to intensify or reduce such threats. The importance of threat perception lies in the very logic of partial autocracies: To endure, they must implicitly or explicitly allow some opposition forces certain kinds of social, political, or ideological power—but things must never reach a point where the regime feels deterred from using force when its deems fit. If a regime can keep up this balancing act, reformists within the government will find it easier to convince hard-liners that the benefits of accommodation outweigh the costs. Conversely, where it is hard to make this case, rulers will prefer total autocracy. As to the conditions that encourage a choice in favor of one or the other, these can be summarized as follows: States that promote competitive or *dissonant* politics will tend to feel surer that Islamist ambitions can be limited and so will be more willing to consider accommodating opposition, while states that promote hegemonic or *harmonic* politics will tend to invite more radical "counterhegemonic" Islamist opposition movements whose presence increases the expected cost of political liberalization.

## The Dead End of Hegemony

Iraq, Saudi Arabia, and Syria are total autocracies whose endurance is often attributed to three conditions, each of which bears a word of comment. The first, oil money, is necessary but not sufficient: Some other Arab countries receive oil income but are not *total* autocracies. The second condition is the "harmonic" foundation of legitimacy: Total autocracies spread the idea that the state's mission is to defend the supposedly unified nature of the Arab nation or the Islamic community (the danger that Islamists might "outbid" the regime on the second score should be obvious). The third condition is the hegemonic reach of state institutions: Total autocracies create powerful organizations whose main job is to absorb or repress rival political voices. Here too there is a potential danger for the regime. As the ambivalent alliance between the House of Saud and the Wahabi religious establishment shows, state control of Islamic institutions can be both central to this hegemonic strategy and a threat to it. Because Islam is a transcendent religion that can never be fully coopted, governments must cede some autonomy to state-supported religious institutions or elites, thereby raising the prospect that elements of the religious establishment could defect to the Islamist opposition.

To deter this and all other possible rebellions, total autocracies have large and brutal security agencies. Yet the more force is used, the longer grows the list of revenge-seeking enemies—a drawback that is especially acute when the rulers belong to ethnic or religious minorities (in Syria, Alawites; in Iraq, Sunni Arabs). Harmonic ideologies and their pretenses of "Islamic" or "Arab" unity may aspire to hide such narrow power bases, but the reality of minority rule is apparent enough, further alienating key religious groups and making the expected costs of reform that much higher.

One way out of this vicious circle might be to emphasize instrumental over symbolic legitimacy—by handing out more oil rents to key groups, for instance. Such strategies have obvious limits. An alternative (or complementary) approach is to rob your neighbor's bank, as Iraq tried to do by invading Kuwait in 1990. But barring such desperate measures, some leaders might conclude that a limited political opening is worth the risk. After all, what value is there in maintaining decades of hegemonic rule if the instruments of domination cannot be used to ensure the ruling elite's continued good health?

This was certainly the motive behind Algeria's dramatic political opening in 1989. At the time, Algeria was a classic harmonic state. For nearly 30 years, its generals and ruling-party hacks had been absorbing all potential opposition into a quasi-socialist order that celebrated the alleged harmony of "the Algerian people." Islamic leaders and institutions were drafted into this hegemonic project, thereby ironically ensuring that, in the wake of liberalization, populist Islam would emerge as *the* counterhegemonic force. The Islamic Salvation Front (FIS) and its revolutionary—if nebulous—vision of an Islamic state galvanized an estranged generation which had come to believe that the rhetoric of unity spouted by the ruling National Liberation Front (FLN) was mere window-dressing for the corrupt rule of a minority that was more French than Arab, or more Berber than Muslim. Despite this growing estrangement, in 1991 the FLN foolishly wagered that it could reproduce its hegemony through competitive elections. While a proportional system might have limited the FIS's electoral gains and thus made some kind of power sharing possible, the FIS's revolutionary ideology created so grave a perceived threat that no such arrangement could likely have survived the military's quest for total certainty, or the preference of many secular would-be democrats for the protection that the generals promised.

This illusory quest for safety set the stage for a civil war that has claimed some 100,000 lives. In the wake of this disaster, Algeria's leaders tried to put together a power-sharing system in which the identity claims of Berbers, secularists, Islamists, and (implicitly) the military would be recognized, institutionalized, and perhaps negotiated. But the mixed system that was born with the 1997 parliamentary elections produced mixed results. It certainly provided unprecedented opportunities for elites with opposing ideologies to pursue dialogue.[6] But to give such a system credibility, regimes must promote genuine (even if circumscribed) representation, while leaders must project an understanding of the populace's elemental fears and aspirations. President Abdelaziz Bouteflika got off to a good start in 1999, but the high abstention rate in the 2002 parliamentary elections suggests that much work remains to be done if the regime is to consolidate whatever gains it can claim.

Algeria's recent experience suggests that leadership and political learning can play a role in helping regimes and oppositions to exit autocracy, but the lesson seems lost on some. Syria's brief opening is a case in point. When President Bashar al-Assad assumed the reigns of power from his late father in June 2000, observers wondered if the son would honor his public promises to open up the system.[7] The answer was clear by the autumn of 2001, when some liberal intellectuals were arrested for holding informal meetings to discuss democracy. Thus was the door slammed shut on the briefest Arab-world political opening to date.

What did Assad fear? His security chiefs probably convinced him that the tiniest reform was a slippery slope to oblivion. While the regime had decimated its radical Islamist opposition in 1982 by massacring 10,000 citizens in the town of Hama, and while it had coopted some businessmen from the Sunni merchant elite, a combination of economic crisis, anger at corruption, and a growing contempt for "Ba'athist socialist" ideology and Assad's contrived cult of personality all gave the regime reason for concern.[8] In the face of these and other worries, the new president could not pin his hopes on a few liberal intellectuals with no organized following. These knowns and unknowns, as well as the imposing shadow of his late father, proved far more relevant than Bashar's optometry studies in London or his exposure to the Internet. With oil rents still flowing in, it seems a wonder that it took so long for him to conclude that full autocracy was the only option.

While Tunisia's President Ben Ali has reached a similar conclusion, the origins of total autocracy in his country differ from those in Saudi Arabia, Iraq, or Syria. Instead of oil money and ideology, there is Ben Ali's obsession with power and the determination of business interests and the ruling elite to emulate the Asian model of state-driven, export-oriented industrialization. With a small population whose well-educated workers and professionals include a large percentage of women, Tunisia had significant constituencies *within and outside* the regime that chose not to contest the "nonideological" hegemony of the ruling Democratic Constitutional Rally (RCD). The spectacle of the bloodshed next door in Algeria helped to cement this tacit consensus against rocking the boat.

By the late 1990s, the effort to create an "Asian-style" economic miracle in North Africa had run into many obstacles, not least of which has been the regime's abuse of civil and human rights. Moreover, in the

absence of accountability and the rule of law, state-driven industrialization was feeding rent-seeking and corruption.[9] By 1999 there was
clearly a demand for political opening, but the voting that year ended
with the RCD controlling 92 percent of the seats in the Chamber of
Deputies and Ben Ali winning another term with a claimed mandate of
99.4 percent of the vote. Islamists remained banned, revealing the
regime's continued anxieties about threats from that quarter. Since then,
Ben Ali has rammed through a set of constitutional amendments to extend his term from four to six years and arrested human rights activists,
thereby signaling his determination to maintain total power.

## Why "Dissonance" Is Good

Total autocracy is the exception rather than the rule in the Arab
world. Most Arabs live under autocracies that allow a measure of
openness. Three factors have generated and sustained such regimes.
First, the rulers of Morocco, Egypt, Jordan, Kuwait, and Lebanon have
not tried to impose a single vision of political community, or to
completely swallow up every vestige of organized pluralism in society.
Instead, they have put a certain symbolic distance between the state
and society in ways that leave room for competitive or *dissonant*
politics. By not nailing the state's legitimacy to the mast of one
ideological vessel with a putatively sacred national or religious mission,
they have helped to short-circuit the growth of counterhegemonic
Islamist movements. Second, partial autocracies are *nonhegemonic*.
Within limits, they allow contending groups and ideas to put down
institutional roots outside the state. This ensures competition not only
between Islamists and non-Islamists, but among Islamist parties as well.
The more such contention there is, the likelier it is that rulers will risk
an opening. Third, partial autocracies have enough economic
development and competition to free the state from obsessive concern
with any single interest, class, or resource. In many such regimes, for
instance, one finds public-sector employees and bureaucrats vying with
independent professionals and private businessmen for the state's
political and economic support.

Such economic and political dissonance facilitates the juggling act
that is central to regime survival. Rulers of liberalized autocracies strive
to pit one group against another in ways that maximize the rulers' room
for maneuver and restrict the opposition's capacity to work together.
Yet such divide-and-rule tactics also give oppositionists scope for influence that they might not have in an open political competition that
yields clear winners and losers. Consensus politics and state-enforced
power sharing can form an alternative to either full democracy or full
autocracy, particularly when rival social, ethnic, or religious groups fear
that either type of rule will lead to their political exclusion. In Kuwait,

Lebanon, Jordan, Morocco, and to some extent Egypt, the peaceful accommodation of such forces depends in part on the arbitrating role of the ruler.

No ruler is completely autonomous in relation to society. The kings of Morocco and Jordan may have a better perch from which to arbitrate conflicts than do Arab presidents, whose fates are usually tied to a ruling party or its interests. But since both monarchs derive their legitimacy at least *partly* from their purported lineage ties to Mohammad, they are, as Abdeslam Maghraoui notes, at once modern leaders of a nation *(watan)* and traditional patrons of the Islamic community *(ummah)*. Similarly, while Egypt's rulers long ago distanced themselves from the Arab-nationalist rhetoric of Gamal Abdel Nasser, they have not fully repudiated the basic ideological premises of the populist state that he founded. The legitimacy of the Egyptian state still rests partly on its role as a defender of communal Islamic values.

That the rulers of some liberalized autocracies are both the chief arbiters within society and the major patrons of religious institutions is central to these regimes' survival strategies. As arbiters, those who hold power in Egypt, Morocco, and Jordan use cultural, religious, and ideological dissonance to divide the opposition. As patrons of religion, these same powerholders use their ties to Islamic institutions to limit the influence of secular political forces. Over time, this Islamization strategy has led to acute dilemmas. For in their efforts to coopt conservative Islamic ideas these regimes have hindered the creation of alternatives to the illiberalism that is characteristic of *mainstream* (and not merely radical) Islamism.

Consider the case of Egypt, where indulging Islamist sensibilities is an old art form. With parliamentary elections looming in the fall of 2000, the culture minister, backed by the top religious authorities at the leading state-funded Islamic university, banned the obscure Syrian Haidar Haidar's novel *A Banquet for Seaweed* on the grounds that it dangerously departed from "accepted religious understanding" and threatened "the solidarity of the nation." Having thus defended the faith, the government then shut down the very opposition newspaper that had exposed the offending book![10] However cynical, the move made perfect sense. The political party that published the paper had close ties to the mainstream Muslim Brotherhood, and the state was out to underscore its own role as the supreme arbiter of matters Islamic (for good measure, the authorities had two hundred Muslim Brothers arrested). In a stinging judgment that actually understates the problem, Max Rodenbeck observes that the cumulative effect of actions like this has been to "compel an 'orthodoxy' that is both amorphous and restricted, preventing Islamist thought from moving beyond denunciation of heresy and repetition of formulas from the Koran."[11] Even Al-Wasat—a party led by Islamists who advocate a more pluralistic vision of Islam—has had its application for party certification repeatedly turned down. Egypt's rulers are not interested in promoting a liberal Islamic party, either because they fear that radicals might capture it or because they do not want a successful liberal Islamist party to ally with secular parties in ways that might undermine the regime's strategy of survival through a delicate balancing act.

Variations of this Islamization strategy can be found in other regimes which, unlike Egypt's, permit legal Islamist parties. Partial inclusion is a more useful way of buttressing liberalized autocracies because it requires Islamists to renounce violence, act openly, and most importantly, play by what are ultimately the government's rules. Yet the Islamists may reap advantages, since even limited participation in parliaments or cabinets gives them means to extend their influence. Following the 1991 unification of North and South Yemen, for example, the General People's Congress (GPC) became the ruling party by cutting a deal with the tribal-cum-Islamist Islah party, whose religious wing thereby gained control of public education. Indeed, in 1994 President Ali Abdallah Salih "gave money to Sheikh Abdel Meguid al-Zindani, an Afghan veteran and former associate of Osama Bin Laden's, to build Al Eman University on government land near Sanaa."[12] Still, once the deal with Islah had served the purpose of marginalizing the South, the GPC engineered an election in 1997 that ushered many of Islah's Islamists out of parliament while leaving the tribal members with their seats. More recently, the government has tried in the wake of September 11 to assert more control over Islah's schools.

By comparison with other hybrid regimes, Yemen's experience is unique. While a patrimonialist vision of authority colors public education in much of the Arab world, there is little evidence that the governments of Egypt, Jordan, Morocco, and Kuwait promote a particularly radical or anti-Western vision of Islam. Yet neither do they imbue their curricula with anything like liberal democratic values. Absent such a positive effort, the state-sponsored "traditional" view of Islam (with its emphasis on state authority and the claims of community) will remain vulnerable to the allure of radical Islam. Periodic attempts to placate Islamists by unleashing state-subsidized clerics against "apostates" can produce the same result. Apart from the danger that such efforts may backfire—as they did when the ceding of the Jordanian education ministry to Islamists in 1994 provoked an uproar from liberals—over time Islamization strategies undercut the careful juggling acts at the heart of regime survival strategies.

## The Need for *Political* Society

One way of escaping the dilemmas created by partial autocracies might be to advocate liberal Islam. But no leader has embraced this option, for obvious reasons. Liberal Islam, moreover, constitutes a limited intellectual trend that has thus far not sunk deep organizational roots in Arab societies. Nor have civil society organizations been able to pierce the armor of liberalized autocracy. On the contrary, in Egypt, Morocco, and Jordan the sheer proliferation of small NGOs—riven by fierce ideological divisions and hamstrung by official regulations—has made "divide and rule" easier.

By themselves, civil society organizations cannot make up for the lack of a functioning political society, meaning an autonomous realm of self-regulating political parties that have the constitutional authority to represent organized constituencies in parliaments.[13] Autocratic rulers know this, of course—their survival strategies are designed to *prevent* the emergence of any effective political society. Partial autocracies use patronage as well as laws governing parties and elections to stop opposition elites from creating organic political parties. As a result, most Arab-world political parties are better at negotiating with powerful rulers than at articulating the aspirations of each party's disorganized followers. Under such conditions, apathy reigns, while elections rarely attract more than 35 percent of the potential voting public.

As for legislatures, constitutions hobble rather than bolster their authority, as does the lack of a rule of law (which is not the same thing as a state that makes lots of laws). Such constitutions are rife with loopholes that "guarantee" freedoms of speech and assembly so long as such liberties do not infringe upon "national" or "Islamic" values. Indeed, what used to be said of the old Soviet Constitution can be said of most Arab constitutions: They guarantee freedom of speech, but not freedom *after* speech. Arab "reformers" since Anwar Sadat have been great advocates of "a state of laws," by which they have meant laws passed by compliant legislatures and upheld by compliant judges in order to legitimate the regime's survival strategies. Such laws not only inhibit democratization, they give legal sanction to forms of economic corruption that only further delegitimate the so-called capitalism of liberalized autocracies.

Because the absence or presence of political society is largely a function of official policy, it will not emerge unless Arab leaders redefine the relationship between citizen and state. Sadly, it is now clear that the new generation of leaders in Jordan and Morocco are not up to this task. Indeed, insofar as survival strategies have increased the perceived costs of democratization while not providing for effective economic development, the young kings of these lands have shown themselves unwilling or unable to cross anxious hard-liners in the military, the security forces, and the business community. Thus while Morocco's King Mohammed VI spoke early on of shifting to a "new concept of authority," he soon fell back on one of the hoariest defenses of partial autocracy, pleading lamely that "each country has to have its own specific features of democracy."[14]

## "Reform" versus Democratic Gradualism

If an exit from liberalized autocracy to competitive democracy is improbable, can we detect movement in the opposite direction? As noted above, events in Egypt and Yemen as well as Jordan—where there has been a crackdown on the press and two postponements of national elections since November 2001—seem to suggest that the answer is unfortunately "yes." This "deliberalizing" trend, as Jason Brownlee calls it, has at least four causes. First, there is the decline in external rents. This process has pushed regimes to adopt the kinds of structural economic reforms that they had previously skirted in their efforts to accommodate key constituencies. But such reforms have not produced enough "winners" to defend them successfully under conditions of open political competition, so rulers see a need to clamp down on previous political openings. Second, there is the growing influence of *mainstream* Islamism. Radical Islamism may be declining in some quarters of the Arab world, but Islamist movements that seek *peacefully* to advance illiberal cultural projects by playing according to the rules of partial autocracy are getting stronger.[15] Although these movements may not command electoral majorities, the disarray besetting secular democrats means that Islamists would certainly win at least powerful pluralities in any open election. Third, the failure of the Palestinian-Israeli peace process has not only given Islamists across the Arab world a powerful symbol, it has also facilitated the forging of ideologically heterogeneous alliances between secularists and Islamists that rulers find increasingly threatening.[16] Finally, in the context of a U.S.-led war on terrorism that requires the support or good will of many Arab leaders, Washington has until very recently evinced a certain tolerance for democracy.

Yet past experience suggests that the deliberalizing trend we are seeing is an inflection point in a long-term cycle. Perhaps the current shift toward tightening will be more protracted than previous ones, but in the longer run rulers and oppositionists are unlikely to forgo the advantages that partial autocracy offers to both. Even in Jordan, with its volatile combination of a Palestinian majority whose most effective leaders are Islamists, a new king who is still establishing his authority, a fragile economy, and the looming prospect of a U.S.-led regional war, it is unlikely that either King Abdallah or the Islamists (who in fact boycotted the 1997 elections) will give up a tradition of uneasy but mutually beneficial accommodation.[17]

Indeed, while Egypt and Jordan may be moving, for the time being, in a more authoritarian direction, there is some evidence that liberalized autocracies might be growing *more* rather than less common in the

Middle East. As Michael Herb notes, in 1999 and 2000, respectively, the leaders of Qatar and Bahrain initiated political openings after years of full autocracy. Bahrain held parliamentary elections in October 2002 while Qatar will hold parliamentary elections to replace its 35-member Consultative Council in 2003.[18] Morocco, which was holding parliamentary elections as this essay first went to press in September 2002, might also expand the boundaries of liberalized autocracy by creating more space for Islamist opposition. It is not a coincidence that all these countries are monarchies. Arab monarchs have more institutional and symbolic room to improvise reforms than do Arab presidents, who are invariably trapped by ruling parties and their constituencies. That said, and as I have argued, not all monarchies are equally capable of promoting political reform. Totalizing monarchies that rule in the name of harmonic ideologies—one thinks of the House of Saud—engender radical oppositions and thus are unlikely to countenance more than the slightest opening.

As for kings who rule partial autocracies, those who serve as both arbiters of the nation and spokesmen for the Islamic community find themselves constrained by the very Islamic elites whose teachings the kings often echo or encourage. As Abdeslam Maghraoui notes, Morocco's Mohammed VI might confront this paradoxical fact of life as a result of the coming elections. If the Islamist Justice and Development party makes major gains in the upcoming election but does not overplay its hand by rejecting membership in a multiparty majority coalition that limits its ideological reach, Morocco might follow the lead of other Arab states by allowing for partial inclusion of Islamists in a mixed system. But if the Islamists score a large victory and then challenge the king's *religious* authority, Morocco's leaders may eventually decide to move toward less rather than more political openness.

There is no doubt, as Jean-François Seznec observes, that one factor pushing Arab regimes to engage in even modest political openings is that oil just does not pay the way it used to. With external rents declining, the implicit bargain by means of which rulers bought popular acquiescence in return for various forms of petroleum-funded largesse has fallen on hard times. Yet we should be careful not to lapse into structural determinism, for social, institutional, and ideological factors can raise or lower the expected costs of political change in dramatic and unexpected ways.

None of this excuses partial autocrats, of course. After all, for the most part they have embraced only such "reforms" as *hinder* the emergence of an effective political society. Moreover, because their survival strategies have often boosted Islamists rather than an expanded political arena as such, these rulers have sustained a cycle of conflict, stalemate, and reform. This makes it hard for even reformers with the best of intentions to envision a different future, and easy for the most cynical to rationalize their opposition to anything deeper than cosmetic reforms. Given the paucity of will and the imposing constraints, there is not likely to be much substantive change until at least two conditions emerge: first, when *both* mainstream Islamists and ruling elites offer a pluralistic vision of political community that does not make the state the enforcer of any particular vision of Islamic identity. And second, when the United States presses its Arab allies to transcend an involuted gradualism whose small steps trace the sad contours of an unvirtuous circle rather than the hopeful lineaments of a real path forward. Rather than espouse a fuzzy notion of "reform," such a policy of *democratic gradualism* must not only push for the creation of effective political parties, representative parliaments, and the rule of law; it must also be accompanied by international support for effective monitoring of local and national elections. Without international observers, the silent pluralities of the Arab world— large groups of people who often have little sympathy for illiberal Islamism—will never be able to make their voices heard.

## NOTES

1. Adam Przeworski, "The Games of Transition," in Scott Mainwaring et al., eds., *Issues in Democratic Consolidation: The New South American Democracies in Comparative Perspective* (Notre Dame: Notre Dame University Press, 1992), 109. Przeworksi argues that "what normally happens is . . . a melting of the iceberg of civil society which overflows the dams of the authoritarian regime." While he later observes that "liberalization could substitute for genuine democratization, thereby maintaining the political exclusion of subaltern groups" (111), the thrust of his conceptualization is that transitions move forward or back to reach a new equilibrium.

2. Thomas Carothers, "The End of the Transition Paradigm," *Journal of Democracy* 13 (January 2002): 5–21. Carothers (9) notes that "of the nearly 100 countries considered as 'transitional' in recent years, only a relatively small number—probably fewer than 20—are clearly en route to becoming successful, well-functioning democracies or at least have made some democratic progress and still enjoy a positive dynamic of democratization."

3. For several excellent discussions of this phenomenon see the essays in the section on "Elections Without Democracy?" by Larry Diamond, Andreas Schedler, and Steven Levitsky and Lucan Way in the April 2002 issue of the *Journal of Democracy*. These articles highlight the *exceptional* character of democratic transitions.

4. On 18 March 2003, the Court of Cassation—Egypt's supreme appeals court— aquitted Saad Eddin Ibrahim and his four codefendants of all charges. The court's verdict is final; the Egyptian government cannot appeal.

5. Thomas Carothers, "End of the Transition Paradigm," 9. He defines the "gray zone" as one in which regimes are "neither dictatorial nor clearly headed toward democracy."

6. The interviews that I conducted in Algiers in May and June 2002 with members of the 1997 parliament, Islamist and non-Islamist alike, suggest that political learning beyond the merely tactical level took place.

7. See Scott Peterson, "The Grooming of Syria's Bashar al-Assad," *Christian Sci-*

*ence Monitor,* 13 June 2002; Susan Sachs, "Bashar al-Assad: The Shy Young Doctor at Syria's Helm," *New York Times,* 14 June 2000.

8. Bassam Haddad, "Business as Usual in Syria?" MERIP Press Information Note 68, 7 September 2001.

9. Christopher Alexander, "Authoritarianism and Civil Society in Tunisia," *Middle East Report* 205 (October–December 1997).

10. The party was the Labor Socialists and its newspaper was *Al-Shaab,* which in fact got Haidar's book wrong. See Max Rodenbeck, "Witch Hunt in Egypt," *New York Review of Books,* 16 November 2000, 39. The quotes condemning Haidar come from Al-Azhar University's Islamic Research Academy and can be found in the first note to Rodenbeck's essay.

11. Max Rodenbeck, "Witch Hunt in Egypt," 41.

12. "Yemen's Religious Academies: From Defender of the Faith to Terrorist," *Economist,* 1 June 2002, 48.

13. See Manuel Antonio Garretón and Edward Newman, eds., *Democracy in Latin American (Re)Constructing Political Society* (New York: United Nations University Press, 2001).

14. Lisa Anderson, "Arab Democracy," 55–60. Quote from page 58; originally cited in Roxanne Roberts, "Morocco's King of Hearts," *Washington Post,* 23 June 2000.

15. See Gilles Kepel, *Jihad: Expansion et déclin de l'islamisme* (Paris: Gallimard, 2002).

16. See Dina Shehata, "The International Dimensions of Authoritarianism: The Case of Egypt," paper presented at the Annual Meeting of the American Political Science Association, Boston, 28–30 August 2002.

17. As Russell Lucas notes in his analysis of Jordan included in this volume, King Abdallah dissolved the parliament in June 2002 and has twice postponed elections since then. Opposition to the peace process has played an important role in his decisions.

18. The recent decision by the main opposition groups in Bahrain to boycott the parliamentary elections due to the government's failure to address concerns over the narrow boundaries of political reform indicates that a transition to liberalized autocracy is far from inevitable.

# 5

# THE DECLINE OF PLURALISM IN MUBARAK'S EGYPT

*Jason Brownlee*

*Jason Brownlee, a doctoral candidate in Princeton University's politics department, has been visiting Egypt frequently since 1995. His dissertation examines electoral authoritarianism in Egypt, Iran, Malaysia, and the Philippines under Marcos. This essay originally appeared in the October 2002 issue of the* Journal of Democracy.

Discussions of the prospects for expanded freedom in the Arab world often invoke Egypt as a leading candidate for gradual political reform.[1] The country's intermediate level of economic development, its extensive array of nongovernmental organizations (NGOs), and its multiparty system all seem to favor a democratic future. President Hosni Mubarak himself recently claimed that Egypt enjoys "all kinds of democracy." But the truth of the matter is that participation and pluralism are now at lower levels than at any time since Mubarak assumed the presidency in the wake of Anwar Sadat's assassination 21 years ago.[2] After a tenuous period of political opening in the 1980s and very early 1990s, the regime has progressively limited opportunities for the dispersal of power beyond the president, let alone for an actual alternation in power.

If any form of "freedom" has been expanded in Egypt, meanwhile, it has been the freedom of the presidency from the informal constraints that earlier limited its authority. Over the past two decades, Mubarak has acquired substantial liberty to have his opponents convicted in military trials, for example, or to shut down newspapers and professional syndicates, or to jail human rights activists. Overall, pluralism has declined markedly since the outset of his rule. And unless domestic and—perhaps more importantly—international actors compel the Egyptian president to cede power to other branches of government and to allow civil society organizations to operate independently, the outlook for organized political contestation in Egypt will only continue to dim.

Since 1967, Egypt has spent all but five months under a declared "state of emergency" by which the regime has rationalized the outlawing of demonstrations, the use of indefinite detentions without trial, and the endowment of presidential decrees with the power of law. President Sadat had terminated the provisions of emergency rule in the spring of 1981, but following his assassination by Islamist militants in October of that year, his vice-president and successor Mubarak quickly reinstated them. In 2000, the People's Assembly—the lower house of the Egyptian parliament, which is dominated by the president's National Democratic Party (NDP)—voted yet again to extend emergency provisions for a further three years.

Early in his presidency, Mubarak applied few of the emergency measures at his disposal. Echoing Sadat, he spoke of administering "democracy in doses," while releasing political prisoners and allowing press criticism of government ministers. The opposition's representation in parliament rose to a record 20 percent in the 1987 elections; nongovernmental associations grew by the thousands; and professional syndicates provided additional forums for debate and protest. These developments, and the regime's decision not to use force against its opponents, suggested that the government was genuinely ceding political space. One early 1990s report from the U.S. Agency for International Development hopefully concluded:

> The Mubarak government . . . clearly prefers to use the tactic of repression sparingly, and by regional standards, successfully limits its recourse to "the stick." Whether from calculation or conviction, the government is committed to a process of consultation with important social actors and of political reform. The government's style, in marked contrast to that of its predecessors, has been one of consensus building.[3]

But soon thereafter, the prospects for further political reform started to deteriorate sharply. Indulging in executive decrees, the extensive use of military courts, and the broad deployment of security forces, Mubarak reversed Egypt's course and began to "deliberalize"—renewing controls on opposition parties, elections, Islamist activity, civil society organizations, and the press.

The regime's ongoing and costly military campaign against Islamist militants (the annual death toll from which peaked in 1993 at more than 1,000) provided the pretext for a new drive of repression against nonviolent political opponents as well. When members of the Muslim Brotherhood (MB)—which was formally outlawed but allowed to organize without formal party status—won the leadership elections of the doctors', engineers', pharmacists', and lawyers' syndicates in the early and mid-1990s, legislation was enacted to bring most of the syndicates under the management of government-appointed judicial committees. The regime sent 54 Brotherhood members to prison by military trial in 1995 and detained thousands more without charge.[4] Today the government still deploys the same "state of emergency" rationale for similarly repressive measures against nonviolent Islamist political actors, even though the primary target of its military campaign—the Islamic Group—surrendered in 1998 and there have been no domestic attacks by militant Islamists in five years.

Nor was government repression restricted to Islamists. The 1995 elections, rife with violence and fraud, gave Mubarak's NDP a record 94 percent majority in parliament. Meanwhile, the regime's Political Parties Committee—which regulates the creation of new parties—had rejected every application made to it during the 1990s, including a proposal from the explicitly "consensus-building" Center Party, composed of prodemocratic Muslims and Christians.[5] At the same time, the regime dictated that all NGOs would have to receive government approval of both their establishment and activities, and particularly for the receipt of foreign funds. Operating since 1985, the Egyptian Organization for Human Rights, the oldest human rights group in the country, was denied a license to operate officially, and in 1998—after state-security forces arrested the organization's secretary general, Hafez Abu Saeda—it was forced to turn down Western funding and to scale back its activities.

Ultimately, the freedoms that opposition activists enjoyed during the 1980s easily slipped away. And they easily slipped away because the "openings" of that earlier decade had no institutional basis, coming as they did solely at the discretion of the regime. Mubarak's first years in power thus never represented a genuine move toward liberal democracy but only a tactical and precarious *tolerance*.

## The Courts Defend the Ballot

An unusual court decision mandating judicial supervision over the 2000 parliamentary elections momentarily reintroduced meaningful contestation into Egyptian political life. In November 1999, Mubarak—fresh from a plebiscite giving him six more years in power—had announced that the coming elections to the People's Assembly would be "subject at all stages to supervision by the judiciary."[6] But the legislation that was subsequently passed by parliament merely empowered committees of judges to float between polling stations, which was a transparently weak means of preventing electoral fraud. In the summer of 2000, however, the country's Supreme Constitutional Court (SCC)—playing on the government's rhetoric of democratic reform—ruled that members of the judiciary *had to* monitor *every* station as voting took place. Members of the judiciary—long considered the branch of Egypt's government least dominated by the executive and most likely to advocate greater political freedom—then supervised three rounds of elections and runoffs, from October 18 through November 24, across Egypt's 222 electoral districts (and 15,502 polling stations), providing unprecedented assurance that a vote cast would be a vote counted. (It is an open question as to why Mubarak called for the judicial supervision in the first place. Some think he expected the judiciary's decision and was trying to coopt the announcement. Most agree that he did not anticipate the seriousness with which the judiciary would ultimately attempt to implement his proclamation.)

Hoping they could still rig the results, NDP officials grew frustrated when watchful judges stopped unregistered voters from casting ballots and refused to turn ballot boxes over to policemen offering to "transport them to tallying stations." But with almost a week between each stage of voting, the regime developed countermeasures, especially using security forces to block voters from entering polling stations in the first place (often assaulting the voters in the process). Judges, confined to monitoring the election process inside the stations, could do nothing about these abuses. The regime's voter-deterrence efforts were mainly concentrated on Muslim Brotherhood supporters. As one NDP member explained candidly, "Sometimes we *had* to stop the Muslim Brothers . . . especially in the third stage," when several of the organization's leaders were in the running.[7] Because of the security-force blockades, only two Brotherhood candidates gained seats in the final round.

The unanticipated level of competition at the district level publicly stung the NDP, but it did not come close to transferring power from it. True, two-thirds of incumbent candidates were defeated, eight parliamentary committee chairs among them. And only 172 (39 percent) of the NDP's official candidates were elected. But another 181 "NDP independents"—members who had run in the elections despite not having received the party's nomination—won seats and subsequently rejoined the party. In addition, 35 actual independents joined the NDP after winning their seats, topping off the party's current 88 percent parliamentary majority—a margin comfortably above the two-thirds needed to pass legislation and rubber-stamp the president's decisions.

If the elections embarrassed the ruling party, they disgraced the official opposition. In total, the Liberal, Nasserist, National Gathering, and Wafd parties ran 352 candidates but took only a disheartening 16 seats (a mere 3.5 percent of all the seats in the People's Assembly). By contrast, the Muslim Brotherhood, operating without official party status, won just as many races with only 63 candidates. In 1995, none of the MB's 148 candidates had been successful. Their victories in 2000, despite the regime's efforts to thwart them, demonstrated the impact of the SCC ruling.[8] Through the institution of judicial supervision, members of the SCC and others in the judiciary exercised significant independence from the regime's designs and broke the pattern of noncompetitive elections that had developed over the previous decade.

Yet the influence of judicial supervision may wane considerably before the parliamentary elections scheduled for 2005. Last year, Mubarak dealt a crippling blow to the SCC's autonomy when he appointed as head of the Court Fathi Naguib, who, as assistant minister of justice, had helped to craft many of the laws that restricted civil society in the 1990s. Accordingly, the SCC may prove far more pliant in the future, particularly if given the opportunity to revisit the supervision of elections.

Although the 2000 elections raised the competitiveness of Egypt's parliamentary elections, they did not derail the trend of physical repression and political closure. Since 2000, state-security forces have continued to arrest MB members, often now in raids on private residences, and to detain them—sometimes for months—without trial on charges of belonging to an illegal organization or plotting to overthrow the government. In the summer of 2001, a state-security court sentenced Saad Eddin Ibrahim, the liberal sociologist and founder of the Ibn Khaldun Center for Development Studies, to seven years hard labor on charges that included tarnishing Egypt's reputation and illicitly accepting foreign funding. Outside observers have judged both the original trial and a July 2002 retrial, which upheld the original ruling (finally revered in early 2003), as seriously flawed and politically motivated. Meanwhile, recent elections —the reform of which was the focus of Ibrahim's Center—have been largely noncompetitive. In the 2001 contests for the Consultative Assembly (the parliament's upper house), the NDP took 74 out of the 88 seats at stake. And in January 2002, the People's Assembly exempted all local council elections from judicial supervision, assisting the NDP in winning a 98 percent majority.

## Competition Within the NDP?

While the 2000 elections did not alter the authoritarian character of regime-society relations, they did trigger a debate within the NDP on how best to prepare the party for future competition. Through the last parliamentary elections, NDP candidates were chosen by the party's general secretariat, under the leadership of its three-member politburo: Minister of Information Safwat El-Sherif, Minister of Parliamentary Affairs Kamal El-Shazli, and NDP secretary-general Youssef Wali. In the summer of 2000, several recent entrants into the general secretariat, most prominently the president's son, Gamal Mubarak, sought to incorporate "new blood" in the form of younger and better-qualified candidates.[9] But the selections—444 finalists chosen from a pool of 3,000 younger NDP members—ended up being chosen by El-Shazli, the head of party membership. About 1,400 of those not chosen ran as "NDP independents," and when most of the party's official candidates lost, Wali and El-Shazli portrayed the results as harmonious "corrections" of their earlier choices.

Gamal Mubarak, however, spoke publicly about the need for internal party reforms and introduced a formal method for selecting candidates. Beginning with the Consultative Assembly elections and continuing through local council races, holders of internal party posts were able to vote in electoral caucuses on their preferred nominees. The system broadens internal participation, but it functions mainly as an advisory process, while the general secretariat continues to have the final say on candidacies. And the old guard of Wali, El-Shazli, and El-Sherif has manipulated the caucuses to favor more conservative candidates.[10] Seeking an institutional base for himself, the younger Mubarak must now work to make the system fairer and more meaningful. He has gained ground against the old guard, recently joining the NDP politburo along with outspoken MP Zakariya Azmi and Alieddin Hilal, the minister of youth and former dean of Cairo University's Faculty of Economics and Political Science.

The drive for pluralism within the NDP does not, however, seem to extend outward to society at large. For example, no NDP parliamentarians voted against a law passed earlier this year that reinforces the government's authority to approve and dissolve nongovernmental organizations. So even if Gamal Mubarak and a "new guard" gain control of the party, they are unlikely to promote a competitive multiparty system without pressure from outside the regime.

## External Relations and the Possibility of Change

As U.S. president George W. Bush recently stated, "Opposition parties should have the freedom to organize, assemble, and speak, with equal access to all airwaves. All political prisoners must be released and allowed to participate in the election process. Human rights organizations should be free to visit . . . [in order] to ensure that the conditions for free elections are being created."[11] The president was, in fact, referring to Cuba, but his words could apply verbatim to Egypt. With respect to its levels of opposition activity and its space for institutions of civil society, the Egyptian regime now bears more resemblance to Fidel Castro's dictatorship than to any of the struggling democracies in Eastern Europe or sub-Saharan Africa. Mubarak's capacity for neutralizing his opponents approaches the kind of arbitrary dominance common in "sultanistic" systems, where "[t]he ruler exercises his power without constraint, at his own discretion . . . unencumbered by rules or by any commitment to an ideology or value system."[12] Nor can liberalization begin without Egypt's executive first being "encumbered." But whence could the necessary checks on the regime's power originate?

Mubarak has subdued Egypt's Islamists, leftists, and human rights community to the point where little domestic impetus for reform remains. Accordingly, external backers may hold the most potential for gradually limiting executive power while supporting the parties and an embattled civil society. The United States, in particular, provides Egypt with $2 billion a year in development and military aid and helps bring in still larger economic relief packages, such as last spring's multilateral pledge for $10 billion in loans and grants over three years—including an immediate grant of $2 billion to compensate for the country's post–September 11 drop in tourism revenues. The United States accordingly has Mubarak's ear. Its officials could pressure him into allowing opposition groups to contest the NDP's hegemony and letting human rights organizations operate freely.

Successive U.S. administrations have tended to oppose democratization in Egypt—as they have in the Muslim Middle East generally—believing that a push to check the Egyptian president's power might bring about an "Algerian scenario" in which Islamists would take hold of government.[13] But these fears are misplaced. The Egyptian president is effectively elected by the People's Assembly, which offers a single candidate for a plebiscite every six years, and is thus highly insulated from the general electorate. At the same time, although the Muslim Brotherhood poses the most viable challenge to the NDP in parliament, the Brothers' popular support remains modest.[14] Completely fair elections would likely give the MB about 15 percent (66) of the contested seats, a share well short of the one-third (approximately 150) needed to nominate a presidential candidate.[15] Since tremendous authority rests in a chief executive who is for all intents and purposes elected by his own party, Egypt does not stand on the brink of a "one man, one vote, one time" crisis. Both the security of the president's position and the modesty of the MB's political base allow for competitive parliamentary elections without the "risk" of regime change.

Moreover, the existing opposition parties represent outdated bases of support. Current restrictions on the creation of new parties maintain an artificial and skewed two-party "competition" between the NDP and the MB. If the system is to reach an equilibrium that reflects contemporary Egyptian society, new parties must be allowed to form legally. Such an opening would have to be accomplished informally, party proposal by party proposal, but it could begin with the dissolution of the Political Parties Committee and the transfer of its responsibilities to the courts. A competitive multiparty system would then reduce, rather than increase, Islamist representation in parliament by offering anti-NDP voters alternatives to the Muslim Brotherhood. Similarly, for Egyptian civil society organizations to be able to support human rights as their peers in other developing countries have done, they must be free to accept foreign funding and operate without fear that their members will be detained or imprisoned. Finally, a formal end to the "state of emergency" would be the most important single act toward building an active political society working independently of the president's will.

As with judicial supervision of the 2000 elections, these measures would help to impose institutional boundaries, constrain the president's powers, and end the charade of "liberalization" that cloaks the current pattern of repression. Empowering non-NDP actors in these areas would not threaten a sudden turnover of power to Islamists. On the contrary, broadening the space for political activity in Egypt would strengthen alternative non-Islamist currents for a day when competition for the presidency is more likely.

None of this will happen without acute and sustained pressure on Hosni Mubarak. At present, however, Egypt's closest ally appears committed simply to backing the president. Even before September 11, the United States consistently supported the Egyptian government, despite that government's aggression against its domestic political opponents. The war on terrorism has only reinforced that position and offered a new source of legitimation for the regime's political use of extralegal detentions and military trials. Remarkably, U.S. secretary of state Colin Powell has even portrayed Mubarak's heavy-handed approach to domestic security as a model for emulation, stating his "appreciation for the commitment that Egypt has made to working with us as we move forward to deal with the scourge of terrorism. Egypt, as all of you know, is really ahead of us on this issue. They have had to deal with acts of terrorism in recent years. . . . And we have much to learn from them and there is much we can do together."[16] What Egypt and the United States  can accomplish together, and what they should cooperate on, are matters of important debate. But if a narrow and simplistic focus on security trumps the potential gains of political opening, one can expect a persistence of authoritarianism in Egypt that simply negates USAID programs promoting democracy and better governance.[17]

In a surprise move on 14 August 2002, however, the Bush adminis-  tration announced that unless and until Egypt's domestic human rights situation improved, Cairo would not receive additional U.S. aid beyond the nearly $2 billion per year guaranteed by the Camp David peace accord with Israel.[18] This unprecedented linkage of U.S. foreign assistance with political reform in a Middle Eastern state focused upon the imprisonment of Saad Eddin Ibrahim, who holds U.S. citizenship. The aid cap may thus represent a narrow effort to free Ibrahim, or at least to placate his supporters in America, without altering the United States' overall relationship with Egypt and its backing for Mubarak.

On the other hand, if U.S. policy makers sincerely seek a more democratic Egypt, they must take further steps to help liberalize Egypt's political system, specifically by restraining its ruler. Through sustained criticism of the regime's martial-law policies and its suppression of civil society, the United States could show that it is adopting a principled position that leads it to stand with the Egyptian people. Unless such a shift occurs—and unless Washington, along with other external actors, balances support for the regime with advocacy of Egyptians' political and civil rights—Egypt's domestic opposition will make scant progress under Mubarak or any of his immediate successors.

## NOTES

I thank Robert Vitalis, Josh Stacher, Dan Slater, and Najla Mostafa for helpful comments on an earlier version of this essay. I am grateful also to the American Research Center in Egypt for supporting my research there. Responsibility for the arguments offered here rests with me alone.

1. Fareed Zakaria, "How to Save the Arab World," *Newsweek,* 24 December 2001, 22–28; Thomas Friedman, "The Free-Speech Bind," *New York Times,* 27 March 2002, A23.

2. Patrick E. Tyler and Neil MacFarquhar, "Mubarak to Press Bush on Palestinian Statehood," *New York Times,* 4 June 2002.

3. Alan Richards and Raymond Baker, *Political Economy Review of Egypt: Prepared for USAID's Governance and Democracy Program* (Washington, D.C.: Management Systems International, 1992), 36.

4. See Eberhard Kienle, *A Grand Delusion: Democracy and Economic Reform in Egypt* (London: I.B. Tauris, 2001).

5. For more on the Center (Wasat) Party project, see Joshua Stacher, "Discontent Beyond Discontent: Post-Islamist Rumblings in Egypt," *Middle East Journal* (forthcoming, 2002).

6. "The President's Speech Before a Joint Meeting of the People's Assembly and Consultative Assembly," *Al-Ahram* (Cairo) [original in Arabic], 14 November 1999, 14.

7. Author's interview with senior NDP official, Cairo, Egypt, 25 April 2002.

8. Hala Mustafa, "Introduction: The 2000 Elections—General Indicators," in Hala Mustafa, ed., *The 2000 People's Assembly Elections* (Cairo: Al-Ahram Center for Political and Strategic Studies, 2001), 10 [original in Arabic].

9. Jihad Ouda, Negad El-Borai, and Abu Se'ada, *A Door onto the Desert: The Egyptian Parliamentary Elections of 2000—Course, Dilemmas, and Recommendations for the Future* (Cairo: United Group, 2001), 57–58.

10. Author's interview with NDP member of the Consultative Assembly, Cairo, Egypt, 4 April 2002.

11. "President Bush Announces Initiative for a New Cuba," Washington, D.C., 20 May 2002 *(www.whitehouse.gov/news/releases/2002/05/20020520-1.html).*

12. H.E. Chehabi and Juan J. Linz, "A Theory of Sultanism: A Type of Nondemocratic Rule," in H.E. Chehabi and Juan J. Linz, eds., *Sultanistic Regimes* (Baltimore: Johns Hopkins University Press, 1998), 7. For an analysis of "neopatrimonialism" under Mubarak, see May Kassem, *In the Guise of Democracy: Governance in Contemporary Egypt* (Ithaca, N.Y.: Ithaca University Press, 2000).

13. See Fawaz A. Gerges, *America and Political Islam: Clash of Cultures or Clash of Interests?* (New York: Cambridge University Press, 1999).

14. For statements by one MB leader, Abdel Mene'im Abu al-Futuh, affirming the group's belief in the peaceful rotation of power, see "A kinder, gentler Brother," *Cairo Times,* 18–24 January 2001, 25.

15. This figure is drawn from the MB's success rate in the early, fairer rounds of the

2000 elections and from consultations with MB members and political observers in Egypt.

16. Colin Powell, "Remarks with Egyptian Minister of Foreign Affairs Ahmed Maher," Washington, D.C., 26 September 2001 *(www.state.gov/secretary/rm/2001/5066.htm).*

17. Thomas Carothers, "Ousting Foreign Strongmen: Lessons from Serbia," *Carnegie Endowment for International Peace Policy Brief* 1 (May 2001).

18. See Peter Slevin, "Bush, in Shift on Egypt, Links New Aid to Rights," *Washington Post,* 15 August 2002, A1.

# 6

# ALGERIA'S UNEASY PEACE

### William B. Quandt

**William B. Quandt** *is Edward R. Stettinius, Jr., Professor of Politics at the University of Virginia. His books include* Peace Process: American Diplomacy Toward the Arab-Israeli Conflict Since 1967 *(2001) and* Between Ballots and Bullets: Algeria's Transition from Authoritarianism *(1998). This essay originally appeared in the October 2002 issue of the* Journal of Democracy.

Among Arab countries, it was Algeria that took the most convincing steps toward liberal democracy in the period from 1989 to 1991, when the old one-party system was formally ended, a flowering of civil society occurred, and honest competitive elections were held for the first time. More than ten years later, however, the country appears stalled between its authoritarian past and a democratic future—even while a clearly rising number of its citizens aspire to the latter.

No one today would be apt to describe Algeria as a model for political emulation—whether elsewhere in the Arab world or beyond. If current analysts are asked what they take to be most characteristic of Algerian political life, they are more likely to note its persistent violence and deadly factionalism than its periodic elections, multiparty parliament, or remarkably free press. But to understand the enigma of contemporary Algeria, we must see all these elements together.

The country's move toward greater political openness in 1989 was prompted by a long-simmering crisis that had come to a boil in October of the previous year.[1] The generation that had come of age after Algeria won its independence from France in 1962, and for whom jobs had become scarce following the oil-price collapse of the mid-1980s, had taken to the streets in revolt. Many others who had endured the dreariness and deprivations of the one-party era had cheered the angry young men on. Taking in the extraordinary breadth and depth of popular support for the protesters, the regime—dominated since independence in 1962 by the National Liberation Front (FLN) and its military and state-security apparatus—eschewed a policy of pure repression, opting instead for extensive political reform.[2]

A new constitution, ratified in a February 1989 referendum, opened the way to the end of the FLN's political monopoly. Within a short time, Algeria was teeming with new political organizations, civic associations, and a free press. The most popular of the new political groups was the Islamic Salvation Front (FIS), an expansive coalition comprising a small number of radical Islamists, a few veterans of the war against the Soviets in Afghanistan, the traditionally pious urban classes, and vast numbers of alienated youths.[3]

President Chadli Bendjedid, underestimating the strength of the FIS, seemed to think that he could leverage its support among the public to weaken the unpopular FLN, without endangering his own prerogatives as president or alarming his military backers. Bendjedid himself was a product of the FLN-dominated system, of course, but he had become aware that his own political survival required that he take his distance from a party widely blamed for the failures of the past decade. In thinking that he could endure the weakening of the FLN, he was mistaken, rather like Mikhail Gorbachev, who tried to distance himself from the Communist Party in the last days of the Soviet Union.

## Islamists Rising

In 1990, the FIS made a remarkable showing in municipal elections, unseating the FLN in more than half the country's municipalities and setting the stage for the dramatic National Assembly contest of 1991. Although the FIS polled nearly a million votes fewer in 1991 than it had garnered the previous year, it still won twice as many as the FLN and was poised to win a majority in the new National Assembly. Then the military intervened. In January 1992, the generals canceled the second stage of the election, deposed President Bendjedid, and soon thereafter banned the FIS from politics altogether.[4]

In the first round of the aborted election, the FIS had managed to win the votes of only about a quarter of all eligible voters (only about 55 percent of the electorate had cast valid ballots, the rest having either not voted or cast blank ballots), but given the disarray of the other parties, that would have been enough for it to claim a major victory and establish itself as the dominant voice in Algerian politics.

Although the military did preempt democratic elections, it could not—or would not—try to turn back the clock entirely. Some post-1989 liberal reforms survived, most notably a formal commitment to a pluralistic political system, along with a relatively free and outspoken press. But the military and state-security services were clearly the ultimate arbiters of power: Algerians refer to them as "les décideurs," the "seraglio," the "nomenklatura," or simply "le pouvoir"—"the power." Yet it would be wrong to assume that they had no social support, particularly among the many Algerians who felt anxious about the prospect of the FIS bringing about a "Tehran on the Mediterranean."

Since the aborted election of 1991, Algeria has held five more: for the presidency in 1995 and 1999, for the National Assembly in 1997 and 2002, and for municipal and provincial assemblies in 1997. The 1995 presidential election witnessed a surprisingly large turnout, reported to be some three-quarters of eligible voters. Most of these voters favored Liamine Zeroual, a general backed by the military. But Mahfoud Nahnah, a moderate Islamist, won about three million votes, just slightly fewer in absolute terms than the FIS took in 1991. Despite widespread skepticism about the precision of the reported figures, Algerians took the election generally to reflect a keen desire for a return to order after the bloody years of 1994 and 1995, the nadir of a bitter and devastating civil conflict between the regime and armed Islamist militants.

The 1997 parliamentary elections also saw a relatively big turnout—reportedly about two-thirds of eligible voters. A new regime-backed party, the National Democratic Rally (RND), took first place in what many thought was a fraudulent result. Nahnah's party, the Movement of a Society for Peace (MSP), placed second, and the FLN came in third, with about the same number of votes as it had won in 1991. While the regime-favored RND officially won a third of the vote and 40 percent of the seats in the lower house of Parliament, it had to find coalition partners if it was to govern effectively. Accordingly, at the outset of the new assembly the exchanges between deputies were often vigorous, galvanizing public debate as they were broadcast on live television.

The 1999 presidential election had the makings of a return to openly democratic contestation. Seven candidates took part, among whom at least four were serious political contenders with distinct agendas. The campaign seemed at the outset to be free and fair, but on the eve of the election six of the seven candidates withdrew, claiming to have evidence that the election was being rigged. Only longtime FLN member Abdelaziz Bouteflika remained in the race. Official figures gave him a landslide victory with just under 74 percent, but his actual numbers look to have been much smaller. According to a source inside the Algerian administration at the time, only about a quarter of the electorate went to the polls, and of these some 30 percent voted for Bouteflika.[5]

By the time Algerians were called to the polls again in May 2002, the political landscape had been strongly colored by a decade of upheaval. At least 100,000 Algerians—mostly noncombatants—had died in the violence between the regime and radical Islamists, despite the fact that most Algerians stayed on the sidelines (a reason for doubting that the term "civil war" captures the reality of the case). In 1997, the country's principal armed Islamic movement, the military wing of the FIS known as the Islamic Salvation Army, reached a truce with the regime. And following his election in 1999, Bouteflika offered amnesty to those who laid down their arms. While this did not end the violence entirely, it did reduce it substantially.[6]

With the easing of the security situation in the late 1990s, social and economic issues came to the forefront of politics. Unemployment, poor education, wretched housing, and a host of other problems—including political corruption and the lack of democracy—were suddenly all on the public agenda. In 2001, a sustained protest movement began in the ethnically Berber area of Kabylia, but the issues raised were of nationwide interest. The regime made concessions to the Berbers' demands that their language be recognized nationally, while stonewalling on most of the broader public demands.

## The Current Stalemate

It was against this backdrop of social urgency that the May 2002 National Assembly elections went forward. Several parties, especially the two Berber-based formations, called for a boycott and many Algerians professed a lack of interest. The campaign was generally uninspiring, despite notable efforts by Prime Minister Ali Benflis to rejuvenate the FLN by actively campaigning in the countryside and bringing new and younger people into the party. A public opinion poll on the eve of elections showed that a bare majority intended to vote and that the FLN, the party of order and stability, would win.

The election results were basically credible, if not necessarily exact.[7] Only 46 percent of the electorate turned out, many of whom cast blank ballots as an act of protest, so that only 41 percent actually voted. In Kabylia, there was a near-total boycott of the election. The final tally gave the FLN a majority of the seats with about 36 percent of the vote. The previously dominant, regime-sponsored RND suffered a major setback, winning only 8.5 percent. Similarly, the MSP lost significant support while a rival Islamist party, the Movement for National Reform (MRN)—led by Abdallah Djaballah—won about 10 percent. Prime Minister Benflis's new cabinet included a number of the old guard but also a significant number of new, young personalities, including five women—the largest number ever to serve in an Algerian government.

After more than ten years of elections of varying degrees of probity, Algeria shows a number of enduring political patterns:

First, the society seems to be divided into at least three main ideological blocs: 1) a nationalist group backed by between 25 and 30 percent of the population—officials, state workers, and rural voters—that reliably votes for the FLN or other government-endorsed parties; 2) an Islamist bloc that commands the loyalties of some 15 to 20 percent; and 3) a Berber-nationalist bloc that has the support of another 10 to 15 percent. Political allegiances within the remainder of Algerian society are scattered among small groups of democrats, regionalists, and independents. No single bloc has a majority, and none can easily govern without some support from at least one of the others.

Second, elections have revealed the main fissures in Algerian society, but they have done little either to legitimize governance or to challenge the positions of those in power. Nor have democratic procedures taken root as a way of resolving conflicts. While elected officials are by no means mere puppets of the military, they know that the latter potentially has veto power over major decisions.

Third, multiparty democracy is no longer a disparaged concept in Algeria, as it was in the early days following independence. Most Algerians today say that they would welcome democracy, greater accountability, the rule of law, and more transparency. They are tired of the contempt with which the regime treats ordinary citizens. And Algerians have become skeptical of ideologues, both within the power structure and among the Islamists. Although concrete evidence is hard to come by, opinion polls do show that Algerians are deeply alienated from all political parties, and most express a fairly cynical view of politics altogether. Concrete social issues now seem of greater concern than they were in the early 1990s, when partisans of democracy and an Islamic state were engaging in vigorous ideological debate.

Finally, a vibrant free press and growing access to satellite dishes and the Internet have made for lively political discussion within the country. Satire, political cartoons, *rai* music, and a rich political slang in dialectical Arabic provide outlets for political sentiment. The large community of Algerian expatriates living in nearby Europe also helps to ensure that ideas of modernity and democracy are well understood by Algerians back home, many of whom are fluent in one or more foreign languages—principally French, but increasingly English as well.

## The Outlook

What, then, are the prospects that Algeria's limited degree of liberalization will be transformed into genuine and sustained democratization? The society is structurally pluralistic; popular sentiment seems to favor democracy; and the formal political system, while inclined toward a very strong executive, is not the major obstacle. So where is the problem?

Some argue that it lies deep within Algerian culture. One version of this view—commonly asserted about all Muslim countries—is that Islam and democracy are simply incompatible. Any religion that recognizes the sovereignty of God, the reasoning goes, is going to have trouble with the idea of the sovereignty of the people.[8] Indeed, some of the hard-liners in the FIS once made this argument themselves, asserting that democracy was a false Western import with no substantive value in Muslim society. Scholars now generally dismiss this claim as a form of erroneous cultural essentialism, but the argument nevertheless lives on in some circles. A variant on the culturalist argument is a historical reading of Algeria's past, holding that an engrained pattern of resorting to violence for the achievement of political ends has prevailed for hundreds of years.[9] Both arguments share the problem of explaining both too much and too little. If cultural arguments can explain Algerian political violence, can they also explain the prolonged period of calm from about the mid-1960s until the late 1980s? Or do cultural analysts maintain that Algerian culture actually changed during this period? In the end, seeking "cultural" causes here begs more questions than it answers.

Closer to the mark are specific features of Algeria's recent history and economy that make it difficult to change the locus of power. First, Algerian nationalism was from the outset fiercely egalitarian, populist, and antipluralistic. From the colonial period onward, parties have been seen as a source of weakness. Because the French had destroyed much of the Algerian elite during 132 years of colonial rule, the new nationalist leaders generally came from modest backgrounds and tended to believe that only they could speak authentically for "the people." Both during and after the struggle for independence, there was very little in the way of a hierarchy capable of winning automatic respect in Algerian society. In a sense, it was thought that "the people" had won the revolution and that no single individual should stand out above anyone else.[10] The FLN quickly splintered, and political power eventually ended up in the hands of the one institution that did have some structure and hierarchy—namely, the military—where it has remained ever since.

Why has it been so hard to wrest power from the military's hands? First of all, the military has never split into warring factions. Second, it has been able to use the threat of internal disorder as a justification for its rule. And third, the flow of oil wealth enabled the military to provide strong financial incentives to those who collaborate with it. This is something of a familiar pattern in resource-rich rentier states, and it makes it difficult to break the monopolies held by those who control the flow of rents. At the same time, when oil prices go down, as they did in the mid-1980s, the regime may feel the need to engage in at least the appearance of political opening in order to diffuse responsibility for the cuts in benefits inevitable at such times.[11]

In brief, then, a populist form of nationalism paved the way for the military to take power in the name of the people; the military's relatively cohesive organizational structure has given it a comparative political advantage; and petrodollars have helped to keep soldiers in place by giving an unpopular regime a means of buying acquiescence from many citizens. The system is nevertheless under strain, and we ought not to discount the prospect that there could be change in the direction of greater participation and accountability.

If Algeria is to experience real and sustained progress toward democracy, the military must move to the sidelines. This could take the form of a Chilean-style "pact," a deal with the democrats that offers a high degree of autonomy and immunity from prosecution; or it could follow the Turkish model, with a powerful military assuming a special role as guardian of the constitution—a kind of "national security council"—but with day-to-day responsibility clearly in the hands of elected politicians. As the generals advance in age, it may be possible to negotiate a pact of this type. Most are of the generation that came of age in the 1950s and are reaching the natural ends of their careers, and it is not clear whether they can or will put in place successors to themselves.[12]

Were Algeria to make a transition to democracy in the near future, it would probably be an untidy affair—as democracy often is—but there is no reason to think that it would prove unmanageable or throw the country back into a state of strife. Algeria has already had the experience of a fairly vigorous and pluralistic national movement during the 1930s and 1940s; it has sustained a meaningful measure of pluralism over the past decade, despite enormous challenges; and few Algerians now want to go back to the constraints of a one-party state.

An Algerian democracy would probably begin with a strongly presidential model. The constitution, which has been tailor-made by each president except the current incumbent, already tends to privilege executive power and leave parliament in a relatively weak position. But the legislature would also likely become a forum in which coalitions would have to be forged in order for government to work at all—which, in turn, could be an important basis for a more general habituation to the arts of compromise that Algerians have been chronically unaccustomed to practicing.

## Democrats and Others

Algeria is not exactly a case of a potential "democracy without democrats": There are some convinced democrats, but there are probably many more Algerians who have a narrowly instrumental view of democracy—in particular, viewing it as a means to get rid of a political order that they detest. None of the country's existing political parties, even those most ostensibly democratic in ideology, is governed internally by democratic procedures. In fact, most are simply groupings gathered around some prominent personality. There is certainly no Algerian Nelson Mandela—no single political figure around whom democrats would naturally rally. Still, there are several individuals who could appeal to democrats: the current prime minister, Ali Benflis, a modern and competent technocrat with reformist inclinations; Mouloud Hamrouche, the prime minister who presided over the first phase of Algeria's democratization in the early 1990s; and possibly Ahmed Taleb Ibrahimi, a moderate Islamist with good nationalist credentials, although he is now getting on in years. Any one of these figures could count on significant levels of support from Algeria's alienated young, women, Berbers, and moderate Islamists.

While in the mid-1990s the military could plausibly claim that it needed to hold power in order to defeat radical Islamists, it has now succeeded in reducing the chances of an Islamist victory—whether by force of arms or at the polls—to almost nil. The extremism of Algerian Islamists, especially from 1995 to 1997, alienated most citizens, even among those who had been initially sympathetic. Conflict fatigue has decidedly set in, and the population is showing a keen desire to return to a more tranquil and normal life. The appeal of ideologues must now compete with a profound and pervasive skepticism, which is felt even by those youths who would previously have been most inclined to seek salvation in the radicals' millenarian vision of an Islamist state.

Moreover, most Algerians are politically well-informed and would support the change to a more responsive and accountable government. The media would also be on board, having already established themselves as robust guardians of free expression. Furthermore, democracy in Algeria would have several important assets: The expatriate community would likely be willing to repatriate part of its wealth to an Algeria that seemed to be on the mend. Europe and the United States would provide tangible new support. And the country has enough oil and gas income to enable a democratic government to address issues of social concern such as housing and education.

So I remain a guarded optimist, not about the possibility of a sudden transition to democracy, but about an eventual change in that direction. Recall the conditions set out by Dankwart Rustow in his seminal article on the conditions needed for a democratic transition: a sense of national identity; a hot family feud that no single party can win; the adoption of rules to regulate competition; and a period of habituation to nonviolent handovers of power from one group to another.[13] Algeria is nearing the point where the third of these conditions may be met: Its political system offers the makings of a set of rules regulating political competition among major groups in Algerian society, groups that for decades have been engaged in an acute struggle. We may not quite know what to label the country at this point. It is still fundamentally an authoritarian system, but it is not enough to note that power remains concentrated in the hands of a few. Much else is happening to suggest that its future need not resemble its past. Whether democracy is, in fact, in Algeria's future is uncertain—and up to Algerians to decide— but those on the outside should not be dismissive of the prospects or indifferent to the possibility. A democratic Algeria, were it to come about soon, could again place the country among the pacesetters for the entire region.

## NOTES

1. See M'Hammed Boukhobza, *Octobre 88: Evolution ou rupture?* (Algiers: Editions Bouchène, 1991), 49–68.

2. Abed Charef, *Algérie: Le grand dérapage* (Saint-Amand-Montrond: Editions de l'Aube, 1994), 6–41.

3. Séverine Labat, *Les islamistes algériens: Entre les urnes et le maquis* (Paris: Editions du Seuil, 1995), 95–127; and Ahmed Rouadjia, *Les frères et la mosquée: Enquête sur le mouvement islamiste en Algérie* (Paris: Editions Karthala, 1990), 111–39.

4. Lahouari Addi, *L'Algérie et la démocratie: Pouvoir et crise du politique dans l'Algérie contemporaine* (Paris: Editions la Découverte, 1994), 160–83. Addi (188) puts forward the idea of a "regression féconde," meaning that if the FIS had been allowed to assume power, this would have had the effect of demystifying and discrediting the Islamist movement, paving the way for real democracy in future elections. In a sense, the extremism of the Islamists in the mid-1990s had the effect of discrediting them in the eyes of many, without the Islamists ever coming to power.

5. William B. Quandt, "Algerian Puzzles," *EUI Working Papers* (Florence: European University Institute, 2000).

6. Gilles Kepel, *Jihad: The Trail of Political Islam* (Cambridge: Harvard University Press, 2002), 254–75.

7. Hugh Roberts, "Musical Chairs in Algeria," MERIP Press Information Note 97, 4 June 2002.

8. Bernard Lewis, "Islam and Liberal Democracy," *Atlantic Monthly,* February 1995, 89–98. See also Bernard Lewis, "Islam and Liberal Democracy: A Historical Overview," *Journal of Democracy* 7 (April 1996): 53–63.

9. Luis Martinez, *La guerre civile en Algérie* (Paris: Karthala, 1998), 23–26. Martinez (377) concludes his important book with the following summary: "Of the factors capable of explaining Algeria's descent into civil war after its short multiparty experience in 1990–91, the most central is the 'imaginaire de la guerre.' We have shown that the failure of the 'democratic transition' in Algeria is explained by the belief in the virtues of violence as the means of changing leadership."

10. William B. Quandt, *Revolution and Political Leadership: Algeria, 1954–1968* (Cambridge: MIT Press, 1969), 148–74.

11. Giacomo Luciani, "The Oil Rent, the Fiscal Crisis of the State and Democratization," in Ghassan Salamé, ed., *Democracy Without Democrats? The Renewal of Politics in the Muslim World* (New York: I.B. Tauris, 1994), 130–55.

12. For a thoughtful discussion of these possibilities, see Omar Belhouchet, "ANP et l'Algérie," *El Watan* (Algiers), 24 June 2002.

13. Dankwart Rustow, "Transitions to Democracy: Toward a Dynamic Model," *Comparative Politics* 2 (April 1970): 1033–53.

# 7

# DEPOLITICIZATION IN MOROCCO

*Abdeslam M. Maghraoui*

*Abdeslam M. Maghraoui, a Moroccan political scientist, is a visiting professor in the department of politics at Princeton University. Previously, he was a research fellow at Princeton's Transregional Institute and taught Middle East politics at Georgetown University and the University of Michigan–Ann Arbor. This essay originally appeared in the October 2002 issue of the* Journal of Democracy.

In the 1950s, Morocco was one of the rare newly independent states to embark on a path of political pluralism and market economics. The following decades saw successive governments enact reforms establishing a relatively open political and economic system. And yet, almost half a century on, the country remains authoritarian.

Why? Though favorable to democracy on the surface, Morocco's liberal reforms have actually worked against it by *depoliticizing* the public sphere. By "depoliticization" I mean the marginalization of questions of legitimacy or sovereignty and—in the Moroccan case especially—the concomitant political primacy given to economic issues. Having unremittingly framed economic questions in strictly technical terms, the monarchy has succeeded in sidestepping a fundamental debate on the sources and distribution of power in the Moroccan political system. Parties that might have spearheaded democratic reform have meanwhile diluted their demands and embraced the monarchy's claim that the country simply needs better economic management.

Morocco's trajectory over the past five decades sheds light on both the slow advance of democratization throughout the Arab world and the relationship between political and economic reform in the region—indicating that hopes placed in gradual liberalization there may be misplaced. Throughout the region, one can find widespread support for the rationalization of economic relations (particularly among business representatives and technocratic elites), economic justice and equity (among nationalist parties, trade unions, and Islamic groups), or civil entitlements abstracted from a clear political philosophy of rights (among human and cultural rights groups). But support for democratic principles remains sparse and ambivalent.

My contention is that this imbalance results from the depoliticization of Arab societies. By the 1990s, significant economic liberalization had also occurred in Algeria, Egypt, Jordan, Kuwait, Lebanon, Syria, and Yemen.[1] But political reforms have not only lagged behind economic adjustment;[2] economic imperatives have been used strategically, across the board, to delay political reform. For example, Morocco's late King Hassan II (r. 1962–99) asked the World Bank to provide a report on the state of that country's economy, and then used the report to argue in parliament for the priority of economic reforms over constitutional change. Recently, the heads of state of Jordan, Syria, and Algeria have made similar arguments. Indeed, the strategy of putting political rights on hold in the name of social or economic imperatives has been a characteristic of most Arab political regimes since the end of colonial rule.[3]

## Economic Liberalization and the Retreat of Politics

Since the time of its independence in 1956, Morocco has engaged in three cycles of economic liberalization: 1) a period of monetary stabilization (1965–83); 2) a structural adjustment program (1983–92); and 3) a program of *mise à niveau* (or "upgrading") intended to restructure Moroccan firms so as to increase their capacity and competitiveness in preparation for free trade with Europe (1995 to the present).

*Stabilization.* In 1960, Morocco abruptly canceled its first National Plan, which had followed the state-centered model then popular among newly independent nations. The government embarked on a new "mixed economy," in which the public sector assumed the role of stimulator to free enterprise, and signed a series of aid and loan conventions with the World Bank and the International Monetary Fund (IMF) to strengthen private entrepreneurship. Stabilization programs lasted roughly until 1983 and focused on budgetary savings through higher taxes and cuts in social programs and subsidies.[4] However, the measures ultimately failed to solve Morocco's economic problems because the very political structure that created them in the first place remained untouched.

Through the creation of state companies in the country's more profitable industries (such as irrigated agriculture, food processing, tourism, banking, construction, and manufacturing), the monarchy used the public sector to control and reward prominent domestic allies. Typically, the state bought out failing companies and resold them at nominal prices to the king's associates once they became profitable—that is, once the public treasury paid for new infrastructure and the public sector ensured advantageous contracts. Rather than creating a dynamic business class, the use of the public sector to nourish private enterprise has made Moroccan entrepreneurs dependent on the state for technical services, fiscal favors, and subsidized loans.[5]

A pivotal event in this first wave of depoliticization was the decision by King Hassan II to launch the "Green March" into the Western Sahara in November 1975. Following Spain's withdrawal from the area earlier that year, the king ordered 300,000 unarmed subjects to enter and "recover" it for Morocco. Parliamentary debates on budget deficits, the misuse of public assets, and deteriorating social conditions were marginalized by speeches about Morocco's territorial integrity and the controversy with Spain. Opposition parties that derived their legitimacy from their association with the independence movement now found themselves trapped in a "sacred national consensus" on the Western Sahara issue, unable to challenge economic and social policies other than on technical or narrowly moralistic grounds. The resulting neutralization of the political opposition, at a time when economic and social conditions were worsening, led to tensions between the political parties and their affiliated trade unions. The locus of contestation shifted to the streets, where it has since remained (and where deadly riots broke out in the 1980s and 1990s).

*Structural Adjustment.* The stabilization phase came to an end when it became clear that Morocco's profound economic problems required regulatory and administrative reforms. Under the supervision of the World Bank and the IMF, a second, more aggressive cycle of economic liberalization took place between 1983 and 1992. Successive governments boldly pursued structural adjustment programs (SAPs). These typically involved privatization, an end to subsidies and price controls, and the lowering of trade barriers. Despite the considerable social costs and political risks that these reforms brought, Morocco implemented them diligently and became an apparent textbook-case for success in structural adjustment.

While Morocco's SAPs resulted in some significant achievements, including reductions in macroeconomic imbalances and increased international competitiveness, the country's economic growth remained erratic and dependent on rainfall and remittances—the latter mostly from Moroccans working in Europe.[6] Once again, the fundamental problem was political, and once again it was largely ignored. Most of the measures called for by the SAPs—whether fiscal, budgetary, or commercial—assumed transparent, technocratic, and relatively autonomous state institutions, none of which Morocco had. While parliamentary majorities were reform-minded in this period, ministers were accountable to the king alone. And while the Moroccan Central Bank has always been formally autonomous, the reality is that the king handpicks its

director and senior executives. Moreover, with each minister of state
answering individually and almost exclusively to the king, there was no
coherent reform strategy or coordination among the ministries of finance, trade, investment, tourism, commerce, and privatization. At the
same time, parliamentary and public debates on structural adjustment
policies hardly even mentioned the connection between Morocco's economic crisis and the political structure that created it.

*Mise à niveau.* Even today, in the midst of the current cycle of liberal reform that began in 1995 and has since been dubbed *mise à niveau,*
the political nature of Morocco's economic problems remains ignored.
Although the government, business representatives, and trade unions
each emphasize different elements of these reforms, the basic idea is
that the free trade agreement with Europe signed in 1995, and its full
implementation by 2010, will force Moroccan firms to be more transparent and more productive. The "spontaneous" restructuring of free
enterprise that this will ostensibly bring is widely seen as a model for
the economy and the polity as a whole.[7] Here again, any renegotiation
of the division of powers between the various branches of the government has been kept off the agenda, as has any clear redefinition of the
monarchy's political prerogatives.

## A History of Depoliticization

In the Moroccan context, depoliticization does not mean the absence
of partisan politics. In fact, the country's first constitution, adopted in
1962, outlawed the one-party system and provided for a multiparty legislature elected by universal suffrage. Since 1963, a dozen national and
local elections have been held, while popular referenda on constitutional
amendments have made Morocco's political system more open and liberal. During the last decade, the country has witnessed further reforms
in the area of human rights and allowed more freedom of expression
and association. But postindependence reform has scarcely touched the
basic configuration of political power. An unaccountable monarchy
continues to govern. Given that the most significant liberal advances
were made only after 1975, when the monarchy's prerogatives were no
longer overtly contested, one could even argue that the foreclosure of
any serious debate on the king's prerogatives was a necessary condition
for political liberalization.

Morocco's experiments with constitutional reform and legislative
politics are best seen as falling into three main periods. The first of
these, which lasted from 1962 to 1975, was the most "political." These
were the years of the power struggle pitting the monarchy against the
two major parties that had emerged from the independence movement:
the conservative-nationalist Istiqlal and the left-leaning National Union

of Popular Forces (UNFP). This period saw substantial political debate over the king's prerogatives, the role of the legislature and cabinet, and the distribution of powers among the various branches of government. But King Hassan mobilized influential traditional networks—tribal chiefs, rural notables, Sufi orders, prominent urban families, and the like—to offset the city-based nationalist parties. In the end, the king won and tightened his control. Morocco's first constitutions and early experiments with parliamentary politics resulted in the consolidation of a closed political system.[8]

The 1962 Constitution vested regulatory powers in a National Assembly composed of a directly elected House of Representatives and an indirectly elected House of Councilors. But these powers were effectively delegated at the king's pleasure. The king appointed and dismissed the prime minister and cabinet, and could dissolve parliament and assume residual powers under emergency laws. In 1970, a new constitution formalized the weakness of the legislature and executive government, effectively establishing emergency legislation that the king had (unconstitutionally) decreed after severe rioting shook Casablanca in 1965. Following two coup attempts, another constitution was ratified in 1972. While this one enhanced the regulatory powers of the legislature and executive government, it also formalized the process of depoliticization. Article 19, for example, established the sanctity of the king as both the "Supreme Representative of the Nation" and the "Commander of the Faithful," thereby formally lodging national sovereignty with a monarchy that claims divine legitimacy. A series of other articles forbade critical debates over royal messages to parliament or the people at large, and removed parliamentary immunity from legislators deemed to be questioning the monarchy, Islam, or the laws of the nation.

Morocco's first legislative elections were held in 1963. They resulted in a deadlock in the House of Representatives, with a royalist coalition squaring off against the two main opposition parties. The near-equal distribution of seats between the two blocs gave rise to lively debates not only on social and economic policies, but on the distribution of power and the nature of the regime as well. Some legislators from Istiqlal and UNFP demanded that the king "reign but not rule"—a demand not heard again in parliament until the late 1970s, after the king had twice suspended the legislature (first from 1965 to 1970, and then again from 1972 to 1977) and ruled on his own.

Whereas the period from 1962 to 1975 was dominated by a power struggle between the monarchy and nationalist opposition parties over the nature and future of the polity, the second period (1975–92) saw the forging of a national consensus that removed such political issues from the reform agenda. Two major events precipitated this consensus: The Western Sahara campaign in 1975 and the promulgation of a new communal charter in 1976.

In November 1975, King Hassan ordered the massive, nonviolent "Green March" to dramatically assert his country's claim to the formerly Moroccan provinces of the Western Sahara, annexed by Spain in the late nineteenth and early twentieth centuries. The Western Sahara issue greatly increased the king's legitimacy as defender of the country's territorial integrity and symbol of its national sovereignty, and tilted the balance of power in his favor until he died at the age of 70 in 1999. With such political unanimity secured around the monarchy, the king made conciliatory gestures to "normalize" political life.[9] Political control and repression were relaxed and opposition parties were now "consulted" and allowed to criticize government policies and to carry out mobilization campaigns. In official discourse, these reforms were labeled "the democratic process" in order to suggest a commitment to the revival of democratic institutions. The new consensus did improve the political environment and favor liberalization, but it did nothing for democratization. Although opposition parties now used the parliament to denounce the economic inefficiencies and social costs of the adjustment program, these parties affected no policies and framed no laws. More damagingly still, they failed to formulate their basic politics in terms of representation and sovereignty, adhering stagnantly to a language that spoke only of efficiency and honesty, dwelling on the "rationalization" and "moralization" of the public sphere. With potential critics self-constrained in this way, the monarchy and its claimed prerogatives only came to seem more legitimate.

Ironically, the opposition parties' decision to end a 15-year boycott and take part in the 1976 local elections made matters worse. To lure the opposition parties to run in urban municipalities and rural communes, the Ministry of the Interior—which answers directly and exclusively to the king—promulgated a new communal charter in 1976. The new charter expanded the budgets, independence, and powers of local councils. In addition, voting registration procedures were revised and updated for more transparency—a longstanding demand of the opposition—and a national council for the supervision of elections was established that included representatives of all political parties. But even the modest objective of efficiently running local administrations and setting examples for the national government was not achieved. Lacking the necessary political structure to compete nationally, Istiqlal and the Socialist Union of Popular Forces (USFP) enlisted popular local candidates who had no commitment to their parties and who were therefore willing to change political affiliation under administrative pressures, or if it otherwise suited their interests. Accordingly, while opposition parties won majorities of council seats in several municipalities, they were paralyzed by shifting party affiliations (and, furthermore, hamstrung by corruption scandals, as the councils were sources of immense wealth).

During its third phase of political liberalization, covering the decade from 1992 to 2002, Morocco enacted a series of reforms to enforce the rule of law, held two constitutional referenda that expanded the powers of parliament, and elected two national assemblies in which the opposition won strong shares of seats. In a series of decrees, the king also established a Consultative Council on Human Rights and a Ministry of Human Rights, a set of administrative tribunals empowered to investigate abuses of power, a Constitutional Council to resolve conflicts over the constitutionality of laws, and a Consultative Council for Social Dialogue to mediate labor disputes. The 1992 Constitution for the first time gave the parliament the authority to approve or reject a new government appointed by the king, and to dissolve a government through a vote of no confidence. A 1996 amendment, moreover, established the direct election of all members of the House of Representatives (a major demand of opposition parties) and reestablished a House of Councilors (elected indirectly by professional associations, labor unions, municipal councils, and interest groups). The process of liberalization culminated in a long-awaited alternation of power when in 1998 King Hassan asked a socialist leader, Abderrahmane Youssoufi, to lead the government in 1998. The legislative elections of September 2002 will mark the first time since independence that an opposition-led coalition government has served its full term in office.

## No Closer to Democracy

Yet it is likely that Morocco is no closer today to a decisive democratic breakthrough than it was four decades ago. The Constitution still plainly locates sovereignty with the king, limiting the role of the government and the parliament to managing social and economic affairs. Moreover, the major parties have accepted this "division of labor" and virtually disengaged from the political sphere. The stability of this arrangement became apparent recently when top officials who had been appointed by King Hassan were involved in a series of shocking public-sector financial frauds. (In one case alone, the sum embezzled was equal to 80 percent of Morocco's total external debt.) To calm public anger, the government put before parliament a law to improve the "management" of public enterprises, utterly marginalizing the question of political accountability that was at the root of the scandals. In the meantime, since coming to the throne in 1999, King Mohammed VI has proceeded with the appointment of an apolitical, technocratic elite to key positions in the administration and the economy.[10] Even if these appointments are at times effective (technocrats are generally more efficient in delivering services to the citizens because they are not involved in the bickering of partisan politics), they amount to the establishment of a shadow government that operates alongside and often against the official cabinet.

Another sign of ongoing depoliticization is the campaign for the September 2002 legislative elections. Almost across the board, the political parties are downplaying their political programs and touting their technocratic and managerial credentials instead. At the same time, private economic actors are threatening to enter the political fray with the intention of applying their *mise à niveau* policies in the political sphere.

Morocco's long and gradual liberalization has advanced relatively smoothly in both the economic and political spheres, but it has not led to democracy. Defenders of Morocco's liberalization strategy might point to the country's relative success in checking Islamist forces, and it is true that the two main Islamic groups, Adl wal Ihsan (Justice and Charity) and Adl wa Tanmiya (Justice and Development), have thus far been off balance. The former, which has disdained participation in the electoral process, has been weakened by the king's strategic backing of social programs and remains politically isolated; apart from having been able to mobilize support in opposition to the 1991 war in Iraq, or on behalf of the Palestinians, or against women's rights, it has shown no real political potential. The latter, Justice and Development, does participate in the political process, and it has sought to broaden its support by calling for serious political and constitutional changes. But its appeal has been diluted by the emergence of alternative groups—new-left coalitions, youths from the traditional opposition parties, some NGOs, and the independent press—now demanding similar reforms. Recently, the dismantling of an al-Qaeda cell planning to blow up a cafe in Marrakesh and a bus, along with the arrest of nine extremists involved in a series of religiously motivated executions in Fez and Casablanca, badly damaged the image of Islamic groups in Morocco. So there is little reason to fear any strong electoral showing by the Islamists in the September 2002 parliamentary elections.

Still, a reform strategy that keeps Islamists off balance without leading to democracy is short-sighted. The relative weakness of Morocco's Islamist movement likely has more to do with the tremendous heterogeneity of religious life in the country than with the regime's strategy of cautious liberalization. And in the long run, the logic of depoliticization could in fact play into the hands of the Islamists, given their insistence that the best safeguard against social injustice, economic corruption, and the abuse of political power is the strict application of a religious moral code: Insofar as the regime itself claims that political sovereignty ultimately resides with the "Commander of the Faithful" and not a popularly elected body, the regime adheres to a conception of authority very much like the Islamists' own, and leaves itself vulnerable to their ideological challenge. If there is to be enduring stability and prosperity in Morocco, the regime must go beyond its strategy of political control through liberal reform and embark decisively on the path of genuine democracy.

## NOTES

1. Bahgat Korany et al., *Political Liberalization and Democratization in the Arab World, Vol. 2: Comparative Experiences* (Boulder, Colo.: Lynne Rienner, 1998).

2. Daniel Brumberg, "Authoritarian Legacies and Reform Strategies in the Arab World," in Rex Brynen et al., eds., *Political Liberalization and Democratization in the Arab World, Vol. 1: Theoretical Perspectives* (Boulder, Colo.: Lynne Rienner, 1995), 229–59.

3. See, for example, Hazem Beblawi and Giacomo Luciani, eds., *The Rentier State* (New York: Croom Helm, 1987).

4. Brendan Horton, *Morocco: Analysis and Reform of Economic Policy* (Washington, D.C.: World Bank, 1990).

5. Habib El Malki, *Trente ans d'économie marocaine: 1960–1990* (Paris: CNRS, 1989).

6. For a complete analysis and evaluation of the SAP, see Guilain P. Denoeux and Abdeslam Maghraoui, "The Political Economy of Structural Adjustment in Morocco," in Azzedine Layyachi, ed., *Economic Crisis and Political Change in North Africa* (Westport, Conn.: Praeger, 1998), 55–87.

7. Nourredine El Aoufi, "La reforme économique: Stratégies, institutions, acteurs," *Monde Arabe Maghreb-Machrek* 164 (April–June 1999): 36–52.

8. I. William Zartman, "King Hassan's New Morocco," in I.William Zartman, ed., *The Political Economy of Morocco* (New York: Praeger, 1987).

9. Jean-Claude Santucci, "La question saharienne dans la vie politique marocaine," in P.R. Baudel et al., eds., *Enjeux sahariens* (Paris: CNRS, 1984).

10. Abdeslam M. Maghraoui, "Monarchy and Political Reform in Morocco," *Journal of Democracy* 12 (January 2001): 73–86.

# 8

# STIRRINGS IN SAUDI ARABIA

*Jean-François Seznec*

**Jean-François Seznec,** *adjunct professor at Columbia University's Middle East Institute and Georgetown University's Center for Contemporary Arab Studies, is the author of* The Financial Markets of the Persian Gulf *(1987) and a founding member and managing partner of the Lafayette Group LLC, an investment company in Annapolis, Maryland. This essay originally appeared in the October 2002 issue of the* Journal of Democracy.

At first blush, an article on democracy in Saudi Arabia—a state often described as an absolute monarchy—could be very short indeed. The secret services are strong and imposing. Most nongovernmental organizations and associations are forbidden. The press is entirely controlled, and the largest press groups are actually owned by members of the royal family. Elections, local or national, have never been held, and King Fahd has said that there is "no place" for them. There are no political parties. Arrests are arbitrary. The judicial establishment is politically dependent. And, while the political clout of radical Islamists is greatly overplayed in the Western media, the regime actively sponsors a conservative form of Islam that is highly repressive, particularly regarding the freedom and equality of women. Given this litany of nondemocratic features, Saudi Arabia would seem to be a perfect example of an authoritarian state.

On the ground, however, Saudi Arabia's authoritarian character is not so obvious. One can even detect protodemocratic stirrings. Granted, if we were to plot the country on Robert Dahl's famous chart ranging regimes between "closed hegemonies" and "polyarchies," we would find it very near the former end of the spectrum.[1] But its political trajectory today is discernibly toward the latter. Since 1992, Saudi Arabia's rulers have allowed for more consultation with those whom they rule, more inclusiveness in institutions, a limited liberalization of the press, and less repression of the Shi'ite Muslims who make up an estimated 3 to 5 percent of the kingdom's total population of approximately 22 million.

It has been a custom of the king and the major princes to open their doors to petitioners once a week in well-publicized—and now televised—meetings called *majlis* (the word refers to the salon or reception room where these meetings take place). While today the king's poor health precludes his own involvement, one can see a senior prince receiving thousands of petitioners at each *majlis*. The petitioners will kiss him deferentially and usually hand him a piece of paper bearing a request, perhaps for a land grant or a small sum of money. This paper is passed on to the prince's staff, which will then provide a response. It is a system in which the princes dole out largesse in order to display and reaffirm their eminence.

The royal family, and the king in particular, traditionally wield enormous power, but it is power that traces its roots to a Bedouin society which was itself quite egalitarian. Tribal leaders were normally chosen for their valor and wisdom, not their birth. Today, the king is named according to a procedure defined in the Basic Law of 1992, but that law only codifies a Bedouin tradition long followed by the House of Saud: A king-to-be is *not* born heir apparent. He must be approved by the rest of the family, even if also ultimately endorsed by the existing king. One of the consequences of this arrangement is that a potential king must show his ability to negotiate, to maneuver, and to manage his family and some affairs of state before being chosen and enthroned. De facto, then, the king is elected by his family members. And since the family is very large—there may be as many as 15,000 royal princes—the competition for power is keen. It can be argued that while the Saudi state is authoritarian, the ruling class governs itself internally in ways that at least approximate democratic procedures.[2]

This tradition of choosing the princely candidate who seems most able to win acceptance and cooperation from his relatives has been the key to the kingdom's political stability. In one form or another, aside from two hiatuses totaling 35 years, the Al Saud family has been in power in central Arabia since 1744. Unlike other ruling Bedouin families in the region, they have tended to transfer power to one another peacefully, which has limited vengeful transitions and helped to keep the family unified.

The royal family is also bound to other families in the kingdom. Since 1744, the Al Saud have allied themselves (often through marriage) with the Al Sheikh, the descendants of Abdel Wahab (1703–92), the famous radical religious reformer whose name is now attached to Wahabism, the most influential form of conservative Sunni Islam in the region. The Al Sheikh, who hail from the same west-central Arabian province of Najd as the Al Saud, have traditionally handled the religious establishment while the Al Saud have provided the sword and the purse.

A certain degree of political competition within the closed circle of the family and its allies does not, of course, translate into democracy for the rest of the population. The latter has customarily been patronized and helped, but only to the extent that it has remained in basic harmony with its rulers. Yet with the discovery of oil and subsequent improvements in health and education, the country has seen huge and politically consequential demographic changes. The population, thought to be about 4.5 million in 1970, is probably almost five times that number now, although that figure includes roughly six million foreign workers who will not stay in the country and have no claims to any of the benefits of being Saudi. But the rest of the population—over half of which is younger than 16—*is* Saudi and views itself as a citizenry with rights, not as a class of servants indentured to the Al Saud. Accordingly, the leaders of that family, including King Fahd, have come to act as if they must co-opt a large number of commoners (that is, those outside the royal family) to stay in power.

Since 1975, economic change and more widespread education have nurtured a population that is more sophisticated and outspoken than ever. The king could have chosen to open up the political system so as to include and consult with the increasingly diverse elements that have gained significant social and economic clout, but this would have meant risking the royal family's grip on power. Instead, he chose to continue a policy, dating from the mid-1960s, of sharing a substantial part of the regime's oil benefits with commoners in return for their tacit agreement not to challenge the royal family's ultimate prerogatives.

By 1998, when King Fahd's health began to fail, the entire economy had by royal design gradually become "binary": Any activity that has to do with oil, finance, industry, and, to a large extent, commerce is handled by commoners, while anything having to do with the military, the interior, and agriculture remains within the purview of the royal family.[3] Each half of this binary system receives about 50 percent of the oil income, distributed through state contracts and industrial investments to the commoners and through military contracts to the royal family.[4]

From 1970 to about 1998, the interaction between commoners and royals was minimal, but this implicit social contract kept peace in the valley. Had the arrangement been different, with princes in command of the oil ministry or the ministry of finance, so much of the oil wealth would have flowed directly to the royal family that the commoners would have felt dangerously disenfranchised. By spending $432 billion on the military between 1984 and 2001,[5] the king was able as well to satisfy his family, which profited directly. By limiting the family's involvement in the rest of the economy, he was able to keep the commoners happy.

## Pressures for Change

This arrangement has kept Saudi Arabia stable for more than 30 years, and until now it has staved off pressure for mass participation in public life. In short, by fostering a commoner-controlled civil service and economy, King Fahd has limited the influence of his family for the sake of its own long-term preservation—absorbing protodemocratic social pressures and containing them through politically institutionalized economic incentives.

Nevertheless, the pressures for change are intensifying. The greatest challenge to the system is the country's demographic explosion. With population growth averaging about 3.5 percent annually, the country must create between 260,000 and 500,000 new jobs every year.[6] Theoretically, the new generation of young Saudi graduates and job seekers could replace the six million foreign workers, and to a certain extent this is happening in some service industries such as banking and the hotel trade. But on the whole, the number of foreign workers has actually increased, and with it the unemployment rate among locals. Part of the problem is the Saudi "social contract" itself: The government does not want to push the merchants too hard to hire Saudis for fear of losing the merchants' support. The merchants and industrialists, for their part, want to be competitive in world markets and so need to keep labor costs down. It is easier to hire well-educated Indians or Pakistanis, who cost a fraction of what Saudi workers do and are totally at the mercy of their employers in a way that Saudi workers are not.

Massive government and private investments in industry and related services could lead to further employment, but the state's ability to invest more in petrochemicals and related industries has limits. Income from petroleum is about US$50 billion per year when oil is at $24 a barrel, as was the case from 1999 through 2001. Since 1980, however, deficits have been the rule. In 1998, oil income was $37 billion, leaving a budget deficit of $13 billion. To invest more in industry, the state and parastatal agencies would have to rely on further borrowing on local and international financial markets. Major new debts would hurt Saudi Arabia's blue-chip image and subject it to vastly increased international pressure. An obvious alternative to borrowing would be for the state to divert its large military expenditures into industrialization, but this would weaken the royal family's position in the "social contract." Only the private sector, which keeps $200 to $500 billion overseas (the figure is debated), could make the necessary investments.

In spite of the demand for capital, very little private investment has occurred. The bureaucracy has made the establishment of large new private industries so difficult that few ever get off the ground. This is unlikely to change unless financial and commercial regulations become independent of civil-service control.[7] But the civil service knows very well that true economic liberalization, especially in the financial and energy sectors, would expose these sectors to purchase by the major princes. Commoners would be crowded out, and tensions between the royal family and the rest of Saudi society would mount. Thus it seems that the civil service—tacitly supporting the strategy of King Fahd—

strives to limit the power of the royal family in order ultimately to protect the binary economic system, and with it the entire Saudi social
bargain.

Since King Fahd became infirm in 1998, there have been a few al-
terations in this arrangement. Princes have become more involved in
the previously protected sectors of finance and oil. Saudi American Bank,
for example, one of the largest banks in the kingdom, is now controlled
by al-Walid bin Talal bin Abdel Aziz—a well-known, if not politically
powerful prince. The energy sector is now managed by a committee of
technocrats and princes under the leadership of Prince Saud al-Faisal
bin Abdel Aziz and Crown Prince Abdullah, not solely by the minister
of oil and the king as in the past. But the economic system is still tightly
controlled; the stock markets remain small; and the ability to create companies that float capital is very limited, even though all indications are
that the markets would boom if liberalized.

The elements in Saudi society most destabilizing to its "social contract"—and so, to its incipient process of liberalization—tend to come
from the ranks of Wahabi Islamic reformists. As part of the deal between the Al Saud and the Al Sheikh, the Wahabi religious establishment
has long been pampered and indulged with access to state funding and
the state-controlled media. But while religion is central to the everyday
life of Saudis, there is between the Al Saud and the religious establishment a marked distance that has kept the Wahabis from assuming a major
role in the political evolution now taking place.

Moreover, the Wahabis themselves are very much divided: There are
the traditionalist proponents of a "purer" Islam who support the regime,
advocate reform by peaceful means, and are seen mainly on Saudi television—mostly as boring old men best ignored. Then there are the
"jihadis," who are generally younger, advocate change through violence—they include the followers of Osama bin Laden—and are widely
disparaged as unstable hotheads.[8] Their ideas frighten most Saudis,
particularly the middle class. Despite Western impressions that a broad
and deep stream of radical, antidemocratic Islamism runs just beneath
the surface of Saudi society, the jihadis' support is slim. And so, ironically, Wahabi jihadism is more apt to abet liberalization indirectly—by
maintaining some anxiety among the royal family and the commoners
about what might be waiting for Saudi society should their "social contract" fail—than it is to threaten the regime directly.

## Petitions, Portents—and Proto-Parliaments?

In 1991 and 1992, King Fahd himself had a taste of the pressures that
have been building in Saudi society over the past few decades when he
received two particularly significant petitions, one from a "liberal" group
and a second from a "conservative" one. After avowing their support for

the monarchy, both sets of petitioners asked that there be increased consultation with the people generally; both complained about bureaucratic delays and corruption, and both warned that judges were not acting independently and were failing to render justice according to Islamic law *(shari'a)*.[9]

The very fact that petitions such as these, mild though they may have appeared on the surface, were even offered was a sign of serious tension. The king not only heard the petitions but acted on them by royal decree, laying down the Basic Law of 1992, which created a 60-member appointed body called the Shura Council.[10]

The Shura is only a consultative body—it has no power to pass laws and can offer advice only when the government asks. Yet in the course of the decade the Shura has become more and more active. In 2001, it doubled in size. The new members are mostly technocrats, businessmen, and academics (no royals belong), and their ranks include—remarkably—two Shi'ites.

The significance of this inclusion in Wahabi Saudi Arabia is hard to overstress. Since the kingdom's earliest days, Shi'ites have been subject to severe repression by the Wahabis, who regard Shi'ism as heresy. Only very recently has the state made efforts to stop anti-Shi'ite discrimination and assaults, to provide Shi'ites with more funds for their schools, and to include them in the kingdom's economic development.

The significance of the Shura itself is likewise hard to overstress. Its meetings are widely reported in the local press and on television. They take place regularly each year for a number of weeks in a very large and luxurious custom-built hall in the palace district of Riyadh. The annual opening of the Shura's session looks almost like that of the British Parliament: The king and the major princes come and proclaim the Council open, and state-run television shows selected excerpts from the deliberations. The Shura is now a major institution in Saudi Arabia.

Perhaps even more surprising to frequent visitors to the kingdom is the amount of private and semiprivate discussion one hears regarding national affairs. There are no public opinion polls, so reports on the views of "the people" can only be anecdotal. It seems, however, that everyone with whom a visitor speaks will complain about corruption, especially corruption in the royal family. People complain about the dearth of jobs for Saudis as well, and they often question the right of the Wahabi establishment and its religious police to control everyday life. But no one challenges the legitimacy of the king or the royal family. It is also striking to the visitor that over the years the same people, however closely or distantly related to the state they might happen to be, have become more and more vocal about their disagreements with the current state of affairs. Semi-public meetings (likewise called *majlis*) are often held during early-evening hours in private homes, where male Saudis will gather to talk politics.

This new political ferment is striking and vigorous, and one sees it taking place at all social levels, even that of the royal family. Though Saudi Arabia is still in the lower left-hand corner of Dahl's chart—that is, in the "closed hegemony" segment—it is at present slowly but discernibly moving upward and to the right, toward more liberalization and inclusiveness.

## "Democratization" from the Top Down

If further evolution in this direction is to take place, however, it can only be with the encouragement, or at least approval, of the king. A current rumor in the kingdom is that Crown Prince Abdullah wishes to allow municipal elections. It is of course unlikely that King Fahd would agree to such a move, so the question depends very much on whether and when Abdullah officially becomes king. All indications are that most of the Saudi people and the main social groups—including even some circles within the royal family—would like more liberalization and participation. But no actual decisions can take place on this front until the issue of succession is resolved.

It is highly likely that extensive negotiations are now taking place among various clans of the royal family over who will hold the leadership in the future. These negotiations will be decisive, because only skillful and courageous leaders will be able to channel and accelerate the protodemocratic trends currently at play in Saudi Arabia. There are those in the royal family who are capable of making the necessary policy choices, and the process of selecting a new leadership does allow for the most able to be promoted. But the kingdom is under tremendous social pressure to change rapidly, and it is not clear that a transition on the political level will happen soon enough to cope with the needs of the entire population, as opposed to those of a few senior princes.

Despite appearances, then, there is some hope for democratization in Saudi Arabia: It has a preexisting culture of consultation and discussion inherited from the Bedouin and Arab traditions of *majlis*. It has a leadership that is used to negotiation on most issues within its own group (and to a certain extent with other groups). It has relatively low levels of tension among social groups, due in great part to the "share the wealth" policies of King Fahd. And the royal family has begun to include more ethnic and religious (though solely male and Muslim) groups in the discussion of public affairs.

Yet elements remain in place that can only raise doubts for democrats: The Saudi state, in order to maintain the country's relatively low levels of social tension, has become heavily bureaucratic, and there are no elected officials to control it. The civil service will not relax its grip until the bureaucrats feel sure that the royal family will not muscle its way into ownership of the main industries, crowding out the private sector and creating tensions. Finally, the lack of an independent judiciary means that the royal family stays above the law. Until this changes, and the Al Saud is placed strictly on the same legal footing as commoners, the state will remain imperious. And this will not happen through any pressure from below: Equality under the law can be imposed on the family and the judiciary only by a strong and well-respected king. Paradoxically, an authoritarian ruler of stature will be needed to establish the institutional structures that can push Saudi Arabia further away from "closed hegemony." Until the question of succession is definitively settled, then, the country's protodemocratic reforms will necessarily remain stalled.

## NOTES

1. Robert A Dahl, *Polyarchy: Participation and Opposition* (New Haven: Yale University Press, 1971), 7.

2. Jean-François Seznec, "The Politics of the Financial Markets in Saudi Arabia, Kuwait and Bahrain," unpubl. diss., Yale University, 1994, 50–54.

3. Jean-François Seznec, "WTO and the Perils of Privatization: A Case Analysis of Saudi Arabia," in Kartik Roy and Joern Sideras, eds., *Institutions, Globalization and Empowerment* (Cheltenham, England: Edward Elgar Publishing, 2002).

4. Military expenses have hovered around $10 to $15 billion per year, and spending on other security agencies such as the Ministry of Interior may be about $5 billion. Oil income has been in the range of $15 billion to $50 billion since 1980, for a total of about $1.2 trillion between 1974 and 2000 (figures extrapolated from the *Middle East Economic Survey*).

5. Totaled from Anthony Cordesman, *The Conventional Military Balance in the Gulf in 2000* (Washington, D.C.: Center for Strategic and International Studies, 2000), 12–14, and *Saudi Military Forces Enter the 21st Century* (Washington, D.C.: Center for Strategic and International Studies, 2002), 43.

6. Youssef Courbage, "L'Arabie Saoudite: Une démographie en changement," in *Monde Arabe Maghreb-Machrek* (Paris), October–December 2001, 36.

7. A new institution called Saudi Arabian General Investment Authority (SAGIA) has been established to help foreign investors establish firms in the kingdom. SAGIA lobbies to simplify the laws and regulations, and pushes the potential investors' files in the various ministries. This new organization has had some success in the past year, but it is too early yet to see whether it can truly break down bureaucracy.

8. Quintan Wiktorowicz, "The New Global Threat: Transnational Salafis and Jihad," *Middle East Policy* 8 (December 2001): 18–38.

9. See F. Gregory Gause III, *Oil Monarchies: Domestic and Security Challenges in the Arab Gulf States* (New York: Council on Foreign Relations, 1994), ch. 4.

10. The Basic Law established the first informal constitution of the kingdom. Among the most important provisions were the formalizing of the rules of succession, a regulation governing state contracting and spending, and the setting forth of the principle that the resources of the country belong to the state rather than the royal family.

# 9

# EMIRS AND PARLIAMENTS IN THE GULF

*Michael Herb*

**Michael Herb** *is assistant professor of political science at Georgia State University. He is the author of* All in the Family: Absolutism, Revolution and Democracy in the Middle Eastern Monarchies *(1999). This essay originally appeared in the October 2002 issue of the* Journal of Democracy.

Talk of democracy in the states of the Persian Gulf often inspires skepticism. There is, first and foremost, the anxiety that even modest moves toward democracy will lead to their "Talibanization." But fears that an Islamist takeover will result from a partial transition are exaggerated. As much as the sad experience of Algeria shows the very real dangers of ill-considered attempts at democratization, it is unlikely in the extreme that an Algerian scenario will play out in the Gulf: The ruling families there are too deeply ensconced to be ousted by Islamists. In each country, the ruling family holds a monopoly on the cabinet portfolios of defense, interior, and foreign affairs (the "ministries of sovereignty," as they are called), along with numerous other posts—all of which afford the dynasties tremendous political security. To be sure, the intrafamilial diffusion of power that results can and does lead to disputes within the dynasties, but because each also has effective mechanisms for internal dispute resolution, they remain durable.[1]

The resilience of the Gulf autocracies makes full democratization a distant prospect, but there is a silver lining of sorts to this: Monarchical stability lowers the risks of partial democratization in the form of free elections for a parliament of limited authority. Among the Gulf states, only Kuwait has extensive experience with such a legislature, its parliament having sat in most years since 1963. Nor can this parliament be dismissed as mere window dressing or as a token of liberalization without democratization. Elections matter in Kuwait. Its parliament has substantial legislative powers and more influence still in setting the public agenda, although only limited control over the cabinet. And other states of the Gulf Cooperation Council (GCC)—Bahrain, Qatar, and Oman—are moving in the same direction. Parliamentary elections were scheduled for October 2002 in Bahrain, and for sometime in 2003 in Qatar. Oman's Majlis al-Shura (Consultative Council) is already elected, though under restrictive conditions that ensure results amenable to the government.

Islamists form the single largest political tendency in the Kuwaiti parliament, and they swept the May 2002 local elections in Bahrain. The Kuwaiti National Assembly is best known in the West for its 1999 rejection of the emir's proposal to allow women to vote. Islamist illiberality on other issues should not be underestimated or glossed over. On issues related to religion or to the role of women, the ruling families are still generally more liberal than many of those who are—or might be— elected to parliament. All of this prompts further skepticism about parliaments, and gives grounds to wonder if there is a serious disconnect between democracy and liberalism in the Gulf: Modestly democratic parliaments generate a good deal of illiberal policy.

On balance, however, parliamentary life does more good than harm. Kuwait's system of government is far more transparent than that of, say, Saudi Arabia. Citizens (or some of them) have a voice in how they are governed. Liberals and other non-Islamists have a public platform from which they can set out their views, something Saudi liberals lack. And, at least in these Gulf monarchies, parliamentary life does seem to promote some degree of moderation among Islamists. In Kuwait and Bahrain, they plainly benefit from liberal political freedoms—the alternative being ruling-family repression. For there to be free elections, there must be substantial freedom of the press, speech, assembly, and so forth, and Islamists recognize that they depend on these freedoms. This creates an arena for public debate in which Islamist ideas can be contested. Kuwaiti women are not free to vote, but they can publicly argue that they *ought* to be. And the most durable victory for women's suffrage will be achieved when most Kuwaitis are convinced, via public debate, that women should have full political rights. In a region where autocracy tends to clear civil society of all groups but Islamist ones, liberals and others in Kuwait are able to give voice to their ideas, form organizations, and contest elections.

## Kuwait's Parliament

Any discussion of Gulf parliaments by necessity centers on the Kuwaiti National Assembly (only Bahrain has had any previous parliamentary experience, and it was short). Elections in Kuwait are free. The government did purchase some votes in the past two elections, in 1996 and 1999, but the results largely reflected voters' intentions.[2] At the same time, Kuwait has an unusual constitutional provision that gives all cabinet members seats in the unicameral parliament along with the right to vote on most issues. The cabinet can include up to 16 members (the Assembly has 50 elected members). Since only one of those must be an elected member of parliament, the government enjoys a reliably loyal bloc of up to 15 additional voting MPs, some of whom belong to the ruling family, the Al Sabah. (Sheikhs of the Al Sabah never run for election.) Furthermore, the cabinet votes are supplemented by the votes of "service deputies," a bloc within the parliament that reliably supports the government in exchange for constituent services. And yet, despite these advantages, the government does sometimes lose important votes, as was the case with parliament's refusal to give women the vote.

The monarchical nature of the Kuwaiti regime shapes the likely path of any further democratization, which will not revolve around more or freer elections, but will instead require making the cabinet responsible to parliament rather than to the emir. Today Kuwait's emir selects the prime minister—who is invariably also the crown prince—and the prime minister selects the other ministers in turn. The family allocates the ministries of sovereignty among its own members, while the remaining ministers are appointed following wide consultations with various groups and individuals throughout Kuwaiti society. While the ruling family determines the final formula, it does give serious attention to balancing the political forces in parliament. The resulting cabinet need not win an immediate vote of confidence from parliament, nor indeed does the 1962 Constitution provide for a vote of confidence in the government as a whole.[3] Following a practice found in some older Western constitutions, however, the Kuwaiti Constitution allows for votes of confidence in *individual* ministers. Such a vote is preceded by an interpellation in which deputies formally question the minister (members of the cabinet do not vote on motions of confidence). On the request of at least ten deputies, the interpellation proceeds to a vote of confidence. If the minister loses the vote, he is dismissed.

Kuwait's parliamentary system has seen a considerable degree of consolidation. Elections have become an accepted part of the country's political life and, crucially, Kuwaitis have come to expect that they will be fairly conducted for the most part. An unconstitutional suspension of the parliament is less likely now than at any time in the past. Over time, the constituency for absolutism in Kuwaiti society has dwindled. From the 1960s through the 1980s, the ruling family gave citizenship (and the right to vote) to many tribal members in order to counterbalance the urban-nationalist and merchant opposition, although today the tribes are themselves more often in the opposition than they are with the government. The same holds true for two older sometime allies of the government, the Islamists and the Shi'ites.

Formidable obstacles nonetheless stand in the way of any further movement toward making the cabinet answer to parliament. First, the ruling family will not lightly give up its control of the ministries of sovereignty, nor is it likely to allow the parliament to decide which Al Sabah sheikhs get which posts. These are core prerogatives of the family, tied directly to its internal balance of power and to its method of resolving internal disputes. Second, while there is a strong desire for more democracy in some quarters, the ruling family enjoys real legitimacy. Republicanism has no support in Kuwait, and the 1962 Constitution, which itself enjoys wide support, calls for a parliament but also grants the ruling family a major role in government.

Perhaps the greatest obstacle to further democratization is the opposition's own lack of common purpose. Islamists and liberals agree that there ought to be a parliament, and they cooperated in demanding a resumption of parliamentary life after the suspension of the Assembly in 1986. But that is about the extent of their common program. They have certainly not cooperated much in recent years to further trim the power of the Al Sabah.

Recent Kuwaiti politics affords a sense of how the issue of further democratization gets lost in the political shuffle. In July 2002 a formidable parliamentary coalition of Islamists, Shi'ites, and tribal deputies interpellated the minister of finance, himself a respected liberal. The interpellation proceeded to a vote of confidence, and Sheikh Sabah, the acting prime minister, declared that the government would resign if the minister lost the vote. This raised the prospect that the crisis could turn into an opportunity to establish the principle that the cabinet as a whole could be brought down by a vote of the Assembly. But in the event, the political battle did not turn on the issue of further democratization. Instead, as the journalist Hamid al-Jasir of *Al-Hayat* put it, the interpellation brought three divisions to the fore: 1) the split between the competing wings of the ruling family; 2) the divide separating liberals and Islamists; and 3) the rift between "economic neo-liberals" and those defending the interests of the poor (which is also a distinction between the *hadar*— or city families—and the more recently settled tribes).[4] The divide among the sheikhs of the Al Sabah is particularly important. The allocation of posts to members of the ruling family inevitably leaves some dissatisfied, and unhappy sheikhs have used parliamentary interpellations to attack governments and try to force redistributions of cabinet posts. This does not mean that the deputies are mere pawns of the sheikhs, but it does indicate why Kuwaiti politics is much more complicated than a straightforward battle between the autocratic monarchy and the democratic opposition.

Sheikh Sabah, the acting prime minister, has long had good relations with Kuwait's liberals. The nominal prime minister, Sheikh Saad, has health problems, and the emir asked Sheikh Sabah to form the current government in early 2001. In the recent crisis, liberals in the parliament rallied around Sheikh Sabah, their champion in the ruling family, putting them in an awkward position for a group that has long sought to trim the powers of the government. In the end, the finance minister narrowly survived, drawing on votes from liberals, urban deputies, and reliably progovernment service deputies. But victory had a cost: Even the government's liberal supporters criticized it for shoveling largesse at wavering deputies. The government also backed down on some of its economic and administrative reform plans, which made up the core of its program. And the political system came to yet another paralyzing halt over issues that were seen to be as much about personalities as about issues. The combination of a fractious ruling family with parliamentary horse-trading gets in the way of coherent government and makes the Kuwaiti model less attractive to the rest of the region.[5]

One solution would be to let parliament form governments rather than merely attack them. But there are no signs that a move in this direction is imminent. Such a move would require that the prime minister's post be given up to someone from outside the family, though the ruling family might still reserve the ministries of sovereignty for its members. Further democratic development in Kuwait, if it occurs, will almost certainly be on a parliamentary model: No president will replace the emir. Parties operate informally, but they are weak. The current electoral system (25 small two-member districts) produces a parliament composed largely of independents, some associated with the government, others with liberal or Islamist political groups. A different electoral system could produce stronger parties, especially if they could form governments. But it is unlikely that even this would produce a party capable of forming a government without a coalition. The cleavages in Kuwaiti society are deep: between liberals and Islamists, Sunnis and Shi'ites, tribes and *hadar*. Of course, all of this may be to the good: The prospect of an electorally dominant Islamist party in a more democratic Kuwait, however unlikely, gives reason for pause.

## Bahrain and Qatar

The new ruler of Bahrain—a tiny island country with about half a million citizens that sits between Qatar and the Saudi coast—recently launched an ambitious political opening, releasing political prisoners, inviting the opposition back from exile, reforming the security forces, and promising elections. All this marked a vast improvement over the situation in the 1990s, when the regime busied itself with brutally repressing its opposition. Bahrain's Shi'ite majority distinguishes it from Kuwait, Qatar, and Saudi Arabia, where Sunni ruling families preside over mostly Sunni citizens. The Sunni Al Khalifa family took over Bahrain in 1783 and has long treated the Shi'ites as a conquered people. Bahrain's divisive history has created a deep reservoir of ill will between the Al Khalifa and most of the populace. While the sectarian divide poses an obstacle to partial democratization not found in other GCC states, it is far too simple to blame Bahrain's past lack of success with parliamentary life on the sectarian issue alone. Bahrain's previous experiment with a parliament, from 1973 to 1975, foundered not on the sectarian issue but because the ruling family grew exasperated at the legislature's refusal to agree to a restrictive law on public security. The main Shi'ite opposition group in the 1990s has been quite moderate, focusing its demands on the restoration of the 1973 Constitution and eschewing any demand that the ruling family be removed from power. Given the ruling family's iron grip on the almost wholly Sunni security and military forces, the country's Shi'ites have little other choice. The ruling family's brutal repression of the opposition in the 1990s was not necessary to avoid an Iranian-style revolution, but instead merely served the desire of the ruling family to avoid any accountability to the subjects of their family fiefdom.

> *The presence of active parliaments can lay the foundation for further democratization, especially to the degree that a tradition of free elections continues.*

Bahrain modeled its 1973 Constitution closely on Kuwait's. In February 2002, the ruler revised this constitution by decree, further limiting the powers of parliament. The revisions created an appointive upper house and dropped the provision that calls for the cabinet as a whole to sit in the elected lower house. Disagreements between the elected lower house and the appointive upper house are to be resolved by a vote of all members of both houses in joint session. Since both houses will be the same size, with 40 members each, this gives elected deputies less power than they enjoyed under the 1973 Constitution, which called for a set of institutions closely resembling those found in Kuwait today. Only the lower house votes on interpellations and motions of confidence, but the vote succeeds only if two-thirds of the deputies vote against the minister. The opposition is unhappy about these unilateral changes to the constitution, but it is not clear that it would gain much by rejecting them and refusing to participate in the upcoming elections. It is primarily the attitude of the ruling family that will determine the fate of the current opening; the family will have to make the concessions necessary to keep the moderate opposition engaged. Opposition leaders, for their part, will need to balance their desire to keep the game going with their need to remain responsive to the demands of their constituents.

A draft of Qatar's new constitution was presented to the emir in July 2002. It calls for a unicameral legislature. Qataris—including women—will elect two-thirds of the members in direct and secret elections, while the emir will appoint the remaining members. The parliament will have the power to approve the budget, to interpellate ministers, and to vote them out of office through a vote of confidence. The constitution was drafted by a committee appointed by the emir, which took a very deliberate three years to complete its task. Qatar has already had local elections, in 1999, and observers commented positively on their fairness. Women were allowed to run as candidates and to vote, though none won a seat. The most marked difference between Qatar and both Bahrain and Kuwait lies in the absence, to this point, of a really vocal opposition. Qatari moves toward liberalization appear to be tactical concessions by the emir, who overthrew his father in 1995 and seems to have calculated that a slow process of liberalization, followed by the opening of a parliament, would help place his rule on a firmer basis.

Full parliamentary democracy in Kuwait, Qatar and Bahrain will not be achieved any time soon. But the parliamentary life that is underway in Kuwait, and on the way in Bahrain and Qatar, should not be dismissed lightly. Nor will partial democratization lead to an Islamist takeover. Today in Kuwait citizens have a real—if still constrained—voice in how they are governed, and even Islamists find they have a stake in defending the liberal freedoms that accompany parliamentary life. The presence of active parliaments can lay the foundation for further democratization, especially to the degree that a tradition of free elections continues. There are certainly real blemishes. Parliaments reflect the illiberal views of the Islamists elected to them. And the way in which Kuwait's parliament has become entangled in disputes within the ruling family contributes to a sense of political and societal drift. Yet Kuwait is also the freest of the Gulf states, and it has the most transparent government among them. Efforts to set up parliaments in the Gulf—especially in Bahrain—should be encouraged, as should their spread to other nearby states, particularly Saudi Arabia.

## NOTES

1. See Michael Herb, *All in the Family: Absolutism, Revolution and Democracy in the Middle Eastern Monarchies* (Albany: State University of New York Press, 1999).

2. On Kuwaiti politics see Mary Ann Tétreault, *Stories of Democracy: Politics and Society in Contemporary Kuwait* (New York: Columbia University Press, 2000) and Jill Crystal, *Oil and Politics in the Gulf: Rulers and Merchants in Kuwait and Qatar* (Cambridge: Cambridge University Press, 1995).

3. An unused constitutional provision gives parliament the power to declare that it cannot work with the prime minister. Should this happen, the emir dismisses either the parliament or the cabinet.

4. *Al-Hayat* (London), 14 June 2002.

5. See, for example, Khalid al-Dukhail in *Al-Hayat* (London), 18 February 2001.

# 10

# YEMEN'S ABORTED OPENING

## Jillian Schwedler

***Jillian Schwedler*** *is assistant professor of government and politics at the University of Maryland and chair of the Board of Directors of the Middle East Research and Information Project (MERIP), publisher of* Middle East Report. *This essay originally appeared in the October 2002 issue of the* Journal of Democracy.

In 1990, North and South Yemen surprised the world by announcing that, along with the unification of the two countries, the new Republic of Yemen would bring democracy to the Arabian Peninsula. Rapid democratization seemed unlikely, given that Yemen is a mostly rural country with poor economic development, a lack of basic services in many areas, and low levels of literacy. But the first years after unification were promising. The country had a vibrant public sphere and the 1993 national elections produced a pluralistic parliament. Today, however, the government more closely resembles the autocracy of the pre-unification North than a country in democratic transition. Although President Ali Abdallah Salih continues to call Yemen an "emerging democracy,"[1] he seems uninterested in moving the country beyond tactical liberalization and toward a genuinely open political system.

The Republic of Yemen was formed in May 1990, when the leaders of the Yemen Arab Republic (North Yemen) and the People's Democratic Republic of Yemen (South Yemen)—the Arab world's only Marxist state since winning independence from Britain in 1967—agreed to unify their countries.[2] While the embrace of democracy was largely a strategic choice by which each intended to prevent the other from dominating, talk of unification dated to the 1970s, and South Yemen's leaders had been debating democratic reforms since the 1980s. With unification, each believed that it would do relatively well in the elections, maintaining its own base while winning support in the territory of the other.

Unification took place fairly quickly. While some aspects of the North-South power-sharing arrangement were formalized, such as having the government based for six months of the year in Sana'a (the capital of the North) and for the other six in Aden (that of the South), other aspects were agreed to informally by the North's President Salih and the South's President Ali Salim al-Bayd. They decided that a five-person transitional Presidential Council would consist of three northerners and two southerners, while the transitional parliament would simply combine the two existing assemblies. Salih would be the first president, with al-Bayd as his vice-president. And regardless of electoral returns, the two would form a coalition "unity" government, although separate armies would be maintained until the system was institutionalized and mutual trust was established. The North's political elite became a party called the General Popular Congress (GPC), the name of the former North's umbrella assembly, while the leaders of the South kept their preunification name as the Yemeni Socialist Party (YSP).

## Opening and Closing the Political System

By the time of the first national elections in 1993, Yemen already had a well-developed civil society, North Yemen having benefited from a lively public arena even before unification.[3] Some two dozen political parties had emerged,[4] as well as research institutes, women's and human rights groups, and some 20 newspapers. Tribal organizations, political parties, and civil society groups all organized conferences and rallies as the elections approached, and the press published quite freely. Most of this went on in the major cities, and the majority of Yemen's then 14 million citizens lived in villages and rural areas. Yet even among the tribes of outlying areas, there were open debates about liberalization, and major political parties held lectures and rallies organized through their local branches. Mosques served as important locations for public debate, as did afternoon *diwan* gatherings (where qat leaves are chewed for their mild stimulant effect). Meanwhile, Salih created a number of "shadow" civil society organizations that mirrored the goals and activities of—and endeavored to divert support away from—independent groups. Nevertheless, Yemen had the makings of a meaningfully pluralistic political system.

The largely free and fair elections of April 1993 returned a multiparty assembly:[5] The GPC won 123 of 301 seats, and the YSP, 56. The new Yemeni Islah party, a coalition of tribal and Islamist groups established in 1990, won 62.[6] Although the GPC and YSP had orchestrated their power-sharing arrangement in advance of the elections, the Islah party, having won more seats than the YSP, was brought in as a junior coalition partner and given several cabinet portfolios. This frustrated YSP leaders, particularly given Islah's connections with the GPC elite, but the YSP's own performance at the polls gave them little leverage for argument.

For the YSP, the problem was not only that Islah was a conservative Islamist party, but that its coalition of businessmen, Islamist groups, and prominent tribal leaders was formed from many long-time supporters of Salih. The tribal connection is important. The chair of the Islah party, Sheikh Abdallah al-Ahmar, also heads the Hashid tribal confederation, of which Salih's own Sanhan tribe is a member. While the Islah party and its Islamist focus have led to the development of support bases distinct from those of the GPC, its inclusion in the coalition government was less as a "third" party than as a partner of northern power bases that diminished the influence of the YSP.[7]

Almost immediately, YSP ministers and Vice-President al-Bayd began to complain that the transitional agreement was not being honored. Meanwhile, the GPC accused the YSP of plotting the secession of the South, particularly when Bayd failed in August 1993 to return from a Washington visit made without Salih's knowledge. By February 1994, parts of the YSP army had already been transferred north and incorporated under a single GPC-dominated Ministry of Defense, and the YSP began acquiring arms and recruiting for its own army. Although YSP leaders did not have a clear or unified position on the question of secession, conflict between the two parties' armies broke out in May, upon which the YSP declared the establishment of the Democratic Republic of Yemen in the South. By July, however, the Southern army was defeated and many YSP leaders went into exile.

Today political parties remain legal and active; a dozen or so newspapers publish regularly; and at least a handful of independent civil society organizations still function, including secular and Islamist think tanks that regularly address issues such as corruption and the need for political reform. But real power resides with Salih and the GPC.

The Islah party, nevertheless, retains enough support to pose a challenge to the regime. Following the 1994 war, the GPC and Islah divided the government's cabinet positions, and Islah leaders set about implementing their planned reforms. Among Islah's portfolios was the Ministry of Education, the control of which they saw as decisive to building a "purer" Islamic society from the ground up. Within a few years, the public school curriculum was reformed, numerous Islamist teachers were hired, the class time allotted for Koranic studies was increased, and new school texts were issued with expanded Islamist content. Islah leaders also succeeded in changing the wording of the 1994 Constitution to stipulate Islamic law as its "unique" source, overturning the language of the 1991 Constitution, which had Islamic law as its "principal" source. At the same time, Islah ministers encountered a deeply entrenched system of corruption and patronage, one that served to concentrate Salih's authority by maintaining a diverse network of allies who depended mainly on him. Within two years, Islah saw its political clout within the government decline rapidly, and most Islah

ministers resigned in frustration. Some Islah leaders remain in the closest circles of Salih's power, but these ties have little to do with Islah as
a party and much to do with patronage, kinship networks, and personal
relations.

A second set of national elections was held in April 1997. In the
months before the polling, an unofficial but widely acknowledged agreement between the GPC and Islah—whereby the two would not oppose
each other in specific districts—fell apart. Many "independents" turned
out to be GPC candidates, running in districts where it had been agreed
that Islah would prevail. In the end, the vote returned an overwhelmingly pro-GPC assembly, and the veneer of pluralism was gone. The
GPC won 188 seats and Islah, 53, although the actual GPC bloc—which
includes the nominally independent GPC loyalists—is closer to 226 seats,
about 75 percent of the assembly.[8] The YSP, still a legal political party,
boycotted the vote.  Educated Yemenis continue to speak enthusiasti-
cally of the prospects for democracy, though when asked whether Yemen
is democratic, their answer is invariably no.

## Obstacles to Democracy

Salih came to power in North Yemen in 1978 through a coup. Under
the terms of the unification pact, he became provisional president, having eventually to run for election and be limited to two terms. In the fall
of 1999, almost ten years after unification, he defeated an "alternative"
GPC candidate—parliament having disqualified the only real opposition candidate, from the YSP—and began his "first" five-year term in
office. During this first term, Salih and 144 members of the GPC-dominated assembly proposed amending the constitution by popular
referendum to extend parliamentary terms from four to six years and
presidential terms from five to seven. Yemenis went to the polls in February 2001, just two months before the scheduled parliamentary
elections; of the reported 30 percent of eligible voters casting ballots,
75 percent supported the amendments. Salih will now likely rule Yemen
"democratically" through 2013, at which time his son Ahmad will be of
eligible age to run for the office.

Beyond Salih's overriding commitment to keeping power, two additional factors tend to be cited as obstacles to meaningful democratic
change in Yemen: tribalism and the political strength of Islamists. There
is little doubt that tribalism remains strong in Yemen, but precisely what
"tribalism" is, and what it means for democratic prospects, are often
misunderstood. First of all, only about 20 percent of Yemen's population is tribal. Second, throughout the liberalization of the early 1990s,
tribal leaders were more interested in preserving their economic assets—
land, natural resources, access to the few oil fields (which together pump
less than a million barrels a day), and particularly control of local mar-

kets—than they were in promoting or opposing democratization as such. Even the kidnapping of foreigners is often an effective means of extracting basic services: electricity, roads, teachers, and cell phone towers. Nor are Yemeni tribes "great blocs of persons, aligned with each other on 'traditional' grounds," as is commonly thought. Rather, they are better understood as "networks of individuals who control both trade and real estate," in which kinship is just one catalyst of relations.[9]

*If a meaningfully democratic political arena were to emerge in Yemen, there is little doubt that tribal leaders would participate in order to protect their interests and promote their agendas.*

If a meaningfully democratic political arena were to emerge in Yemen, there is little doubt that tribal leaders would participate in order to protect their interests and promote their agendas, as all political parties seek to do. Tribal networks have survived the country's many political upheavals over the past century, not by preserving some premodern past, but by adapting quickly. While tribal networks may not be bastions of democratization, neither are they "relics" that necessarily impede reform. A number of prominent tribal leaders are active in government and party politics, and in many strongly tribal areas parliamentary elections are even occasions for celebration.

Despite the alliance of conservatism that brought tribal leaders together with Islamists in the Islah party, the latter generally possess distinct political agendas and even oppose the extended kinship networks on which tribalism is based. And Yemen's Islamists hardly form a solid bloc, in part because Yemenis follow many different schools of Islam. The Yemeni branch of the Muslim Brotherhood, for example, advocates reform in large part through increased literacy (for both women and men) in the service of universal Islamic education. The Brotherhood forms a key segment of the Islah party and is committed to working through democratic, legal channels to realize its goal of achieving political, social, and economic reform in line with the teachings of the Koran. For this group, democracy is a form of government completely in line with Islamic teachings.

Yet the Islah party also includes the controversial Sheikh Abdel Meguid al-Zindani, one of the party's "spiritual guides," though not the one respected by the Brotherhood members who lead Islah's administrative units. Zindani headed the Muslim Brotherhood in the 1970s until he was forced out by a younger, reform-minded leadership. He is wealthy and extremely conservative, has a modest personal following, and is by far the most prominent extremist in the Islah party, but he has little influence over routine party activities. Zindani has been particu-

larly alienated since the September 11 attacks, as Salih continues working with the United States to destroy al-Qaeda cells and sympathizers
in Yemen.

The most influential Islamists outside of the Islah party are the highly
conservative Salafis, fundamentalists who seek literal application of Islamist teachings. Some Salafis are also called Wahabis because of their
ties to Saudi Arabia. Salafis are much more conservative than Brotherhood members, particularly concerning pluralism and the role of women.
Whereas Brotherhood members accept the right of socialist and communist parties to function—provided members do not practice or
advocate atheism—Salafis reject pluralism in any form. The importance
of Salafis in Yemen has less to do with their beliefs, however, than with
their ties to neighboring Saudi Arabia. Saudi influence in Yemen has
waxed and waned over the years, but it remains consistently strong in a
number of regions, particularly along the hazily defined border between
the two countries. (Saudi Arabia opposed Yemeni unification, supporting both YSP leaders and Northern elites in an effort to keep the country
divided.) Salafis have been provocative and confrontational in promoting their brand of Islam,[10] and the breadth of their activities would not
be possible without Saudi financing.

The number of Yemen's "Afghan Arabs"—Arabs who trained with
Islamist militants in Afghanistan—has long been a subject of controversy. Tariq al-Fadli, the most famous of this group, abandoned his
extremism when he married into Salih's Sanhan tribe soon after unification and quickly became the lead GPC representative in his region.[11]
Most of the remaining Afghan Arabs joined forces with extremist Salafis
in the southern Abyan region, just east of Aden, forming the Aden-Abyan
Islamic Army (AAIA). This group of no more than two dozen guerrillas
was responsible for a series of bombings around Aden and in the eastern
Hadramawt region of Yemen. In December 1998, the AAIA kidnapped
16 foreign tourists, four of whom were killed during a government rescue attempt. Zein al-Abidine al-Mihdar, the leader of the AAIA, was
captured, tried, and executed in October 1999; other members received
long prison terms. After years of denying the AAIA's existence, Salih
declared the group completely destroyed upon Mihdar's execution. Since
then the AAIA has been inactive, though two offshoots—Muhammad's
Army and the Islamic Deterrence Forces—claimed responsibility for the
October 2000 attack on the U.S.S. *Cole* in Aden harbor.[12]

In sum, we cannot pronounce categorically on whether Islamists
would help or hinder democratization in Yemen. Most Islamists within
the Islah party are reformers, and many have been outspoken within
local and transnational Islamist debates about the compatibility of Islam and democracy. Within the past year, Islah joined the Joint Meeting
of Parties, a group of eight Islamist and leftist opposition parties. This
bodes very well for pluralism, as it signals a willingness on the part of

diverse groups to cooperate across significant ideological divides. The Joint Meeting seeks to pressure the GPC and the government for better representation, and it has opened a dialogue on alternatives to the current electoral system, including representation on local councils and the limited introduction of proportional representation. This Islah rapprochement with the YSP also contains an element of democratic learning, as the Joint Meeting serves to coordinate those who wish to preserve and expand what few democratic openings remain.  Meanwhile, Islamist extremists such as Zindani and most Salafis reject even limited political liberalization as an imperialist import, and they are likewise critical of Salih for courting Washington and allowing FBI agents latitude in seeking out possible al-Qaeda cells and sympathizers.

## Democrats and Protodemocrats

Yemen has numerous committed democrats, even if most do not enjoy high levels of public support. The country's democratic reformers include intellectuals, moderate Islamists, jurists, business leaders, most socialists, and even some tribal leaders. The strongest obstacle to political liberalization comes neither from extreme Islamists nor tribal leaders, but rather from the regime itself, from the bureaucrats who flourish in the existing patronage networks, and from local notables who fear losing control of regional trade and resources.

Under Salih's tight control, the likelihood that Yemen will move toward a genuine political opening is extremely remote. Salih's every move over the past decade has demonstrated a clear focus on maintaining his authority, despite periodic openings, efforts at limited reform, and a constant stream of democratic rhetoric. Those committed to democratic reforms (such as the YSP) and those who became committed (such as elements within the Islah party) have been gradually shut out. Local and international journalists are harassed for covering issues the state deems sensitive. In summer 2002, for example, several foreign correspondents for Arabic-language publications were arrested for covering armed conflicts between Yemeni troops and tribe members in the al-Jawf region, reporting on military issues having been deemed a risk to state security and thus prosecutable under the penal code.

Were meaningful liberalization to occur, Yemen would not be without capable individuals and potential leaders committed to change. The country already has a multiparty system, a relatively free press, and a vibrant public sphere—far more so, on all counts, than most other Arab nations. Sustained contacts between socialists and reform-minded Islamists over the past few years suggest the emergence of a coalition that could ultimately pressure Salih to open the system, particularly if the economic situation—a per capita annual income of $300, mounting reliance on foreign aid, and poverty that has doubled in six years—continues to deteriorate. For the time being, however, Yemen's "emerging democracy" remains a hostage of Salih's regime.

## NOTES

This article draws on research in Yemen from 1995 to 1998, supported by the American Institute for Yemeni Studies, the Fulbright Foundation, and the Social Science Research Council.

1. Salih has used this phrase frequently since June 1999, when Yemen hosted the National Democratic Institute's conference on "Emerging Democracies," in which 15 countries participated.

2. For a history of Yemen, including an analysis of the impetus for unification, see Paul Dresch, *A History of Modern Yemen* (New York: Cambridge University Press, 2000).

3. Sheila Carapico, *Civil Society in Yemen: The Political Economy of Activism in Modern Arabia* (New York: Cambridge University Press, 1997).

4. Ilham Manea, *Al-Ahzab wa al-tanthimat al-siyasiyyah fi al-Yaman, 1948–1993* [Parties and political organizations in Yemen, 1948–93] (Sana‘a: Kitb al-Thawabit 2, 1994). At one point there were more than 40 parties. See Paul Dresch, *A History of Modern Yemen,* 190.

5. Renaud Detalle, "Les élections législatives du 27 avril 1993," *Monde Arabe Maghreb-Machrek* 141 (July–September 1994): 3–36.

6. Iris Glosemeyer, "The First Yemeni Parliamentary Elections in 1993: Practising Democracy," *Orient* 34 (1993): 439–51.

7. Jillian Schwedler, "The Yemeni Islah Party," in Quintan Wiktorowicz, ed., *Islamist Activism: A Social Movement Theory Approach* (Bloomington: Indiana University Press, forthcoming).

8. Paul Dresch, *A History of Modern Yemen,* 209.

9. Paul Dresch, *A History of Modern Yemen,* 198.

10. See Shelagh Weir, "A Clash of Fundamentalisms: Wahabism in Yemen," *Middle East Report* 204 (July–September 1997): 22–23, 26.

11. Paul Dresch, *A History of Modern Yemen,* 198.

12. Sheila Carapico, "Yemen and the Aden-Abyan Islamic Army," MERIP Press Information Note 35, 18 October 2000.

# 11

# DELIBERALIZATION
# IN JORDAN

*Russell E. Lucas*

**Russell E. Lucas** is assistant professor in the department of political science and the School for International and Area Studies at the University of Oklahoma. He is the author of *Institutions and the Politics of Survival in Jordan* (forthcoming, SUNY Press). *This essay originally appeared in the January 2003 issue of the* Journal of Democracy.

In 1989, with the first Palestinian *intifada* (uprising) raging just across the Jordan River in the West Bank, domestic discontent spilling into his own streets, and his country's finances in tatters, Jordan's King Hussein (r. 1953–99) began taking a series of extraordinary steps toward political opening. He ended repression, called new elections to replace the National Assembly that he had dissolved in 1988, and forged a national pact that put Jordan at the forefront of liberalization in the Arab world. As the late king's son and designated successor Abdallah II faces a similar situation more than a decade later, however, the regime is nearing the completion of a full circle back to martial law.

Jordan has not fully returned to military rule, but the legislature has again been indefinitely suspended, and most public protests are banned. While the majority of Jordanians today do not question their monarch's legitimacy, they do increasingly resent his policies—particularly his continued alliance with the United States at a time when U.S. policy toward Iraq and the Israeli-Palestinian conflict have made that alliance less popular than ever. As of late 2002, it seemed possible that a U.S. military presence in Jordan during a war against Saddam Hussein's regime in Iraq could provoke an insurrection against Abdallah II and the Hashemite dynasty. The Jordanian monarchy has managed to hang on through the tumults of the past decade-and-a-half by adroitly wielding the twin survival strategies of liberalization and deliberalization—using the former when royal interests seemed to dictate and reversing the process when the opposition threatened to get too strong.

Jordan's population of 5.3 million is overwhelmingly composed of Sunni Muslim Arabs. About half the population is of Palestinian lineage. Many of these Jordanian Palestinians have roots in the West Bank or in what today is Israel, and a personal or family history of displacement due to the Israeli-Arab conflicts since 1948. Their sometimes-uneasy presence, as well as the history of strife between Palestinian nationalist groups and the Hashemite monarchy, make for a societal divide that threatens to exacerbate whatever domestic tensions may arise over regional political developments.

Jordan's political liberalization in the 1990s was not a deliberate process of democratization, but rather a survival strategy chosen by a monarchy anxious to shore up its legitimacy in the face of domestic discontent over peace with Israel and the pain caused by structural adjustment in this small, resource-poor country. In time, after critics of the king's foreign and economic policies gained more ability to speak out forcefully than he liked, the strategy was gradually abandoned and the reforms were slowly rolled back. Liberalization gave way to its opposite, deliberalization.

Even with political liberties at their lowest ebb in years, as they are today, Jordanians feel that they enjoy far more pluralism and openness than do their neighbors in Saudi Arabia, Syria, or Iraq. Jordan's relative openness has much to do with a legacy of regime-led state-building dating back to the creation of the Jordanian state. Hussein's grandfather, Emir (later King) Abdallah I (d. 1951) founded what was then called Transjordan in the 1920s under British auspices out of the wreckage of the collapsed Ottoman Turkish Empire. Over the ensuing eight decades, a modern state has been built with the Hashemite monarchy at its core. That monarchy has survived the acquisition of the West Bank as a result of the 1948 war with Israel; the original King Abdallah's assassination; his son Talal's deposition in 1952; the turbulence surrounding Arab nationalism in the 1950s; the loss of the West Bank to Israel during the Six Day War of June 1967; and bloody domestic clashes between royal troops and Palestinian nationalists during the "Black September" of 1970.

The monarchy weathered each of these crises in turn, emerging more firmly entrenched and at the head of a more expansive supporting coalition than ever before. The oil boom of the late 1970s invigorated the economy of Jordan, which itself has no oil but occupies an advantageous position near the oil-rich Gulf region. (An upsurge in aid from other Arab countries helped as well.) When the oil boom went bust in the 1980s, however, the country's financial strength began to erode. In 1988, in response to forceful calls for Palestinian self-determination vis-à-vis Israel, King Hussein decided to sever ties with the West Bank. The decision prompted capital flight by nervous Jordanian Palestinian businessmen—the main financiers of Jordan's private sector. The resulting currency devaluation intensified the fiscal crisis, sending Jordan into the arms of Western donors for a bailout.[1]

## Crisis and Opening

The monarchy then introduced a number of unpopular economic reforms in order to satisfy its creditors, leading many average Jordanians to protest against the resultant cuts in daily subsidies. Riots broke out in a number of traditional bastions of support for the regime.[2] Instead of using coercion, King Hussein opted for tactical political opening. He shook up his cabinet and in November 1989 held the first full parliamentary elections in more than 20 years. Soon thereafter, he called for a National Charter, signed in 1991, in which a broad cross-section of Jordan's elites agreed on plans for institutional reform. The new National Assembly subsequently re-legalized political parties (which had been banned since 1957) and eased press censorship. Martial law formally ended in 1991, and Jordan appeared to be stepping off on a march toward democracy.

The elections of 1989 were the freest that Jordan had ever seen. They also revealed what the balance of power between the regime's supporters and the opposition looked like after decades of martial law. Although the king still appointed the upper House of Notables, the 80-member House of Representatives was elected by universal suffrage—albeit in a gerrymandered system that strongly favored the regime's rural supporters over the ideologically mobilized urban opposition. Proregime forces therefore fared well, though not as well as expected. The big story was that despite glaring malapportionment, the opposition factions combined to win 39 House seats. The moderate Islamist party, the Muslim Brotherhood (MB), won the largest single share with 23 seats. The Jordanian MB, unlike its counterparts in Syria and Egypt, had enjoyed a relatively cooperative relationship with the regime, though in the 1980s the MB began to back a reformist agenda increasingly opposed to royal policies, if not to the monarchy itself. Traditional opposition groupings of leftists and Arab nationalists rounded out the ranks of elected legislators. This new parliament used its constitutional powers to test successive prime ministers and cabinets in confidence votes and grill them in budget debates. It also helped push King Hussein into his neutralist policy during the Gulf War, which was popular at home even as it dismayed Jordan's Western allies.[3]

Despite official claims to the contrary, the political openings of the early 1990s were never designed to produce full-fledged democracy in Jordan. As one of King Hussein's key advisors during this period remarked, liberalization was intended to invite more guests into the living room for "coffee talk," with a few welcome to stay for dinner. None were to be invited into the kitchen, though, and certainly none were welcome in the rest of the house.[4] Parliament could debate some internal issues, in other words, but its involvement in foreign and economic policies was not welcomed. And yet foreign and economic policies were matters of acute concern to most Jordanians; when the threat of the opposition mobilizing those concerns became apparent, the regime began to have second thoughts about the usefulness of political liberalization.[5]

During the 1990s, King Hussein pledged his country's support for the U.S.-led Middle East peace process and robustly implemented an IMF-sponsored economic reform package. As early as 1991, however, the regime began to see the difficulties of simultaneously accommodating a shift toward negotiations with Israel *and* increased political opening. In response to Jordan's participation in the Madrid peace conference—which opened a new chapter in Arab negotiations with Israel—Prime Minister Tahir al-Masri lost his support in parliament and resigned in anticipation of losing a confidence vote. In spite of this episode, which affirmed parliament's constitutional role in holding the executive responsible, cabinet ministers in Jordan still worry more about retaining the king's than the legislature's confidence.

In August 1993, as peace with Israel drew palpably closer through peace talks in Washington, King Hussein decreed new electoral rules designed to shrink the opposition's seat share. By introducing a system based on the single, nontransferable vote (SNTV), he rewarded rural and tribal allies while further rigging electoral outcomes against city-based opposition candidates, particularly those from the MB. As a result of the new electoral law, the opposition lost nearly half its seats in the November 1993 elections. After Israel and the Palestinian Liberation Organization (PLO) signed the Oslo Accords in September 1993, Jordan moved to make peace with Israel as well. In October 1994, the two countries signed a full peace treaty that the weakened opposition was unable even to delay, let alone block. Instead, the new legislature speedily ratified the treaty, which was not signed until the monarchy had taken the precaution of imposing a ban on public demonstrations.[6]

The regime tried to sell the virtues of peace with Israel to a skeptical but apathetic public by promising that the United States would shower Jordan with the kind of aid that Egypt got after the 1978 Camp David Accords. But Western assistance was a trickle rather than a flood, and Jordan's economy continued to struggle. When the peace process began to stall after Israel's Prime Minister Yitzhak Rabin was assassinated by a Jewish extremist in 1995, King Hussein responded by deepening Jordan's implementation of IMF structural-adjustment reforms. By 1996, Jordan had raised taxes, cut government spending (especially on public-sector salaries), and begun, albeit hesitantly, a program of privatization. It had not, however, tackled consumer subsidies—one of the major requirements of the IMF package. In August of the same year, the cabinet ignored the widespread objections that were being heard even in parliament and raised the price of bread. Riots against subsidy cuts broke out in many of the same cities that had revolted in 1989. Whereas the violent protests of that earlier year had prompted political opening, in 1996 the regime responded with force.

## The Years of Rollback

In the late 1990s, the regime continued to roll back its earlier political liberalization. The opposition threatened to mobilize a public angry at the pain caused by economic reform, while the unpopularity of normalized relations with Israel compounded their potential to do so. In contrast to Egypt's stable but distant relationship with Israel, King Hussein saw the peace process as leading toward a new regional order in which Jordan would act as Israel's intermediary in the Arab world. As the peace process slowed under Israeli prime minister Benjamin Netanyahu, however, Jordanian supporters of peace began to see their vision of "a new Middle East" fading. The opposition capitalized on this by calling on Jordanians to reject the normalization of political and economic relations with Israel. Although the opposition could not block the legislation by which such normalization would be carried out, it did succeed in uniting its disparate ranks around opposition to normalization. For example, Jordan's professional associations—its syndicates of middle-class professionals, nearly all controlled by the opposition—began to expel members who visited Israel. The opposition also managed to close a trade fair put on by Israeli companies in Amman in January 1997 through peaceful protests that drew nearly 4,000 demonstrators.

The regime came to perceive the growing institutionalization of antinormalization forces as a potentially serious threat not merely to the monarchy's policies but to its very survival. King Hussein feared that the link pervasively made between the pain of economic reforms, on the one hand, and the growing consensus against normalization of relations with Israel, on the other, could become not just the basis for a series of disjointed, spontaneous demonstrations but a viable opposition platform that might be enough to support a full-scale antiregime mobilization. With parliamentary elections due in November 1997, King Hussein ordered further limits on political liberties, hoping that the crackdown would prevent opposition electoral gains that could upset his plans to push further economic reforms through parliament.[7]

To silence critics of its economic and foreign policies, the regime decreed restrictive amendments to the press law in May 1997. This sparked an outcry not only from the opposition and international human rights observers, but from liberal regime supporters as well. When the newly amended law was invoked in order to shut down most of Jordan's weekly newspapers, the aggrieved asked the courts to overturn the decree. The courts did so, but did not hand down their decision until long after the November elections were over.

The changing by decree of the election and press laws, as well as the signing of the peace treaty with Israel, led the MB to call for a boycott of the 1997 elections. Most opposition parties joined the boycott, as did a range of disillusioned liberals who had traditionally backed the regime. The boycotters demanded a repeal of the press and election decrees and a reversal of the normalization process with Israel. The regime refused to budge, and the upshot was that the opposition wound up shutting itself out of the legislature which was chosen that autumn with nothing to show for the sacrifice of its seats. While overall voter participation was lower than it had been in 1989 or 1993, it was not so low that it embarrassed the monarchy, which benefited from record levels of rural turnout. Only a token opposition presence remained in parliament, and most deputies were strong supporters of the regime.

The regime's pliant new parliament quickly passed legislation to curb the press. The 1998 press law even earned new Prime Minister Abd al-Salem al-Majali a spot on the New York-based Committee to Protect Journalists' list of the "Ten Worst Enemies of the Press." The opposition could do little to oppose the changes, which prompted the editor of the *Jordan Times* to lament that with respect to the freedom of the press, Jordan had sadly come "full circle . . . to martial law."[8]

As parliament debated the new press law, King Hussein gave regency powers to his younger brother, Crown Prince Hassan, and left the country to seek cancer treatment in the United States. Jordanians spent months preparing themselves for the end of Hussein's almost half-century–long reign, which came with his death in February 1999. What they did not anticipate was the surprise emergence of Hussein's son, Abdallah, as heir to the throne: Less than two weeks before he succumbed, the dying king had decided to displace his younger brother and name Abdallah as successor. In contrast with his father's focus on regional politics, Abdallah II placed greatest stress on Jordan's economic reform and its integration into the world economy. He requested that parliament remove some of the provisions of the restrictive press law, and even ventured out into the public in disguise in order to uncover administrative inefficiencies, earning public accolades.

But King Abdallah's taste for liberalization would prove short-lived. In 1999, as negotiations got underway on a final-status agreement between the PLO and Israel, Abdallah pledged Jordanian support for the peace process while further limiting the scope for public opposition to it: A September 1999 crackdown on the Jordanian offices of the Palestinian Islamic Resistance Movement (Hamas) demonstrated that the regime's tolerance of dissent had reached a limit. When the second *intifada* erupted in September 2000 and the Palestinian-Israeli final-status negotiations broke down, the renewed conflict in the West Bank echoed in Jordanian domestic politics—just as it had during the first *intifada,* which began in 1987. The king and his cabinet perceived the new uprising as a threat not only to Jordan's peace agreement with Israel but also to the survival of the regime itself. Externally, Jordan maintained its peace treaty with Israel, but it cooled Jordanian-Israeli relations: When Jordan's ambassador to Israel finished his term in November 2000, he was not replaced.

Meanwhile, the regime showed little tolerance for public manifestations of support for the uprising. A ban on demonstrations was imposed after rallies in early October 2000 led to property damage and one shooting death. When the opposition staged a march in the Jordan Valley that drew almost 20,000 people, security forces broke it up with violence. In May 2001 and April 2002, masses of demonstrators returned to the streets of the capital city of Amman, once again meeting with forceful suppression—although those few demonstrations that officials had permitted had generally been peaceful.

The parliament elected in 1997 finished its term in 2001. Although the House of Representatives was overwhelmingly proregime, it often resisted royal initiatives to cut government spending and to integrate Jordan further into the global economy. The House, for example, rejected plans to raise taxes and strengthen antitrust laws. When the legislature's term ended in June 2001, King Abdallah dissolved the assembly and began to rule by decree, announcing that parliament would return after new elections.

One of the first decrees simplified voting registration and added 24 seats to the House of Representatives, but did little else to change the controversial electoral system. The cabinet claimed that the elections slated for November 2001 would be delayed for at least 10 months in order to allow voters to register into the new electoral system. In August 2002, elections were again postponed at least until the spring of 2003. Although ostensibly for procedural reasons, it seemed clear that the delays were actually motivated by the regime's fear of holding elections with the *intifada* raging next door and U.S.-led military action against Iraq possibly imminent.[9] Since June 2001, more than 80 other laws have been decreed.[10]

The second *intifada* and related regional developments have led the cautious Jordanian regime to stifle domestic discontent, with force if necessary. With parliament suspended indefinitely, rallies banned, laws being decreed at a dizzying pace, former parliamentarians being jailed, and round-ups of militants leading to curfews, there is widespread speculation both within and outside the country that a full return to martial law is pending. Moreover, Jordan's economy remains weak and aid-dependent despite nearly 15 years of structural adjustment. Jordan's liberalization project was intended to generate support for foreign and economic policies that the regime saw as necessary for its survival. Inadvertently, liberalization gave voice to opposition critics who could not reconcile themselves to peace with Israel. Liberalization also allowed domestic vested interests to veto structural-adjustment measures. Eventually, with little or no tangible benefits accruing from either economic or foreign policies, the regime saw that domestic public opinion could be mobilized against the regime's policies if not the monarchy itself. This realization led to increasing deliberalization, thus bringing Jordan nearly full circle back to martial law. Currently, though, Jordan's liberalized autocracy seems perilously close to veering sharply enough in the direction of deliberalization to become autocracy plain and simple.

## NOTES

I wish to acknowledge the financial support provided for my research by the American Center for Oriental Research, the Fulbright program, the University of Haifa, and the Truman Institute. I alone bear responsibility for the arguments presented in this essay.

1. Rex Brynen, "Economic Crisis and Post-Rentier Democratization in the Arab World: The Case of Jordan," *Canadian Journal of Political Science* 25 (March 1992): 69–97.

2. In contrast, the Palestinian refugee camps around the capital Amman remained quiet.

3. Laurie Brand, "Liberalization and Changing Political Coalitions: The Bases of Jordan's 1990–1991 Gulf Crisis Policy," *The Jerusalem Journal of International Relations* 13 (December 1991): 1–46.

4. Author's interview with Adnan Abu Odeh, former chief of the Royal Hashemite Court, Amman, Jordan, 9 March 1998.

5. Glenn Robinson, "Defensive Democratization in Jordan," *International Journal of Middle East Studies* 30 (August 1998): 387–410.

6. Laurie Brand, "The Effects of the Peace Process on Political Liberalization in Jordan," *Journal of Palestine Studies* 28 (Winter 1999): 52–67.

7. Curtis Ryan, "Peace, Bread and Riots: Jordan and the International Monetary Fund," *Middle East Policy* 6 (October 1998): 54–66.

8. Committee to Protect Journalists, *Attacks on the Press 1997* (New York: Committee to Protect Journalists, 1998). Author's interview with Abdullah Hassanat, editor of the *Jordan Times,* Amman, Jordan, 23 June 1998.

9. *Jordan Times* (Amman), 16 August 2002.

10. *Middle East International,* 31 May 2002; *The Economist,* 6 June 2002.

# II

## Iran and Turkey

# 12

# IRAN'S REMARKABLE ELECTION

*Shaul Bakhash*

**Shaul Bakhash** *is Robinson Professor of Middle East History at George Mason University in Fairfax, Virginia, and a member of the editorial board of the* Journal of Democracy. *He is the author of* The Reign of the Ayatollahs: Iran and the Islamic Revolution *(1990). During the 1960s and 1970s, he was an editor with* Kayhan Newspapers *in Tehran, and reported from Tehran for the* Economist, *the* London Times, *and the* Financial Times. *This essay originally appeared in the January 1998 issue of the* Journal of Democracy.

In May 1997, the Islamic Republic of Iran presented the world the re- markable spectacle of an autocratic, repressive regime that bans politi- cal parties holding a free and fair presidential election. In a hard-fought and highly competitive contest, former minister of culture Mohammad Khatami gained an upset victory over Speaker of the Majlis (parlia- ment) Ali Akbar Nateq-Nuri, winning almost 70 percent of the vote to become the Islamic Republic's fifth president. According to the gov- ernment, turnout topped 80 percent, a figure not reached since the early years of the revolution. Even allowing for the possibility of some offi- cial inflation of turnout statistics, anecdotal evidence suggests that large numbers of people (especially women, young people, and members of the middle class) went to the polls this time after not having bothered to vote in several previous elections. Moreover, the ballots were properly counted, the results publicly announced, and the voters' mandate ac- cepted by the regime.

In evaluating the significance of this election, of course, certain un- usual institutional features of the Islamic Republic must be kept in mind. First, although Iran's president runs the government and appoints cabi- net ministers (subject to confirmation by the Majlis), he does not hold the country's highest office. Ultimate authority rests with the Supreme Leader or *rahbar*—also known as the *faqih* (Islamic jurist)—who is se- lected from among the country's leading clerics by the clerically dominated but popularly elected Assembly of Experts. The Supreme Leader, not the president, appoints the chiefs of the military and security forces, the head of the judiciary and of the broadcasting services, and the clerical members of the Council of Guardians, a watchdog body that can strike down any legislation that it deems violative of Islam or the 1979 Constitution. The Supreme Leader is constitutionally empowered to set the broad policies of the Islamic Republic, and in practice he has acquired additional means of interfering in the running of the government.

Second, the Islamic Republic requires that anyone wishing to run for the presidency must be approved by the Council of Guardians. In 1997, with two-term incumbent Ali Akbar Hashemi Rafsanjani barred by the Constitution from running again, the Council approved only four out of a large field of such applicants. While most of those rejected were not serious candidates, a number of representatives from legitimate, if officially unrecognized, political groups were barred from running. The election was basically a restricted competition among members of the ruling elite, and became a race between the two front-runners, Nateq-Nuri and Khatami.

Yet this does not mean that no significant differences separated the two leading candidates. Although Khatami is also a member of the clerical elite, the ruling establishment clearly favored the more conservative Nateq-Nuri. The country's most powerful clerical organization, the influential Friday prayer leaders in almost all the major cities, the majority of members of parliament, the majority of members of the Council of Guardians, the minister of intelligence, and, most important, Supreme Leader Ayatollah Ali Khamenei all explicitly or implicitly endorsed Nateq-Nuri. The overwhelming popular vote for Khatami in the face of these endorsements represented an incontrovertible "No" to the ruling clerical establishment and a demand for change—for an easing of political, social, and cultural restrictions; for improved economic conditions; and for a greater say in determining the country's policies. Khatami won, moreover, with a campaign that stressed the rule of law, tolerance for a multiplicity of views, wider political participation, social justice, and the need to strengthen the institutions of civil society. It was this message, along with Khatami's palpable moderation, that powerfully resonated with the electorate.

## Rise of the Hard-Liners

The election of Khatami was the more striking because hard-liners had been gaining ground in the years preceding the election. In the three years immediately following the death of Ayatollah Ruhollah Khomeini in 1989, a period that coincided with Rafsanjani's first term as president, social and cultural (though not political) controls had actually been eased. Beginning in 1992, however, this limited liberalization ran into

trouble. A conservative Majlis banned satellite-television dish anten-
nas; secured the resignation of Khatami as minister of culture and Islamic guidance because his policies toward film, theater, and publishing
were considered too liberal; and then forced the resignation of
Rafsanjani's brother as head of the state-controlled radio and television
networks for similar reasons. The Supreme Leader himself led a campaign against the Western "cultural onslaught," shorthand for the Western music, films, television programs, and forms of dress attractive to
the younger generation, and a thinly disguised attack on Iran's West-
ern-oriented intelligentsia and their prominence in the arts.

The security services, led by the Ministry of Intelligence, also gained
greater influence and freedom from accountability during these years.
For example, in November 1994, writer and translator Ali Akbar Saidi-
Sirjani, who had been arrested on fabricated charges of spying, homo-
sexuality, and drug use, died in police custody, allegedly of a heart attack.
A number of other writers were found dead in suspicious circumstances.
Several newspapers and magazines were suspended or shut down.

In April 1997, much to the anger and embarrassment of the government, a German court indicted Iranian intelligence minister Reza
Fallahian and implicated Iran's highest officials in the 1992 assassination of the leader of Iran's Kurdish Democratic Party and three
companions in a Berlin restaurant. This was one of several assassina-
tions of Iranian opposition figures in Europe attributed to the Ministry
of Intelligence.

With the government's connivance, or at least acquiescence, some
clerics began once again to deploy squads of club-wielding bully-boys,
known as the Ansar-e Hezbollah (Helpers of the Party of God), to break
up meetings organized by the political opposition or by those advocating views unwelcome to the regime. The Ansar trashed the offices of
the publisher of a novel deemed disrespectful to Islam, torched a book-
store, and attacked female bicyclists in a Tehran park. They were also
utilized to prevent the Islamic thinker and philosopher Abdul Karim
Soroush from addressing university students on at least three campuses
in Tehran and Isfahan. Soroush has built up a large following among
students, lay intellectuals, and even seminarians by arguing for an Islam that is pluralistic, tolerant, open to change and interpretation, and
compatible with democracy. By arguing against the clerical monopoly
over the interpretation of the sources of Islamic law, he has implicitly
challenged the clerical claim to a monopoly of political authority.

The politicization of the Council of Guardians was a further indication of the erosion of constitutional checks and balances. One Council
member, Ayatollah Ahmad Jannati, championed the Ansar on the
grounds that devoted Muslims were required to act when the government failed to suppress corruption and un-Islamic activities. The Council of Guardians handed down decisions that significantly reduced the

representation of the radical clerical faction in the 1992 parliament and that favored conservative clerics in the 1996 voting for the Majlis.

The rise of hard-liners was also evident in the shift that took place in the relative influence of Rafsanjani and Khamenei, who had run Iran as a diumvirate following Khomeini's death. The two worked closely together, but whereas Rafsanjani was inclined to moderate Iran's foreign policy and to ease social, cultural, and press restrictions, Khamenei favored the hard-liners. After 1992, Khamenei increasingly came to dominate the relationship.

The presidential election thus took place against a background that appeared particularly inhospitable to a "reform" candidate, to a campaign that offered a real choice to the voters, or to the fair conduct of the balloting. The history of past presidential elections pointed in the same direction. Aside from the first election for president in 1980, the outcome of each subsequent election (1981, 1985, 1989, and 1993) was for all intents and purposes predetermined.

That the 1997 election turned out differently is attributable to four factors: 1) the continuing vibrancy and energy of Iranian civil society; 2) a political system that is severely restricted but still offers opportunities for intraregime factionalism and competition; 3) fortuitous events—the ebb and flow of daily politics and the small and large decisions taken by individuals and key players as they responded to day-to-day developments; and 4) the personality of Khatami himself.

## Civil Society: Precarious but Vigorous

While the Iranian regime is autocratic, often ruthless in its treatment of critics, and, at least in certain areas, totalitarian in intent, its reach has limits. Iran has a large and vigorous middle class. Literacy is high among school-age children. The revolution and the political upheavals of the last 20 years have politicized important segments of the populace. The hand of the state rests heavily on all Iranians, and few professional associations or publications operate without some interference by the government. But there is also a sense in which society stands apart from and in opposition to the state. Women have carved out space for themselves by resisting the Islamic dress code, insisting on the right to work, and securing the restoration of some legal rights introduced under the monarchy and suspended after the revolution. In the privacy of their homes, Iranians watch CNN, *Baywatch,* and other foreign broadcasts via satellite; they listen to popular music, dance, play cards, and drink alcohol. Young men and women cannot fraternize on university campuses, but they meet, right under the watchful eyes of the morals police, while hiking and picnicking on Fridays among the foothills of Tehran. These may not appear as acts of great political consequence, but they reflect the many ways in which society, or groups within it, keep at bay the repressive instincts of the state. In small ways, these acts also turn homes and streets into a sphere of contestation where people from all walks of life seek to widen the space in which the state allows them to operate.

Although the press is censored and outspoken editors and writers are punished, literary and quasi-political journals such as *Kiyan, Goftegu, Kelk,* and *Iran-e Farda* have managed to keep alive a vigorous debate on literary issues and such subjects as civil society, the relationship of state and religion, and the role of clerics in government. *Kiyan* publishes the essays through which Soroush has dramatically altered the context and the very language in which religion and even politics are discussed in Iran.

Why the state permits these magazines to publish is not so great a puzzle as it might at first appear to be. The censors have assumed (wrongly as it turned out) that discussions of concepts such as civil society are not harmful as long as discourse remains general and avoids direct criticism of the form of government prevailing in the Islamic Republic. Officials wish to provide some outlet for students, the educated, and the intellectually restless. The Ministry of Culture may wish to control the content of films, but independent directors like Abbas Kiarostami make movies that win prestigious international prizes like the Palme d'Or at Cannes, providing a reflected glory in which the Ministry can bask.

Even though the separation between state and society in certain areas is sharp and confrontational, in others it is more complex and ambiguous. Most Iranians look on the security agencies, the morals police, and the revolutionary committees as instruments of repression, pure and simple. To the intelligentsia, censorship is a deadening and threatening presence. The judiciary is not an independent shield for rights, but a tool that the state uses to punish dissidents and confiscate the property of supposed miscreants for the benefit of the ruling elite and their minions. Publishing firms, professional associations, and nonregime political groups operate at state sufferance and with some state interference. Even independent publications, lacking foreign exchange, depend on state-subsidized newsprint that the Culture Ministry doles out generously to friends and parsimoniously to critics. Independent film makers, theater groups, and dramatists may need official funding or access to state-run facilities in order to operate. The government interferes in the elections of professional bodies such as the bar association and the medical association (though the latter enjoys limited autonomy). Various government agencies operate publishing houses, newspapers, film studios, think tanks, and cultural centers that compete with the private sector in the production of culture.

Yet public space exists, even if in a restricted form. Publications and associations are not simply instruments of the state, and some constantly test the limits of the freedom that the government will allow. Many of those who work in the official cultural and intellectual institutions resemble their nongovernmental counterparts in their desire to engage the cultural and political issues that are current in the outside world. At times the level of repression and control is high; at other times, as in the 1997 presidential elections, a confluence of factors broadens the scope of free civic space. Independent publications and loose groups of citizens will then move, as they did during the presidential campaign, to occupy part of the public space, to speak out, and to influence the political process.

## The Wages of Elite Factionalism

The clerical community dominates the state and politics, but it is not united. There are divisions between the "political" clerics who hold power and those who, fearing for the integrity of the religious establishment, eschew involvement with the state. Since the 1979 revolution, the regime has both repressed and tolerated dissidents among its own ranks. It has dealt harshly with senior clerics who question the involvement of the clergy in politics or the constitutional principle—on which the very foundations of the Islamic Republic rest—that ultimate authority is vested in the Supreme Leader. Ayatollah Hosain Ali Montazeri was dismissed in 1989 as Khomeini's designated successor after he criticized the mistreatment and execution of political prisoners, the suppression of the press, and inadequate consultation by Khomeini with his colleagues. Several senior clerics, Montazeri among them, remain under virtual house arrest. They are not allowed to speak on public issues and are limited to teaching only small numbers of students because they have questioned Khamenei's qualifications to hold the highest office or claim rights to it for themselves.

The regime also tolerates within its own ranks factions that differ significantly over major questions of policy and ideology. These groups are permitted in part because their basic loyalty to the revolution and the Islamic Republic is not in doubt. Besides, the ruling clerics are linked together by family ties and intermarriage, patronage networks, and durable friendships formed in the seminary or during the struggle against the monarchy. In practice, this means that while political infighting and rivalries can be quite sharp, the losers survive. After 1992, for instance, left-wing clerics were squeezed out of parliament and government, but two of the most radical among them were permitted to establish newspapers. One of these papers, *Salaam,* has become an important voice of dissent within the ruling elite.

The most senior clerics have traditionally enjoyed a degree of independence as regards their opinions on religious matters—an independence which, in highly politicized times, spills over into the political sphere. They enjoy large followings among seminarians and believers, whose donations give them quasi-independent revenues. For example, Ayatollah Taheri, the Friday prayer leader of Isfahan, sided with his own townspeople in protesting the decision of the Council of Guardians to void the election of a controversial independent candidate during the 1996 parliamentary elections.

The ruling clerics and their lay allies are organized in a number of loosely structured associations that reflect political divisions and a range of views. The two most important clerical organizations are the Association of the Combatant Clerics of Tehran and the Society of Militant Clerics. The Combatant Clerics number among their ranks most of the leading "political" clerics and are conservative on social, cultural, and women's issues. They depict themselves as committed to the deprived classes, but have close ties to the bazaar merchants and the shopkeepers. A defender of clerical prerogatives, the Combatant Clerics' Association has also strongly supported the claim that the Supreme Leader deserves the absolute obedience of all Iranians.

The Militant Clerics—whom the Iranian press describes as belonging to the "leftist" or "radical" part of the political spectrum—began as a breakaway faction of the Combatant Clerics, from whom they split over issues of both policy and personality. The Militant Clerics and their nonclerical allies dominated the government in the late 1980s. Committed to state control of the economy (including prices), subsidies for the poor, and distributive justice, the group opposed the privatization program that Rafsanjani pursued (with limited success) in the 1990s. Under their leader Mehdi Karrubi, they charged that these policies resulted in windfall profits, income disparities, and the rise of an undeserving business class. They also argued for the prerogatives of the Majlis against the claims of the Supreme Leader. Through a kind of constitutional gerrymandering (and with some help from the Council of Guardians), Rafsanjani managed virtually to exclude the Militant Clerics from the Majlis that was elected in 1992, and then gradually shut them out of senior government positions as well. They reemerged to play an active role in the 1997 presidential elections, however.

A third group, calling itself the Servants of Construction, was formed by 16 high-ranking civil servants only three months before the 1996 parliamentary elections. Its founders included ten cabinet ministers, four deputies to the president, the governor of the Central Bank, and the mayor of Tehran—all men closely associated with President Rafsanjani. The group was put together to keep alive Rafsanjani's policies and legacy in the face of the increasingly conservative, bazaar-oriented trend in parliament. In contrast to the Association of Combatant Clerics (of which Rafsanjani is himself a prominent member), the Servants of Construction is an organization composed primarily of lay technocrats. In the elections it presented itself as a group committed to encouraging entrepreneurial and industrial capitalism rather than traders and the bazaar, and inclined to allow more freedom in social and cultural affairs. Despite its late entry into the field, the Construction group and its allies managed to elect 80 candidates, giving them almost 30 percent of the seats in the 270-member Majlis. The Combatant Clerics and their allies, however, held on to as many as 140 seats.

A number of smaller groups also matter, as do certain associations that are not organized for the purpose of electoral politics but which carry political weight. The Association of the Seminary Teachers of Qum speaks for the senior instructors in the complex of religious colleges there. In recent years it has played an important, if informal, role in according recognition to the most senior and respected Islamic jurists, and its endorsement is eagerly sought by candidates and by officials eager to have clerical sanction for controversial policy initiatives. The Friday prayer leaders in the big provincial cities often play an important role in the politics of their regions.

Although political parties are not permitted in the Islamic Republic, the large factions display some, though not all, of the attributes of parties. They elect officers, hold regular meetings, present slates of candidates and (generally vague) platforms in elections, form parliamentary caucuses, and negotiate and form alliances with one another for electoral and parliamentary purposes. But membership is tiny, generally no more than several dozen activists and their acolytes. Patronage and mosque and clerical networks provide these factions with rudimentary means for mobilizing voters. But in towns and cities especially, appeals must reach the wider, unorganized public. In the 1997 presidential election, Khatami's organization proved especially adept at mobilizing the unorganized voter and cutting into the traditional support bases of the Combatant Clerics' Association and the clerical establishment.

The existence of these political factions (along with daily newspapers that support them) does not invariably translate into meaningful political competition, even within the ruling elite. The years following the 1992 parliamentary elections, for example, were generally politically quiescent. The dominant Khamenei-Rafsanjani diumvirate marginalized the Society of Militant Clerics and its left-wing allies. Yet the existence of different political "lines" (as the Iranian press calls them) among the elite means that there is *potential* for meaningful politics. This turned out to be the case to a limited degree in the 1996 parliamentary elections, and to a fuller degree in the 1997 presidential balloting. In these instances, the issues and competing visions advanced by the leading factions were posed in clearer terms. The search for allies drew in the smaller factions. Infighting spilled over into the daily press; as it grew more outspoken, so did the independent weekly and monthly journals. In the competition for votes, the factions were compelled to appeal to a larger public, making wider political participation possible.

The 1996 parliamentary elections were shaped primarily by a split between Rafsanjani's technocrats, who controlled the cabinet and government, and the Association of Combatant Clerics under Nateq-Nuri, who controlled parliament and looked set to win the presidency in 1997. Ironically, the Rafsanjani technocrats decided to form the Servants of Construction and go their own way only after the Combatant Clerics rejected their proposal to form a joint slate of 5 pro-Rafsanjani candidates and 25 Combatant Clerics candidates to run for the 30 seats in the Tehran-area Majlis district. This rebuff turned the election into a contest, encouraging smaller groups to campaign energetically as well. (The Militant Clerics, still nursing their wounds and skeptical that the elections would be fair even in a narrow sense, sat out the campaign.)

The Servants of Construction proved effective campaigners despite their inexperience. They set up a network of offices and support groups in many parts of the country. In this they were helped by their identification with Rafsanjani, a formidable political figure who has contacts and is owed favors all over the country. The emergence of a centrist, technocratic faction—something of a first for the Islamic Republic—also drew followers. Bazaar merchants and businessmen poured money into both sides in the campaign. In the end, the Combatant Clerics retained their majority, while the Servants of Construction won their large 80-seat bloc. The Construction group, moreover, had created a new political organization, had given respectability to the idea of a political faction not centered on clerics and religious issues, and had utilized new ways (for Iran) of campaigning. They had also aroused voter interest by creating an open breach within the ruling coalition. The 1996 elections were a dress rehearsal for the more significant presidential race of the following year.

## The Politics of the 1997 Election

The 1997 presidential race might easily have gone the way of previous such elections. Khatami's candidacy was more the result of happenstance than planning; and Nateq-Nuri appeared to have an early lock. A number of developments helped to sharpen factional rivalries, however, and the campaign that resulted gave voters a real choice.

The regime, hungry for proof of its continued popularity, wanted a large turnout (Khamenei himself called for a vote of 30 million). Since this would require a credible contest, the leaders needed at least one believable candidate to run against Nateq-Nuri. The Servants of Construction, disheartened by Nateq-Nuri's early lead, deliberated for weeks but could not come up with a viable candidate. In the meantime, Khamenei had been encouraging the Society of Militant Clerics to end their boycott and participate in the elections. He may have seen this as a means of increasing voter interest and bolstering his own role as final arbiter among factions. The Militant Clerics, ruing their decision to sit out the 1996 parliamentary elections (the smaller factions, after all, had picked up seats), responded to the invitation with alacrity.

They turned to Khatami only by default, after the Supreme Leader discouraged their first choice, former prime minister Mir Hosain Musavi, from running.[1] A reluctant Khatami agreed to run only on the condition that he could be an independent candidate rather than the official standardbearer of the Militant Clerics. So unpromising did his candidacy appear that the Servants of Construction took another two weeks before they agreed to join the Militant Clerics in endorsing him.

A number of factors combined to turn Khatami's tentative campaign into a winning one. First, the official endorsements of Nateq-Nuri appear to have backfired. Many Iranians resented the sense that Nateq-Nuri was being forced down their throats. It was widely known that the Supreme Leader preferred Nateq-Nuri. The Friday prayer leaders in major cities who endorsed Nateq-Nuri were all Khamenei appointees. On the eve of the balloting, Khamenei said that Iranians would not vote for a candidate who would be "soft" toward America, a remark widely interpreted as a reference to Khatami. Clerics were everywhere urging Iranians to vote; but when Khamenei instructed them also to indicate who was "the best qualified" to be president, this became an excuse for the abandonment of any pretense at neutrality and the wholesale endorsement of Nateq-Nuri by most clerics. Some clerics told the faithful it was their "religious duty" to vote for Nateq-Nuri. When it became clear that most of the members of the artistic community favored and might campaign for Khatami, the minister of culture issued a directive instructing cultural associations to avoid endorsing specific candidates— a move that aroused considerable resentment. A number of clerics backing Nateq-Nuri charged that the Khatami camp wanted to exclude the clergy from politics and create a secular state. For a public already disillusioned with the ruling clerics, these official endorsements provided further reason to vote for Khatami.

Second, officials grew concerned that the impression the election was being rigged in Nateq-Nuri's favor would result in a low turnout. This led both Khamenei and Rafsanjani to issue statements guaranteeing the freedom of the elections. Somehow these pledges were believed in the closing days of the campaign, and helped to ensure a large turnout.

Third, Khatami benefited from effective organization. The Servants of Construction put to good use the experience they had acquired during the 1996 parliamentary elections to organize for Khatami a nationwide campaign of posters, speeches, newspaper supplements, and the like. Khatami also was able to attract many enthusiastic young volunteers to his campaign. By election day, his campaign claimed that it had four hundred campaign offices across the country. If true, this would suggest a new style of campaign organization in Iran, with implications for future parliamentary and presidential campaigns. Tehran mayor Gholam Hosain Karbaschi, a Rafsanjani protégé, threw behind the Khatami campaign the support of his widely read newspaper *Hamshahri* and the considerable resources that his office made available to him in the capital city, which is home to more than a tenth of Iran's population of about 60 million.

Nateq-Nuri was far more successful than Khatami in gaining clerical endorsements. Yet the scramble for endorsements, which always play a role in Iranian elections, led the factions to seek and secure the endorsement of student associations, cultural associations, artists, athletes, associations of ethnic groups resident in the capital, and the like, involving larger numbers of people in the campaign. Although many members of the artistic community initially were cowed by the minister of culture's directive and adopted a posture of public neutrality toward the race, by the end of the campaign they were signing manifestoes on Khatami's behalf.

Fourth, while the state-controlled television network appeared to favor Nateq-Nuri in its election coverage, the press played an important role in providing a forum for a wide range of views during the election campaign. Much of this was partisan, but it created a better informed public, and analysis of the politics of the election in the weekly and monthly press was often very good. Finally, Khatami himself and his message played a highly significant role in determining the outcome of the election. The election showed once again that personality—and one man's ideas—can be a force in politics.

## The Accidental President

Khatami had little previous experience as a campaigner, having run only once for election (to the first parliament in 1981). During the last three years of his long tenure (1982–92) as minister of culture and Islamic guidance, he lifted many restrictions on magazine and book publishing, cinema, theater, and the arts. This, along with the fact that parliament had forced his resignation, stood him in good stead with the intelligentsia and the politically aware. His reputation for financial probity became more widely known in the course of the campaign and stood in sharp contrast to the corruption or business connections and wealth attributed to most of the other ruling clerics.

The little-known Khatami proved to have a winning personality. He spoke well, dispensed with the trappings of power that surround high officials in Iran, and adopted an attractive simplicity. Whereas Rafsanjani, as president, and Nateq-Nuri, as Speaker of the Majlis, often used helicopters on provincial tours or campaign stops, Khatami drove around in a Paykan, the small car that most ordinary Iranian motorists own.

Khatami's message was perhaps even more important than his style. His emphasis on the rule of law resonated with a public used to arbitrary behavior by the courts and the security agencies. In a country where the morals police enter homes to confiscate satellite dishes or arrest young boys and girls for partying or listening to Western music together, Khatami said the government should not interfere with what people do in the privacy of their homes. When Khatami said intellectuals have a right to personal security, listeners understood the reference to the secret arrests and mysterious deaths of writers over the last few years. His remark that political authority should not be the monopoly of one group pointed to clerical monopoly of the state. He repeatedly emphasized the need for a society-wide dialogue on issues before the country. In contrast to the routine demonization of the West in clerical discourse, he said Iran had much to learn from Western civilization and spoke not of a "clash" but rather a "dialogue" between civilizations.

Khatami also paid particular attention to youth and women, who voted for him in large numbers. The minimum voting age in Iran is only 15, and slightly more than a quarter of all Iranians are between that age and 30. Job opportunities are scarce, even for university graduates. The young are frustrated by the many restrictions that the regime imposes on dress, music, films, and intermixing between men and women. The educated among them yearn for a more open political environment. Women, through courageous struggle, have gained more rights then they enjoyed in the early years of the revolution, but they still chafe at dress restrictions, limited access to top jobs, and a tradition-bound clergy that, with its emphasis on woman as wives and mothers, still advocates for them what many regard as second-class status.

The vote for Khatami was not merely a protest vote against Nateq-Nuri and the ruling clerics; it was a vote for Khatami himself. The support for Khatami built up slowly, in a groundswell. My impression is that many Iranians decided to vote only in the closing days of the campaign. This would confirm that Khatami gained votes as individuals grew familiar with his ideas, gained confidence in his sincerity, and, finally, came to believe that he could make a difference. Endorsements not forthcoming early on multiplied in the later stages of the campaign. Women and the young played a major role in ensuring Khatami's victory. For example, Khatami gave a frank and full interview to the women's magazine *Zanan,* while Nateq-Nuri refused to answer its written questions.

The themes propounded by Khatami have become the common currency of public discussion since the election. If Soroush injected the idea of civil society into debates among the intelligentsia, Khatami introduced this concept to a much wider public, turning it into a subject for discussion among the political class and the public at large. Today it is difficult to pick up a political journal or newspaper and not run across the idea of "civil society" being either attacked or defended. The Supreme Leader himself has tried to co-opt Khatami's campaign themes. Since the election, he has instructed the judiciary to root out official corruption, stressed the importance of addressing the problems of youth, and spoken repeatedly about women's issues. In October, a few days after a major Khatami speech on women's rights, a hundred thousand women were pulled together at a Tehran sports stadium to hear an address by Khamenei on the same issue.

Khatami does not want to overthrow the existing system. He wants to make it work better, but he wants to do so in interesting ways. For example, he notes that in the age of satellite dishes and the Internet, Iran cannot shut out the outside world, and he argues that the young can be "immunized" against the attractions of Western popular culture only through open debate and the free exchange of ideas. He knows that the Iranian Constitution enshrines the idea of religious rule, but seeks ways to make the principle of clerical supremacy compatible with individual rights and liberties.

## "A Moment of Enthusiasm"?

The 1997 presidential election reflected both the possibilities of and the obstacles to meaningful politics in Iran. There exists a factional politics of elites that at times can offer real competition and choice and, through its own internal dynamics, engage a wider public in politics. There exists a press that, despite restrictions, can quickly seize opportunities to act as a watchdog and to engage in trenchant reporting and analysis. There exists, finally, a vibrant middle class eager to take part in politics but not quite sure how to do so. A confluence of factors brought these elements together to produce an election that captured the imagination of ordinary citizens and shook up the ruling establishment. Yet in some ways, public participation in the election resulted from what political scientist Leonard Binder has described in another context as "a moment of enthusiasm." The intriguing question is whether the moment will pass—whether Iran will continue to be a generally if unevenly repressive autocracy relieved by occasions when elite factionalism ushers in heady but evanescent periods of political openness; or whether Khatami (and others who think like him) will find the means to sustain this "moment," to strengthen the institutions of civil society, and to make possible a politics that is both meaningful and durable.

On the plus side, Khatami has come into office with a huge public mandate. He has used his clout to make important changes in the cabinet, including the removal of the notorious minister of intelligence, Reza Fallahian. His minister of interior has been replacing Ministry officials and provincial governors and, although nothing is certain, this could augur well for the conduct of future elections. His minister of culture has already lifted many restrictions on the press and publishing. The debate in the Iranian press today is more open, and factional politics more intense, than at almost any time since the early days of the revolution. This is creating a better informed public, reviving the idea of politics as a choice among competing programs, and encouraging more groups to organize. Writers and journalists, for example, recently formed (or re-formed) a professional association.

On the other hand, factions opposed to the new president—in the Majlis, the clerical establishment, the security agencies, and elsewhere—will resist changes that they see as threats to their interests and livelihoods. Already there is evidence of attempts to frustrate, embarrass, and neutralize Khatami and his ministers. Even larger issues are at stake. Freer debate has reopened the issue of the Supreme Leader's authority, and at least one group has called for a limitation of his powers. Such talk has no doubt already alarmed Khamenei, and if it spreads from the fringes to the center of political debate, will reinforce his inclination to silence dissident voices. The 1998 elections for the Assembly of Experts, which selects the Supreme Leader, will be another flash point. These races will likely be hotly contested, tempting the hard-liners to crack down. The judiciary, the security forces, and the military establishment all remain under the control not of the president, but of the Supreme Leader. The institutions of civil society cannot continue to grow in strength without his support or at least his acquiescence. Some members of the clerical elite, including Khamenei himself, fear that Khatami's reforms could touch off a process that will threaten the regime itself. The security forces may find reason to crack down if the changes attempted by Khatami and the resistance to them severely fracture the ruling elite and lead to disorder in the streets.

Although such a return to repression cannot be ruled out, the experience of the recent elections, the freeing of the press, and the recent rise in political activity will make a new crackdown much more difficult to bring off. The ruling elite will have to pay a price in coin they prefer to avoid—possibly in bloodshed, certainly in an indifferent, disaffected, or even hostile public. To alienate the younger generation could prove particularly costly.

What seems to be missing in Iran are the institutions that will keep the larger public, and especially those members of it who are at the center of the political spectrum, durably engaged in politics. The political organizations of the formal clerical factions are too narrowly based to take on this task. Khatami has no political organization of his own, nor does he appear temperamentally inclined to do what it would take to build one. Such professional and civic associations as do exist are not organized to mobilize large groups of people from the political center. The danger is that those who voted for change and moderation in the elections, having no means to keep themselves engaged, will now sit back and wait for "their" president to bring about the changes for which they voted. The disengagement of the center, of course, will raise the danger of polarization, with the radicals at the two ends of the political spectrum setting the tone of politics.

The principal task of Khatami and those who support his endeavor will be to create and strengthen political, professional, and civil associations among the broad political center and to keep them engaged in politics. This will be a hugely difficult undertaking, but a start has been made. If it is successfully followed through, one can envision an Iran in which Iranians will secure, on a more durable basis, the freedom to associate, to speak out on issues through an independent press, to hold government officials answerable to elected representatives, and to check the worst excesses of the security agencies. This would be a modest, yet astonishing, achievement.

## NOTE

1. Musavi, who had led the cabinet during the harsh years of the war with Iraq, was a staunch advocate of state control over the economy, and hence highly unpopular with the bazaar merchants and their allies among the conservative clergy.

# 13

# IS IRAN DEMOCRATIZING? OBSERVATIONS ON ELECTION DAY

*Haleh Esfandiari*

**Haleh Esfandiari** *is consulting director of the Middle East Project at the Woodrow Wilson International Center for Scholars. From 1980 to 1994, she taught Persian language and literature at Princeton University. Prior to that, she served as deputy secretary general of the Women's Organization of Iran and worked as a journalist in Iran. She is the author of* Reconstructed Lives: Women and Iran's Islamic Revolution *(1997), written in part while she was a visiting fellow at the International Forum for Democratic Studies in 1995. This essay, which originally appeared in the October 2000 issue of the* Journal of Democracy, *draws upon remarks that she presented on 8 March 2000 at a symposium sponsored by the Wilson Center and the Center for Middle East Peace and Economic Cooperation.*

Iran's 2000 parliamentary elections dramatically underscored how far the country has moved in the direction of competitive, if far from fully democratic, politics. Representing a variety of factions and coalitions, more than 5,000 candidates campaigned vigorously for the 290 seats in the Majlis, or parliament. In two rounds of hotly contested voting on February 18 and May 5, a broad reformist coalition supportive of the policies of President Mohammad Khatami won a decisive victory.

It must be kept in mind, however, that in the Islamic Republic there are restrictions on who is eligible to run for office. The Council of Guardians screens candidates for parliamentary elections from a list submitted by the Ministry of Interior. In other words, candidates are vetted first by the Ministry of the Interior and then by the Council. In the runup to the February elections, the Council of Guardians disqualified 569 candidates, many of them prominent figures in Iranian politics, but the exclusions were not across the board and were fewer than in the past. Candidates had the right to appeal, although that did not help them in most cases.

Those candidates who made it through the vetting process competed for votes in multimember districts, ranging in size from a single seat to

Tehran's 30 seats (the latter were contested by 871 candidates). Voters mark their ballots for individual candidates, recording as many choices as their district has seats. Thus, in Tehran, the 30 individuals receiving the highest number of votes were awarded seats in the Majlis. To be elected in the first round, however, candidates also must receive at least 25 percent of the votes in their district. (The old parliament had lowered this minimum requirement from 35 to 25 percent, hoping that this would benefit conservative candidates.) If, for example, two seats in a multiseat district are forced into runoffs, the four top vote-getters below the 25 percent threshold compete in the second round. This year, 224 seats were decided in the first round, with the remaining 66 requiring runoffs.

Although the electoral system does not officially recognize parties, political groups in Iran today sometimes refer to themselves as parties and often combine with other factions to form large, loosely knit coalitions. In 2000, the elections were dominated by two broad coalitions—the reformists and the conservatives. The reformist alliance, which came to be known as the Second of Khordad coalition (after the date in 1997 on which Mohammad Khatami was elected to the presidency), embraced 18 groups but contained two main tendencies: The forces most strongly committed to President Khatami's reforms were led by the newly founded Islamic Iran Participation Front, headed by the president's brother Mohammad Reza Khatami. The other, more centrist tendency among the reformists was led by the Executives of Construction, a party of technocrats close to former president Ali Akbar Hashemi Rafsanjani. The conservative camp, consisting of a coalition of about 15 parties, was dominated by clerics sympathetic to Iran's Supreme Leader, Mohammed Ali Khamenei.

In preparation for election day, these coalitions and the groups within them tried to agree on informal lists of their preferred candidates. Lists were also put together by associations of journalists, educators, religious groups, and the like. For an entire week preceding the elections, newspapers published the lists put out by the various political groups, with each newspaper featuring lists that reflected its own political affiliation. As the lists did not appear on the official ballot, voters would take them into the polling booths in order to copy them onto the ballot papers. The same candidate often appeared on several lists, and there was considerable overlap among some of them.

In the days prior to the election, the talk of the town in Tehran was the candidacy of former president Rafsanjani, a man of great political weight. He had been warned by his supporters and critics alike not to run, as a poor showing might jeopardize his standing in the community as the head of the powerful Expediency Council. Nonetheless, he decided to present himself as a candidate from Tehran, opening himself up to a barrage of criticism and accusations regarding his political past.

The Participation Front and the Executives of Construction were able to agree on a joint list of 200 candidates in the provinces, but in Tehran the Participation Front refused to endorse Rafsanjani. The Executives of Construction reciprocated by not including Reza Khatami on its list. By election day, the Participation Front and the Executives of Construction had each put out its own list in Tehran.

When Rafsanjani first decided to run, people spoke as if they expected him to lead the voting in Tehran, thereby positioning himself to become the next speaker of parliament. But as election day grew closer and the reformist press continued to vilify him, some believed that he might not be among the top finishers in Tehran. Nobody, not even those most opposed to his candidacy, realized that he had grown so unpopular among voters that he would barely make it through.

## The Campaign

I spent ten days in Tehran, five before and five after the February 18 elections, and was thus able to get a good feel for the atmosphere in which they took place. Meetings, pamphleteering, press conferences, and advertisements in the press were all very much in evidence. After the city council elections of 1999, when the whole of Tehran had been plastered with pictures of candidates, the conservatives had attributed the victory of the reformists to a Western-style electioneering campaign that had included posters and banners in the streets and public proclamations from loudspeakers in cars. This time around, the hard-liners probably thought that it would be better if voters did not get to see the parliamentary candidates, especially since so many of them were not clerics but smiling young men and women. Some of the latter were even wearing robes and scarves rather than the usual black veil that had become the official attire of women running for office. So I was not surprised when I found out that the government had forbidden putting up posters of the parliamentary candidates in the streets.

The conservatives, however, underestimated the power of pamphlets, leaflets, the free press, and election rallies in mosques, stadiums, and universities. People simply ignored the ban on posters, pasting their pamphlets on walls and billboards put up by their municipality. They put up not one leaflet, but rows of them. During the days leading up to the elections, Iran's streets were littered with paper. At every street corner, someone would lean into a passing car and hand out leaflets. In the north of Tehran, where the middle and upper-middle classes reside, schoolgirls could be seen actively distributing leaflets and urging people to vote for the reformist candidates.

Most of the pamphlets were in color. They bore pictures and short biographies of the candidates, as well as manifestos of the parties to which they belonged. I was told that some of the advertisements were paid for by the parties rather than by the candidates themselves. This suggests that political groups now are able to make significant expenditures on elections and to raise money from their supporters to do so.

In 2000, the parties and some of the more affluent candidates set up campaign headquarters and branch offices in different parts of Tehran— a first for an Iranian election. One could obtain all the relevant information about a particular candidate from his or her headquarters. I passed several campaign offices for Mohsen Rezai, the former commander of the Revolutionary Guards, now posing as a reformist. (He was not elected.) These offices were usually storefronts in crowded streets and neighborhoods, leased to candidates for the duration of the campaign. Leasing a shop on a busy street is not a cheap affair.

Election meetings took place mainly in universities, sports stadiums, and mosques. The Participation Front held one of its largest meetings in a sports stadium. It was an unprecedented sight for Islamic Iran. Several thousand people attended the meeting, most of them young men and women who could be seen clapping and cheering. Among the speakers was the president's brother, Reza Khatami. His wife, who is the granddaughter of Ayatollah Khomeini, was standing at her husband's side, again a first for Iran. Several of the Participation Front's candidates gave their stump speeches, endorsing the president's reform program and urging people to vote for them. A student who was there told me that those attending the rally were afraid that they would be attacked by vigilantes when they left the stadium, but there was no sign of them. Even the Morals Police were little in evidence during the elections.

In the mosques, the atmosphere was more serene and subdued. The reformists continued to criticize the conservatives for their obstructionist policies in parliament, while the conservatives warned people against the "cultural onslaught" of the West and the ideas espoused by the reformist newspapers. Breaking with tradition, one of the Participation Front's candidates, a university professor in her early forties, delivered a speech in a mosque wearing a robe and a scarf rather than a long veil. In the past, the police would not have let her enter, or would have physically attacked her.

Another meeting that I attended, organized by the student movement's Office for Solidarity, was held outdoors in front of the mosque at Tehran University. While waiting for the speakers to arrive, the organizers played "Oh Iran," a nationalist song dating back to the era of the first Pahlavi king. Once again, the majority of the participants were young people, particularly students.

That same afternoon, I walked over to one of the large halls of Tehran University, where a meeting was being organized by the conservatives. As I entered the hall, I saw 16 youngsters singing marches—and no one else. I was told that the speakers had come and gone, since no one had turned up to listen to them. A student told me: "After what happened last summer, this is the wrong place for the conservatives to hold a meeting." This was a reference to the authorities' attack on student dormitories following the student protests of 1999.

It was interesting to see the themes emphasized by the pamphlets and handouts of various groups. The Participation Front and the Executives of Construction chose to emphasize nationalist, rather than Islamic, slogans in their pamphlets. The Participation Front's motto was "Iran for All Iranians"; the Executives of Construction's was "Security, Freedom, Prosperity." The conservative Combatant Clerics used as their motto "Piety, Prosperity, Employment, and Justice."

Among the most interesting pamphlets was one depicting Rafsanjani with an open book on his lap and his grandson at his side. In the photograph this prominent cleric appeared without a turban in what was clearly an effort to make him look like a benign grandfather. Another leaflet bore a picture of Mr. Rafsanjani's daughter Faezeh Hashemi, an outspoken member of parliament and the head of the Women's Olympic Committee in Iran. She was seated on a stool in jeans and boots, her black veil draped over a polka-dot scarf. In the background, a group of young women carried Olympic banners. Still another pamphlet displayed Mohammed Mossadegh (the popular nationalist leader of the 1950s), Ali Shariati (the Islamic thinker), and Mehdi Bazargan (the first prime minister of the Islamic Republic), reflecting a return to the old nationalist figures as heroes. Most of the groups talked about freedom, justice, prosperity, the rule of law, popular participation, civil society, and the like.

Another new development was the sheer number of press conferences held by different parties, especially the reformists. The Participation Front had set up its headquarters in central Tehran, and almost every day one or more of its candidates talked to the press about the party's stance on domestic and foreign policy. The same was true of the other parties.

Foreign policy was not prominent in the election campaign. Foreign journalists interrogated the candidates—particularly the ones from the Participation Front—about Iran's relations with the United States and received the standard answer that Iran has given in the past: Iran promotes goodwill; it is up to the United States to take the first step. The candidates did not object to discussions with the United States, provided that Iran's national interests were acknowledged and respected. The principal issues debated during the elections, however, were domestic concerns, especially judicial reform.

## Going to the Polls

On election day, the polling stations opened at 9 a.m. in Tehran. By 9:30 a.m., when I started my tour of the city, long lines had already begun to form. The people's participation in the election was eye-catching and impressive. Both young and old, women and men, waited for hours at a time to cast their vote. There were instances where men and women stood in line together and others where men and women queued up in separate lines. I was told by a woman voter that these things just happened. A woman would be the first in line, another woman would stand behind her, and soon you had a line only for women. The voting stations included mosques, schools, and also special trucks that acted as mobile polling stations, moving from street to street in more populated areas where there were long queues. Turnout nationwide was just under 70 percent.

The Ministry of Interior and almost every political group running in the elections had representatives watching over the ballot boxes. For the most part, the elections were fair, at least as far as reports indicate. Ballot boxes were not stuffed or altered. Voters were not bused to polling stations. In a few places where interference was suspected, skirmishes and fist fights broke out between the two sides. Some vote tampering may well have taken place at certain polling stations, but on the whole, the elections were clean. As one journalist told me, even if 5 percent of the votes in Tehran were tampered with, it made little difference, as the reformists won a clear victory.

The reformists emerged from the first round guaranteed of a large majority, but the official vote count was disputed among the authorities, and the announcement of the final results was delayed. As a result, the second round, originally scheduled for April, was pushed off until May 5. It is hard to be precise about the final overall results of the two rounds, since some of those elected ran as independents, but it appears that less than 60 seats in the new Majlis are held by conservatives, while reformists hold somewhere in the range of 180 seats. The results for 13 seats (11 nullified by the Council of Guardians, 2 unfilled) will be decided in by-elections in May 2001.

Some other statistics regarding the election are worthy of mention. Only 70 incumbents were reelected, meaning that the new Majlis is predominantly composed of first-time parliamentarians. The number of clerics in the Majlis took a sharp drop from 53 to 33 (there had been 153 in the first Majlis). At the same time, the number of women elected declined, going from 14 to 11.

The most important outcome, however, remains the clear victory of the reformists. They won because they were identified with President Khatami, who is still very popular and highly respected. The voters indicated their desire to give him a cooperative parliament, hoping that this would enable him to implement his program to open up the country.

# 14

# IS IRAN DEMOCRATIZING?
# REFORM AT AN IMPASSE

## Ladan Boroumand and Roya Boroumand

**Ladan Boroumand,** *a Visiting Fellow at the International Forum for Democratic Studies, is a historian from Iran with a doctorate from the Ecole des Hautes Etudes en Sciences Sociales in Paris. She is the author of* La Guerre des principes *(1999), an extensive study of the tensions throughout the French Revolution between the rights of man and the sovereignty of the nation. Her sister **Roya Boroumand,** a historian from Iran with a doctorate from the Sorbonne, is a specialist in Iran's contemporary history and has been a consultant for Human Rights Watch. They are working on a study of the Iranian Revolution. This essay originally appeared in the October 2000 issue of the* Journal of Democracy.

In parliamentary elections on 18 February 2000, Iranians cast their ballots overwhelmingly in favor of candidates who supported the reforms advocated by President Mohammad Khatami. Named after the day of Khatami's 1997 election to the presidency, the Second of Khordad coalition, which brings together 18 reformist groups, captured 189 seats in the 290-member Majlis. Heading the list of winners with 60 seats was one of the coalition's principal members, the Islamic Iran Participation Front (IIPF), founded in 1999 and led by the president's brother, Mohammad Reza Khatami. The IIPF and most of the 17 other groups in the coalition belong to the left wing of the political and religious establishment that has ruled Iran for the past 20 years. The coalition also contains some "centrist" factions, notably the Executives of Construction, a grouping of technocrats close to former president Ali Akbar Hashemi Rafsanjani (1989–97).

Divided over the nature and extent of the reforms, the groups composing the reformist coalition failed to agree on a single list of parliamentary candidates; they formed five different ones. Regardless of their differences, however, all the coalition members concur in supporting the freedom of the press and the protection of people's rights strictly within the constitutional framework of the Islamic Republic of Iran. Reforming the press law, amending the electoral law, and adopting legislation that clearly defines a political offense form the basis of their political program. The reformists are also committed to modifying the country's administrative and economic structures and easing the senseless constraints on people's everyday lives. The reformist coalition has a relatively more modern conception of both Islamic precepts and the state than its conservative rivals, who do not draw a clear dividing line between the public and private spheres.

In winning the 2000 legislative elections, the reformists consolidated their success in the 1999 municipal elections. The international media generally described the 2000 elections as free and democratic. One might thus assume that, with the reformists' takeover of the executive, legislative, and municipal branches of government, Iran is in the process of inventing a new form of Islamic democracy.

A close look at Iranian politics, however, reveals a more complex story. The electoral victories of Khatami's supporters do not seem to have facilitated the implementation of his program of restoring people's rights. In June 1998, nine months after coming to office and at the height of his popularity, Khatami suffered a political setback when his Interior Minister, Abdullah Nuri, who had begun to implement his policy of reform, was impeached. President Khatami called for a more active public role for women, but Mohsen Saïd Zadeh, a theologian and promoter of women's rights, was arrested and tried for his liberal interpretation of Koranic precepts; Saïd Zadeh was convicted, defrocked, and silenced for five years. About a year after Khatami's election, his policy of tolerance toward secular activists was challenged by the serial killing of five dissidents, Parvaneh and Dariush Forouhar, Mohammad Jafar Pouyandeh, Mohammad Mokhtari, and Pirouz Davani. Following the success of the reformists in the February 1999 municipal elections, Mohsen Kadivar, a cleric who called for the reform of the political and judicial systems, was arrested and sentenced to 18 months in prison on charges of subversion.

More than two months later, the newspaper *Salam* revealed ties between the killers of the dissidents and high-ranking officials. These revelations resulted in the newspaper's immediate closure, which, in turn, prompted peaceful student protests. Backed by the security forces, the regime's thugs retaliated with a ferocious attack on student dormitories. The ensuing street demonstrations led to a massive wave of arrests among students and leading dissidents, many of whom were not involved in the demonstrations. Trials were held behind close doors. Special "revolutionary" courts issued death sentences and extensive prison terms for several students and secular activists. In November 1999, Abdullah Nuri, who had led the reformist candidates to victory in the municipal elections, was tried before the Special Court for the Clergy and sentenced to a five-year prison term for allegedly maligning religion, insulting the founder of the Islamic Republic, and disseminating false rumors through articles published in his newspaper. On 12 March 2000, less than a month after the reformists' spectacular victory in the parliamentary elections, Saïd Hajarian, a former intelligence director and one of the artisans of the reformist electoral victory, was seriously wounded in an attack allegedly carried out by members of the Revolutionary Guards. In May 2000, a massive crackdown on the press resulted in the arrest of leading reformist journalists. As the new parliament began its work, another wave of arrests targeted student leaders. Despite the president's assurances, justice has yet to be dispensed in the slayings of the secular dissidents.

What is disturbing and paradoxical in Iranian politics is the pattern of reformist electoral victories and political defeats. In electing a reformist-dominated parliament, Iranians seem to have lost the relative freedom of the press that had been their main gain since Khatami's accession to power. This paradox underscores the discrepancy between "reform" and real democratization in Iran. To understand this gap, one must first examine the unique character of Iran's constitutional regime.

## Cooptation and Elections

The Islamic Republic of Iran is unique. Though its political structure incorporates elements borrowed from the modern nation-state, and some of its traits evoke the Soviet system, it cannot be identified with either model. It is a theocracy founded on the political privileges of a clerical oligarchy. Its institutions and procedures, including elections, must be analyzed within their own philosophical and constitutional context.

In the Islamic Republic of Iran, sovereignty is the exclusive prerogative of God, who delegates it to an Islamic Jurisprudent, the Supreme Leader. This is clearly spelled out in the Iranian Constitution:

> The Islamic Republic is a system based on belief in: 1. The One God . . . His exclusive sovereignty and right to legislate, and the necessity of submission to His commands; 2. Divine revelation and its fundamental role in setting forth the laws; 3. The return to God in the Hereafter, and the constructive role of this belief in the course of man's ascent toward God; 4. The justice of God in creation and legislation; 5. Continuous leadership *(imamat)* and perpetual guidance, and its fundamental role in ensuring the uninterrupted process of the revolution of Islam (Article 2).
>
> [T]he *wilayah* [guardianship] and leadership of the *Ummah* [community of the faithful] devolve upon the *'adil muttaqi faqih* [the just and pious Islamic Jurisprudent], who is fully aware of the circumstances of his age; courageous, resourceful, and possessed of administrative ability, [he] will assume the responsibilities of this office in accordance with Article 107 (Article 5).
>
> The powers of government in the Islamic Republic are vested in the legislature, the judiciary, and the executive powers, functioning under the supervision of the absolute *wilayat al-'amr* [guardianship] and the leadership of the *Ummah* (Article 57).

The theocratic nature of the regime requires that all laws and political decisions be in conformity with Islamic precepts and canon law. For that purpose, two constitutional levers are provided: the absolute power of the Supreme Leader and the oversight of the Council of Guardians. The Supreme Leader, through his absolute power and guardianship of the rights of God in the body politic, is above the constitution. He is appointed by the Assembly of Experts, an elective assembly composed of theologians. The Council of Guardians is composed of six theologians designated by the Supreme Leader and six jurists elected by the parliament from a list presented by the head of the judiciary. The latter is also designated by the Supreme Leader.

The Council of Guardians enjoys veto power over all laws and an approbatory and supervisory function with regard to elections to the presidency, the parliament, and the Assembly of Experts. All candidates seeking elective office must first be approved by the Council of Guardians, which must then validate the results of completed elections. Thus the country's elected officials must, in effect, submit to two elections, first that of the Council of Guardians, and second, that of universal suffrage.

The Islamic Republic of Iran is a system that has been operated through cooptation from the outset. The founder of the Islamic Republic, Ayatollah Khomeini, never submitted his mandate to the people's vote. He was carried to power by popular fervor and by mass demonstrations, but he exercised his trusteeship prior to and irrespective of any popular vote. Before his death, Khomeini himself designated his successor, Ayatollah Khamenei, whose nomination was subsequently approved by the Assembly of Experts. Yet the system also incorporates an elective mechanism. It is the interaction between cooptation and elections that makes the Iranian regime unique.

In contrast with modern representative democracies, where elections form the basis of legitimacy and political sovereignty, the Iranian constitution reduces elections to the mere manifestation of public opinion: "In the Islamic Republic of Iran, the affairs of the country must be administered with the support of public opinion expressed by means of elections. . ." (Article 6). The Islamic Republic thus distinguishes itself from totalitarian states, where ideology subsumes public opinion and elections are a political ritual automatically consecrating the only party candidate. The constitutional function of public opinion is a specific feature of the Iranian theocracy.

## The Parliamentary Elections of 2000

There is a logical connection between the function of elections in Iran and the paradoxes of political life, including the gap between reformism and democratization. To be registered on an electoral list as a candidate, a person must first sign a form affirming allegiance to the

Constitution and the absolute Guardianship of the Islamic Jurisprudent over the polity. Since democracy and absolute power are antithetical, all prospective candidates must, in effect, make a profession of faith against democracy. To grasp the significance of such a profession of faith, one must remember that even a majority of the Shi'ite clergy consider the setting up of the theologian as the people's political guardian—an innovation of Ayatollah Khomeini's—to be heterodox and reject it.[1] Thus eligibility becomes impossible not only for a democrat but also for an orthodox Shi'ite—unless either betrays his beliefs.

The requirement of signing the candidacy form in order to gain access to any elective functions significantly limits citizens' participation in the political life of their country. The authorities reject the candidacies of those who modify the candidacy form. Once they sign it, candidates are screened to determine their "legitimacy." The most important aspects of this process are the reports of the Ministry of Information (the political police) and the Office of the Prosecutor General, both of which are under the control of the clerical oligarchy. It is worth noting that all independent political parties—democrat, liberal, nationalist, socialist, and religious-nationalist—were banned by Ayatollah Khomeini. Because his command is above the law and survives him, the Ministry of Information automatically vetoes the candidacy of anyone who has been a member, or a sympathizer, of any of these groups. This, in turn, results in the disqualification of the candidate by the Ministry of Interior. The authorities refer to these would-be candidates as "outsiders," in contrast with "insiders," the only people permitted to participate in the country's political life.[2]

Once a potential candidate is approved by the Ministry of Information and the Prosecutor General's office, the Council of Guardians subjects his opinions and behavior to a meticulous evaluation. In each province, the morality militia (Basij), the Revolutionary Guards, and the Friday Imams have to fill out questionnaires on specific candidates, responding to questions such as these: Do women in the candidate's family wear the *chador*? Does the candidate vote regularly in elections? Does he attend the Friday sermons and participate in demonstrations of support for the regime? Has he ever criticized the Islamic Republic or the absolute power of the Supreme Leader? Does he observe all his religious duties? Disqualified candidates have a right to appeal, but the Council of Guardian itself judges these appeals.

In 2000, the Council of Guardians disqualified more than 500 of the 6,000 candidates approved by the Ministry of Interior. Needless to say, candidates considered "outsiders" were systematically disqualified from the race. Also disqualified, however, were some prominent figures within the ruling oligarchy (that is, the "insiders"), including Abdullah Nuri, former minister of the interior; Abbas Abdi, one of the founders of the IIPF; and several reformist journalists. These candidates all had impeccable revolutionary credentials.

Due to the ideological constraints placed on candidates, the parliamentary campaign in 2000 was full of vague electoral promises. In fact, the most specific commitments came from disqualified candidates, who played an active role in the campaign, leading the most important rallies in the week preceding the elections. Of course, whether the election winners intend to implement the reforms demanded by their disqualified colleagues remains to be seen.

The prescreening of candidates is not the only constraint on the electoral process. The counting of the votes and their validation also fall within the purview of the Council of Guardians. Even though the Ministry of Interior is in charge of organizing the elections, the Council of Guardians appoints representatives to monitor the voting at each polling station. These representatives must sign off on election reports. In 2000, the proreform Ministry of Interior and the conservative-backed Council of Guardians arm-wrestled over the election results, the latter nullifying results in a number of constituencies, including four in Tehran. The Ministry of Interior protested against the nullifications, which worked to the detriment of the reformists, sparking off demonstrations in many parts of the country and leading to clashes with the security forces in which eight people died and several were wounded.

Although its actions did not alter the overall election result, the Council of Guardians prevented about 10 reformist deputies from taking their seats in parliament. The ensuing controversy between the reformist and conservative factions of the oligarchy over the counting of the votes offers crucial evidence for evaluating the reformists' prospects for democratizing the regime. While differing on the outcome of the election, the Ministry of Interior and the Council of Guardians both claimed to be defending the rights of the people and accused each other of electoral fraud. An analysis of the Tehran results, the focus of a serious confrontation between reformists and conservatives, reveals how a common appeal to the rights of the people can lead to conflicting interpretations of the electorate's will.

The candidacy of former president Hashemi Rafsanjani lay at the heart of the Tehran election controversy. A former student and close collaborator of Ayatollah Khomeini, Rafsanjani has held several of the state's highest offices in the past 20 years. Reformist journalists have accused him of complicity in the assassination of dissidents and have decried his administrative and economic policies for being at the root of the corruption plaguing all areas of government. Rafsanjani's name appeared on all the conservative electoral lists, as well as on some reformist lists.

The vote for Tehran's 30 parliamentary seats was counted several times. The proreform Ministry of Interior proceeded with an electronic count of the vote, while the Council of Guardians ordered a manual count. Less than 48 hours after the polls closed, the Ministry of Interior declared that it had completed the electronic count; it did not, however, announce the results until the manual count had also been completed.[3] After much suspense, Rafsanjani was declared elected, with the lowest number of votes of the 30 deputies elected from Tehran. The Council of Guardians ordered a second count of 1,000 ballot boxes, which confirmed the prevailing rumors of Rafsanjani's defeat. Thereupon, the Ministry of Interior and the Council of Guardians agreed to suspend the second count and to confirm Rafsanjani's election as the thirtieth deputy from Tehran. Both the conservatives and the candidate edged out by Rafsanjani alleged electoral fraud. In light of these allegations, the Council of Guardians cancelled parts of the elections and, after more than 50 days of bickering with the Ministry of Interior, decided to augment Rafsanjani's votes, making him the twentieth deputy elected from Tehran. Just as the Supreme Leader confirmed these results, Rafsanjani renounced his seat.

This episode reveals the relationship between the ballot and the people's will. According to anonymous official sources, the electronic counting of the votes signaled Rafsanjani's defeat, ranking him fiftieth on the list of candidates. The two rounds of manual counting, however, announced him first as the thirtieth and then as the twentieth highest vote-getter in Tehran. Let us remember these three figures—50, 30, and 20—for they represent perfectly the parameters of the Iranian political game. Never officially announced, the figure 50 was skillfully leaked by the reformist faction of the oligarchy in order to increase its bargaining power with the conservatives;[4] the figure 30 was what the reformist authorities struggled to establish; and the figure 20 represented the Council of Guardians' interpretation of the people's will. The two factions of the oligarchy agreed to ignore the figure 50, while stressing that they were each defending the people's rights. Which of Rafsanjani's three scores expresses the people's will? The fact that the two sides could not come up with a mutually satisfactory answer reflects both the unusual role of elections in Iran and the ambiguity of the concept of "the people."

## The Definition of "the People"

What constitutes "the people"? In modern representative democracies, the people is the sum of free and equal individuals who, through their representatives, exercise their natural right to participate in the making of the laws to which they submit. The essence of popular sovereignty is the capacity to legislate. But what becomes of popular sovereignty when God is the sole legislator in the body politic? Either the people are excluded from sovereignty or the concept of the people mutates. In other words, instead of comprising free and equal individuals, the concept of the people comes to refer to the mass of believers.

This is precisely what happened in Iran in 1979. A referendum on an undefined Islamic Republic (the people did not know what kind of regime they were voting for) consecrated the transformation of the "people as individuals" into the "people as the faithful." From then on, there could be no contradiction between the rights of God and the rights of the people. The individual's free will and autonomy ceased to be an element of the people. Faith constituted the people and established the sovereignty of God, whose commands were known only by the ayatollahs. Responding to those protesting against the new constitution, Khomeini defined the sovereignty of the "people as the faithful" in the following terms: "Where there is no Guardianship of the Islamic Jurisprudent, there is idolatry. . . . Idols disappear only if God designates authorities."[5] He added: "People want Islam, people want the *Velayat-e-Faqih* (Guardianship of the Islamic Jurisprudent), which is God's command. . . . If you submit to a referendum the principle of the Guardianship of the Islamic Jurisprudent . . . people would vote for it."[6]

From its inception, the very principle of the *Velayat-e-Faqih* has been opposed to universal suffrage and the sovereignty of the people:

> There are societies and social regimes which are founded on . . . people's suffrage. . . . But there are other societies that are ideological and doctrinal. This means that the people in these societies opt . . . for a doctrine, and by doing so they declare that from then on all must be in accord with this particular doctrine. . . . The Islamic Republic is a doctrinal republic. . . . It is different from a democratic republic. We cannot allow the popular suffrage to be in command without any restrictions, as this is incompatible with the constitution and with an ideological regime.[7]

We owe this definition to Mohammad Beheshti, vice president of the first Assembly of Experts, which formulated the Islamic Republic's constitution in 1979. It was with this definition in mind that the authorities declared that a 99.5 percent majority had ratified the draft of the constitution, put forth in a second referendum (held in December 1979). Little did it matter that 50 percent of the electorate had boycotted the referendum. The 99.5 percent reflected an abstract entity defined by Khomeini as the embodiment of the faithful.

Far from being institutional anomalies or abuses of power on the part of the conservatives, the "insider-outsider" dichotomy that divides the Iranian population into first-class and second-class citizens, the numerous candidate-screening procedures, and the veto power of the Council of Guardians are the ideological and institutional instruments essential to the survival of the "people as the faithful." In the words of Hojatoleslam Masoudpour, the Council of Guardians' elections director: "If those who do not care about Iran, about the values, the beliefs, and the faith of the people, enter the parliament and betray people's ideals, then the blame would be on the Council of Guardians."[8] It is thus in the name of people's rights that the Council of Guardians disqualifies a large number of candidates.

The Supreme Leader has reminded Iran's new generation of the ideological foundations of the Council of Guardians' veto power:

> When, at the beginning of the revolution, the terms "democracy" and
> "democratic" were common currency, and the phrase "the Islamic demo-
> cratic republic" was sometimes used, the late Ahmad Agha [Khomeini's
> son] communicated a message on behalf of the Imam forbidding us from
> pronouncing the word "democratic." . . . The importance of the Imam's
> gesture lay in the fact that he was affirming the principle of the reign of
> Islam, which does not translate into the rule of the Muslims. If it were
> meant as the rule of Muslims, this would mean, at most, that a Muslim
> would be named as head of state and that he would deter, at least on the
> outside, debauchery, immodesty, and the perversion of mores. But the
> country's regime and its administration would not be based on Islam. . .
> . [D]emocracy and liberalism, both of which are inspired by Western
> culture, must not become encrusted in the foundations of Islamic regimes.[9]

The above sheds light on how the Council of Guardians screened
reformist candidates. It is not so much their past as revolutionaries that
was questioned, but rather their interpretation of the people's rights under the constitution. Most (though not all) of the elected reformers, in
stressing the rights of the people, defined the people as those who conformed to the faith. This is the view expressed by President Khatami
himself. For Khatami, the revolution and the Islamic Republic, based
on God's sovereignty and the Guardianship of the Islamic Jurisprudent,
offer the best path to salvation.[10] "Today, the Islamic Revolution is challenged by a decaying Western civilization," he asserts. "What makes
things difficult," he continues, "is that this civilization is founded on
freedom. In the face of salvation, which is Islam's ideal, the West bran-
dishes freedom." In introducing Western freedom to his Iranian readers
as it is defined by the social-contract thinkers and formulated in legal
and political terms in the Universal Declaration of Human Rights,
Khatami recognizes the seriousness of the challenge: "Freedom, as professed in the West, is natural to man, whereas we found our regime on
virtue. What we require of our citizens is virtue. Virtue is not natural to
man, and must be acquired through effort, deprivation, and abnegation.
We ask the citizen to sacrifice his natural passions."[11]

To address this situation, Khatami proposes cultural openness, since
in a world dominated by communications, it is impossible to prevent
the intrusion of Western values. Cultural openness aims at immunizing
Iranian believers against Western freedom. "Just as a body receives the
attenuated form of a microbe through vaccination, so too must society
be exposed to the thinking of dissidents. Revolutionaries must be able
to respond to dissident ideas with the strength of their thoughts and
valid arguments."[12]

"The people as the faithful" is a key postulate of Khatami's concept
of democracy; faith, and not individual freedom, is the substance of the
people. The distinction between Western democracy and Islamic democracy, founded on a "new kind of popular sovereignty,"[13] has been a
recurrent theme of his political speeches since 1997: "If we put aside

religion and this new experience [that of the Islamic revolution], what would we replace them with? That would be a great mistake. Is the West our model? The West itself needs reforms. . . . The experience of popular sovereignty based on religion is the greatest achievement of the Islamic revolution."[14]

It is for this reason that, in spite of all of his moderation and good will, Khatami cannot acknowledge the political rights of dissidents. Tolerating them as long as they do not propagate their ideas is the most he can do. What he seeks to reform are the abuses that derive from what is, in his view, the legitimate oligarchic nature of the regime. Thus he asked for forgiveness from those who had been unjustly disqualified from the 2000 parliamentary elections, but at the same time he praised the Council of Guardians, thereby implicitly approving its role: "Such a large-scale task [that of qualifying several thousand candidates] necessarily involves difficulties, shortcomings, and discontent. . . . But in any case and overall, one must praise the positive aspect of this episode."[15] This explains why Khatami enjoys the support of the Supreme Leader, whom he has never hesitated to back in times of crisis. The president strongly condemned the student uprising of July 1999 and endorsed the Supreme Leader's decision to ban most of the reformist newspapers in April 2000. Yet Khatami strives for a more efficient and rational theocracy and strongly supports a more modern interpretation of Islamic precepts. It is his opposition to the archaic views of his conservative colleagues that wins him popularity.

Within the ranks of Khatami's supporters, however, there are some reformists who do not share his definition of the people. It is precisely these "insiders" whose candidacies were rejected, or who have run into problems with the legal system during the last three years. They hold that the rights of the people, understood as the entirety of the electorate, take precedence over the rights and prerogatives of the clerical oligarchy. These reformists base their claim on Article 56 of the Constitution, which states that a human being is the "master of his social destiny." But by opting for a democratic interpretation of Article 56, they put themselves at odds with the spirit and letter of the constitution. It is easy for their opponents to remind them that "social destiny" does not extend to the religious and political realms, as attested by all the articles concerning the rights of the people.[16] It is therefore neither surprising nor paradoxical that this group of reformers, having converted to democracy, should pay the price of their allies' electoral victory.

For the conservatives, the authorized reforms must be founded on the concept of the "people as the faithful" and not the "people as individuals." This is why repression goes hand-in-hand with the reformists' victories. By disqualifying 10 percent of the proreform candidates, the Council of Guardians did nothing more than carry out its constitutional duties: "The real electoral fraud consists in letting uncommitted people enter the parliament."[17] The screening of candidates and electoral fraud are not accidental occurrences; they are an ideological necessity. From the first Assembly of Experts election in 1979 through the parliamentary elections of 2000, electoral fraud has afflicted the popular vote in Iran.

## The Role of Public Opinion

This is not to suggest that elections in Iran are a mere masquerade. Since 1997, changes in the rate of electoral participation point to an interesting interplay between the electorate and the oligarchy. To capture the nature of this relationship, we must first distinguish between two periods in the history of the Islamic Republic. In the first decade following the revolution, elections were little more than an ideological and religious ritual. Presidents Rajai (1981), Khamenei (1981 and 1985), and Rafsanjani (for his first-term election in 1989) were each elected with more than 85 percent of the vote. Indeed, as the embodiment both of the people and of the faithful, Khomeini would choose the victor before the elections actually took place.

Khomeini and his friends had found themselves governing a modern society based on a developing economy. Canon law, whose prescriptions are based on tribal societies living in a barter economy, proved inadequate to run the country. In order to survive, Khomeini forged alliances with Muslims who were strongly influenced by Marxism-Leninism. The Soviet model proved better-suited to the needs of the Islamic Republic than was liberalism. The Soviet concept of the people could be seen to coincide with the Islamic concept of the *ummah,* or community of believers. Throughout the first decade of the Islamic Republic, the official rhetoric conflated the masses of the deprived *(mostaz'afin)* with the working masses, heavily stressing antiliberal and anticapitalist themes. Consequently, Iran shifted its international alliances, establishing political and commercial ties with the Soviet Union and its satellites.

On the domestic front, religious socialists took control of the administration. For 10 years, the regime pursued a policy of nationalization and expropriation in an atmosphere of terror and repression. At the same time, to avoid being engulfed by communism, Khomeini made a point of nominating conservative *ulemas* to the Council of Guardians. He also protected the right wing of the clerical oligarchy against the totalitarian tendencies of the left.

Two major events changed the course of electoral history in Iran: Khomeini's death in 1989 and the fall of the Soviet Union. Khomeini's death revealed the differences between communist revolutions and the Islamic revolution. While communist ideology is rooted in history and provides for a specific model of social and economic organization, the ideological foundations of the Iranian revolution are metaphysical and

metahistorical. In fact, though canon law *(fiqh)* is a compilation of juridical prescriptions that organize the daily life of believers, like the
Koran it does not prescribe any specific form of political organization.
By the same token, apart from the fact that private property is considered a right, religious law does not seem to favor a particular economic
system. It can accommodate an economy based on slavery as well as a
socialist economy. This indeterminacy gives rise to pluralism within
the clerical oligarchy, engenders political tension, and creates the conditions for genuine political rivalry. Such pluralism has been present
within the oligarchy ever since the advent of the Islamic regime.

Barely two years after Khomeini's death, the Soviet Union collapsed,
depriving the Iranian regime of its communist allies abroad. Ideologically destabilized by the failure of the Soviet socialist model, the leftist
members of the ruling elite were easily ousted by their conservative
adversaries. The old left-right tension resurfaced in the shape of a conflict between modernist technocrats and hard-line conservatives. To
avoid factional violence, and in accordance with the constitution, the
clerical oligarchy decided to use elections as a means of resolving its
internal conflicts.

In this way elections emerged as a vehicle of public opinion. Though
barred from voting for its true representatives and still lacking sovereignty, the Iranian electorate has become an important player in the
country's political life. The vote may not be fully protected and the
oligarchy may commit electoral fraud with impunity, but it is nonetheless well-advised to take into account public opinion in order to settle
the differences among its various factions. For instance, when the hard-
line conservatives tried to defeat their leftist opponents in the 1992
parliamentary elections, they relied on public opinion. The middle
classes, which until then had not voted, went to the polls in order to rid
themselves of the left, whose political and economic performance had
been catastrophic. In 1997, President Rafsanjani ordered the organizers
of the presidential elections to prevent electoral fraud. As a result,
Khatami was elected president by a sweeping majority.

The Rafsanjani saga in 2000 further illustrates the role that elections
play in Iran's theocracy. Recall the three results: 50, 30, and 20. The
vote count and the unofficial announcement of Rafsanjani's real total
facilitated negotiations between the oligarchy's two factions. While the
reformists accepted Rafsanjani's election, provided that he be last on
the Tehran list, the conservatives would not accept such a humiliation
for so historic a figure of the revolution; they accorded him twentieth
place. The reformers officially lost this tug of war. Yet (and this is where
the number 50 gains importance), by leaking Rafsanjani's real place-
ment and inciting public anger, the reformers ultimately won their case.
The sovereign people of the Islamic Republic officially elected
Rafsanjani, but he decided to resign from parliament because of the

"smear campaign" launched against him and his deteriorating image in the public eye.

Given that not a single outsider was allowed into the electoral race, the parliamentary elections enabled the left wing of the oligarchy (which after 1991 had begun to adopt a more liberal discourse) to reconquer much of the political power that it had lost in the early 1990s. Leaning on public opinion, the victors negotiated their comeback with their rivals.

In their current form, the elections will not lead to the regime's democratization. By signing the candidacy form, the newly elected deputies reiterated their submission to the absolute power of the Supreme Leader, undermining from the outset their own ability to democratize the regime. The new parliament's inability to reform the press law is a case in point: The reformist faction had presented a draft that sought to eliminate a few of the numerous constraints on freedom of the press in Iran. In a letter read to the parliament on 6 August 2000, however, the Supreme Leader ordered the deputies to withdraw the draft, claiming that it was detrimental to Islam and harmful to the regime. Deputies who protested against the Supreme Leader's infringement of the legislative power were reminded by the reformist speaker of the parliament of their required obedience to the constitutionally sanctioned absolute power of the Supreme Leader, and the draft was ultimately withdrawn.

In the short term, the regime can benefit from holding elections insofar as they help allay internal tensions and improve Iran's international image. Over the long term, however, a price will be attached to this recourse to public opinion. The regime has introduced a subversive element within a closed ideological system; in going to the polls, the electorate seeks to achieve its own objectives.

Indeed, since 1997 the electorate has used each election not to choose its own representatives but to reject the theocracy. According to Saïd Hajarian, advisor to President Khatami:

> The phenomenon of the Second of Khordad [the election of Khatami in 1997] is a structural phenomenon, caused by the accumulation of the masses' unsatisfied demands. . . . Until right before 1997, the rate of participation in the elections was 40 percent; the electoral campaign and the conservatives' attack against Khatami turned the attention of the population—the discontented silent majority—toward Khatami. Part of the remaining 60 percent entered the electoral arena in order to peacefully declare its opposition and to give an ultimatum to those holding power.[18]

Many voters confirmed this analysis, often asserting that they cast their vote not *for* particular candidates but *against* those representing the regime's orthodoxy. A leading figure of Iranian literature explained: "I will not miss the opportunity to vote against those I do not like. . . . Of course, we would have liked to have the freedom to vote for the candidate of our own choice, those in whom we believe, but unfortunately, our choices are limited."[19] Figures from civil society stressed that their participation in the elections did not constitute approval of the electoral process. "Unfortunately," said a lawyer and human rights activist, "as long as the approval and the veto power of the Council of Guardians exist, our vote does not indicate a participation in political decision making."[20] "A republican regime," said a disqualified candidate, "is by definition a popular and democratic regime where the people freely chooses its representatives. If a number of people are excluded for any reason . . . a great number of individuals who trust these people are deprived of the chance to elect them; thus their rights as citizens are violated."[21]

Despite these shortcomings, the Iranian people have used elections to gain a minimum of political visibility and to exert pressure on the ruling oligarchy. By making a number of promises, reformists encouraged people to vote. Saïd Hajarian insisted that no authority should prevail over that of the parliament elected by the people. Akbar Ganji stated: "If we want freedom, democracy, human rights, and security, we must all be present at the polling stations. . . . If 30 million Iranian citizens go to the ballot boxes and send democratic reformists to the parliament, it will be possible to reform all the laws contrary to human rights, civil rights, and the constitution."[22]

These are the hopes that have led the Iranian people to the ballot box in recent years. In return, they expect results. Yet three years have already passed without significant improvements since 83 percent of voters took to the polls to elect a president who recognized the existence and dignity of civil society. The 2000 parliamentary elections attracted 69 percent of the electorate, a fall in turnout of 14 percent, reflecting a loss of popularity on the part of the reformists. The political repression following the recent elections has left Iran's public with the growing sense that it has once again been fooled by its rulers. Yet the clerical oligarchy cannot manipulate public opinion indefinitely. Sooner or later, the regime will have to make a choice. It can return to the pre-1992 system and limit elections to a form of ritual with a high rate of abstention, thereby exacerbating its tensions with civil society. Or, in return for electoral participation, it can grant the freedoms that voters demand. In that case, however, the "people as the faithful" is bound to succumb to the "people as individuals"—and there is reason to doubt whether the Islamic Republic of Iran can survive the sovereignty of the "people as individuals."

## NOTES

1. See S. Amir Arjomand, *The Shadow of God and the Hidden Imam* (Chicago: University of Chicago Press, 1984), 268–70; and S. Amir Arjomand, *The Turban for the Crown: The Islamic Revolution in Iran* (New York: Oxford University Press, 1988), 156.

2. Here is how the regime's dignitaries justify this dichotomy: "The debate on insiders and outsiders has its roots in Islam. . . . The enemy wishes to suppress the barrier between the insiders and the outsiders. The enemy wants to come in under the guise of the

insiders . . . and make our surprised youth say that there is no barrier. No my brother, it is not so." (M. Rayshahri, Friday sermon at Tehran University, 4 February 2000, quoted in the daily *Fatth* [Tehran], 5 February 2000.) To ordinary citizens, the distinction between insiders and outsiders looks rather different: "Insiders enjoy all constitutional and civil rights and benefit from the privileges of *citizenship*. . . . Outsiders must pass an ideological and moral test before they can be employed or continue with their studies. . . . Outsiders are not authorized to publish newspapers or books. They do not have the right to produce films or organize themselves into political parties. They are never promoted to high managerial positions. . . . They cannot be candidates in presidential or legislative elections. They cannot even organize funerals for their dead. . . . Outsiders have the right only to participate in the elections of insiders." M. Mohammadi, "The Foundation of the Two Concepts of Insiders and Outsiders," in *Iran Farda* (Tehran) 43 (May–June 1998): 10–12.

3. See *Iran Mania Election News,* www.iranmania.com, 22 February 2000.

4. See B. Moqaddam's editorial in the daily *Resalat* (Tehran), 3 April 2000.

5. Khomeini, *Sahife-ye-Noor* (Tehran), 4 October 1979, vol. 6, 34.

6. Khomeini, *Sahife-ye-Noor* (Tehran), 23 October 1979, vol. 6, 118.

7. *Minutes of the Debates of the Assembly of Experts,* 1 September 1979, vol. 1, 376.

8. *Kayhan* (Tehran), 11 January 2000.

9. *Kayhan* (Tehran), 26 January 2000, 1, 14.

10. M. Khatami, *Bim-e-Moj* (Fear of the wave), Tehran: Simaye Javan, 1997, 147. First published in 1993, *Bim-e-Moj* is Khatami's political manifesto. It was reprinted twice in 1997 after Khatami's election to the presidency and again in 1998 and 1999.

11. Ibid., 154–55.

12. Ibid., 152–53.

13. Interview with Khatami in the daily *Hayate-No* (Tehran), 23 August 2000, 2.

14. In *Asr Azadegan* (Tehran), 23 April 2000, 2. On the paradoxes of Khatami's political thinking, see our "Illusion and Reality of Civil Society in Iran: An Ideological Debate," *Social Research* 67 (Summer 2000): 303–44.

15. The daily *Mosharekat* (Tehran), 9 February 2000, 2.

16. Article 24 of the Constitution, for instance, provides for freedom of expression "except when it is detrimental to the principles of Islam." In Article 26, the Constitution guarantees citizens the freedom of association unless such associations violate "the criteria of Islam, or the basis of the Islamic Republic."

17. H. Shariat-Madari, *Kayhan* (Tehran), 17 February 2000, 3.

18. E. Baqi, interview with S. Hajarian, *Fatth* (Tehran), 3 April 2000.

19. *Arya* (Tehran), 17 February 2000, 3.

20. *Fatth* (Tehran), 29 January 2000, 3.

21. "Bazi-e naqes-e democracy" (The deficient game of democracy), *Asr Azadegan* (Tehran), 19 January 2000, 5.

22. Akbar Ganji, *Asr Azadegan* (Tehran), 15 February 2000.

# 15

# IS IRAN DEMOCRATIZING?
# A COMPARATIVIST'S PERSPECTIVE

*Daniel Brumberg*

**Daniel Brumberg,** *assistant professor of government at Georgetown University, is the author of* Reinventing Khomeini: The Struggle for Reform in Iran *(2001). This essay originally appeared in the October 2000 issue of the* Journal of Democracy.

One of the uncomfortable facts of life confronting students of comparative politics is that all political systems are, to some extent, unique. Indeed, it seems that the more we know about a particular place, the harder it becomes to compare it to others. Squeezing a given case into a tight theoretical mold offers no easy solutions to this problem, a lesson nicely illustrated by Brazil, whose experience partly inspired the theory of "bureaucratic authoritarianism." Yet Brazilian authoritarianism never quite matched the expectations that animated this theory, or for that matter, its paradoxical offspring—the theory of "democratic transitions." As Guillermo O'Donnell and Philippe Schmitter once noted: "Brazil is an interesting exception. . . . No serious attempt was made in Brazil to create distinctively authoritarian institutions. Rather, the generals [ruled] . . . by distorting rather than by disbanding the basic institutions of political democracy."[1]

One might quibble with the assertion that Brazil lacked distinctively authoritarian institutions and insist instead that the grafting together of democratic and patrimonialist structures during the 1960s is precisely what created an "exceptional" political beast, one that subsequently resisted a full transition to democracy for nearly 15 years. Yet then we would have to concede that this protracted dynamic was not wholly unique to Brazil, or even to Latin America. Many of my Egyptian colleagues still complain that their country is mired in a *marhalla intiqaliyya mustamira*—a continuing transitional stage. This ailment sounds familiar. For a long time, Mexican political scientists lamented their country's "painful and indefinite transition."[2]

Whether the Islamic Republic of Iran is floating in a similar political purgatory, or is instead trapped in an Islamic variant that reflects Iran's distinctive culture and politics, is an interesting question—one that Ladan and Roya Boroumand's chapter in this volume, "Is Iran Democratizing? Reform at an Impasse," compels us to ask. The central premise of their argument is that politics in Iran is unique because that country is ruled by a "theocratic system." While I agree with the authors' overall assessment of the internal workings of that system, I doubt that the "discrepancy between 'reform' and real democratization in Iran" is as paradoxical or as unique as the authors suggest. The use of "survival strategies"—selective political openings that *forestall* competitive democratization and lend a measure of legitimacy to authoritarian regimes—is a widely practiced art in the Middle East and elsewhere.[3] Moreover, in Morocco, Jordan, and Kuwait, monarchs have regularly invoked patrimonialist symbols to give a purported cultural authenticity to their claims that collective rights (as they define them) must take precedence over those of the individual. While there is no guarantee that such claims can be sustained indefinitely, we should not preclude the possibility that Iran's reformists and conservatives will together find ways to accommodate such contradictions and thus to "muddle along," as Houchang Chehabi has suggested.[4]

The uneasy accommodation of competing visions of authority that has animated Iran's political system since the 1979 Revolution is a familiar phenomenon in the Middle East. While some scholars use concepts like "corporatism" or "Islamic democracy" to capture this phenomenon, I prefer the term "dissonance" because it points *not* to a coherent system (or ideological synthesis) but rather to the deliberate and uneasy linking of competing notions of political community. The resulting political music may lack harmony, but it often plays quite well. Thus Morocco's King Hassan II survived for four decades by *institutionalizing* both legal-rational and traditional notions of authority. His role as master arbiter of these contending visions was enshrined in the 1992 Constitution, which declares that as "Commander of the Faithful, Supreme Representative of the nation," and "symbol of its unity," he can "dissolve the Chamber of Deputies by decree."[5] Today Morocco may be governed by a seven-party coalition, but this admirable example of reform cannot be equated with the victory of competitive democracy.

Dissonant systems and the survival strategies on which they often rely succeed because of—rather than despite—a heritage of cultural and ideological pluralism. When Anwar Sadat, the late president of Egypt, declared that "democracy is a safety valve *(siman al-amin)* because at least all of us will know when sedition occurs,"[6] he not only reminded his foes that political openings *(infitah)* could be used to expose opponents; he also implied that pluralism could be manipulated to divide (and rule) Egypt's fractious society, in which contending visions of authority—and the leaders who espoused them—had withstood decades of authoritarianism.

The success of survival strategies in Egypt, Morocco, Kuwait, and Jordan has also been due to at least two other factors. The first is the ambiguous nature of the term "democracy." As is well known, the word implies at least two ideas—pluralism (or contestation) and mass participation (or inclusiveness).[7] The calculated use of Islamic symbols to justify the subordination of the first to the second has been a popular strategy, one that Sadat cleverly deployed to make sure that the quest for "political democracy" would never threaten the social gains *(makasib)* of Gamal Abdel Nasser's revolution. But sustaining survival strategies also requires at least one other condition: a delinking of elite and mass, or of political parties and their constituencies. After all, as long as this link remains, it is always possible that opposition leaders will mobilize followers in a struggle to redefine democracy in ways that defy or impugn collectivist ideologies.

## Dissonant Politics in Iran

Despite the best efforts of Supreme Leader Ayatollah Ali Khamenei and his allies to forge and legitimate their own survival strategy, Iran's reformists have succeeded on at least one front: They have discredited the notion of the "people as the faithful." That feat is a tribute to the dissonant nature of politics in the Islamic Republic. The late Ayatollah Khomeini may have aspired to a harmonic vision of politics, but he never quite realized that goal. Although Khomeini wanted a "theocracy" (and proclaimed its existence), I am not sure that our understanding of politics in the Islamic Republic is advanced by using this term. As the Boroumands note, Islamic socialists played a key role in the Revolution and its ruling institutions. Indeed, the Islamic vision of revolution upheld by intellectuals like Ali Shariati had as much—if not more—to do with Karl Marx and Jean-Paul Sartre than it did with the Prophet Mohammad or the first Shi'ite Imam.[8] Although Khomeini and his allies violently dispensed with many proponents of this dissonant vision, and although they rejected the very word "democracy," the term remained in the lexicon of Iran's revolutionary leaders, to be appropriated and used for different ideological, social, and political purposes. It is this struggle to redefine democracy—as much, if not more, than the existence of any hegemonic concept of "public opinion"—that explains the curious twists and turns of Iranian politics both during and after the 1990s.

Former president Ali Akbar Hashemi Rafsanjani may have inadvertently inaugurated this struggle when he declared in 1988 that in Iran "democracy is present in a form better than in the West," because a "government of the people, by the people" exists "with the permission of the *Velayat-e-Faqih*" (that is, the Islamic Jurisprudent, who at the time was Khomeini).[9] This, of course, was no small qualification, coming as it did from a president who, in 1991, eagerly joined the new *Faqih*

(Ayatollah Khamenei) in a five-year campaign to repress their opponents on the Islamic left. But the fact that Rafsanjani used words that momentarily placed him closer to Gettysburg than Tehran reminds us of the diverse ideologies that animate the Islamic Republic.

It is true that these anomalies did not begin to shake up the political system until Islamic leftists like Abdul Karim Soroush and Abbas Abdi found themselves repressed by the very state that they had once helped to legitimate. Yet the shift from Islamic Bolshevism to Islamic Menshevism was genuine: It reflected widespread disillusionment with collectivist notions of democracy, as well as an abiding hope that a pluralistic vision of the "people as individuals" could eventually coexist with, and even support, an Islamic state.

Ladan and Roya Boroumand believe that President Mohammad Khatami does not subscribe to this liberal vision. According to them, his assertion that "freedom, as professed in the West, is natural to man, whereas we founded our regime on virtue" shows that he upholds a collectivist notion of authority. This may very well be, but by itself this statement does not tell us very much. Khatami's ideas have evolved in tandem with the ideological changes that have unfolded within the Islamic left, of which he is a part. Hints of his evolving views are to be found in his *Fear of the Wave,* the book that the authors cite in their analysis of his views. Published in 1993, years before Khatami could have ever dreamed of being elected president, and only one year after Majlis hard-liners had forced him to resign from his post as Minister of Islamic Guidance, the book's arguments appear couched in language designed to push the envelope about as far as Khatami could under these trying circumstances. Thus while holding that West and East have fundamentally different conceptions of freedom, he also asserts that "Western civilization rests on the idea of 'liberty' or 'freedom,'" and that it was through such ideas that the "West . . . freed humans from the shackles of many oppressive traditions" such as those "imposed on the masses in the name of religion."[10] My own analysis suggests that, as the reform movement has gained strength, Khatami's thinking has become bolder and implicitly more liberal. When he calls for an "Iran for all Iranians," when he asserts that "the legitimacy of the government stems from the people's vote . . . [and that] the Islamic government is the servant of the people and not their master," or when he makes the controversial suggestion that the Supreme Leader is *also* "the leader of all those who do *not* believe in religion but who have accepted the system," Khatami subverts, rather than bolsters, the collectivist ideology of the Revolution.[11]

It is surely the case that the Council of Guardians has recently used its constitutional powers to close down the opposition press and to keep the most vociferous and well-known exponents of competitive democracy out of the recently elected Majlis. The reformists have a decisive majority, but lay intellectuals such as Akbar Ganji, or maverick clerics like Abdullah Nuri and Mohsen Kadivar, have been arrested or branded as "outsiders" and thus cannot compete in elections. Yet many of their colleagues in the new Majlis share their aspirations for a more liberal society. The "insider-outsider" distinction is thus less important than it may seem, particularly given that reformists on the inside have the support of millions of young people, for whom the notion of the "people as the faithful" makes little sense. The more important question is one that the Boroumands address: In the long run, can these reformists make a difference and, if so, how?

## The Logic of Survival

One possible answer is that they can, but only by using the system to bring it crashing down. Such a possibility exists because, as the authors note, elections and parties (however disorganized) now provide vehicles through which the people (however defined) can at least try to express their aspirations independently of the ruling clerics. As I have noted above, the emergence of mass political parties—such as Iran's Second of Khordad Front—makes it difficult to maintain control of political openings, particularly when such parties break the rules of the "accommodation game" by taking control of parliament and thus threatening the ruling powers. We should not forget that the final collapse of survival strategies in Mexico—an event signaled by the July 2000 presidential-election victory by Vicente Fox of the National Action Party (PAN)—was preceded by the ruling Institutional Revolutionary Party's loss of the lower house in 1997. Could it be that the Second of Khordad Front will eventually become Iran's PAN?

Although the Boroumands confidently predict that the "'people as the faithful' is bound to succumb to the 'people as individuals,'" much of their analysis suggests that Iran will *not* follow in the path of Brazil and Mexico. But even if Iran does not, perhaps it will eventually emulate some of its Arab neighbors. The negotiation of political accommodations is clearly an option that both Khatami and Khamenei prefer to being pushed over the brink by their most militant supporters. From the perspective of Khatami's allies, a fragile experiment in cohabitation that often subordinates their vision of constitutionalism and the rule of law to Khamenei's patrimonialist ethos is hardly ideal. To postpone, perhaps indefinitely, the transition from a hobbled political opening to competitive democracy is a risky strategy, particularly when Khatami's young followers expect, at the very least, that he will get the clerics out of the business of telling the youth how to be good Muslims.

Apart from such cultural and political concerns, there is the question of the economy, which cannot be easily addressed by a politics of accommodation with the old order. As many cases in Latin America and

Eastern Europe demonstrate, political and social pacts that allow *apparatchiks* to survive have a corrosive effect on market reforms.[12] Although Khatami's allies cannot succeed without tackling the economy, their efforts will invite a cynical response from conservative clerics, who will undoubtedly denounce market reforms as they simultaneously line their own pockets.

In short, fashioning and sustaining survival strategies will not be easy. Still, my guess is that the Islamic Republic of Iran will remain for years to come a land of profound contradictions and testy alliances. While we all may hope that such anomalies will one day surrender to a new dawn, we should not be surprised if Iran's leaders devise solutions that leave the country's changing political system suspended somewhere between Heaven and Hades.

## NOTES

1. Guillermo O'Donnell and Philippe Schmitter, *Transitions from Authoritarian Rule* Vol. 4 (Baltimore: Johns Hopkins University Press, 1984), 22.

2. Jorge G. Castañeda, "Two Roads Await Mexico's Next Chief," *New York Times,* 8 October 1987.

3. See Daniel Brumberg, "Authoritarian Legacies and Reform Strategies in the Arab World," in Rex Brynen, Baghat Korany, and Paul Noble, eds., *Political Liberalization and Democratization in the Arab World* (Boulder, Colo.: Lynne Rienner, 1995), 229–59.

4. Houchang Chehabi, remarks delivered at a seminar on "Democratization in Iran" at the Woodrow Wilson International Center for Scholars in Washington, D.C., 13 June 2000.

5. Moroccan Constitution, Articles 19 and 70. Article 23 also stipulates that: "The King's person is inviolable and sacred."

6. See "Liqimat al-Ra'is al-Sadat fi Liq'a bi a'da' al-Majlis al-'ila lil Jaim'aat," remarks by President Anwar Sadat at the Higher Universities Council on 30 January 1977, published in *Kitab al-Ra'is Anwar al-Sadat* (Speeches of President Anwar Sadat) (Cairo: Ministry of Information, 1980).

7. Robert Dahl, *Polyarchy* (New Haven: Yale University Press, 1971).

8. See Mehrzad Boroujerdi, *Iranian Intellectuals and the West: The Tormented Triumph of Nativism* (Syracuse, N.Y.: Syracuse University Press, 1966).

9. "First Sermon on Islamic Government," *Foreign Broadcast Information Service,* Near East/South Asia, 19 January 1988.

10. Mohammad Khatami, *Hope and Challenge: The Iranian President Speaks* (Binghamton, N.Y.: Institute of Global Cultural Studies, 1997), 17.

11. "Ettela'at," *Foreign Broadcast Information Service,* Near East/South Asia, 27 February 1997 (emphasis added).

12. Frances Hagopian, "Democracy by Undemocratic Means? Elites, Political Pacts, and Regime Transition in Brazil," *Comparative Political Studies* 23 (July 1990): 147–70.

# 16

# THE DEADLOCK IN IRAN: PRESSURES FROM BELOW

*Ramin Jahanbegloo*

*Ramin Jahanbegloo is head of the Department of Research on Contemporary Thought at the Cultural Research Bureau in Tehran. His books include* Conversations with Isaiah Berlin *(1991),* Gandhi: Aux sources de la nonviolence *(1998), and* Iran and Modernity *(2000). During 2001–2002 he was a Reagan-Fascell Democracy Fellow at the International Forum for Democratic Studies in Washington, D.C. This essay originally appeared in the January 2003 issue of the* Journal of Democracy.

Predicting the outcome of the struggle for political leadership in Iran has become a popular parlor game in some circles in Washington and other Western capitals. But there is also genuine anxiety about this struggle throughout the world, quite understandably given Iran's vital regional and international importance, along with the huge stakes involved not only for Iranians but for Americans and Europeans, not to mention Iran's immediate neighbors. The outcome will resonate across the Middle East and have major strategic implications for the war against terrorism.

Today, Iran is facing a crisis generated by fundamental contradictions in the political system that has ruled the country during the quarter-century since the Iranian Revolution and the rise of the Islamic Republic. In that time, the country has made an amazing passage from infatuation with Islamist martyrdom and fierce anti-Americanism to preoccupation with free markets, economic-growth rates, and Western ways of life. The resulting "dot Islamism" of contemporary Iran—characterized by the co-existence of a capitalist economy and clerical rule—has only disguised these contradictions. For the historical trajectory of contemporary Iran may point not only to a deepening of economic liberalization but to the implementation of genuinely democratic political reforms and an empowering of civil society that would threaten to end the conservative monopoly on power that has been in place from the outset of the regime.

More than five years after the midranking reformist cleric Mohammad

Khatami won his first landslide victory in presidential balloting, Iran's leadership is deeply divided over the country's future. While Khatami easily won reelection in June 2001, he has remained unable to persuade the powerful conservative clerical and internal-security establishments to embrace his reformist project of bringing dialogue, tolerance, and pluralism to Iran's political system. The clerics and security officials still control most key power centers, including the armed forces, the intelligence agencies, and the judiciary. The reformists remain exposed to pressure and coercion from these quarters, and thus can find themselves blocked in their efforts to take such constructive steps as reestablishing normal diplomatic relations with the United States.

And yet Iranian political reality is complex and fluid in ways that cannot be reduced to a simple dichotomy between reformists and conservatives within the regime. There is not actually a single clear-cut political struggle in Iran. Rather, the country's domestic politics is characterized by multiple and competing power centers whose rivalries have created a chaotic situation in which various shades and types of "reformism" and "conservatism" interact in often bewildering ways—generating, for example, contradictions and inconsistencies in Iranian foreign policy that tend to baffle outside observers.

Indeed, the Iranian political order is perhaps best described as a chaotically divided political system that is now frozen in a state of institutional gridlock. The executive branch, led by President Khatami, and the 290-member parliament (Majlis) are both generally reformist. The judiciary is largely in conservative hands. Finally, there is Ayatollah Ali Khamenei (the successor to Ruhollah Khomeini), whose official title is Leader of the Islamic Revolution and whose prerogative it is to overrule any of the other branches. As supreme leader, Khamenei has the power to choose the head of the judiciary and the chief of the state broadcasting agency, as well as primary responsibility for military and security affairs. The combined result of this constitutional structure and the political forces inhabiting it is that the branches often work at cross-purposes and little gets done. For example, in recent years the executive branch has been handing out newspaper licenses for the purpose of promoting a free press and vibrant civil society, while courts and the security forces have been shutting down papers and arresting or aggressively interrogating journalists and editors.

To be sure, the framers of the Islamic Republic's 1979 Constitution meant for there to be a degree of institutional tension in the system they designed. But the tensions were supposed to be limited, while the constitutional scheme as a whole clearly presupposed a profound harmony of interests and goals among those who would fill the key posts. The reformists' electoral predominance since 1997 has plainly shown this presupposition to be faulty, polarizing Iran's governing groups and threatening to drive the tensions beyond the point where the system can contain them.

These tensions within the regime are hardly playing out in a social vacuum: After two overwhelming electoral victories for Khatami's reformism, the genie of democratization is out of the bottle. One of the most important effects of these victories has been the spread of the language of democracy, not only among young people but throughout the population generally—no mean feat in a country with so long-established a tradition of authoritarianism. By far the most important and widely repeated slogan associated with the president and his successful campaigns for office has been "the rule of law" *(hukumat-e-qanun)*, which draws an implicit contrast with the regime's official call for "the rule of Islam" *(hukumat-e-eslami)*. And since 1997, popular political discourse has set aside talk of "revolutionary charisma and divine mandate" in favor of the idea that popular election is the true basis of governmental legitimacy.

Yet Khatami's conservative foes have blocked his reform program and thrust Iran into a legitimacy crisis. The gap between the Islamists who dominate the state and the rising liberal and modern tendencies within Iranian society is fast becoming an abyss. Almost 70 percent of Iran's population of 67 million—and more than 50 percent of the electorate (the voting age is 16)—is younger than 30. And notwithstanding the persistence of such phenomena as buses segregated by sex, the wearing of veils, and other superficial signs of Islamist dominance, Iran's younger generation is today almost completely "de-Islamized." Among the most forceful contemporary political voices are new student groups such as the Organization for Strengthening Unity, which calls for a referendum by which the popular will may determine Iran's future. The leader of this group, Heshmatollah Tabarzadi, recently issued a strongly worded statement charging that the conservatives had lost their legitimacy, were intellectually ossified, and had no grasp of Iran's problems. It is no exaggeration to say that Tabarzadi was voicing an opinion prevalent among Iran's young people, most of whom were born after 1979 and see the Revolution supported by their parents mainly as having failed to provide them with meaningful freedom and economic security.

## Stirrings of Reform?

The repression to which students and intellectuals have been subjected over the past six years has failed to check the spread of democratic ideas. Some of the reasons for this are negative, such as the philosophical exhaustion of the conservative-theocratic and leftist alternatives, but there are positive reasons as well. These include the emergence of an ethic of individualism that is displacing the ethic of obedience to political or religious authority, and the advent of a new generation of intellectuals—including some clerics—friendly to modern democratic ideas. Meanwhile, since Khomeini's death in 1989, some within the narrow but disproportionately influential religious establishment have come to criticize his doctrine of "the supremacy of the Islamic jurisprudent" *(Velayat-e-Faqih)* on religious grounds and to defend parliamentary democracy as consistent with Islam. The existence of this reformist camp within the clerical-religious world has forced the conservatives to defend themselves on a second front against proponents of a *religious* civil society (for example, Mohsen Kadivar or Abdul Karim Soroush) who call for an Iranian democracy that is based on Islam but ultimately directed by popular vote.

To be sure, the reform process in Iran has recently shown signs of fatigue. The same young people who brought Khatami to power have grown frustrated by his failures. Within 18 months of his second electoral victory, young demonstrators were urging him to step down. With Khatami's relevance waning, the locus of the struggle for civil liberties and human rights has shifted from the presidency to the chambers of parliament and the offices of reformist journals. In truth, the reformist record of the Majlis is scarcely more impressive than that of the executive branch, but this is attributable less to the shortcomings of reformist legislators than to the clergy-dominated Guardian Council. This latter body has repeatedly exercised its constitutional prerogative to reject bills passed by parliament, and has used its control over the judiciary to bring politically motivated charges against reformist legislators, all the while obstructing any effort to secure independent appraisals of how the judiciary or other state institutions actually function. This intense conflict makes plain just how much political practice in the Islamic Republic has belied the ideology of the Islamic Revolution, which postulates an absolute convergence between Islamic orthodoxy and the popular will. Today, Iran is a country where the people are rapidly turning against radical Islam and toward democracy.

Growing popular discontent may wind up leading to spontaneous local upheavals in such large cities as Tehran, Isfahan, Mashad, and Tabriz—largely due to the sickness of the Iranian economy. Despite rising prices for oil, Iran's main export, the governor of the nation's central bank announced in March 2002 that the foreign debt stood at $20 billion. Productivity is low; underemployment and outright joblessness are high; inflation ranges from 20 to 50 percent; and the living standards of most Iranians are below what people enjoyed under the Pahlavi monarchy during the oil-boom years of the 1970s. Each year, more than 750,000 Iranians enter a labor market that has been adding only about 300,000 new jobs annually. According to Iran's labor ministry, more than four million Iranians are unemployed. For those who do have work, wages stagnate while inflation eats away at their buying power. Less-skilled workers are hit especially hard. According to a November 2001 report by the Iranian Statistics Center, a government agency, 5 percent of Iranians live in "absolute poverty" and the vast majority of others need to hold two jobs just to pay for basic needs. According to the reformist daily *Hayat-e-No,* real housing and energy costs have risen 70 percent since 1998, while goods and services have grown 50 percent more expensive.

These harsh economic conditions have come with predictably distressing social costs: marked increases in drug addiction, crime, and prostitution. A July 2000 report by Mohammad Ali Zam, a Tehran official in charge of cultural affairs, claimed that prostitution had skyrocketed in Iran between 1998 and 1999. According to a January 2002 report published in the daily *Entekhab,* there are now 20,000 professional prostitutes in Tehran, mainly runaway girls who have been hired by the city's criminal gangs. And principally because of the dramatic increases in drug addiction, crime, and prostitution, Iran now has serious problems with HIV/AIDS.

## Demonstrations and Popular Mobilization

It is not surprising, then, that in the last decade Iran has seen growing unrest and a greater number of antigovernment demonstrations throughout the country. Most recently, in November 2002, a death sentence for blasphemy imposed on Hashem Aghajari—a history professor from the west-central city of Hamadan—angered a wide spectrum of Iranians, prompting a week of student protests in Tehran and raising the temperature of the power struggle between reformists and hard-liners. To quell the tension, Ayatollah Khamenei ordered the judiciary to review the case against Aghajari, while warning the students to stand down lest "the forces of the people" intervene against them. Fistfights broke out between the students and several hundred vigilantes aligned with the ayatollah. Although the scope of each of these demonstrations was limited, taken together they indicate a general dissatisfaction with the performance of the Iranian government among the population as a whole and among young people in particular.

Popular mobilization around these issues has led to a widespread and deeply felt yearning among the people at large for greater reform and democracy. Despite the intensity of their desire for change, however, relatively few Iranians favor violent confrontation with the regime, and it seems unlikely that a full-scale national popular uprising will take place in the next few years. The Islamic Republic, unlike the shah's regime, enjoys real support from significant sectors of the Iranian power pyramid, including the paramilitary Basij force (otherwise known as "the Guardians of the Revolution") and even reformists, such as Khatami or Abbas Abdi (the former hostage-taker and the editor-in-chief of the daily *Salam*), who feel that their politics of "active calm" (as their movement understands its *modus operandi*) is not working very well.

Overall, the struggle for power between reformists and their foes is going nowhere, and it is likely that the deadlock will continue until Khatami's tenure ends in 2005 (he is constitutionally barred from running again). Equally important, relations with the United States remain poor, with domestic challenges and contradictions often blocking a genuine desire for normalization.

That said, the failure of the reform movement and the growing dissatisfaction of the Iranian people suggest three other possible scenarios for the near-term future. In the first, the hard-liners, acting with Khamenei's blessing, try to stop the reform movement in its tracks by mounting a coup against Khatami. In the second, a series of violent and sporadic outbursts against the regime have cumulative effects that crack the foundations of the current power structure and lead to a takeover by elements of the security services acting in league with organized criminal gangs in the major cities.

In the third scenario—which is simultaneously the most optimistic and the least probable—the democratic movement of students and intellectuals topples the forces of repression and leads Iran toward freedom and democracy. But perhaps this last and most hopeful scenario is not so far-fetched. For even if political events remain hard to predict and even if the current political forms continue to defy abolition, it is certain that the vitality of Iranian intellectual and artistic life is asserting itself and winning the war of ideas against radical Islam and a militant but sclerotic fundamentalism. Connected to this and equally certain is the change that is taking hold in the hearts and minds of Iran's vast numbers of young people. Here indeed may lie the greatest challenge— and the greatest opportunity—for Iranian society, since as Gandhi says: "The spirit of democracy is not a mechanical thing to be adjusted by abolition of forms. It requires change of the heart."[1]

## NOTE

1. Richard Attenborough, ed., *The Words of Gandhi* (New York: Newmarket, 1999), 19.

# 17

# THE DEADLOCK IN IRAN: CONSTITUTIONAL CONSTRAINTS

*Mehrangiz Kar*

*Mehrangiz Kar is an Iranian human rights attorney and activist currently residing in the United States. The author of 13 books, she was jailed in Iran in April 2000 on charges of "threatening national security," and remains barred from appearing publicly there. In 2001–02, she was a Reagan-Fascell Democracy Fellow at the International Forum for Democratic Studies. In 2002, she received the Ludovic Trarieux Prize for her work in defense of human rights. The following essay, which originally appeared in the January 2003 issue of the* Journal of Democracy, *is based on remarks that she delivered at the National Endowment for Democracy in Washington, D.C., on 30 May 2002. They were originally translated by Hormoz Hekmat, editor of* Iran Nameh, *a social-science journal published in Persian by the Foundation for Iranian Studies.*

In assessing the prospects for democratic change in Iran, one must attend not only to broad social pressures throughout the country, or even to the concrete reform initiatives that come from within the government, but to the ultimate institutional determinant of contemporary Iranian politics: the Revolutionary Constitution of the Islamic Republic. In what follows, then, I will discuss the impediments and obstacles to political reform that Iran's Constitution poses, and explain why such reform cannot be realized without radical constitutional change.

Since the election of pro-reform president Mohammad Khatami in 1997, there have been two basic approaches, two outlooks, toward the achievement of reform in Iran: "Reformists" within the regime essentially believe that the Constitution has the capacity—indeed, the positive potential—to lead the Revolutionary government of Iran toward democracy. By contrast, "secularists," who remain outside the regime, basically think that the Constitution contains impediments profound enough to block meaningful reform. It is not uncommon for reformists and secularists to take shared positions on immediate political questions. And they share some broad, long-range political goals that set them together in opposition to conservatives. But there are profound stakes between them when it comes to evaluating the conditions for a transition to democracy in Iran.

To be sure, there are articles in the Constitution that allow for the implementation of the basic rights and freedoms for the Iranian people. Certain articles speak of the rights of the accused, due process of law, and other concepts that can be considered essentially liberal-democratic and conducive to the realization of human rights in Iran. But there are other articles that negate these liberal concepts altogether, for which reason one can fairly say that, in the aggregate, the mechanisms afforded by the Islamic Republic's Constitution are quite clearly not conducive to liberal-democratic reform.

When Khatami became president, the Fifth Majlis was dominated by the most conservative elements. To prevent Khatami from being able to carry out his reform agenda, conservatives wasted little time in passing new laws to further restrict those few and limited rights and freedoms that Iranians then enjoyed. For example, they passed newly repressive laws on criminal procedure in cases of press-law violations, further limiting the rights of the accused. And this was just one of the areas in which they tried to tie President Khatami's hands as he attempted to implement the reform program on the basis of which he was elected.

Because of the obstructionist posture of the Fifth Majlis, reformists naturally came to believe that the realization of their goals depended on whether they could gain control of the parliament. Prior to the elections for the Sixth Majlis in 2000, reformists started devising slogans and programs aimed at overhauling the legal system—talking about amending laws that limited people's right to run for public office, restricted the press, and dealt unfairly with women and religious minorities. The reformists also proposed laws intended to ameliorate Iran's catastrophic economic situation. Running on this agenda, they won overwhelming voter support and 200 of the parliament's then-270 seats.

More than two years have passed since the inauguration of the Majlis's sixth term, and despite the presence in that body of a number of very courageous representatives who have discussed in detail, and assiduously promoted, the reformists' program, nothing concrete has yet been accomplished. Indeed, conservatives have accused a number of Majlis deputies of breaching Islamic law and the Iranian penal code merely by criticizing conservative-controlled institutions in the course of parliamentary debate. Some deputies have been tried, and one—Hossein Loghmanian, a deputy from the west-central city of Hamadan—was jailed for a number of weeks. Loghmanian was subsequently released so as to preempt public outcry, but the judiciary has made and kept extensive files on him, as they have on numerous other reformists in the Majlis, for the purposes of political intimidation. Reformist deputies, then, have been denied even limited parliamentary immunity, creating a new source of political tension in Iran and, at the same time, a new source for public awareness and protest against the situation in the Majlis.

## The Nature of the Obstacles

Ultimately, however, it is not the whims of reactionary jurists that are obstructing the legislative activities of the reformist legislature. The barriers faced by the Majlis are fundamentally constitutional.

To begin with, the Constitution has contradictory provisions regarding the functions and prerogatives of the Majlis. On the one hand, the Constitution clearly stipulates that the Majlis is to be an independent legislature. On the other hand, however, the Majlis's freedom to enact laws is subject to the will of another body, the Guardian Council. The members of this Council—six jurists and six high-ranking clerics—are appointed, either directly or indirectly, by the highest official in the executive branch, the Supreme Leader (currently Ali Khamenei).

Bills passed by the Majlis are not legally binding until the Guardian Council attests, first, that the presumptive law does not contradict the basic tenets and provisions of Islamic law and, second, that it does not contradict the basic principles of the Constitution. Strikingly, *every single* reform law that the Majlis has passed over the last two yeas has been stopped in its tracks by the Guardian Council.

Once the Guardian Council rejects a particular law, it sends that law back to the Majlis with specific objections. The Majlis must then, on the basis of the directives given by the Council, revise and amend the law and send it back. This has continued over the past two years, with many reformist laws held in abeyance; the tension between the Majlis and the Guardian Council is, in other words, paralyzing Iran's legislative process.

In the first years following the adoption of the Constitution in 1979, Ayatollah Khomeini decided that a device was needed to overcome any impasse that might arise between the Majlis and the Guardian Council. He therefore decreed into existence a separate body, one effectively appointed by the Supreme Leader, to handle this problem. The exact translation of its name is a bit difficult; in full, it is something like "board to make decisions on the basis of the interests of the Islamic Republic of Iran," or, for short, the Expediency Council. Expediency in this case means the interests of the Islamic Republic, the regime; there is no reference to the public. This body—which was formally added to the Constitution in 1990—is the final arbiter in contemporary Iranian politics: When there is no agreement between the Majlis and the Guardian Council on a particular law, it goes to the Expediency Council, which has the final word.

Before the election of the reformist-dominated Sixth Majlis in 2000, the Expediency Council had sometimes permitted the final passage of laws that the Guardian Council had rejected as contradictory to Islam. At the time, the Expediency Council was more interested in solving problems than in seeing to it that legislation was indeed compatible with Islamic law. During the Sixth Majlis, however, both supervising bodies—the Guardian Council and the Expediency Council—have been completely dominated by conservative, antireformist elements, leaving the reformist majority in the Majlis totally blocked.

There are a number of bills that have gone from the Majlis to the Guardian Council which the Guardian Council has either rejected or left undecided. And even where bills have reached the Expediency Council, the latter has so far refused to make any decision on them. Included among these acts are a proposed law that would reduce restrictions on foreign investment in Iran (a very important issue for the Iranian economy), as well as one on women's rights.

## Why Iran Has No Real Parliament

Thus the Iranian Majlis is not a genuine parliament, given that it must by law accept the views of two other superior organs. And since the Supreme Leader has remained unwilling to change the composition of these two bodies by appointing to them individuals more amenable to the reformist movement that animates the Majlis, the situation is not likely to change.

In addition to its lawmaking role, the Majlis has constitutional duties: to investigate and oversee the performance of the executive and judicial branches of government, and to receive and investigate complaints and criticisms from the public. In these two areas, likewise, the Majlis has been completely unable to fulfill its responsibilities. For example, it intended to investigate and audit the records and activities of the Foundation for the Dispossessed, one of Iran's most powerful *bonyads* ("charitable foundations" under the control of the Supreme Leader that operate hundreds of companies, receive more than half of the state's expenditures, and account for up to 40 percent of the country's economy). But legislators found their plans scotched when the Guardian Council declared that parliament had no right to investigate these organizations, which are under his direct control. The Expediency Council has decided that the Majlis can investigate organizations under the control of the Supreme Leader when, and only when, he expressly grants the Majlis that right. Although Article 90 of the Constitution empowers a Majlis committee to investigate complaints from citizens about the judicial branch, the judiciary, which is also under the control of the Supreme Leader, has not allowed this committee to be active. In fact, the judiciary has refused to respond to repeated parliamentary inquiries regarding the citizen complaints that the Majlis has received.

One might think that the emergence of a reformist legislature would naturally lead toward democratic progress. But this has not happened in Iran, and one would have to be idealistic to the point of naivety to think that genuine democratization will come simply by a continuation of the current process. The obstacles in the Constitution and legal framework of Iran are simply too profound.

There is no chance that the Majlis will be able to interpret away the Constitution's antidemocratic principles, for only the Guardian Council enjoys the right of constitutional interpretation. Moreover, although the Majlis is the closest thing that Iran has to an elected governing body, the powers of the Guardian and Expediency councils to purge candidates and validate results mean that even the Majlis is not chosen by truly democratic means. In Iran, in other words, there is no real distinction between appointed and elected organs. And those in which there is any nascent agenda for democratic reform are, by constitutional design, politically powerless to bring it about.

And yet profound social tensions persist. University-student demonstrations erupted this past November after the Islamic Court voted to execute a reformist professor, Hashem Aghajari—a well-known reformist and advocate of democracy and the freedom of speech—for the crime of blasphemy. The Court ultimately withdrew the sentence at the behest of the Supreme Leader, who sought to placate the protesters after a week of demonstrations, but not before threatening them with suppression by "the forces of the people" should they not stand down. The result was a small victory for Iranian democrats, but it also served to reaffirm a status quo in which they, and their representatives in government, remain thoroughly marginalized by the country's real—and constitutionally entrenched—ruling powers.

Considering that the Constitution of the Islamic Republic includes such overwhelmingly antidemocratic features and precludes meaningful change, it is probably inevitable that opponents of the conservatives who rule Iran will eventually turn to violence.

# 18

# TURKEY AT THE POLLS: AFTER THE TSUNAMI

*Soli Özel*

**Soli Özel** *teaches in the Department of International Relations at Bilgi University in Istanbul. He is the editor of the Turkish edition of* Foreign Policy *and a columnist for the daily newspaper* Sabah. *His "Eye on Turkey" commentaries for the U.S. affiliate of the Turkish Industrialists' and Businessmen's Association (TÜSIAD) can be accessed at www.tusiad.us. This essay originally appeared in the April 2003 issue of the* Journal of Democracy.

The elections of 3 November 2002 were more widely discussed, more intensely scrutinized, and of more interest to foreign publics than any in the 80-year history of the Turkish Republic. Why did Turkey come under the glare of this spotlight? Because the frontrunner in all the polls and the eventual winner of just over a third of the vote and just under two-thirds of the seats in the 550-member Grand National Assembly, Turkey's unicameral parliament, was the Islamic-rooted Justice and Development Party (AKP), a successor to two previously banned Islamist parties that now rejects the Islamist label. In a fit of rage, it seemed, Turkish voters had swept aside a whole cohort of established but corruption-tainted parties, possibly in defiance of the country's politically powerful military, and opted instead for a group of self-avowed "Muslim Democrats" led by the charismatic former mayor of Istanbul, Recep Tayyip Erdoğan. (See the Table on p. 180 of this volume.)

Ordinarily, these events would have been of interest mainly to specialists, and then mostly because of the huge disproportion between votes received and seats gained: Thanks to the 10 percent national threshold that the outgoing military regime wrote into the constitution back in 1982, both the AKP and the only other group to win a place in parliament, the Republican People's Party (CHP), reaped enormous "seat bonuses." But the ascent to power of a party rooted in Turkey's Islamist movement drew wide international attention and prompted some of the usual (and sometimes poorly informed) ques-

tions about Islam and democracy that have become so pressing since
9/11: Could Turkey, this most militantly secular, predominantly Muslim country, turn fundamentalist? Was this going to be an example of
"one man, one vote, one time" even though Turkey had a long history
of pluralism and vigorously competitive electoral politics? Was a clash
with the secular establishment (including perhaps the military) inevitable even though the AKP refused the "Islamist" label and ran on a
platform calling for Turkey's full membership in the European Union
(EU)? So the image that these elections evoked was Iran for some and
Algeria for others, although Turkey is neither.

The parliament that the elections have brought into being has just
two parties: the AKP with 363 seats and the CHP with 178 (there are 9
independent deputies). Several things leap out from the election results:
First, voters were merciless in punishing nearly all the traditionally established parties, whether or not they were part of the government. The
three parties that formed the incumbent governing coalition—the left-
ist-cum-nationalist Democratic Left Party (DSP) of Prime Minister
Bülent Ecevit, the center-right Motherland Party (ANAP), and the right-
wing Nationalist Action Party (MHP)—saw their combined vote share
fall from 53.4 percent in 1999 to a humiliating 14.6 percent in 2002.
Likewise, one of the major traditional formations then in opposition
ranks, the True Path Party (DYP) of former prime minister Tansu Çiller,
also lost vote share, going from 12 percent in 1999 to a seatless 9.6
percent total in 2002. The traditional Islamists fared poorly as well.
Their vehicle, the Felicity Party, won a mere 2.5 percent.

A second aspect of the 2002 balloting was the electorate's anxious
search for new options. According to a survey taken by pollster Tarhan
Erdem, nearly a third of the voters said that they had been intent on
"trying out a new party."[1] Erdem suggested that 38 percent of AKP
voters were from this group. This volatility is probably a symptom of
the eroding support bases of the DYP and ANAP plus the two other
traditional centrist parties: The four saw their combined vote share drop
from almost 83 percent in 1991 to just over 36 percent in 2002.

The dark horse of the elections and a probable beneficiary of the
voters' restless mood was the Youth Party (GP), a brand-new grouping
that serves as the political vehicle of 37-year-old media tycoon Cem
Uzan. Relying on concerts and shows, bereft of organization, and touting a message of unabashed, even fascistic nationalism and xenophobic
populism, the GP pulled a surprising and perhaps ominous 7.2 percent
of the vote. A typical Uzan stump speech—I took the following from
the 30 October 2002 edition of *Star,* his Istanbul-based newspaper—
would avow that: "Turkey has all the wealth it needs to become a world
power. This is what scares the foreigners . . . the strengthening of Turkey will be a propaganda boost for Turkishness and Islam. . . . This is
exactly what they don't want. . . . Either the IMF or Turkey!" Given

Uzan's age, wealth, and skill at exploiting modern mass communications, his GP could become a force to be reckoned with.

A third notable characteristic of the 2002 races was the comparatively low turnout. With nearly a quarter of the electorate (up from about 18 percent in 1999) either not voting or casting spoiled ballots, voter participation was at its lowest in 30 years, though in absolute terms it still included more than 30 million people, or slightly less than half of Turkey's total population. Voting is nearly the only institutionalized act of political participation that most Turks perform, so the drop may bespeak rising alienation from the political system, or at least the established parties.

Finally, the high threshold ensured that nearly one out of every two votes cast (46 percent) was wasted. The legitimacy questions that this raises could constitute a rallying point for extraparliamentary opposition to the AKP government. The Kurdish-nationalist formation that appeared on the ballot under the hastily devised acronym DEHAP after courts had threatened to outlaw its mother-party fell short of the threshold with 6.2 percent of the total nationwide vote, and yet took 45 percent or more of the vote in five of Turkey's 82 provinces, and in fact topped 10 percent in nine more, all of which were clustered in the southeast, where Kurds predominate. And yet none of this was enough to send a single DEHAP candidate to Ankara.

After the elections, party leaders Tansu Çiller of DYP and Mesut Yılmaz of ANAP resigned their posts. Devlet Bahçeli of the MHP was the first to declare an intention to resign but as of this writing in early March 2003 still has not done so. The new head of the DYP is a former minister of both the Interior and Justice departments, Mehmet Ağar. His background, record, and involvement in a grave scandal of the late 1990s may signal a significant shift in the DYP's identity. ANAP elected to its chair a former cabinet minister named Ali Talip Özdemir; he has impressed few among the public with either his personality or his vision.

## Surprising Election, Not-So-Surprising Result

Like Santiago Nasar in Gabriel García Márquez's novella *Chronicle of a Death Foretold,* the three parties in the coalition that had held power since May 1999 moved toward their own obliteration. By calling elections for the fall of 2002, 18 months ahead of schedule, the DSP, MHP, and ANAP were putting their tenure on the line before voters could feel any payoff from the painful but necessary economic-stabilization measures that these parties had adopted in order to solve the worst economic and financial crisis in modern Turkish history. Had the bickering coalition partners been able to contain for just a few more months their disagreements over such matters as the internal political and legal reforms demanded by the EU-accession process, they might well have

caught the voters in a much better mood. Whatever the coalition partners' reasons for not wishing to wait, one thing is clear: Their decision
to call the country to the polls flung wide the door to power for the
AKP, which stepped smartly through it.

Exit polls overseen by Yılmaz Esmer show that the AKP got almost
equal numbers of votes from men and women and was highly favored
by 18-to-25-year-olds, many of them first-time voters. The AKP also
drew heavily on support from the less-educated and less well-off while
polling about equally strongly in big cities, medium-sized towns, and
rural areas. Esmer found that most AKP voters favored EU accession
even if they doubted that the EU was sincere about the process. Fully
half of AKP voters wished to end relations with the International Monetary Fund, whose loan conditionalities had spurred the coalition
government to enact its unpopular austerity measures. Finally and most
significantly, the AKP attracted voters who had previously supported
other parties across the political spectrum. Only a quarter of all AKP
voters were people who had voted for the Virtue Party (FP), the AKP's
Islamist predecessor, in 1999.[2]

There is little doubt that Erdoğan was a strong campaign asset for the
AKP. Still a popular figure in Istanbul, he had since 1998 been barred
from holding office because a court found him guilty of inciting hatred
after he publicly recited a poem by the nationalist writer Ziya Gökalp
(1876–1924) that referred to minarets as "our spears" and mosques as
"our barracks." The determination of the secular-statist establishment
to keep Erdoğan out of politics probably only enhanced his mystique
and his party's appeal.

While the 2002 balloting was in the most immediate sense a cry of
anger by voters infuriated at the sorry state of Turkey's economy, deeper
analysis suggests that broader and longer-lasting forces are at work. In
the future, we may look back at 2002 as the first in a series of realigning
votes that decisively reshaped Turkish parties, elections, and political
life in general. The AKP certainly shows signs of being a classic realigning party. It appears to have swayed and motivated both new and
existing voters, and represents a winning coalition that is diverse but
held together by a common cultural discourse that resonates with all.
The party's leaders appear to sense this, too, which may explain their
emphasis upon a synthesis of communitarianism and market-based liberalism as well as the remarkable absence of almost any Islamist
references in their major campaign speeches.

If a watershed has been reached, the roots of the shift may be traceable to the 1980s. Under the more liberal economic policies strongly
advocated by Prime Minister (later President) Turgut Özal (1983–91) of
ANAP, including freer capital flows, privatization, and integration into
the EU customs union, there prospered a new provincial business class
that was not dependent on state protectionism but was simultaneously in

touch with world markets, culturally conservative, and religiously observant. For a time, the forces of economic liberalization were held back by an older rent-seeking and rent-granting coalition of small and large business owners, public and unionized employees, wealthier peasants from the Anatolian heartland, and bureaucrats. As beneficiaries of a fading era of high tariffs and other state-led development policies, the members of this coalition feared globalization and free markets.

But theirs was a rear-guard action. The new middle classes began to come into their own in the 1990s, drawing to their ranks traditional provincial shopkeepers and merchants who had learned to adapt to markets and developing a shared sense of "independence from the hegemony of the ruling Republican elites."[3] More free from state patronage networks and the cultural influence of Republican secularism, they are the engine of AKP's expansion, which has gained such momentum that even farmers, small businesspeople, and less-skilled workers who once supported antiglobalization Islamist or nationalist parties now vote for the avowedly pro-market and pro-EU AKP.

The AKP has thus come, through a number of remarkable twists and trends, to represent both many net winners and many net losers from Turkey's integration into the global economy. Can the party reconcile their divergent interests while at the same time carrying on the arduous work of political liberalization and democratization? This, more than any other, is the master question of Turkish politics at the dawn of the twenty-first century.

## The Long Wave

For the Turkish economy, the 1990s were "years that the locust hath eaten." Rampant populism in economic policy fueled wild boom-and-bust cycles that bottomed out in the deep recessions of 1994 and 1999, during each of which the economy shrank by more than 6 percent. Public finances deteriorated and real interest rates shot up (the average inflation rate across the decade topped 80 percent, up from 48.5 percent in the 1980s), while a poorly regulated banking system, uncompetitive state-run utilities, and the exceedingly slow pace of privatization held down growth. Poverty and inequality grew worse.[4]

Instead of summoning the more than 60 million people of Turkey to rise to the new challenges of the post–Cold War world and the global economy, the center-left and center-right parties that dominated the politics of the decade tried to preserve the old spoils system. The bitter harvest of the establishment's inability or unwillingness to let go of its accustomed clientelism and populism was the disastrous 2001 bankrupting of Turkey's public finances and the resulting depression, which saw negative growth rates top 9 percent, unemployment rates hover around 15 percent, and close to a fifth of the population slip below the official poverty line. The establishment's refusal to seek ways to accommodate the aspirations of Turkey's large Kurdish population or of observant and politically active Muslims led on the one hand to increasing restiveness among these groups (indeed, in the Kurdish case an internal war ravaged many corners of the mountainous southeast and probably cost about 30,000 lives between 1984 and 1999), and on the other to a consequent intensification of the worried military's willingness to make its weight felt in political affairs.

The Kurdish insurgency, combined with testy EU dealings, particularly after the Union chose to pass over Turkey's candidacy for full membership in December 1997, spurred the rise of xenophobia and exaggerated nationalism. The military gradually redefined domestic problems as national-security threats, with the influence of the armed forces visibly increasing throughout political life. And yet throughout this very decade pressures for further democratization continued to well up from within Turkish society. The EU helped by asking Turkey to live up to its commitment to democratic reform as a *sine qua non* of the membership process.

While democratic advocacy had long been the province of a small slice of the intelligentsia plus a cluster of NGOs, the 1980s and early 1990s saw some Islamist intellectuals making constructive contributions as well. While human rights and democratic liberties never became a top priority for most ordinary Turks, there were signs of a strong, if latent, desire to civilize and liberalize the polity. Among these were the popularity of the expansive Turgut Özal, and the burst of enthusiasm that greeted the short-lived New Democracy Movement's efforts (1993–95) to promote a more liberal approach to politics and to gain a wider public hearing for Kurdish and Islamist activists. In the 1990s, the prominent industrialists' and business owners' association known as TÜSIAD, which had supported the 1980 military coup, added its voice to the democracy chorus, noting that Turkey's future prosperity hinged on EU accession and thus on further democratization.

The armed forces and other foes of liberalization often rebuffed these and similar appeals, pointing to the threats of surging Islamism and violent Kurdish separatism (and taking little care to distinguish peaceful Kurdish activism from the armed insurgency of the Kurdistan Workers' Party [PKK]). With the 1999 capture of PKK leader Abdullah Öcalan and the winding-down of the internal war, Islamism came to replace Kurdish nationalism as the primary security threat in military eyes.

Paradoxically, then, the 1990s were both good years and bad years for democratization, with Turkey's still-fragile civil society groups, and not its professional political class, doing the lion's share to sustain the case for greater liberty and participation. Looking at this uneven report card, one is reminded of Guillermo O'Donnell's observation that new polyarchies "actually have two extremely important institutions. One is highly formalized but intermittent: elections. The other is informal, permanent, and pervasive: particularism (or clientelism broadly defined)."[5] Even as rampant cronyism feeds a cynical public mood and hampers democratic consolidation, he goes on to note, the democratic ideals that are supposed to underlie the practice of elections are not unimportant. For even the paying of mere lip service to the formal rules of open and accountable government encourages and legitimizes demands that these rules be followed.[6] The effect, loosely speaking, is to create a seesaw battle between a cynically apathetic acknowledgment that clientelism rules and a righteous anger that democracy and transparency do not.

Turkey in the 1990s provided a good illustration of what O'Donnell meant. Throughout the decade, a closed and protected system was kept on artificial life support. Blatant populism and patronage drove corruption to new levels. In case after case, expediency and habits of mutual protection among even rival politicians stymied legal enforcement as the public looked on in disgust. As market-based reforms, global competition, and economic troubles narrowed the opportunities for spoils, the centrist parties developed sharper elbows in their fight for a place at the trough. Cronyism became rampant just as the parties faced the erosion of their electoral base. The center-right parties turned into self-perpetuating, nepotistic, corruption machines that were increasingly alienated from their constituencies. The main center-left Social Democratic People's Party (or SHP, which was absorbed by the CHP in 1995), became a victim of its own incompetence in municipal administration between 1989 and 1994, and began to lose ground to the nationalistic left-wing populism of Bülent Ecevit's DSP.

Under these circumstances the Islamist-based Welfare Party (RP) began its rise. It was the only party that took grassroots organization seriously, put forward ideas, and talked often and openly about justice. After winning the mayors' races in Istanbul and Ankara, the RP became the biggest single vote-getter in the 1995 parliamentary elections with 21.4 percent. In July 1996, Welfare formed a coalition government with the DYP (even though Tansu Çiller had campaigned on an anti-RP platform) and took Turkey down the path toward the "postmodern coup" of early 1997.

## Susurluk and the Postmodern Coup

The AKP's success has proximate as well as structural causes. The former grew out of four events that have shocked the Turkish people over the past six years. The first was the startling set of revelations that came to light after a fatal car crash near the small western town of Susurluk on 3 November 1996. The second was the postmodern coup, which was originally set in train by the military on 28 February 1997. The third was the devastating Izmit earthquake of 17 August 1999. The fourth was the economic meltdown of February 2001. Not only did these developments take place amid larger currents of dramatic economic, social, and political change that eddied about Turkey in the wake of the Cold War, but each hit with the force of a blow heavy enough to change the course of Turkish politics.

In the ill-fated Mercedes sedan that ran into a truck outside Susurluk were a senior police official, an ultra-rightist assassin and drug dealer wanted by (among others) Interpol, his ex–beauty queen girlfriend, and a Kurdish tribal leader–cum–DYP deputy (the wreck's sole survivor) who headed an anti-PKK militia. The car's trunk held an array of pistols and silencers, plus official documents establishing several false identities for Abdullah Çatlı, the fugitive criminal. Like a stone heaved into a cesspool, the Susurluk incident sent out widening riplets of scandal as reporters traced links between these characters and other politicians (including the DYP's Mehmet Ağar, who was forced to resign as justice minister), organized-crime figures, state-security agencies, and unsolved killings from the mid-1990s.

At the scandal's heart was the lawless "dirty war" that Turkey's shadowy "deep state" had been waging in the southeast. Çatlı was a notorious gangster long suspected of involvement in various crimes including the 1978 murders of seven left-wing students in Ankara, the 1979 killing of a prominent journalist, and Mehmet Ali Ağca's 1981 attempt on the life of Pope John Paul II. Dogged reporting by Turkish journalists showed that Çatlı had in all likelihood been acting as a hitman for elements within the security services, which in return had been shielding him and his other illicit activities from the law. Citizens' anger was intense and widespread. The quest for a clean society, a transparent state, and accountable politicians gained strong momentum. Tansu Çiller owned up to her government's actions, insisting that they had all been taken to protect the nation's unity, while RP head Necmettin Erbakan—the chief of the only party with no connection to these events—deliberately did nothing to capitalize on the eruption of public fury.

For Prime Minister Erbakan, however, another sort of reckoning was waiting. On the last day of February 1997, the regular monthly meeting of the military-dominated National Security Council, a constitutional body that comprises top elected officials and the senior armed-service chiefs, gave the Welfare–True Path coalition government a list of 18 measures to be implemented without delay, including a clampdown on "reactionary Islam." With the threat of an actual coup hanging in the air, the military spent the next months waging a relentless public-relations campaign that turned society against the government and eventually forced the resignation on June 18 of Erbakan and his cabinet.[7] The noose on civilian politics remained tight after that. Press freedom was severely curtailed, with many journalists and other public figures targeted by military-orchestrated smear campaigns.

Despite the obvious damage that these machinations did to democracy, a significant segment of the public supported them, most likely for two reasons. The first was the immoderation that the RP's leaders showed in their rhetoric regarding foreign policy and the sacrosanct principle of secularism (both "red zones" for the generals).

The second reason grew out of the failure of Turkey's civilian politicians, particularly those in the center-right parties, to take the initiative in defining the boundaries of legitimate political speech and action, especially as these touched on secularism. The RP's bolder—indeed at times bigoted—claims about the role of religion in politics flanked these parties to the right, exposing their ambivalence on the secularism question and carving away much of their traditional Muslim support base. The military, alarmed by the lack of a robust civilian response to the Islamists' use of religious symbols and values for political purposes, saw itself as stepping in to fill the gap and defend the threatened foundations of the order created by Kemal Atatürk, the founder of both the secular Turkish Republic and its army. And yet: The political system probably would have dealt with the RP eventually and the postmodern military intervention—like the not-so-postmodern coups of 1960, 1971, and 1980—set back not merely one admittedly problematic faction but the whole cause of civil and democratic political order.

The Motherland Party under Mesut Yılmaz opportunistically acquiesced in the intervention and took the ousted RP's place along with Ecevit's DSP and defectors from DYP who just formed a new party. It is a testimony to the complexity of the relations between the military and the parties that Erbakan specifically called on his followers not to riot or even protest when the Constitutional Court later banned Welfare as a threat to the foundations of the Republic. This behavior is in line with the studied ambivalence toward the politically assertive military that Turkish parties have generally shown. Pondering the reasons for this, Ümit Cizre argues:

> A political class threatened by the formal and informal role of the military as the ultimate guardian of the regime has critical problems in relinquishing patronage resources. In that guardianship model, the political class constantly weighs the political pay-off derived from a reform in the system—to put an end to powerlessness, incapacity, corruption and stasis—against the costs of giving up power based on patronage. It is more than likely that the civilian political class will not choose to terminate rent-seeking networks by reforms that would reduce the prominence of the military in politics. Its foremost concern will be a short rather than a long-term one.[8]

What is called within Turkey "the February 28 process" was not limited to the political wing of the Islamist movement. Islamic networks, sects, associations, and individuals were targeted for excoriation and sometimes prosecution or court-ordered bans on their activities. Accustomed to gentle official treatment, the larger community of Islamists was traumatized and left with deep new doubts about the benign character of state authority.

Knocked cold by a mailed fist swathed in the bureaucratic equivalent of a velvet glove, some Islamists awoke from the experience with a newfound appreciation of democratic principles and a systematic resolve—the first ever in their movement's history—to embark on a principled quest to defend not merely their own liberties, but democratic liberties as such. The much-maligned EU and its norms became a key source of support for the persecuted Islamist parties. In an ironic way that no one fully intended, the postmodern coup paved the way for the generational and ideological cleavage and reorganization within the Islamist movement that gave birth to the AKP.

## Goodbye to Big Daddy: The Quake of '99

Amid the fear and anger created by the February 28 process and the breakdown of EU-Ankara relations after the snub at Luxembourg in December 1997, Turkish society turned increasingly inward and even, in some quarters, xenophobic. Under threat of war, Syria at last ended the 20-year stay within its own or Lebanon's borders of Turkey's public enemy number one, PKK chieftain Abdullah Öcalan. After a fugitive interval, he wound up in the Greek embassy in Nairobi, Kenya, where he was caught by U.S. agents in February 1999 and turned over to Turkish authorities.[9] Thereupon nationalist feelings boiled over, and upon such sentiments rode to power the DSP and the MHP—the nationalist parties to the left of center and on the extreme right, respectively.

This heavy nationalism and the reified idea of an omnicompetent, paternalistic *devlet baba* (daddy state) were shattered in the early-morning hours of 17 August 1999, when a powerful earthquake devastated several urban areas in western Turkey. Centered near the city of Izmit at the easternmost tip of the Sea of Marmara, less than 60 miles from Istanbul, and measuring 7.4 on the Richter Scale, the quake's 45-second-long main shock was enough to cause massive loss of life and expose "fissures in the edifice of the Turkish State."[10]

The state apparatus, including the military, utterly failed to come to the rescue of the victims for almost three days. As round-the-clock television coverage broadcast the disaster's aftermath to a horrified nation, it became painfully obvious that the damage had been made much worse by the illegally shoddy construction of so many buildings in the densely populated quake zone. Bribes or patronage deals had caused building codes to be ignored. There were reports of multistory apartment blocks that had lethally collapsed on their sleeping denizens because the buildings' foundations had been made from unstable (but free) beach sand while inspectors looked the other way.

Other countries immediately sent rescue teams, which on several occasions were refused entry into Turkey or otherwise impeded. The Turkish state's disaster-relief agencies were revealed to be dry-rotted with ineptitude and corruption. While authorities sat back in disarray, "thousands of ordinary citizens and NGOs searched for victims in the rubble and provided such goods as medicine, food, legal advice, and educational services to victims."[11] Foreign organizations and governments (including that of Greece, in a gesture which undid much of the damage done by Greek involvement in sheltering Öcalan) rushed help into the disaster zone and impressed Turks with their efficiency, sympathy, and warmth. The earthquake and what it brought to light broke the national mood of sullen isolation and destroyed the old *modus vivendi* between Turkish society and a state that would rather hold tight to its own prerogatives than take help from civic organizations struggling to bring relief to thousands of suffering people.

Because of the neighborhoods it struck, the earthquake heavily affected Turkey's articulate, *status quo*–oriented middle classes. Their sense of having been betrayed by the state that they had once venerated ran deep indeed. The social contract between the state and this important segment of society was broken. Thenceforth the drive toward an accountable, transparent, and efficient government ruled by law would go forward on a stronger social basis than ever before. EU membership became all the more prized as an aid to this cause; some even saw it as a panacea. The outpouring of help and support from abroad also showed Turks that the world was not their enemy. The spell of xenophobia and exaggerated appeals to national security was fast being broken.

As the 1990s waned, there were ample signs that stopgap measures needed to give way to serious efforts at effecting a basic overhaul of Turkey's key political and economic institutions. Yet fierce resistance slowed reform, at least until the twin economic catastrophes of November 2000 and February 2001 showed all but the most incorrigibly obtuse that to try and carry on with "business as usual" would be tantamount to embracing national self-destruction.

With an economy shrinking by more than 9 percent a year, a radical cure was the only way out, and the pain would be widespread. As Ilter Turan argues,

> Economic reforms, taken together, call for nothing less than the total abandonment of the patronage system that has characterized Turkish politics during the last several decades. Each measure inflicts some deprivation on some constituency that rebels against the unfortunate fate that is being imposed on it.[12]

With the twin crises "the existing mode of capital accumulation . . . where gains are private but 'all risks' are socialized has irrevocably ended."[13] The state and the private sector alike have had to bite the bullet and streamline themselves. But as former treasury secretary Mahfi Eğilmez repeatedly stresses, smooth progress toward full EU member-ship is the hook upon which hang so many hopes for solvency and sustained growth. From the foreign direct investment that Turkey needs to meet the IMF's stringent demands to prospects for better governance, governmental efficiency, a deeper rule of law, and genuine moderniza-tion—much hinges on the EU accession process.

The net results of Susurluk, the coup, the quake, and the economic downturn have been surging pro-EU sentiment, a broad-based demand for further democratic reform, and fury directed at any and all institu-tions—no matter how previously sacrosanct—deemed responsible for the calamities of recent years. The popular support for EU membership is new, and suggests that this great goal of Republican Turkey is no longer the special preserve of elites. Ultimately, the push for change, the claims of a rising counterelite to a place in the power structure, and the popularity of EU membership all point to a fundamental fact: Hav-ing undergone a rather unsettling two decades, Turkey is now ready to shake off the shackles of the 1982 military-drafted constitution as well as the mentality that framed it.

It was the tide of these aspirations and this disenchantment with the established order of things that brought the AKP to power as the only untested major party in the running on 3 November 2002. A sign of how well the AKP understood this mood was Erdoğan's decision to visit every EU capital before the Copenhagen Summit on enlargement met in December 2003.

## The Republic's Great Test

The AKP's rise may have been too rapid for its own good. It did not have enough time to consolidate its organization or formulate a detailed program. To this day, the AKP remains a coalition of forces rather than a coherent political apparatus. Its first few months in power also re-vealed its deficits of expertise and experience. The best chance to shape economic policy came and went unexploited. The cabinet could easily mishandle the cross-pressures that will come from the IMF's demand for austerity and party loyalists' demands for largesse, patronage jobs, and the like.

For all its early stumbles, the AKP government has also proven itself to be a quick study, pragmatic, and decisive when it comes to foreign policy and most domestic political matters. From the start, Erdoğan boldly departed from the official line on the now-almost-30-years-old Cyprus issue by calling for it to be resolved, and soon. He has stuck with that position so far, despite bitter criticism from some quarters, probably because he realizes that the Cyprus issue is a litmus test for the AKP. If it cannot recast policy in this area but instead finds itself forced to mouth the words of the old script, the party will reign but not rule.

The difficult issues surrounding Turkey's possible involvement in a military coalition against Saddam Hussein's regime in Iraq have also generated a severe crisis for the AKP. Prime Minister Abdullah Gül's sagacious if half-hearted handling of the matter and the hard negotiations conducted by the United States and Turkey over military, political, and economic issues appeared to end in futility when on 1 March 2003 the Grand National Assembly refused the government's request for permission to invite U.S. ground troops to base themselves in Turkey, and also refused to allow Turkish troops to cross into northern Iraq. Nearly a hundred AKP deputies either defected or abstained—a sign of intraparty power struggles as well as the AKP's responsiveness to public opinion, which was overwhelmingly against a war considered unjust in Turkey. How the mismanagement of this vote—by the AKP government, by Turkish president Ahmet Necdet Sezer, and by the United States—will affect the AKP's future and staying power remains to be seen. Whatever the repercussions, Erdoğan will be the one primarily responsible for dealing with them, since he won a by-election to parliament on March 9 and was expected to take over quickly as prime minister.

During his few months in office, Abdullah Gül's transparent conduct earned the country's respect. The holder of a doctorate in economics and a one-time deputy premier under the government that was ousted by the 1997 coup, he is arguably one of the most levelheaded members of the Islamist establishment. Certainly he kept remarkably cool in the face of scathing verbal sallies against his government by senior military officers and their allies, including judges, who have been warning the public against the Islamist peril, albeit to reactions of ridicule and ire more than concern and support.

The military issued its warning via the chief of the General Staff at the beginning of January. In a speech citing the usual concerns about "national security," he attacked the government's Cyprus and EU policies and above all condemned the possibility of Islamic rule. While established opinion makers voiced little backing for the general's minatory message, the possibility of confrontations with the military will in all probability linger, and this may not be a bad thing. Contrary to what many believe, at some stages of democratization open confrontation may be healthier than a paper-thin, basically phony consensus. An opportunity for the kind of salutary face-off I am talking about could come when the AKP government finally decides to tackle the hot issue of headscarf-wearing by women in universities and the public domain. There has already been one uproar, which arose when the speaker of parliament took his headscarfed wife along to see the president off on a trip.

The AKP faces a formidable challenge, and it is itself a formidable challenge for the established order of the Turkish Republic. Partly this is a result of a conflation of socioeconomic and cultural cleavages that causes symbols such as the headscarf to take on extraordinary political significance. Many doubt the sincerity of the AKP's recent democratic conversion, citing the party's Islamist lineage and the religiously conservative character of its leadership. But this is the wrong line of argument. As Dankwart A. Rustow reminds us in the ur-text of democratization studies, "we should allow for the possibility that circumstances may force, trick, lure or cajole nondemocrats into democratic behavior and that their beliefs may adjust in due course by some process of rationalization or adaptation."[14]

In truth, the AKP, if it continues to hold together, has a historic task and opportunity to be the agent of Turkey's transformation from a spotty and in too many ways illiberal democracy into a fully fledged specimen of the liberal democratic breed. It is worth noting that Turkey's political tradition mostly precludes political liberalism. The Islamist movement is no exception. However, the only way for this party to survive in power and endure is through a liberal transformation of the Turkish polity and its civilianization. This explains why the AKP's drive for EU accession is genuine: It is a matter of enlightened self-interest, and the party clearly knows it. As the events of early 2003 regarding Iraq made clear, the EU is in a state of internal disarray that could render Turkey's goal of full membership very elusive. Moreover, the Iraq war, even as it rehabilitates Turkey's prime strategic value, could harm the cause of democratization. The record shows that when Turkey collects high strategic rents, its democracy is liable to suffer.

The AKP's success or failure at the mission described above will have ramifications far beyond the consolidation of liberal democracy in Turkey. If the communitarian-liberal synthesis works and Turkey's decent secular principles can be rescued from their essentially extrinsic yet historically stubborn entanglement with authoritarianism, if Turkey's Islamic movement reconciles itself to a secularism grounded not only in worry about the dangers of politicized religion but also in an honest desire to protect religion's own integrity and dignity, if the military can at last be brought to see that it is time to let its inordinate political involvements "go gentle into that good night," then the Turkish political system will have managed to remodel itself along democratic lines. Finally, the success of AKP will also and at last make of Turkey what the country had always sought to be: a modern, democratic, secular model for the rest of the Muslim world.

The ingredients are there for the experiment to succeed. As Erik-Jan Zürcher has noted, "Perhaps the greatest success of Turkey's modernizing elite is the very fact that it has lost its monopoly of the political and cultural debate. Through the spread of higher education and wealth there has come into being a large and vocal middle class, important parts of which no longer regard a strong religious identity and a modern way of life as incompatible."[15] To take the measure of what could happen if the AKP fails to become the agent of such a transformation, or if the established elite finds a way to spoil it, one need only look at the nihilistic populism of Cem Uzan and his GP and wonder what might be waiting in the wings.

The challenge and the choice, as always, are Turkey's own.

## NOTES

1. Tarhan Erdem, "Seçmen Profili" (Voter profile), *Radikal* (Istanbul), 6 November 2002, 4.

2. Yılmaz Esmer, "Postelection Analysis," [in Turkish], *Milliyet* (Istanbul), 15–19 November 2002.

3. Ahmet Önsel, "Normalizing Democracy and Modern Traditionalism," [in Turkish], *Birikim,* November–December 2002, 22.

4. Serhan Çevik, "Rock the Vote, *Morgan Stanley Sovereign Research, Europe* (London), 31 October 2002, 2.

5. Guillermo O'Donnell, "Illusions About Consolidation," *Journal of Democracy* 7 (April 1996): 35.

6. Guillermo O'Donnell, "Illusions About Consolidation," 41.

7. On the coup itself and the larger issues of "military politics," see Gareth Jenkins, "Context and Circumstance: The Turkish Military and Politics," *Adelphi Paper* 337, International Institute for Strategic Studies, London, 2001; Cengiz Çandar, "Redefining Turkey's Political Center," *Journal of Democracy* 10 (October 1999): 129–41; and Ümit Cizre, "Demythologizing the National Security Syndrome: The Case of Turkey," *Middle East Journal* 57 (Spring 2003, forthcoming).

8. Ümit Cizre, "From Ruler to Pariah: The Life and Times of TPP [True Path Party]," *Turkish Studies* 3 (Spring 2002): 93.

9. Tuncay Özkan, *Operasyon* (Istanbul: Doğan Yayıncılık, 2000).

10. Paul Kubicek, "The Earthquake, Civil Society, and Political Change in Turkey: Assessment and Comparison with Eastern Europe," *Political Studies* 50 (September 2002): 762.

11. Paul Kubicek, "The Earthquake, Civil Society, and Political Change," 766.

12. Ilter Turan, "Short-Term Pains for Long-Term Pleasures," *Private View* 11 (Spring 2002): 16.

13. Güven Sak, "Recent Gains and the Challenges Ahead," *Private View* 11 (Spring 2002): 24.

14. Dankwart A. Rustow, "Transitions to Democracy: Toward a Dynamic Model," in Lisa Anderson, ed., *Transitions to Democracy* (New York: Columbia University Press, 1999), 20.

15. Erik-Jan Zürcher, "The Rise and Fall of 'Modern' Turkey," (review of Bernard Lewis, *The Emergence of Modern Turkey*), *Turkology Update,* Leiden Project Working Papers Archive, Department of Turkish Studies, Leiden University, The Netherlands (available online at *www.let.leidenuniv.nl/tcimo/tulp/Research/Lewis.htm*).

# 19

# TURKEY AT THE POLLS: A NEW PATH EMERGES

## Ziya Öniş and E. Fuat Keyman

**Ziya Öniş** *is professor of international relations at Koç University in Istanbul. He is the author of* State and Market: The Political Economy of Turkey in Comparative Perspective *(1998) and the co-editor of* Turkey's Economy in Crisis *(forthcoming).* **E. Fuat Keyman** *is an associate professor of international relations at Koç University. He is the author of* Turkey and Radical Democracy *(2000) and the co-editor of* Challenges to Citizenship in a Globalizing World *(forthcoming). This essay originally appeared in the April 2003 issue of the* Journal of Democracy.

The seismic Turkish election of 3 November 2002 was a peaceful, democratic expression of the deep anger felt by Turkish voters toward a political establishment known more for economic populism, clientelism, and corruption than for democratic accountability. Voters turned the tables on the established political class by completely reordering Turkey's parliament and political landscape, bringing the Islamic-rooted Justice and Development Party (AKP) 363 of the 541 elected seats in the unicameral Grand National Assembly, and leaving every other party except Kemal Atatürk's old Republican People's Party (CHP, 178 seats) shut completely out of that institution.

Admittedly and somewhat ironically, the clarity of this democratic verdict was enhanced by the undemocratic 10 percent national threshold, which excluded all of the AKP's and CHP's competitors and gave each of the two successful parties a huge seat bonus: The AKP wound up with two-thirds of parliament on the basis of slightly more than a third of the popular vote, while the CHP gained the remaining third of the legislature's seats with less than a fifth of the total votes cast. And yet producing such a clear two-party verdict was just what the Turkish electoral rules—written into the constitution by Turkey's most recent military government as it prepared to cede control back to civilians in the early 1980s—were designed to do, though in the past had never managed to, giving rise to a series of complicated and sometimes shaky multiparty coalition governments instead.

By 2002, having endured for years the terrible and chronic damage that such problematic governments could do to effective governance and accountability, the voters were ready to cry "Enough!" and to opt instead for a ruling structure that offered the prospect of being more responsive to society and its needs. As a further consequence of these dynamics, the victory of the AKP was welcomed across the various segments of Turkish society despite what some Turks see as that party's questionable provenance: The AKP is one of two parties that succeeded the Islamist-oriented Virtue (Fazilet) Party after the Constitutional Court banned it as a threat to the secular foundations of the Turkish Republic.

Is the postelection optimism about the AKP justified? How successful will the party be at governing Turkey's 68 million people effectively and democratically? How adept will it prove at addressing the problems of joblessness, poverty, and economic growth? To answer these questions, one must analyze both the unique historical circumstances in which the November 2002 voting took place and the AKP's methods of presenting itself to voters and mobilizing support. In our opinion, the key to understanding the events of last fall lies in the insights offered by sociology and the study of political economy. Such an approach, we believe, allows one to assess the AKP without ideological prejudice and yet also to take a sober view of the internal contradictions, inherent limitations, and democratic shortfalls that may rise in salience as this new and largely untested party goes from campaigning as a challenger to governing the Turkish Republic with a decisive parliamentary majority.

## A Peculiar Election

Why did Turkish politics come to a turning point in the fall of 2002 when the next regularly scheduled parliamentary election was not even due to be held until the spring of 2004? How did the AKP benefit—both generally and through its own deliberate actions—from this situation? The answer is twofold, and goes to the heart of what made the 2002 vote so different from previous elections, such as those of 1995 and 1999. First, the central issue was not Kurdish nationalism or political Islam, but the troubled economy. In both 1995 and 1999, parties had relatively little room for political maneuver since the race was dominated by the question of how best to protect the secular and unitary foundations of the Republic against perceived threats from Islamist and Kurdish sources. The prosaic business of proposing ways to solve the problems and meet the needs of society took second place to dramatic questions of state security and political stability. The parties that fared the best, including the Democratic Left Party (DSP) and the Nationalist Action Party (MHP), had state-centered or nationalist agendas.

Second, while the principal *dramatis personae* of the 1995 and 1999 elections were political parties and the state or its organs, the 2002 results were swayed not only by parties but by nonstate actors such as economic pressure groups, civil society organizations, and even international institutions such as the International Monetary Fund (IMF) and the European Union (EU). These indirect actors helped to shape the election by stressing the need for a strong and stable government. They also served as important discursive reference points amid which political parties could position themselves as they framed their own platforms. There seems to be little doubt that the presence of these nonstate actors was significant and favored the AKP and the CHP. The importance of the IMF and the EU (the latter of which Turkey still hopes to join, not least for the economic advantages membership will bring) signaled that the 2002 elections were not merely a national, but also a "globalized" affair with the economy at the center.[1]

The distinctive themes of the 2002 election, in other words, were society and its prosperity rather than the state and its security. The reason for the shift is not hard to see: Recent years have seen the worst economic crisis in modern Turkish history. Every party had to explain how it would attack the devastating problems of economic contraction, unemployment, and poverty. The parlous state of the Turkish economy—and not ideology of any stripe, whether Islamist or otherwise—is what swept the AKP into power and swept all the established parties except the CHP completely out of parliament.

We should note, however, that the centrality of the economy in the minds of Turkish voters signaled neither an unquestioning commitment to the neoliberal ideology of free markets nor a longing for some kind of state-led national-development strategy. What Turks voted for was neither neoliberalism nor *dirigisme,* but rather the promise of an intermediate way between the extremes of freedom and regulation. Or to put this in terms that might seem more plainly relevant to most of the voting public, coping effectively with the crisis had to mean *both* promoting growth after years in which the economy had shrunk by close to 10 percent *and* targeting large and persistent pockets of poverty and unemployment. Economic growth is indispensable; so is social justice. The best chance of obtaining both, as the AKP leadership seems to grasp, is to have an effective state that can underwrite and safeguard a basically free but intelligently regulated market economy.

If this proposition sounds familiar, it should. In the current global context, it goes by the name of "the third way." Perhaps best known today as a concept associated with Tony Blair's New Labour government in Britain, third-way thinking represents an alternative approach to modernization that sees the political order, the economic order, and the question of social justice (including minimal standards of social welfare, distributive fairness, and respect for cultural differences) as

## TABLE—Percentages of Votes and Seats in Turkish Parliamentary Elections, 1983–2002

| Party | 1983 | | 1987 | | 1991 | | 1995 | | 1999 | | 2002 | |
|---|---|---|---|---|---|---|---|---|---|---|---|---|
| | % of Votes | % of Seats | % of Votes | % of Seats | % of Votes | % of Seats | % of Votes | % of Seats | % of Votes | % of Seats | % of Votes | % of Seats |
| Motherland Party (ANAP) | 45.2 | 52.9 | 36.3 | 64.9 | 24.0 | 25.6 | 19.7 | 24.0 | 13.2 | 15.6 | 5.1 | 0 |
| Nationalist Democracy Party (MPD) | 23.3 | 17.8 | - | - | - | - | - | - | - | - | - | - |
| Populist Party (HP)* | 30.5 | 29.3 | - | - | - | - | - | - | - | - | - | - |
| Social Democratic People's Party (SHP)* | - | - | 24.7 | 22.0 | 20.8 | 19.6 | - | - | - | - | - | - |
| Republican People's Party (CHP)* | - | - | - | - | - | - | 10.7 | 8.9 | 8.7 | 0 | 19.4 | 35.6 |
| True Path Party (DYP) | - | - | 19.1 | 13.1 | 27.0 | 39.6 | 19.2 | 24.5 | 12.0 | 15.5 | 9.6 | 0 |
| Democratic Left Party (DSP) | - | - | 8.5 | 0 | 10.8 | 1.6 | 14.6 | 13.8 | 22.2 | 24.7* | 1.2 | 0 |
| Nationalist Action Party (MHP) | - | - | 2.9 | 0 | - | - | 8.2 | 0 | 18.0 | 23.5 | 8.3 | 0 |
| People's Democracy Party (HADEP/DEHAP)** | - | - | - | - | - | - | 4.5 | 0 | 4.8 | 0 | 6.2 | 0 |
| Welfare Party (RP)*** | - | - | 7.2 | 0 | 16.9 | 13.8 | 21.4 | 28.7 | - | - | - | - |
| Virtue Party (FP)*** | - | - | - | - | - | - | - | - | 15.4 | 20.2 | - | - |
| Justice and Development Party (AKP)*** | - | - | - | - | - | - | - | - | - | - | 34.3 | 72.6 |
| Youth Party (GP) | - | - | - | - | - | - | - | - | - | - | 7.2 | 0 |
| Felicity Party (SP)*** | - | - | - | - | - | - | - | - | - | - | 2.5 | 0 |

* In 1985, the HP merged into the SHP, which in turn was absorbed by the CHP prior to the 1995 elections.

** In the 2002 elections, the HADEP contested in conjunction with the Democratic People's Party (DEHAP) due to legal challenges.

*** The AKP and SP are both successors of the Virtue Party (outlawed in 2001), which was a successor to the Welfare Party (outlawed in 1998).

cooperating parts of a dynamic whole governed according to the principle of liberty under law. For Turkey as for other countries, the third way offers a method of handling the challenges with which our globalized age is confronting national societies.[2]

In light of the foregoing, it makes sense to say that what transpired in Turkey last November 3 was a delayed embrace of the global third way. Only those parties that adapted themselves to this new agenda fared well on that day. The rest found themselves sidelined with their futures gravely in doubt.

## How the AKP Succeeded

The centrality of economic issues, the salience of the third way, and the multiplicity of actors involved in the November 2002 election suggest insights into the AKP's victory (as well as the quantitative but not qualitative success of the CHP). The AKP strategy for winning support from the various segments of Turkish society had three dimensions. First, AKP leaders such as Istanbul mayor Recep Tayyip Erdoğan distanced their party from the Islamist label and sought to appeal to the widest possible swath of voters by presenting their party as a center-right formation that was ready to face the urgent problems of the Turkish economy with well-thought-out policies energetically pursued.

Second after this emphasis on competence over ideology was a message of integrity and fairness. Taking aim at things such as "the cronyism and corruption that have hobbled Turkey's banking and financial system for decades,"[3] the AKP argued that sustainable economic recovery could never happen without honesty and accountability in government. Party leaders also pointed out that respect for justice would require not only strict probity, but also the readiness to listen caringly to different segments of society, especially those hardest hit by job losses, poverty, and insecurity. The CHP, by contrast, did not seem as ready to listen and hewed to former economy minister and World Bank vice-president Kemal Derviş's unquestioning acceptance of IMF-mandated structural adjustment as the cornerstone of economic policy. The AKP shrewdly sharpened its difference with the CHP on this point, vowing to keep problems of "social and distributive injustice" at the center of its immediate concerns even if the IMF disapproved.

Third, the AKP said over and over that democracy constitutes the fundamental and effective basis for the long-term solution to Turkey's problems. Since the election, this heavy and special emphasis on democracy has continued to be a major theme in the AKP's discourse on the protection of individual rights and freedoms, as well as in its support for the additional internal reforms that will have to occur if Turkey is ever to accede to full EU membership.

These three themes—competence, integrity, and democracy—were the keys to the AKP's ability to forge organic links with society, convince voters that it was more center-right than Islamist, and win the election. These themes allowed the AKP convincingly to set itself apart from its rivals by: 1) charging that the three governing-coalition parties (DSP and MHP plus the Motherland Party [ANAP]) were too close to the state establishment and too distant from economic lobbying groups and civil society organizations; 2) assuring voters that a wholehearted commitment to democracy, secularism, and religious pluralism made the AKP decisively different from its Islamist forebears; and 3) suggesting that the CHP and Kemal Derviş were too technocratic and too worried about the IMF, yet not worried enough about social justice or the need to support the small and medium-sized enterprises that form the potentially most vibrant sector of the Turkish economy.

## A New Synthesis?

By adroitly highlighting these differences, the AKP built up its support rapidly, especially among the small and medium-scale businesspeople whose numbers and influence have made them a growing force in Turkish society. The AKP also established ties with the poor and mobilized civil-society organizations whose primary aims have less to do with economics than with promoting respect and recognition for Muslim believers. While support from this last set of groups was significant, it remains true that what put the AKP over the top was the economic crisis and voters' urgent desire for solutions to the problems of unemployment, poverty, and economic growth.

The program that the AKP put forward to win public confidence was a synthesis of communitarian (or conservative) and liberal elements. It has three main principles.

The first is an effective and "postdevelopmental" state that is democratic, transparent, and accountable to society, but at the same time "caring" and not afraid to play a role in overseeing the economy. A postdevelopmental state is neither the minimal state envisaged by neoliberalism nor the powerful state performing the dominant role in the economy that characterized the earlier era of import-substitution and planned development. Instead, it is a state that effectively contributes to the development of a free-market economy without actually repressing the market mechanism. In doing so, the postdevelopmental state aspires to play an important role in promoting both economic growth and distributive justice at the same time. In this context, the AKP claims that in its governing, not only will it change the existing state structure which is detached from society, blind to societal needs and demands, and therefore functions as a closed, ineffective and undemocratic system of rule, but also it will create an effective and postdevelopmental state.

The second major pillar of the AKP's approach to governance is a market that is regulated closely enough to keep it honest and to prevent destructive side effects and externalities, but with plenty of free space left for enterprise, innovation, and investment. In this sense, the AKP argues that it promotes a free-market economy and sees it as the basis for the growth that Turkey needs to become fully modernized, financially stable, and robustly industrialized.

Third and finally, there is social justice. To the AKP, this term refers both to the need for some basic level of fairness in the distribution of material goods and services and to the need for full equality of respect and recognition across Turkish society such that no citizen is treated invidiously on the grounds of religious affiliation or ethnocultural identity. Unlike the CHP, the AKP does not see the question of social justice as an indirect problem that will be solved when the primary challenge of economic growth has been met. To bolster its case, the AKP adopts its own version of the logic of indirectness by arguing that promoting fairness and equal respect is an oblique but effective way to foster the widespread social trust that every sophisticated modern economy requires.[4]

At its most general, the communitarian-liberal synthesis means reconciling the free market with community values, religious beliefs, societal norms, and local traditions. More concretely, the communitarian-liberal synthesis calls for a just society organized not on the basis of pure egotistical individualism, but according to the ideal of a democratically regulated state-society relationship in which the "thin" instrumental rationality of the free market is supplemented and guided by the "dense" moral context of what Prime Minister Abdullah Gül calls "moderate and democratic Muslim society."

## How the Center-Left Failed

At first glance, the CHP looks like the other big winner from last November's vote. Certainly the party's showing represented a huge improvement over 1999, when it failed to pass the 10 percent threshold and found itself shut out of parliament. To a degree, the CHP simply reaped the benefits of being an outsider at a time when angry voters were intent on "throwing the rascals out." Also helpful was the "new blood" brought by the highly respected technocrat Kemal Derviş, whose decision in the summer of 2002 to abandon his officially nonpartisan stance and join the CHP gave the party a renovated appearance even while its membership and views on policy remained basically unchanged. Although Derviş's strong identification with the IMF and structural adjustment alienated parts of the traditional CHP base, his presence on the ticket seems clearly to have drawn more voters than it drove away.

When one looks more closely, however, the CHP appears to have fumbled an opportunity so big that its failure as much as the AKP's success should be the headline story of the 2002 election. With voters hungry for change and desperate for a voice, the CHP misgauged the public mood and left a large vacuum that the AKP, to its credit, nimbly filled. What explains the CHP's blunder? First, the party failed to create a strong impression that it cared deeply about the daunting economic hardships and disparities with which voters had to cope. Derviş's vague references to "a social-liberal synthesis" were too little, too late. Second, CHP elites had never bothered to try and build up a grassroots structure that could come close to matching that of the AKP, and also could not rival the record that city governments run by the AKP's predecessor parties had compiled in the 1990s. The contrast between Derviş the former World Bank official and Erdoğan the ex-mayor of Istanbul sums up the asymmetry.

Second, the CHP has been slow to appeal to those who work for or own small and medium-sized enterprises (SMEs). Indeed, the failure of center-left, allegedly social-democratic parties to recruit SMEs into their electoral coalition has been notable for some time, and is another error of omission that Islamist parties have learned to exploit with great skill over the last decade or so.[5]

Third, the CHP suffered from its legacy of close ties to the tradition of Turkish statism, with all the taste for centralization, top-down decision making, and "establishmentarian" thinking this implies. The AKP took pains to show that it cared about the needs and hopes of society at large—including the nonmaterial aspirations for recognition that were at work in such highly charged questions as whether Muslim women can legally wear headscarves in certain public settings. The leaders of the CHP showed little sensitivity on this score and little desire to present innovative solutions to economic problems. On the interconnected issues of democratic reform and full EU membership, the CHP was and remains lukewarm: more or less officially supporting both, but without much energy or conviction.

It is probably not going too far to say that the AKP, in spite of its strong Islamist roots, has looked far more like a European social-democratic party of the "third way" type, repeatedly stressing its commitment to EU-related reforms and the goal of a pluralist and multicultural society both before and after November 3.[6] The CHP, meanwhile, has continued to appear stodgy and even archaic, impervious alike to changing local demands and shifting global dynamics. When one considers the intensity of the contacts that have taken place over the last few years between the CHP and its nominal European counterparts over EU-membership questions and the like, the stubborn passivity of the CHP becomes all the more baffling and paradoxical.

Perhaps part of the explanation for the CHP's hidebound character lies in its strongly hierarchical organization and lack of internal debate over key policy issues. As a result, there has been little challenge from within CHP ranks to the leadership's continuing preoccupation with a rather narrow and outdated notion of national sovereignty. Again, the AKP appears to be reaping the benefits of having taken a different road: It boasts a much wider streak of intraparty democracy and much livelier internal debates over key policy issues, and consequently has been consistently faster and smarter at the art of responding to changing public attitudes and political circumstances.

## Challenges for the AKP

The triumph of the communitarian-liberal ideal last November should not be taken lightly. At long last, it has given Turkey a chance for strong, stable, and responsive government—a chance that may not return soon, if it ever does. There is an opportunity to close the gap between an ineffective state and a changing society that remains one of the worst legacies of the 1990s, and to put political life on a more democratic footing. If this opening can be seized, Turkey's limping economy and all the hopes riding on it will enjoy much better prospects, and the EU will find the grounds on which it can deny Ankara full membership steadily dwindling as the Turkish Republic makes impressive strides toward democratic consolidation and material development.

But can the AKP pull it off? The obstacles are surely formidable, and spring from four major clusters of issues. First is the matter of dealings with the EU and the state of the Cyprus dispute. Second is the question of the IMF and the impact of its conditionalities on the future of Turkish economy. Third is the U.S.-led war against Saddam Hussein's Iraq and the state of Ankara's relations with Washington. Fourth are the unresolved questions that hang in the air between the Islamic-rooted AKP and the resolutely secular Turkish state establishment, particularly the armed forces but also the judicial system and the bureaucracy.

In the argot of political science, these issues are structural and not conjunctural: They touch on deep questions about the basic character of Turkey and its institutions, and they transcend the specific agenda of any particular government. The ones that touch on economics and foreign policy are the most urgent, and indeed are shaping politics in Turkey today.

As soon as it took office in November, the new AKP government began trying to face these challenges forcefully and squarely. With an EU summit slated for Copenhagen in December, the AKP found itself with the tough task of obtaining a definite date for Turkey's accession to full membership. While the AKP did convince the EU that it is not an Islamist formation but a center-right party that strongly supports secular government and the accession process, it received only a "conditional" rather than a "determined" date on which negotiations are to begin, and for 2004 rather than 2003. In the meantime, Turkey is to continue the process of meeting the standards for EU membership laid down at Copenhagen. Turkey has already managed to accomplish important legal changes involving the abolition of capital punishment and the protection of individual rights and freedoms—a key component of which is the granting to minorities the right to express their own cultural identities—in the period leading to the Copenhagen Summit. What is critical from the EU perspective, however, is the proper implementation of these pathbreaking changes.

While the Copenhagen decision was a step forward, the EU could have made the AKP government's work much easier by sending a stronger signal such as a December 2003 conditional date. As it is, Prime Minister Gül and his cabinet must take their half-a-loaf from Copenhagen and push on with the economic program while also making complex, high-stakes decisions regarding Iraq and the dispute-ridden island of Cyprus, where thousands of Turkish troops remain in a northern republic whose government is officially recognized by no capital in the world besides Ankara.

The Copenhagen Summit showed clearly that the possibility of Turkey's accession to Europe depends on the resolution of the Cyprus conflict. Both the application of the Copenhagen criteria, which will mean the end of the strong-state tradition in Turkey, and the Cyprus conflict pose a great challenge to the AKP. And yet it is fair to say that far more than its rivals (including the CHP), the AKP has shown itself ready to move ahead with both the EU-related democratization agenda and innovative solutions to the Cyprus dispute (such as the plan offered by UN secretary-general Kofi Annan).[7] Nevertheless, both issues could create grave tensions in Ankara: There is a serious gap between the AKP's pragmatism and the intense concern for sovereignty that has long been a staple of the Turkish state, and the EU's failure to do more to support Turkey's domestic "pro-EU coalition" is not helping.[8]

Similarly, the AKP's support for the U.S.-led war against Saddam Hussein's regime in Iraq could create a split between the party's leaders and their constituents, especially if it produces problematic results such as the rise of a full-fledged Kurdish state or states in northern Iraq.[9] By the very nature of the case, Turkey's possible direct involvement in a war against another Muslim country would seem to be almost uniquely troublesome for the Islamic-rooted AKP. While the fallout from an invasion remains unknowable at the time of this writing, the stakes are clearly very high for the AKP in particular as well as for Turkey and the region in general. The Gül government stated fairly early that it would support a UN-authorized invasion, and by late February was finishing its bargaining with Washington over the exact terms of Turkey's participation as a member of the "coalition of the willing" in a possible U.S.-led military operation even if no UN Security Council action beyond Resolution 1441 (passed unanimously in November 2002) were taken to sanction the use of force against Saddam Hussein. As the AKP government pressed hard for the best deal that it could get from the United States, one of Foreign Minister Yasar Yakiş's arguments almost surely consisted of pointing to the enormous risk of a domestic backlash that he and his colleagues would be running.

The third possible challenge for the AKP concerns the IMF. Simply put, any Turkish government has to cope with the IMF and the demands that come attached to its loans and credits. This is a fact of life in a developing-world country with a struggling economy, and the AKP government is no exception to the rule. The reality of structural-adjustment and other IMF conditionalities limits the AKP's maneuvering room vis-à-vis economic policy. Attempts by the AKP government to act on its aspirations toward greater social and distributive justice could make for rocky going with the IMF, as could efforts to stimulate activity by small and medium-sized enterprises if IMF officials see those efforts as a threat to macroeconomic stability. And yet both the AKP's principles and its voters call for action on those fronts, so a degree of friction with the IMF will have to be risked.

The formation of the AKP government has raised citizens' and investors' confidence in the economy. After so many years of unsteady or ineffectual coalitions, Turkey has finally elected a single-party government that strongly believes in economic reform, basically respects the IMF framework, and wants full-fledged EU membership. The new government's obvious sense of purpose and resolve helped to lower interest rates and boosted the prospects of economic recovery and a reduced debt burden (Turkey's current debts are massive). But all honeymoons must draw to a close, and the AKP's ended around New Year's 2003 as investors at home and abroad became increasingly concerned about what they saw as a lack of coherence in government policy plus certain deviations from key IMF norms. Exhibit A was parliament's credibility-damaging failure, amid splits in top AKP ranks, to pass crucial corruption-fighting legislation designed to make the process of spending public money more transparent and accountable.

Similar snags have impeded progress in other spheres of economic reform. Critics point to insufficient government support for banking and finance regulators, to a decision to hike pension increases above the level of inflation without spelling out a noninflationary method of financing the raise, and so on. Clearly, the uncertainty surrounding the new government's handling of these and other highly sensitive economic issues has cost it some of its early political capital. Since economic policy is make-or-break territory for the AKP, the tensions that it has already felt between what its constituents demand and what the IMF and the financial community want must give party leaders pause.

Finally, dealings between the AKP and the state establishment could easily grow antagonistic. The likeliest flashpoint is the intensely fraught headscarf issue, which has become a high-profile vehicle for the tensions and anxieties that attend upon a predominantly Muslim society governed by a militantly secular state. Again, the AKP finds itself between a rock and a hard place: If it backs Muslim women who want to wear head coverings wherever they go, the secular elite will fear that political Islam has become dangerous, just as that elite feared six years ago when the military-dominated National Security Council forced the AKP's predecessor party to resign from the governing coalition.[10] Yet should the AKP ignore or straddle the issue, it will anger and disappoint its own most ardent supporters. Since the AKP's predecessors wound up being banned by the Constitutional Court after that body ruled that they had rejected the secular foundations of the Turkish Republic, the danger for the new government here is all too apparent.

During the winter of 2002–03, the AKP leadership focused single-mindedly on urgent economic and foreign policy issues, leaving sensitive topics such as the headscarf question for the future. Postponement is not resolution, however, and a large share of AKP voters clearly expects the government to defend the wearing of headscarves as a matter of right. Party leaders will remain wary, having learned the lesson of what the Kemalist state apparatus did to the AKP's predecessor parties when they waxed too "Islamic." The AKP is also well aware that the EU is watching, and has laid down its own markers regarding the conduct of Turkish domestic politics.[11] The EU's influence cuts two ways: While the nations of Europe endorse the expansion of religious freedom, they also dislike anything that smacks of "religious fundamentalism" and probably share the Turkish state's suspicion that the AKP is an Islamist faction rather than a "normal" center-right formation. Can the AKP thread this particular needle and craft a compromise on this "hot-button" identity issue that will both please its core supporters and stay safely within the "red lines" drawn by the EU and the secular Turkish establishment? Only time will tell.

Among other things, this uncertainty underlines the truth that while the AKP may be the sole party in government, it is not the only power in Turkey and is not yet capable of ruling according to its own economic, political, and cultural agenda. We know that the communitarian-liberal synthesis—or at least the aspiration toward it—succeeded at the polls in November 2002. What we do not know so far is whether it can be put into service as a program for actual governance. Electoral success is one thing; power is another. Will the former translate into the latter? The answer to that question will determine the nature of Turkish politics and the fate of the AKP in the uncertain months ahead.

The voters of Turkey have opened a door that may yet lead to economic stability and fuller democracy for their country. Whether these goals will be realized, however, depends not only on the AKP's willingness to govern democratically but also on society's will to keep up the momentum toward democratic consolidation. Significant challenges are likely to arise, notably in the domain of civil-military relations, the development of a pluralist civil society, and the promotion of intraparty democracy. The AKP cannot advance the cause of democratic consolidation on its own. It will need the help of society if Turkey is going to have any chance of avoiding the risks and reaping the fruits of its delayed encounter with the politics of the third way in the age of globalization.

## NOTES

1. For an attempt to understand the evolution of Turkish politics with explicit reference to complex interactions between global and local phenomena, see Ergun Özbudun and E. Fuat Keyman, "Cultural Globalization in Turkey: Actors, Discourses and Strategies," in Peter L. Berger and Samuel P. Huntington, eds., *Many Globalizations: Cultural Diversity in the Contemporary World* (New York: Oxford University Press, 2002), 296–319.

2. On the broad contours of "global third-way politics," see Anthony Giddens, ed., *The Global Third Way Debate* (Cambridge, England: Polity, 2001); Ulrich Beck, *The Reinvention of Politics: Rethinking Modernity in the Global Social Order* (Cambridge, England: Polity, 1997); and Will Hutton and Anthony Giddens, eds., *On the Edge: Living with Global Capitalism* (London: Vintage, 2000).

3. Owen Matthews, "After the Earthquake," *Newsweek,* 18 November 2002, 24.

4. Clearly, one can see direct parallels here between the broad program of the AKP and the "third way critique" of neoliberal orthodoxy or the emerging "Post-Washington consensus" as expounded by Joseph Stiglitz, for example. See Stiglitz, "An Agenda for Development for the Twenty-First Century," in Anthony Giddens, ed., *The Global Third Way Debate* (Cambridge, England: Polity, 2001), 340–57.

5. For an elaboration of this point, see Ziya Öniş, "The Political Economy of Islamic Resurgence in Turkey: The Rise of the Welfare Party in Perspective," *Third World Quarterly* 18 (September 1997): 743–66.

6. On the basic economic and cultural principles underlying "third way" politics in Europe and an accompanying analysis of the challenges facing new-model social-democratic parties in Europe, see Anthony Giddens, *The Third Way and Its Critiques* (Cambridge, England: Polity, 2000).

7. The comprehensive plan prepared by UN secretary-general Kofi Annan was an attempt to provide a mutually satisfying solution to the Cyprus dispute for all actors involved. The details of the plan are available at *www.mfa.gov.tr/grupa/ad/annan.doc.*

8. For an analysis of the profound impact of the EU Council's decision at the Helsinki Summit of December 1999 to recognize Turkey as a candidate country on the subsequent course of Turkish domestic politics, see Ziya Öniş, "Domestic Politics, International Norms and Challenges to the State: Turkey-EU Relations in the Post-Helsinki Era," *Turkish Studies* 4 (Spring 2003, forthcoming).

9. On the Kurdish issue in Turkish politics, see Doğu Ergil, "The Kurdish Question in Turkey," *Journal of Democracy* 11 (July 2000): 122–35.

10. See Cengiz Çandar, "Redefining Turkey's Political Center," *Journal of Democracy* 10 (October 1999): 129–41.

11. On the sociological basis of Islamic resurgence in Turkey and the role that the EU has played in transforming political Islam in Turkey into a moderate force, see Ziya Öniş, "Political Islam at the Crossroads: From Hegemony to Co-existence," *Contemporary Politics* 7 (December 2001): 281–98.

# III

## Islam and Democracy

# 20

# MUSLIMS AND DEMOCRACY

*Abdou Filali-Ansary*

**Abdou Filali-Ansary** *is editor of the Moroccan quarterly* Prologues: revue maghrébine du livre, *a French-Arabic journal of philosophy, literature, and the social sciences based in Casablanca. He is the editor of the volume* Réformer l'Islam? Une introduction aux débats contemporains *(2003). The present essay, which originally appeared in the July 1999 issue of the* Journal of Democracy, *is based on a talk presented on 13 January 1999 at the International Forum for Democratic Studies in Washington, D.C.*

The past is often held to weigh especially heavily on Muslim countries, particularly as regards their present-day receptivity to democracy. I do not dispute that past history has had an overwhelming and decisive influence in shaping the contemporary features and attitudes of Muslim societies. But the past that is most relevant today is not, as is commonly thought, the early centuries of Islamic history, but rather the nineteenth-century encounter of Muslims with the modernizing West.

It is widely believed that the key to understanding contemporary Muslim societies is to be found in a structure of beliefs and traditions that was devised and implemented at (or shortly after) the moment at which they adopted Islam. This view, often labeled as "Muslim exceptionalism," holds that these societies are, as Ernest Gellner has elegantly put it, permeated by an "implicit constitution" providing a "blueprint" of the social order.[1] This view has been subjected to intense criticism by a number of scholars, but it still influences dominant attitudes in academia and, with much more devastating effects, in the media.

This theory rests on two assumptions: first, that the past is ever-present and is much more determining than present-day conditions; and second, that the character of Muslim societies has been determined by a specific and remote period in their past during which the social and political order that continues to guide them was established. This past has allegedly acquired such a strong grip that it can—and does—chan-

nel, limit, or even block the effects of technological, economic, or social change. In other words, for Muslims alone a remote past has defined,
forever and without any possibility of evolution, the ways in which fundamental issues are perceived and addressed. The ultimate conclusion
lurking behind these considerations is that, due to the overwhelming
presence and influence of that particular part of their past, the societies
in question are incapable of democratization. In other societies history
may take the form of continual change, but in Muslim ones history is
bound to repeat itself.

Apart from the many other criticisms that have been directed against
this set of views, it should be emphasized that it is not based on any
solid historical knowledge about the way in which this "implicit constitution" was shaped and implemented or imposed. Some of its proponents
refer to a normative system that was never really enacted: They invoke
the model of the "rightly guided" caliphate, which lasted, at most, for
about three decades after the death of the Prophet. Many others cite
instead the social order that prevailed during the Middle Ages in societies where Muslims were a majority or where political regimes were
established in the name of Islam. In both of these versions, however,
the power of this past to determine the present remains, by and large,
mysterious. It is simply taken for granted, with no explanation given
about why the past has had such a far-reaching and pervasive effect in
these societies. To understand how the belief in these misconceptions
was born and came to influence contemporary attitudes so powerfully,
we must turn to a particular moment in modern times—the beginning
and middle of the nineteenth century.

## A Tenacious Misunderstanding

The earliest intellectual encounters between Muslims and Europeans
in modern times took the form of sharp confrontations. Jamal-Eddin
Al-Afghani (1838–97), one of the first and most prominent Muslim
thinkers and activists in the struggle against despotism, became famous
for engaging in a controversy against European secularists. He acquired
a high reputation, especially for his efforts to refute European critics of
religion in general and of Islam in particular. An essay that he wrote in
reply to Ernest Renan bore the title *"Ar-Rad 'ala ad-Dahriyin"* ("The
Answer to Temporalists"). He used the term *Dahriyin,* which literally
means "temporalists," to refer to secularists. The word itself, which is
of Koranic origin, had originally been applied to atheists. Al-Afghani
attacked the positivist ideologues of his century, who were deeply convinced that religion was responsible for social backwardness and
stagnation and that scientific progress would soon lead to its disappearance. Through his choice of terminology, Al-Afghani implicitly equated
these nineteenth-century positivists with the seventh-century opponents

of the Prophet. For Muslim readers, this formulation defined the terms of a large and enduring misunderstanding. From then on, secularism was seen as being intimately related to, if not simply the same thing as, atheism. The confusion was taken a step further when, some decades later, other Muslim authors wishing to coin a term for secularism, and either ignoring Al-Afghani's choice of the term *Dahriyin* or feeling that it was inappropriate, chose *ladini,* which literally means "nonreligious" or "areligious."

These initial choices of terminology gave birth to the opposition in the mind of Muslims between, on the one hand, the system of belief and the social order that they inherited and lived in, and on the other, the alternative adopted by the Europeans. Although the term *ladini* was replaced later by another, *'ilmani* ("this-worldly"), the bipolar opposition between the two views was already deeply entrenched. The feeling that has prevailed since then among Muslims is that there is a strict and irreducible opposition between two systems—Islam and non-Islam. To be a secularist has meant to abandon Islam, to reject altogether not only the religious faith but also its attendant morality and the traditions and rules that operate within Muslim societies. It therefore has been understood as a total alienation from the constituent elements of the Islamic personality and as a complete surrender to unbelief, immorality, and self-hatred, leading to a disavowal of the historic identity and civilization inherited from illustrious ancestors. It is worth noting that the vast majority of Muslims in the nineteenth century, even those who were part of the educated elite, lived in total ignorance both of the debates going on in Europe about religion and its role in the social order and of the historical changes reshaping European societies. They were not aware of the distinction between atheism and secularism. The consequences of this misunderstanding still profoundly shape the attitudes of Muslims today.

Thus secularism became known to Muslims for the first time through a controversy against those who were supposed to be their "hereditary enemies." The original distinction within Christianity between "regular" and "secular" members of the clergy,[2] which was the initial step in the long evolution toward the establishment of a separate secular sphere, had no equivalent in the Muslim context. Hence the choice of a term for the concept of secularism was decisive. In the latter part of the nineteenth century and early in the twentieth, the confrontation with the colonial powers, thought to be the carriers and defenders of a mixture of aggressive Christian proselytism and of the new secularism, played an important role in strengthening this dualism. In the diverse conflicts that local populations waged to defend their independence, identity and religion became intimately fused. The oppositions between local and intruder, between Muslim and European, between believer and secularist were, in one way or another, conflated. The resulting polarization came to dominate all attitudes and approaches to questions related to religion, politics, and the social order.

One of the most striking consequences of this evolution is that Islam now appears to be the religion that is most hostile to secularization and to modernity in general. Yet intrinsically, Islam would seem to be the religion closest to modern views and ideals, and thus the one that would most easily accommodate secularization. "The high culture form of Islam," writes Ernest Gellner, "is endowed with a number of features—unitarianism, a rule-ethic, individualism, scriptualism, puritanism, an egalitarian aversion to mediation and hierarchy, a fairly small load of magic—that are congruent, presumably, with requirements of modernity or modernisation."[3] In a similar vein, Mohamed Charfi observes that, on the level of principles, Islam should favor individual freedoms and the capacity for religious choice. The historical developments noted above, however, caused Muslim societies to evolve in the opposite direction—toward the loss of individual autonomy and total submission to the community and the state.[4]

This evolution gave birth at later stages to such dichotomies as "Islam and the West," "Islam and modernity," "Islam and human rights," "Islam and democracy," and others of the sort, which set the framework within which critical issues are addressed, whether in popular, journalistic, or even academic circles. This framework has imposed a particular way of raising questions and building conceptions, imprisoning attitudes in predefined and static formulas.[5] Muslim exceptionalism seems, therefore, to reside in the ways we raise questions about these matters. Although many studies on religion and its influence in the social and political spheres are undertaken in what were formerly referred to as Christian societies, nobody today poses the issue of "Christianity and democracy" in the same way that this question is formulated with respect to Islam. The fact that we still ask questions such as "Is Islam compatible with democracy?" shows how strong this polarization has become. It also shows that a dynamic was established, enabling the polarization that emerged in the nineteenth century to replicate itself as it extends to new fields or expresses itself in new terms.

## From Settlement to System

This polarization, which still determines the type of questions that can be asked, rests on two main prejudices: The first is that Islam is a "system," and should be treated as a structure of rules. The dubious character of this assumption has been clearly pointed out by the eminent scholar of comparative religion Wilfred Cantwell Smith: "[T]he term *nizam* [or] 'system,' is commonplace in the twentieth century in relation to Islam. This term, however, does not occur in the Koran, nor indeed does any word from this root; and there is some reason for wondering whether any Muslim ever used this concept religiously before modern times. The explicit notion that life should be or can be ordered according to a system, even an ideal one, and that it is the business of Islam to provide such a system, seems to be a modern idea (and perhaps a rather questionable one)."[6] Once Islam has been defined in this way, it can be used to assess whether other new or alien concepts can be accommodated within it and to decide the degree of their compatibility with its presumed and predefined content. This stance, however, reflects a particular attitude toward religion, not a particular feature of Islam. In fact, as Leonard Binder has observed, any of the monotheistic religions, if adopted in this manner, can lead to similar conclusions: "In the light of modern liberal democratic thought, Islam is no more, nor any less democratic than Christianity or Judaism. All three monotheistic religions, if proposed as constitutional foundations of the state, and if understood as providing an ineluctable authority for the guidance of all significant human choice, are undemocratic or non-democratic."[7]

The second prejudice is more insidious. It is based on the confusion of Islam as a religion with Islam as a civilization. This confusion is deeply entrenched, again because of prevailing linguistic usages both in Arabic and in European languages. For Islam, no distinction has been drawn comparable to that between "Christianity" and "Christendom." The same word was, and still is, used to refer both to a set of beliefs and rituals and to the life of the community of believers through time and space. Only recently, thanks to the work of historian Marshall G.S. Hodgson, has the necessity of drawing a sharp line between Islam and "Islamdom" been recognized as essential for explaining key phenomena in the history of Muslims.[8] Islamdom, in its golden age, was a social and political order built on norms adopted from Islamic sources but specifically adapted to the conditions of the time. (Only at a later stage were these formulated as explicit rules.) This enabled Muslims in the Middle Ages to create and maintain a world civilization attuned to the circumstances of the era.

Muslims at that time lived within polities bound by *shari'a,* yet did not consider the political regimes to which they were subjected to be in conformity with Islamic principles. The rulers were considered to be legal but not really legitimate. Even though they were not fully legitimate, they had to be obeyed, but only to avoid a greater evil, the *fitna* (the great rebellion or anarchy). For premodern societies of Muslims, the political model remained the early caliphate, which was not bound by *shari'a,* since *shari'a* had not yet been devised. The ideal was a kind of "republican" regime, where caliphs are chosen by members of the community rather than imposed by force, and where the behavior of rulers is clearly dedicated to serving the community instead of satisfying their personal ambitions. Nonetheless, Muslims came to understand that it was no longer possible to implement the fully legitimate system of *Khilafa rachida,* the virtuous or rightly guided caliphate, that the republican ideal was out of reach, and that they had to accept the rule of despots. They could, however, limit the extent of the power accorded to autocratic rulers by invoking *shari'a,* to which a sacred character had come to be attributed. In this way, at least some degree of autonomy from the political authorities, and minimal protection against arbitrariness, could be attained. This is what one may label the "medieval compromise" or "medieval settlement." The sacralization of *shari'a* achieved through this process led to another far-reaching consequence: Ever since, Islam has been seen as a set of eternal rules, standing over society and history, to be used as a standard for judging reality and behavior.

In fact, *shari'a* was never a system of law in the sense in which it is understood nowadays. As was noted by Fazlur Rahman: "Islamic law . . . is not strictly speaking law, since much of it embodies moral and quasi-moral precepts not enforceable in any court. Further, Islamic law, though a certain part of it came to be enforced almost uniformly throughout the Muslim world (and it is primarily this that bestowed homogeneity upon the entire Muslim world), is on closer examination a body of legal opinion or, as Santillana put it, 'an endless discussion on the duties of a Muslim' rather than a neatly formulated code or codes."[9]

What happened in the nineteenth century was the transformation of the medieval settlement into a system in the modern sense of the word. The duality of fact and norm was inverted, as *shari'a*-bound societies were confused with fully legitimate Muslim communities and deemed to be fully realizable through voluntary political action, whether of a peaceful or violent character. We see therefore how the confusion between a "model" and a historical system could arise and spread among Muslims at a time when they were confronted by the challenge of modern ideas. The typical attitudes of premodern Muslims had been based on a sharp distinction between the norm (of the virtuous or rightly guided caliphate) and the actual conditions (including the implementation of the *shari'a*) under which they lived. In the face of this duality, people adopted an attitude of resignation, accepting that the norm was, at least temporarily, out of reach. By contrast, some modern Muslims have elevated the actual conditions and rules under which their medieval forefathers lived to the status of a norm, and decided that they too have to live by these rules if they are to be true Muslims.

This has led to the contradictions of the present day: Secularization has been taking place for decades in Muslim societies, yet prevailing opinion opposes the concept of secularism and everything that comes with it (like modernity and democracy). As a historical process, secularization has so transformed life in Muslim societies that religion, or rather traditions built on religion, no longer supply the norms and rules that govern the social and political order. In almost all countries with substantial communities of Muslims, positive law has replaced *shari'a* (except with regard to matters of "personal status," and more specifically the status of women, where the traditional rules generally continue to be maintained). Modern institutions—nation-states, modern bureaucracies, political parties, labor unions, corporations, associations, educational systems—have been adopted everywhere, while traditional institutions are, at best, relegated to symbolic roles. Similarly, prevailing conceptions and attitudes of everyday life are founded on modern rationality and on doctrines influenced by science and philosophy rather than on traditional or premodern worldviews. Most Muslims now have come to accept the "disenchantment of the world," and this has profoundly transformed expectations and models of behavior within their societies. The evolution from the premodern attitude, combining resignation toward despotism with millennial hopes, to the typically modern combination of sharp political determination and desire for this-worldly progress, is clearly a visible consequence of these very changes, that is, of the secularization that has actually been going on in Muslim societies.

Secularism, however, continues to be rejected as an alien doctrine, allegedly imposed by the traditional enemies of Muslims and their indigenous accomplices. Islam is seen as an eternal and immutable system, encompassing every aspect of social organization and personal morality, and unalterably opposed to all conceptions and systems associated with modernity. This creates an artificial debate and an almost surrealist situation. The changes that are evident in the actual lives of individuals and groups are ignored, while ideological stances are maintained with great determination. Secularists and, more generally, social scientists are often pushed into adopting defensive positions or withdrawing altogether from public debates. Frequently they feel obliged to prove that they are not guilty of hostility toward religious belief, morality, and the achievements of Islamic civilization.

As Mohamed Charfi has pointed out, the policies adopted by some modern states under the influence of nationalist ideologies are partly responsible for this state of affairs. The education systems in many Muslim countries have taught Islam not as a religion, but as an identity and a legal and political system. The consequence is that Islam is presented both as irreducibly opposed to other kinds of self-identification or of social and political organization and as commanding certain specific attitudes regarding political and social matters.[10]

## Attitudes Toward Democracy

We saw that, as a consequence of the inversion of norms that occurred in Muslim societies during the nineteenth century, the traditional rules and usages grouped under the emblem of *shari'a* were transformed into a system and elevated into norms that define the "essence" of being Muslim—that is, simultaneously the ideal status and the specific identity of Muslims. Thus *shari'a*-bound societies are now equated with "truly" Islamic societies. Implementing the *shari'a* has become the slogan for those who seek a "return" to Islam in its original and pure form, which is held to embody the eternal truth and ultimate pattern for Muslims.

What could the status of democracy be in societies that have evolved in this manner? One first must perceive the difference between a question posed in this way, which attempts to interpret the actual evolution of particular societies and their prevailing conceptions, and the kinds of questions frequently asked by fundamentalists and by some scholars, such as "What is the status of democracy with regard to Islam?" This latter formulation posits Islam as a system that one can use to evaluate everything else.

One can discern two possible answers to the question of democracy as I have posed it. The first accepts the strict identification between Islam and *shari'a*-bound systems, and thus rules out any possible future for democracy in this particular environment. The second identifies democracy itself with a kind of religious faith or "mystical ideal." As Tim Niblock has noted: "The Middle East related literature purveys a romanticized conception of the nature and characteristics of liberal democracy. This occurs not through any explicit description of liberal democracy, but precisely through the absence of any analysis of the concept and its practical application. The concept hovers, like a mystical symbol, in the background of the discussion on democratization in the Middle East, with an implied assumption that liberal democracy constitutes an ideal polity where the common good is realized by means of the population deciding issues through the election of individuals who carry out the people's will."[11]

There even appears to be a certain trend toward adopting this second attitude. More and more fundamentalists accept the idea that Islam is not opposed to democracy; some argue that by embracing the principle of *shura* (or "consultation"), for example, Islam has always favored the kind of relationship between rulers and ruled that democracy entails. Democracy may even end up being described as a Western adaptation of an originally Islamic principle. Many fundamentalists are prepared to go as far as possible to support democracy—with the notable reservation that it should be maintained only within the limits set by *shari'a*. A "guided democracy" is the system envisioned by many fundamentalists and traditionalists of different sorts. Iran may be considered as a case where this kind of doctrine has been implemented. In addition to institutions common in all democracies, like elected parliaments and executives, it also has a high council of experts and a religious guide who are entrusted with ensuring that the laws and decisions made by democratically elected bodies are in conformity with religious principles and rules.

This shows how much popularity, or rather prestige, democracy enjoys within contemporary Muslim societies. The renowned contemporary philosopher Mohamed Abed Jabri has said that democracy is the only principle of political legitimacy which is acceptable nowadays in Muslim societies, whatever their religious beliefs and attitudes may be. "Revolutionary" alternatives that postpone the implementation of democracy until other conditions are realized no longer seem to be acceptable to the masses.[12] This support for democracy reflects in some cases a realistic recognition that it responds to the needs of contemporary societies, that it is indeed the only alternative that really works and makes possible the peaceful and rational management of public affairs. In many other cases, however, this newly favorable reception of democracy arises from its being viewed as another utopia.[13] While this may have certain immediate advantages, especially in contexts where democratic systems are in place or where democratization is under way, it may also encourage attitudes that are harmful to the longer-range prospects for democratization. For it may lead to democracy's being seen as an alien or unattainable ideal, and thus strengthen the idea that the Islamic alternative is more workable and better adapted to the conditions of Muslim societies. In other words, democracy may be treated in the same way as other modern ideologies, such as nationalism and socialism, that recently enjoyed a brief ascendancy in some Muslim countries. Both nationalism and socialism were indeed endowed with a quasi-religious aura; they were adopted as ultimate worldviews and total beliefs, and considered as magical remedies to all the ills and problems of society. This kind of approach would only deepen the initial misunderstanding on the part of Muslims of both secularization and democracy. The result would be to strengthen the view that Islam and democracy represent two irreducibly separate and opposing outlooks, even if some mixture of Islam and democracy were to be envisaged and tentatively implemented.

## Replacing Democracy with Its "Building Blocks"

What might be an appropriate strategy for democrats in this situation? For those who are convinced that democracy is not a new religion for humanity, but that it provides the most efficient means to limit abuses of power and protect individual freedoms, enabling individuals to seek their own path to personal accomplishment, there can be a variety of approaches. The most effective ones avoid the reified and "utopianized" version of democracy, either by highlighting such concepts as "good governance" or by supporting some of the "building blocks of democracy," that is, conceptions and systems that are linked to or part of democracy.

Replacing highly prestigious and, at the same time, highly contentious notions with terms that refer to easily understood facts and ideas is neither a retreat from conceptual clarity nor a defeatist position. A few years ago Mohamed Abed Jabri was bitterly attacked by a large number of Arab intellectuals for proposing to replace the slogan of secularization with such notions as rationality and democratization. Secularization, he contended, had become a charged issue for Arab public opinion because it was understood as being more or less equivalent to Westernization; its actual contents, however, such as rational management of collective affairs and democracy, could hardly be rejected once they were understood and accepted in their true meaning. In a similar vein, Niblock has observed: "Focusing on the 'big' issue of democratisation has detracted from the attention which can be given to a range of more specific issues which affect populations critically. Among these are the level of corruption, the effectiveness of bureaucratic organisation, the independence of the judiciary, the existence of well-conceived and clearly-articulated laws, freedom of expression, the respect given to minorities, attitudes to human rights issues, and the extent of inequalities which may create social disorder."[14]

In order to avoid a new and devastating misunderstanding that would present democracy as an alternative to religion and make its adoption appear to be a deviation from religious rectitude, it is essential to renounce quixotic confrontations and to accept some "tactical" concessions—especially when the use of appropriate terminology can bring greater clarification without sacrificing substance. Niblock's suggestion, stressing the importance of specific issues relevant to democracy, is one possible strategy, and it is certainly of real usefulness for the cases at hand. Yet it represents an external point of view, one that seems to be directed primarily at politicians and decision makers who attempt to influence political change in Muslim countries from the outside. It does not take into account the attitudes of Muslims themselves, and especially the need to foster their real acceptance and support of democracy. For this purpose, a more "conceptual" approach is required, one that would help present democracy in terms understandable and acceptable to Muslim publics, and thus bridge the gap between a "mystical" representation and a more realistic comprehension. It would answer the need for analytical terms that can clarify the conceptions and adjust the expectations of Muslims regarding democracy, and that can encourage the kind of *political* support that is equally distant from mythical or ideological fervor on the one hand, and egotistical or individualist attitudes on the other.

This approach, which should be understood not as an alternative but rather as a complement to the one proposed by Niblock, aims at clarifying the issue for a specific public that is influenced by particular worldviews and has expectations of its own. Finding the right terms is not easy. Interpretations of democracy and democratization are so rich and diverse that it may be difficult to reach a consensual view on the subject. All such interpretations, however, seem to point to some basic features as being essential conditions for achieving real democracy. It is possible to underscore at least three such conditions that seem to be required for the particular case of contemporary Muslim societies: 1) the updating of religious conceptions; 2) the rule of law; and 3) economic growth.

1) The *updating of religious conceptions* should be understood not in terms of the Reformation that occurred in sixteenth-century Christian Europe, but rather as the general evolution of religious attitudes that has affected Christians and Jews (except within limited circles of fundamentalists) since the seventeenth or eighteenth centuries and achieved its full effects only in the early decades of this century. The Reformation is a singular event in history, linked to a particular environment and to specific conditions. It cannot, as some observers are suggesting nowadays, be "replicated" in the context of another religion and under twentieth-century conditions.

There is, however, another process of change in religious attitudes that, although it first occurred in one particular environment, is of more universal scope and significance and seems to be related to modernization in general. This process leads the majority of the population to give religious dogmas a symbolic truth-value, and to consider religious narratives as contingent, historical manifestations or expressions of the sacred that are amenable to rational understanding and scientific scrutiny. Religious dogmas and narratives no longer define, in a monolithic way, people's ideas about the world and society, nor do they determine the views that believers are supposed to be guided by in their social and political interactions. This kind of "disenchantment" may discard the literal meaning of sacred words and rituals, but it maintains (and probably reinforces) the overall ethical and moral teachings. Religious attitudes are no longer defined in terms of a combination of strict observance of rituals and the adoption of premodern views, but rather as an informal but deeply felt adherence to principles of morality and a commitment to universal values. Faith becomes a matter of individual choice and commitment, not an obligation imposed upon all members of the community.

An evolution in this direction has proceeded quite far among Christians and Jews, but has made only limited headway among Muslims. The reification of Islam that began in the nineteenth century is the most important obstacle to such progress. Thus it is significant that a number of contemporary Muslim thinkers agree that new attitudes toward religion are now required both by a scrupulous interpretation of sacred sources and by modern conditions. Their teachings imply a strict separation between the sacred message of Islam and Muslim attempts to implement it in the course of history, including the political systems and legislation created in the "golden age." The Egyptian theologian Ali Abderraziq, for example, proposed to consider the early caliphate created by companions of the Prophet not as a religious institution but as a political one, amenable to critical scrutiny in the same way as any normal human institution.[15] Fazlur Rahman and Mohamed Mahmoud Taha suggested a tempered and modernized attitude toward revelation.[16] Mohamed Talbi and Mohamed Charfi introduced and defended a clear distinction between religious principles and the legal prescriptions devised in order to implement them.[17] This trend (if one can so label a collection of otherwise unrelated thinkers who come to similar conclusions) has received little coverage in the media. Its influence has also been restricted by the educational policies of modern states and by intimidation on the part of the fundamentalists.

2) The *rule of law* is a notion that expresses something that Muslims have longed for since the early phases of their history, and have felt to be part of the message of Islam. Muslim travelers to Europe in the nineteenth century were struck by Europeans' adhesion to rules and rule-bound behavior. This made some of them think that these societies were "Muslim" without being aware of it, as Islam was clearly identified with law-abiding attitudes. Fundamentalists claim that the only way of satisfying this aspiration for lawfulness is by implementing *shari'a,* which they present as the sole remedy for the arbitrariness and abuse of power common in most "Muslim" states. This argument can be countered by showing that the modern concept of "rule of law" is clearer, more operational, and easier to monitor, and thus that the dichotomy of "Islam (or rather *shari'a*) versus despotism" trumpeted by fundamentalist propaganda is not the whole story. Experience has revealed that law-abidingness is rather a feature of truly modernized societies, where individuals feel that they have a voice in the making of public decisions.

3) *Economic growth* here refers to the idea of continuous progress, which is a basic component of modernity, replacing the messianic hopes and political resignation dominant in premodern societies with the voluntarism and this-worldly resourcefulness of modern times. Democracy, as an expression of the free will of the citizens, cannot thrive if no collective will is allowed to surface or to have a say about the changes that society is compelled to undergo. It is the direct and visible expression of what Alain Touraine called modernization (in contrast with modernity)—that is, the process through which societies take control of their own affairs, mobilize their forces and their resources, and seek to determine the course of their destiny.[18] Economic growth offers the prospect of an improvement in the conditions of life, which seems to be

required in every modern society, and all the more so in "developing" ones. No prospect of democratization can be envisaged if no economic growth is actually taking place.

## Toward a Universal Rule of Law

It seems obvious that democracy cannot be exported, much less imposed on peoples who are not prepared to accept it and to mobilize themselves to implement it. If great numbers of Muslims today invoke religion rather than democracy as the alternative to despotism, and others consider democracy itself (at least implicitly) as a kind of new religious belief, this is not because of some special characteristics either of Islam or of Muslims. It is rather because of the particular historical circumstances that I have tried to explain. Muslim confrontations with European colonial powers in the nineteenth century gave birth to some great and lasting misunderstandings, as a result of which Muslims have rejected key aspects of modernity (secularization and, to some degree, democratization) as an alienation and a surrender of the historical self to the "Other."

For those who believe that "civilizations" are hard-core realities that last throughout history and that have distinctive and irreducible features, such polarization is understandable, being the "normal" course of history. It should therefore be treated as such, and the appropriate behavior would be to prepare to defend one's own civilization against alien ones in the unavoidable confrontations of the future.

For those, however, who believe that modern history has, for better or worse, put an end to the separate life of different cultures, there can be convergent paths to establishing social and political systems that promote individual freedoms, human rights, and social justice. These convergent paths point to the crucial importance of the international context and especially of the ongoing relationships between established and would-be democracies.

The fact that democracy has been adopted only in some countries (where it defines the ways their interests are promoted) and not in others creates an asymmetry. The collective interests of some communities, and not of others, find a channel for their expression, and therefore for the promotion of their particular national interests. The moral values that prevail within these communities will not prevail in their relationships with others. This asymmetry will fuel deeper antagonism between nations and greater resentment from those who are weaker. It is therefore time to call for a universal rule of law, where law is not considered only as a means for defending selfish national interests, but is respected for its own sake in a "Kantian" way.

We are living, much more than did our ancestors of the nineteenth and early twentieth centuries, in a deeply integrated world. Some form of a "universal rule of law," creating a new balance between the selfish interests of nations and universal principles, would ease the evolution we are seeking. It would help to define a framework—political, cultural, and economic—that is truly compatible with democratic ideals on the scale of humanity, and favorable to their wider acceptance.

## NOTES

1. "Islam is the blueprint of a social order. It holds that a set of rules exists, eternal, divinely ordained, and independent of the will of men, which defines the proper ordering of society. . . . In traditional Islam, no distinction is made between lawyer and common lawyer, and the roles of theologian and lawyer are conflated. Expertise on proper social arrangements, and on matters pertaining to God, are one and the same thing." Ernest Gellner, *Muslim Society* (Cambridge: Cambridge University Press, 1981), 1.

2. Those priests who belong to monastic order and live according to its rules are considered "regular" clergy, while those priests living in the world and not bound by monastic vows or rules are considered "secular" clergy.

3. Quoted by Samuel Huntington, "Democracy's Third Wave," in Marc F. Plattner and Larry Diamond, eds., *The Global Resurgence of Democracy* (Baltimore: Johns Hopkins University Press, 1993), 19.

4. Mohamed Charfi, *Islam et liberté: Le malentendu historique* (Paris: Albin Michel, 1998), 191.

5. Richard K. Khuri gives a very comprehensive description of the way this build-up was achieved. See Richard K. Khuri, *Freedom, Modernity and Islam: Toward a Creative Synthesis* (Syracuse, N.Y.: Syracuse University Press), 1998.

6. Wilfred Cantwell Smith, *The Meaning and End of Religion: A New Approach to the Religious Traditions of Mankind* (New York, 1962), 117.

7. Leonard Binder, "Exceptionalism and Authenticity: The Question of Islam and Democracy," *Arab Studies Journal* 6 (Spring 1998): 33–59.

8. Marshall G.S. Hodgson's main work is *The Venture of Islam,* 3 vols. (Chicago: University of Chicago Press, 1974). A summary of his conclusions appeared in a collection of articles published posthumously under the title *Rethinking World History: Essays on Europe, Islam and World History,* edited, with an introduction and a conclusion, by Edmund Burke, III (Cambridge: Cambridge University Press, 1993).

9. Fazlur Rahman, *Islam and Modernity: Transformation of an Intellectual Tradition* (Chicago: University of Chicago Press, 1982), 32.

10. Mohamed Charfi, *Islam et liberté,* 228.

11. Tim Niblock, "Democratisation: A Theoretical and Practical Debate," *The British Journal of Middle Eastern Studies* 25 (November 1998): 221–34.

12. Mohamed Abed Jabri, *Ad-Dimuqratiya wa Huquq al-Insan* [Democracy and Human Rights] (Beirut: Center for Arab Unity Studies, 1994).

13. Tim Niblock, "Democratisation," 226.

14. Tim Niblock, "Democratisation," 229.

15. Ali Abderraziq (1888–1966) attempted, in a famous and much-debated essay published in 1925, to dispel the misunderstanding and confusions surrounding religion and politics in Islam. His demonstration—for it was intended to be a rigorous demonstration—aimed at showing the strict separation between, on the one hand, religious principles and rules relating to social and political matters and, on the other, the laws and regulations made by theologians and political leaders to implement the faith in the temporal life of their community. He rejected the view, widely held among Sunni Muslims, that the end of the 'rightly guided' caliphate (approximately three decades after the death of the Prophet), which allegedly saw the replacement of the initially religious community by a regular polity and of a religious order by a secular or temporal order, constituted a really basic turn in the history of Muslims. The initiative of Ali Abderraziq was a founding moment in contemporary Muslim thought and politics. It did not succeed in dispelling the "big misunderstanding"; it is, however, the most radical attempt to show that a "new beginning" is possible for Muslims regarding such basic issues as the overall relation between faith and the social and political order. Ali Abderraziq, *L'Islam et les fondements du pouvoir* (Paris: La Découverte, 1994).

16. Fazlur Rahman did so in scholarly and measured terms, while Mohamed Mahmoud Taha wrote a kind of manifesto calling for a reversal of the order of prominence that Muslims give to Koranic verses: Mohamed Mahmoud Taha, *The Second Message of Islam,* Abdullahi Ahmed An-Na'im, trans. (Syracuse, N.Y.: Syracuse University Press, 1987).

17. For Mohamed Talbi, see *Plaidoyer pour un Islam moderne* (Casablanca: Le Fennec, 1996). For Mohamed Charfi, see *Islam et liberté*.

18. Alain Touraine, "Modernité et spécificités culturelles," in *Revue Internationale des Sciences Sociales* 118 (November 1988): 497–512.

# 21

# A HISTORICAL OVERVIEW

*Bernard Lewis*

**Bernard Lewis** *is Cleveland E. Dodge Professor (emeritus) of Near Eastern Studies at Princeton University. Formerly professor of history at the University of London, he is the author of many books, including* The Political Language of Islam *(1988) and* The Arabs in History *(1960). This essay, which originally appeared in the April 1996 issue of the* Journal of Democracy, *is based on remarks he delivered on 13 October 1995 at the International Forum for Democratic Studies in Washington, D.C. Copyright ©Bernard Lewis, 1996.*

In a necessarily brief discussion of major issues, it is fatally easy to go astray by misuse or misinterpretation of some of the words that one uses. Therefore, I ought to say first what I mean by the terms "Islam" and "liberal democracy."

Democracy nowadays is a word much used and even more misused. It has many meanings and has turned up in surprising places—the Spain of General Franco, the Greece of the colonels, the Pakistan of the generals, the Eastern Europe of the commissars—usually prefaced by some qualifying adjective such as "guided," "basic," "organic," "popular," or the like, which serves to dilute, deflect, or even to reverse the meaning of the word.

Another definition of democracy is embraced by those who claim that Islam itself is the only authentic democracy. This statement is perfectly true, *if* one accepts the notion of democracy presupposed by those who advance this view. Since it does not coincide with the definition of democracy that I take as the basis of this discussion, I will leave it aside as irrelevant for present purposes.

The kind of democracy I am talking about is none of these. By liberal democracy, I mean primarily the general method of choosing or removing governments that developed in England and then spread among English-speaking peoples and beyond.

In 1945, the victors of the Second World War imposed parliamentary democracy on the three major Axis powers. It survives in all three, precariously, perhaps, in one. In none of them has it yet confronted any crisis of truly major proportions. Among the Allies, Britain and France bequeathed their own brands of democracy—with varying success—to their former colonies during the postwar retreat from empire.

Perhaps the best rule of thumb by which one can judge the presence of the kind of democracy I mean is Samuel P. Huntington's dictum that you can call a country a democracy when it has made two consecutive, peaceful changes of government via free elections. By specifying *two* elections, Huntington rules out regimes that follow the procedure that one acute observer has called "one man, one vote, once." So I take democracy to mean a polity where the government can be changed by elections as opposed to one where elections are changed by the government.

Americans tend to see democracy and monarchy as antithetical terms. In Europe, however, democracy has fared better in constitutional monarchies than in republics. It is instructive to make a list of those countries in Europe where democracy has developed steadily and without interruption over a long period, and where there is every prospect that it will continue to do so in the foreseeable future. The list of such countries is short and all but one of them are monarchies. The one exception, Switzerland, is like the United States in that it is a special case due to special circumstances. In the French Republic, established by revolution more than two centuries ago, the march of democracy has been punctuated by interruptions, reverses, and digressions. In most of the other republics of Europe, and, for that matter, in the rest of the world, the record is incomparably worse.

In all this, there may be some lesson for the Middle East, where the dynastic principle is still remarkably strong. The most purely Arab and Muslim of Middle Eastern states, Saudi Arabia, derives its name and its identity from its founding and ruling dynasty. So, too, did the Ottoman Empire—the most recent and by far the most enduring of all the Islamic empires. Even such radical revolutionary leaders as Hafiz al-Assad in Syria and Saddam Hussein in Iraq endeavor to secure the succession of their sons. In a political culture where the strain of dynastic legitimacy is so strong, democracy might in some places fare better by going with it rather than against it.

What of our other term, "Islam"? It too has multiple meanings. In one sense, it denotes a religion—a system of belief, worship, doctrine, ideals, and ideas—that belongs to the family of monotheistic, scriptural religions that includes Judaism and Christianity. In another sense, it means the whole civilization that has grown up under the aegis of that religion: something like what is meant by the once-common term "Christendom."

When we in the West today talk of Christian art, we mean votive art, religious art. If we talk of Islamic art, however, we mean any art produced by Muslims or even by non-Muslims within Islamic civilization. Indeed, one can still speak of Islamic astronomy and Islamic chemistry and Islamic mathematics, meaning astronomy, chemistry, and mathematics produced under the aegis of Islamic civilization. There is no corresponding "Christian" astronomy or chemistry or mathematics.

Each of these terms, Islam in the sense of a religion and Islam in the sense of a civilization, is itself subject to many variations. If we talk about Islam as a historical phenomenon, we are speaking of a community that now numbers more than a billion people, most of whom are spread along a vast arc stretching almost 10,000 miles from Morocco to Mindanao; that has a 14-century-long history; and that is the defining characteristic of the 53 sovereign states that currently belong to the Organization of the Islamic Conference (OIC). For obvious reasons, it is extremely difficult (though not impossible) to make any kind of valid generalization about a reality of such age, size, and complexity.

Even if we confine ourselves to speaking of Islam as a religion, significant distinctions must be drawn. First, there is what Muslims themselves would call the original, pristine, pure Islam of the Koran and the *hadith* (the traditions of the Prophet Mohammad) before it became corrupted by the backsliding of later generations. Second, there is the Islam of the doctors of the holy law, of the magnificent intellectual structure of classical Islamic jurisprudence and theology. Most recently, there is the neo-Islam of the so-called fundamentalists who introduce ideas unknown alike to the Koran, the *hadith*, or the classical doctrines of the faith.

Clearly this last version of Islam is incompatible with liberal democracy, as the fundamentalists themselves would be the first to say: they regard liberal democracy with contempt as a corrupt and corrupting form of government. They are willing to see it, at best, as an avenue to power, but an avenue that runs one way only.

## History and Tradition

What then of the two others—historic Islam and Islam as a system of ideas, practices, and cultural traits?

A first look at the historical record is not encouraging. Predominantly Muslim regions show very few functioning democracies. Indeed, of the 53 OIC states, only Turkey can pass Huntington's test of democracy, and it is in many ways a troubled democracy. Among the others, one can find democratic movements and in some cases even promising democratic developments, but one cannot really say that they are democracies even to the extent that the Turkish Republic is a democracy at the present time.

Throughout history, the overwhelmingly most common type of regime in the Islamic world has been autocracy—which is not to be confused with despotism. The dominant political tradition has long been that of command and obedience, and far from weakening it, modern times have actually witnessed its intensification. With traditional restraints on autocracy attenuated, and with new means of surveillance, repression, and wealth-extraction made available to rulers by modern technologies and methods, governments have become less dependent than ever on popular goodwill. This is particularly true of those governments that are enriched by revenues from oil. With no need for taxation, there is no pressure for representation.

Another noteworthy historical and cultural fact is the absence of the notion of citizenship. There is no word in Arabic, Persian, or Turkish for "citizen." The cognate term used in each language means only "compatriot" or "countryman." It has none of the connotations of the English word "citizen," which comes from the Latin *civis* and has the content of the Greek *politēs,* meaning one who participates in the affairs of the *polis.* The word is absent in Arabic and the other languages because the idea—of the citizen as participant, of citizenship as participation—is not there.

At the same time, however, we can discern elements in Islamic law and tradition that could assist the development of one or another form of democracy. Islam boasts a rich political literature. From the earliest times, doctors of the holy law, philosophers, jurists, and others have reflected carefully on the nature of political power, the ways in which political power ought to be acquired and used and may be forfeited, and the duties and responsibilities as well as the rights and privileges of those who hold it.

Islamic tradition strongly disapproves of arbitrary rule. The central institution of sovereignty in the traditional Islamic world, the caliphate, is defined by the Sunni jurists to have contractual and consensual features that distinguish caliphs from despots. The exercise of political power is conceived and presented as a contract, creating bonds of mutual obligation between the ruler and the ruled. Subjects are duty-bound to obey the ruler and carry out his orders, but the ruler also has duties toward the subject, similar to those set forth in most cultures.

The contract can be dissolved if the ruler fails to fulfill or ceases to be capable of fulfilling his obligations. Although rare, there have been instances when such dissolutions took place. There is, therefore, also an element of consent in the traditional Islamic view of government.

Many *hadith* prescribe obedience as an obligation of a subject, but some indicate exceptions. One, for example, says, "Do not obey a creature against his creator"—in other words, do not obey a human command to violate divine law. Another says, similarly, "There is no duty of obedience in sin." That is to say, if the sovereign commands something that is sinful, the duty of obedience lapses. It is worth noting that Prophetic utterances like these point not merely to a *right* of disobedience (such as would be familiar from Western political thought), but to a divinely ordained *duty* of disobedience.

When we descend from the level of principle to the realm of what has actually happened, the story is of course checkered. Still, the central point remains: There are elements in Islamic culture that could favor the development of democratic institutions.

One of the sayings traditionally ascribed to the Prophet is the remark, "Difference of opinion within my community is a sign of God's mercy." In other words, diversity is something to be welcomed, not something to be suppressed. This attitude is typified by the acceptance by Sunni Muslims, even today, of four different schools of Islamic jurisprudence. Muslims believe the holy law to be divinely inspired and guided, yet there are four significantly different schools of thought regarding this law. The idea that it is possible to be orthodox even while differing creates a principle of the acceptance of diversity and of mutual tolerance of differences of opinion that surely cannot be bad for parliamentary government.

The final point worth mentioning in this inventory is Islam's emphasis on the twin qualities of dignity and humility. Subjects—even the humblest subjects—have personal dignity in the traditional Islamic view, and rulers must avoid arrogance. By Ottoman custom, when the sultan received the chief dignitaries of the state on holy days, he stood up to receive them as a sign of his respect for the law. When a new sultan was enthroned, he was greeted with cries of "Sultan, be not proud! God is greater than you!"

## The Influence of the West

For the first thousand years of its history, Islamic civilization's relationship to Christendom was one of dominance. The loss of Spain and Portugal on the remote western periphery had little impact in the heartlands of Islam, and was more than compensated by the advance toward the heart of continental Europe. As late as 1683, an Ottoman army was encamped before the very gates of Vienna. Earlier in the seventeenth century, North African corsairs were raiding as far north as the British Isles. By the early nineteenth century, however, Islamic power was clearly in retreat as European power grew. Finding themselves the targets of conquest and colonization, Muslims naturally began to wonder what had gone wrong. Islam had always been generally "successful" in worldly terms. Unlike the founder of Christianity, who was crucified and whose followers saw their religion made the official faith of the Roman Empire only after centuries as a persecuted minority, Mohammad founded a state during his lifetime, and as ruler he collected taxes, dispensed justice, promulgated laws, commanded armies, and made war and peace.

Educated Muslims, chagrined by the newfound potency of their European rivals, asked: What are they doing right and what are we doing wrong, or not doing at all? Representative, constitutional government was high on the list. The nineteenth century saw the rise of elected assemblies in a number of Western countries, and democracy in our current sense was beginning to take hold. Many Muslims suspected that here—in this most exotic and alien of Western practices—lay the secret to the West's wealth and power, and hoped that the adoption of constitutions and the creation of elected legislatures in the Islamic world would redress the civilizational balance.

Getting used to the idea was not easy; the first Muslim visitors to the West disliked much of what they saw. The earliest detailed description of England by a Muslim traveller is a fascinating account by Mirza Abu Talib Khan, a Turko-Persian resident of Lucknow who was in England between 1798 and 1803. He watched the House of Commons in action, and his comments are enlightening. The government and opposition MPs sitting on their benches facing each other across the chamber reminded him of trees full of parrots squawking at each other, a common sight back home in India. When he learned that the purpose of the noisy assemblage was to make laws, he was shocked. The English, he explained to his readers, had not accepted a divine law and so were reduced to the expedient of making their own laws, in accordance with the experience of their judges and the requirements of their time.

Later accounts were more positive. The first Egyptian student mission went to France in 1826. Their chaplain, a sheikh from al-Azhar, learned a great deal (probably more than his student wards) and wrote a remarkable book about Paris. In it he discusses the National Assembly and the freedom of the press, among other things, and makes the very astute observation that the French, when they speak of freedom, mean roughly what Muslims are getting at when they talk of justice. With this insight, he cuts right to the heart of a key difference between European political culture and its Islamic counterpart.

To Muslims, the use of "freedom" as a political term was an imported novelty, dating only from the time of the French Revolution and General Napoleon Bonaparte's arrival in Egypt in 1798. Before that, it had only legal and social connotations, and meant simply the condition of not being a slave. For Muslim thinkers, as the sheikh from al-Azhar implied, justice is the ideal, the touchstone by which one distinguishes good governments from bad.

By the latter part of the nineteenth century, Islamic rulers were coming to think of a constitution as something that no well-dressed nation could afford to be without. Just as gentlemen were abandoning traditional garb in favor of Western-style frock coats, neckties, and trousers, so the state would sport a constitution and an elected legislature as essential accoutrements.

Yet the idea of freedom—understood as the ability to participate in the formation, the conduct, and even the lawful removal and replacement of government—remained alien. This notion, which belongs to the inner logic of constitutionalism and parliamentarism, is obviously a troublesome one for dynastic autocracies, which can hardly accept it and remain what they are. The real question, then, was whether constitutions, elections, and parliaments—the institutional trappings of democracy—would be only that, or would actually become means that the governed could use to gain some say in their government.

The first serious elections in the Islamic world were held to choose the parliament called for by the Ottoman Constitution of 1876. This parliament was no doubt meant to be a tame body that would supply the ceremonial ratification of the sultan's authority. But the Chamber of Deputies soon developed a mind of its own. On 13 February 1878, the deputies went so far as to demand that three ministers, against whom specific charges had been brought, should appear in the Chamber to defend themselves. The next day, in response, the sultan dissolved the parliament and sent its members home. It did not meet again until the year after the Young Turk Revolution of 1908. That phase, too, was of brief duration, and a military coup ended the stormy interval of parliamentary rule.

Since then, parliamentarism has not fared especially well in the Islamic world. All too often, elections are less a way of choosing a government than a ritual designed to ratify and symbolize a choice that has already been made by other means—something like a presidential inauguration in the United States or a coronation in Britain. This is not always so—there are intervals and cases where elections mean something, and they become more common in the record as one goes from the nineteenth into the twentieth century, in spite of (or perhaps because of) a number of dramatic moves in the opposite direction.

## A Rough Classification of Regimes

Another complication surrounding the term "freedom" is a legacy of imperialism. When outsiders ruled much, though not all, of the Islamic world, freedom came also, or even primarily, to mean communal or national independence, with no reference to the individual's status within the body politic.

Most of the countries in the Islamic world today are free from external domination, but not free internally: they have sovereignty, but lack democracy. This shared lack, however, does not preclude the existence of very great differences among them. Predominantly Muslim societies (Turkey, as we saw earlier, being the great exception) are ruled by a wide variety of authoritarian, autocratic, despotic, tyrannical, and totalitarian regimes. A rough classification would include five categories.

*1) Traditional autocracies.* These are the countries, like Saudi Arabia and the Gulf sheikhdoms, where established dynastic regimes rest on the traditional props of usage, custom, and history. These regimes are firmly authoritarian in character, but the same traditions that sustain them also bind them: their legitimacy relies heavily on acceptance, and too much open repression would shatter it. Their props are not quite what they used to be, however, having been partly undermined by new ideas and forces. The rulers use modern devices to help maintain themselves, but the same devices—especially electronic communications media—are now also available to those who would overthrow the existing order.

The Iranian Revolution, which overthrew the Shah in 1979, was the first electronic revolution in history. It will not be the last. Ayatollah Khomeini could do nothing while he was in Iran, and very little from nearby Iraq. But when he went to Paris and began recording cassette tapes and calling Iran via the direct-dial telephone system that the Shah had installed, he reached a vast audience, with results we know all too well. Satellite television, the fax machine, and electronic mail can all carry the message of subversion in ways difficult to prevent or control. The methods used by the Islamic revolutionaries against the Shah are now being used—in a more sophisticated form—by those who seek to overthrow the Islamic Republic. Other dissident groups—ethnic, religious, ideological—are using the same methods against the regimes that rule in their countries.

*2) Modernizing autocracies.* These are regimes—one thinks of Jordan, Egypt, and Morocco in particular—that have their roots in traditional autocracy but are taking significant steps toward modernization and democratization. None really fits the description of liberal democracy as given above, but none is anything like a total autocracy, either. All three are moving toward greater freedom. Difficulties, setbacks, and problems may abound, but the basic direction of change is clear.

*3) Fascist-style dictatorships.* These regimes, especially the one-party Ba'athist governments in Hafiz al-Assad's Syria and Saddam Hussein's Iraq, are modeled on European fascism. In matters of precept, practice, and style, they owe a great deal to the example of Benito Mussolini and, to a lesser extent, Adolf Hitler.

*4) Radical Islamic regimes.* There are two of these so far, Iran and Sudan. There may be others to follow, perhaps in Afghanistan or Algeria, though the latter possibility now seems to be dwindling rather than growing. Egypt has a potent radical Islamic movement, but the Egyptian political class also has a remarkable knack for maintaining itself in power. Moreover, the threat to the sovereign state posed by pan-Islamic radicalism has been greatly exaggerated. Khomeini used to say that there were no frontiers in Islam, but he also stipulated in the constitution that the president of the Islamic Republic of Iran must be of Iranian birth and origin. In Khomeini's own practice, let alone that of his successors, the Iranian element remained paramount. Elsewhere, there is a similar disinclination among even the most fanatical Islamic groups to sink their national or territorial integrity into some larger whole.

5) *The Central Asian republics.* A final group of countries, classifiable more by history and geography than by regime type, are the six former Soviet republics with mostly Muslim populations, sometimes known nowadays as "the five 'stans" plus Azerbaijan. I can venture no characterization of the regimes in these countries, but will only observe that they seem to be having the same problems disentangling themselves from their former imperial masters as the Egyptians, North Africans, Syrians, and Iraqis had with their respective former masters earlier in this century. After the formal recognition of independence comes the postimperial hangover, a period of interference, unequal treaties, privileges, basing agreements, and so on. The big difference this time, of course, is that the former colonial peoples are dealing not with London or Paris, but with Moscow. This may give rise to different results.

## Muslims Outside the Middle East

There are also hundreds of millions of Muslims in South and Southeast Asia, but space limitations and my own relative ignorance of these lands lead me to offer only a brief and superficial impression of what is happening in them. Pakistan, Bangladesh, Malaysia, and Indonesia all appear to resemble Egypt or Morocco more than Syria or Iraq, which is encouraging. I say that the South Asian countries resemble the Middle Eastern or North African countries (and not vice versa) for a reason. There are almost as many Muslims in Indonesia, for example, as in the whole of the Arab world, but the lines of influence run from the latter to the former. The historical heartlands of Islam have hitherto enjoyed the kind of influence in the Islamic world that the outlying regions could rarely, if ever, achieve. With the overwhelming numerical preponderance of South and Southeast Asian Islam and the growing importance of the Islamic communities in the West, this may change.

Another relatively small group of Muslims who may matter a great deal are those adherents of Islam who have emigrated to non-Muslim countries in Western Europe and North America. These groups are extremely important, not so much because of what is happening in the countries of their present residence, as because of the impact that they have on their countries of origin. As Muslim minorities go, of course, they are a tiny handful. India's Muslim minority (equal to 11 percent of its total population) is by far the largest concentration of Muslims in a non-Muslim country. Indeed, only two other countries (Indonesia and Bangladesh) have more Muslims living within their borders. In the Middle East, there is a sizeable Muslim minority in Israel. Ethiopia, a

Christian country whose church traces its origins to apostolic times, has a significant Muslim minority, and many other countries in sub-Saharan Africa have Muslim majorities or substantial minorities.

There are also old Muslim minorities in Europe, in the Balkan states, and above all in the Russian Federation itself, which may be as much as 15 percent Muslim.

Like Khomeini amid the Iranian-exile community in the 1970s, some of the political groups that move among the new Muslim communities in Europe and North America are seeking to recruit support for struggles against those in power at home. The separatist movement of Turkish Kurds, for instance, is highly active among the Kurdish population in Germany. The Islamic-fundamentalist movement in North Africa collects money, buys weapons, and organizes in France, and various movements are now using the United States in the same way.

The vast majority of Muslim immigrants in Western Europe and North America, it should be noted, has no interest in extremist or revolutionary movements. On the contrary, these immigrants are increasingly taking part (sometimes as citizens) in the democratic processes of their adopted societies while remaining in touch with their countries of origin. The views that they form as a result of their experience of democracy may well be among the most significant factors shaping the political future of the Islamic world.

## Religion and the State

In Islam, as was mentioned above, there is from the beginning an interpenetration, almost an identification, of cult and power, or religion and the state: Mohammad was not only a prophet, but a ruler. In this respect, Islam resembles Old Testament Judaism and looks quite different from Christianity. Christianity, to repeat, began and endured for centuries under official persecution. Even after it became the state religion of Rome under the Emperor Constantine in the fourth century, a distinction was maintained between spiritual and temporal powers. Ever since then, all Christian states without exception have distinguished between throne and altar, church and state. The two powers might be closely associated, as under the caesaropapism of the Byzantine Empire, or they might be separated; they might work in harmony or they might come into conflict; one might dominate for a time and the other might displace it; but the duality remains, corresponding to the distinction in Christian Rome between *imperium* (imperial power) and *sacerdotium* (priestly power).

Islam in its classical form has no organizational equivalent. It has no clergy or clerical hierarchy in anything like the Christian sense of the word, and no ecclesiastical organization. The mosque is a building, not an institution in the sense that the church is. At least this was so until comparatively recently, for Khomeini during his rule seems to have effected a kind of "Christianization" of Iran's Islamic institutions, with himself as an infallible pope, and with the functional equivalent of a hierarchy of archbishops, bishops, and priests. All of this was totally alien to Islamic tradition, and thus constituted an "Islamic revolution" in a sense quite different from the one usually conveyed by references to Khomeini's legacy.

> *As a rule, gradual and unforced change is better than sudden and compulsory change. Democracy cannot be born like Aphrodite from the sea foam.*

Islamic civilization has produced a wealth of theological, philosophical, and juridical literature on virtually every aspect of the state, its powers, and its functions. What is not discussed to any great extent is the difference between religious and temporal powers. The words for "secular" and "secularism" in modern Islamic languages are either loanwords or neologisms. There are still no equivalents for the words "layman" and "laity." Jurists and other Muslim writers on politics have long recognized a distinction between state and religion, between the affairs of this world and those of the next. But this in no way corresponds to the dichotomy expressed in such Western pairs of terms as "spiritual" and "temporal," or "lay" and "ecclesiastical." Conceptually, this dichotomy simply did not arise. It has arisen now, and it may be that Muslims, having contracted a Christian illness, will consider a Christian remedy, that is to say, the separation of religion and the state.

Of course, I am well aware that the Reformation was a stage in the evolution of Christendom and the Enlightenment a stage in the history of Europe, and I am not suggesting that the past of the West can somehow be grafted onto the future of Islam. There is no reason whatever why the Muslims can or should be expected to follow precisely the same pattern, by the same route. If they take up the challenge at all, they will have to tackle it in their own way. So far, alas, there is little sign that they are willing to take it up, but one may hope.

Turkey alone has formally enacted the separation of religion and the state. Its constitution and laws declare it a secular republic. In many practical respects, however, Islam remains an important and indeed a growing factor in the Turkish polity and in the Turks' sense of their own identity.

As a rule, gradual and unforced change is better than sudden and compulsory change. Democracy cannot be born like Aphrodite from the sea foam. It comes in slow stages; for that reason, places like Egypt and Jordan, where there is evolution in a broadly democratic direction, seem to offer the best prospects. In Iraq and Syria, an overthrow of the present dictators is unlikely to lead to the immediate establishment of a workable democracy. The next change of regime in those countries will probably just produce less-brutal dictatorships, which might then evolve into reforming autocracies in the Egyptian or Jordanian style. That would not be democracy, but it would be a huge step forward nonetheless.

The places that offer the best prospects for democracy are those where there is a process of gradual change in the direction of freer institutions. Democracy usually evolves out of a movement toward freedom. The liberal democracies of the West certainly did not come about all at once. One need only think of the history of slavery in the United States or the disenfranchisement of women in most of the Western world to see that, even under favorable conditions, democratic progress takes time and effort and may be hard-won indeed.

Imperialist powers deprived most of the Islamic world of sovereignty; the prime demand, therefore, was for independence. Foreign rule was equated with tyranny, to be ended by whatever means possible. But tyranny means different things to different people. In the traditional Islamic system, the converse of tyranny is justice; in Western political thought, the converse of tyranny is freedom. At the present day, most Islamic countries are discovering that while they have gained independence, they enjoy neither justice nor freedom. There are some—and soon, perhaps, there will be many more—who see in democracy the surest way to attain both.

# 22

# TWO VISIONS OF REFORMATION

*Robin Wright*

**Robin Wright** *is global-affairs correspondent for the* Los Angeles Times *and former Middle East correspondent for the* Sunday Times *of London. She is author of* The Last Great Revolution: Turmoil and Transformation in Iran *(2001),* In the Name of God: The Khomeini Decade *(1990), and* Sacred Rage: The Wrath of Militant Islam *(1985). This essay originally appeared in the April 1996 issue of the* Journal of Democracy.

Of all the challenges facing democracy in the 1990s, one of the greatest lies in the Islamic world. Only a handful of the more than four dozen predominantly Muslim countries have made significant strides toward establishing democratic systems. Among this handful—including Albania, Bangladesh, Jordan, Kyrgyzstan, Lebanon, Mali, Pakistan, and Turkey—not one has yet achieved full, stable, or secure democracy. And the largest single regional bloc holding out against the global trend toward political pluralism comprises the Muslim countries of the Middle East and North Africa.

Yet the resistance to political change associated with the Islamic bloc is not necessarily a function of the Muslim faith. Indeed, the evidence indicates quite the reverse. Rulers in some of the most antidemocratic regimes in the Islamic world—such as Brunei, Indonesia, Iraq, Oman, Qatar, Syria, and Turkmenistan—are secular autocrats who refuse to share power with their brethren.

Overall, the obstacles to political pluralism in Islamic countries are not unlike the problems earlier faced in other parts of the world: secular ideologies such as Ba'athism in Iraq and Syria, Pancasila in Indonesia, or lingering communism in some former Soviet Central Asian states brook no real opposition. Ironically, many of these ideologies were adapted from the West; Ba'athism, for instance, was inspired by the European socialism of the 1930s and 1940s. Rigid government controls over everything from communications in Saudi Arabia and Brunei to foreign visitors in Uzbekistan and Indonesia also isolate their people from democratic ideas and debate on popular empowerment. In the largest and poorest Muslim countries, moreover, problems common to developing states, from illiteracy and disease to poverty, make simple survival a priority and render democratic politics a seeming luxury. Finally, like their non-Muslim neighbors in Asia and Africa, most Muslim societies have no local history of democracy on which to draw. As democracy has blossomed in Western states over the past three centuries, Muslim societies have usually lived under colonial rulers, kings, or tribal and clan leaders.

In other words, neither Islam nor its culture is the major obstacle to political modernity, even if undemocratic rulers sometimes use Islam as their excuse.[1] In Saudi Arabia, for instance, the ruling House of Saud relied on Wahabism, a puritanical brand of Sunni Islam, first to unite the tribes of the Arabian Peninsula and then to justify dynastic rule. Like other monotheistic religions, Islam offers wide-ranging and sometimes contradictory instruction. In Saudi Arabia, Islam's tenets have been selectively shaped to sustain an authoritarian monarchy.

In Iran, the revolution that overthrew the Shah in 1979 put a new spin on Shi'ite traditions. The Iranian Shi'ite community had traditionally avoided direct participation by religious leaders in government as demeaning to spiritual authority. The upheaval led by Ayatollah Ruhollah Khomeini thus represented not only a revolution in Iran, but also a revolution within the Shi'ite branch of Islam. The constitution of the Islamic Republic, the first of its kind, created structures and positions unknown to Islam in the past.

Yet Islam, which acknowledges Judaism and Christianity as its forerunners in a single religious tradition of revelation-based monotheism, also preaches equality, justice, and human dignity—ideals that played a role in developments as diverse as the Christian Reformation of the sixteenth century, the American and French revolutions of the eighteenth century, and even the "liberation theology" of the twentieth century. Islam is not lacking in tenets and practices that are compatible with pluralism. Among these are the traditions of *ijtihad* (interpretation), *ijma* (consensus), and *shura* (consultation).

## Diversity and Reform

Politicized Islam is not a monolith; its spectrum is broad. Only a few groups, such as the Wahabi in Saudi Arabia, are in fact fundamentalist. This term, coined in the early twentieth century to describe a movement among Protestant Christians in the United States, denotes passive adherence to a literal reading of sacred scripture. By contrast, many of today's Islamic movements are trying to adapt the tenets of the faith to changing times and circumstances. In their own way, some even resemble Catholic "liberation theology" movements in their attempts to use religious doctrines to transform temporal life in the modern world. The more accurate word for such Muslim groups is "Islamist." The term is growing in popularity in Western academic and policy-making circles, since it better allows for the forward-looking, interpretive, and often innovative stances that such groups assume as they seek to bring about a reconstruction of the social order.

The common denominator of most Islamist movements, then, is a desire for change. The quest for something different is manifested in a range of activities, from committing acts of violence to running for political office. Reactive groups—motivated by political or economic insecurity, questions of identity, or territorial disputes—are most visible because of their aggressiveness. Extremists have manipulated, misconstrued, and even hijacked Muslim tenets. Similar trends have emerged in religions other than Islam: the words "zealot" and "thug" were coined long ago to refer, respectively, to Jewish and Hindu extremists. Contemporary Islamic extremists have committed acts of terrorism as far afield as Buenos Aires, Paris, and New York, and they have threatened the lives of writers whom they regard as blasphemous from Britain to Bangladesh.

At the opposite end of the spectrum are proactive individuals and groups working for constructive change. In Egypt, Islamists have provided health-care and educational facilities as alternatives to expensive private outlets and inadequate government institutions. In Turkey, they have helped to build housing for the poor and have generally strengthened civil society. In Lebanon, they have established farm cooperatives and provided systematically for the welfare of children, widows, and the poor. In Jordan, Yemen, Kuwait, and elsewhere, they have run for parliament. The specific motives vary from religiously grounded altruism to creating political power bases by winning hearts and minds. But in diverse ways, they are trying to create alternatives to ideas and systems that they believe no longer work.

Less visible but arguably more important—to both Muslims and the world at large—is a growing group of Islamic reformers. While reactive and proactive groups address the immediate problems of Islam's diverse and disparate communities, the reformers are shaping thought about long-term issues. At the center of their reflections is the question of how to modernize and democratize political and economic systems in an Islamic context. The reformers' impact is not merely academic; by stimulating some of the most profound debate since Islam's emergence in the seventh century, they are laying the foundations for an Islamic Reformation.

The stirrings of reform within Islam today should not be compared too closely with the Christian Reformation of almost five hundred years ago. The historical and institutional differences between the two faiths are vast. Nonetheless, many of the issues ultimately addressed by the

respective movements are similar, particularly the inherent rights of
the individual and the relationship between religious and political
authority.

The seeds of an Islamic Reformation were actually planted a century
ago, but only among tiny circles of clerics and intellectuals whose ideas
were never widely communicated to ordinary believers. At the end of
the twentieth century, however, instant mass communications, improved
education, and intercontinental movements of both people and ideas
mean that tens of millions of Muslims are exposed to the debate. In the
1980s, interest in reform gained momentum as the secular ideologies
that succeeded colonialism—mostly variants or hybrids of nationalism
and socialism—failed to provide freedom and security to many people
in the Muslim world. This sense of ferment has only grown more intense amid the global political upheaval of the post–Cold War world.
Muslims now want political, economic, and social systems that better
their lives, and in which they have some say.

The reformers contend that human understanding of Islam is flex-
ible, and that Islam's tenets can be interpreted to accommodate and even
encourage pluralism. They are actively challenging those who argue
that Islam has a single, definitive essence that admits of no change in
the face of time, space, or experience—and that democracy is therefore
incompatible or alien. The central drama of reform is the attempt to
reconcile Islam and modernity by creating a worldview that is compatible with both.[2]

Two Middle Eastern philosophers symbolize the diverse origins of
Islamist reformers and the breadth of their thought. Abdul Karim Soroush
is a Shi'ite Muslim and a Persian from Iran. He is a media-shy academic
who has experienced almost a generation of life inside an Islamic republic. Sheikh Rachid al-Ghannouchi is a Sunni Muslim and a Tunisian Arab.
He is the exiled leader of Hezb Al-Nahda (Party of the Renaissance), a
movement intent on creating an Islamic republic in Tunisia. Over the
past three years, Soroush and Ghannouchi have produced some of the
most far-reaching work on the question of Islam and democracy.

## Abdul Karim Soroush

Soroush supported Iran's 1979 revolution and took an active role in
revising university curricula during its early years. Since then, however, he has articulated ideas that the regime considers highly
controversial. Ranking officials such as Ayatollah Ali Khamenei, the
successor to Ayatollah Khomeini, now Iran's Supreme Guide, have increasingly framed public remarks as implicit but unmistakeable
responses to Soroush's articles and speeches. Some of Soroush's ideas
amount to heresy in the regime's eyes, and the tenor of Khamenei's
statements has become increasingly hostile. In a November 1995 ad-

dress commemorating the 1979 U.S. Embassy takeover, Khamenei spent more time condemning Soroush's ideas than lambasting the United States or Israel.

The degree to which Soroush now frames the debate in Iran was revealed by two unusual events that took place in the autumn of 1995. At Tehran University, more than a hundred young members of Ansar (Helpers of the Party of God) physically attacked and injured Soroush as he attempted to give a special address that the Muslim Students' Association had invited him to deliver. Some among the two thousand students who had assembled to hear him were also injured. The attack then sparked a pro-Soroush demonstration on campus. A new law imposing severe penalties on anyone associating with critics and enemies of the Islamic Republic was widely thought to be aimed at undermining Soroush's growing support.

> *Soroush argues that there is no contradiction between Islam and the freedoms inherent in democracy.*

Educated in London and Tehran in both philosophy and the physical sciences, Soroush has recently taught at the Institute for Human Research and at Tehran University's School of Theology. His columns have been the centerpiece of *Kiyan* (a Farsi word that can mean "foundation" or "universe"), a bimonthly magazine founded in 1991 primarily to air his views and the debate that they have sparked. For years he also gave informal talks at Tehran mosques that were usually packed by followers ranging from young clerics to regime opponents, intellectuals, political independents, and government technocrats. But in the fall of 1995, the government banned him from giving public lectures or instruction and from publishing. He has been effectively forced from public view, and his academic career in Iran has been ended.

Soroush's writings on three subjects are particularly relevant. At the top of the list is democracy. Although Islam literally means "submission," Soroush argues that there is no contradiction between Islam and the freedoms inherent in democracy. "Islam and democracy are not only compatible, their association is inevitable. In a Muslim society, one without the other is not perfect," he said in one of several interviews in Tehran and Washington, D.C., in 1994 and 1995.

His advocacy of democracy for the Islamic world rests on two pillars. First, to be a true believer, one must be free. Belief attested under threat or coercion is not true belief. And if a believer freely submits, this does not mean that he has sacrificed freedom. He must also remain free to leave his faith. The only real contradiction is to be free in order to believe, and then afterward to abolish that freedom. This freedom is the basis of democracy. Soroush goes further: The beliefs and will of the majority must shape the ideal Islamic state. An Islamic democracy

*Excerpts from Notes by Robin Wright on Lectures and Interviews
Given by Abdul Karim Soroush, April–May 1995*

*Freedom of Faith: In a democracy what you really want is freedom
of faith. The other thing is this: justice is important. That is not the
consequence of the rules of the shariʿa, but something that rules over
the shariʿa. The third thing is this: There is no authority on matters
religious. So you have to build a society in such a way as to
accommodate these principles.*

*Text and Context: How do we reconcile the immutable principles of
religion with the changing conditions of the world? The solution will
be like this: We have to find something that is at the same time both
changeable and immutable. And what is that?*

*It is the revealed text itself. It is immutable and changeable at the
same time. It has been revealed to the heart of the Prophet, and so it
should be kept intact and nobody is permitted to tamper with it. At
the same time, there is the interpretation of the text. That is
changeable. No interpretation is without presuppositions. These
presuppositions are changeable since the whole knowledge of
mankind is in flux. It is age-bound, if you like.*

*Now, the knowledge of the age is always in flux. At the end of
history—and I am not sure we are at the end of history, as some
American philosophers suggest—we can know which knowledge is
immutable and which not. But not now.*

*This is how I express the situation: The text is silent. We have to
hear its voice. In order to hear, we need presuppositions. In order to
have presuppositions, we need the knowledge of the age. In order to
have the knowledge of the age, we have to surrender to change. So
we have here the miraculous entity that is changing but at the same
time is immutable.*

*Religion and Reason: The ancient world was based on a single source
of information: religion. The modern world has more than once
source: reason, experience, science, logic. Modernism was a
successful attempt to free mankind from the dictatorship of religion.
Postmodernism is a revolt against modernism—and against the
dictatorship of reason. In the age of postmodernism, reason is humbler
and religion has become more acceptable. To me, the reconciliation
between the two has become potentially more visible.*

cannot be imposed from the top; it is only legitimate if it has been chosen by the majority, including nonbelievers as well as believers.

Second, says Soroush, our understanding of religion is evolving. Sacred texts do not change, but interpretation of them is always in flux
because understanding is influenced by the age and the changing conditions in which believers live. So no interpretation is absolute or fixed
for all time and all places. Furthermore, everyone is entitled to his or
her own understanding. No one group of people, including the clergy,
has the exclusive right to interpret or reinterpret tenets of the faith. Some
understandings may be more learned than others, but no version is automatically more authoritative than another.

Islam is also a religion that can still grow, Soroush argues. It should
not be used as a modern ideology, for it is too likely to become totalitarian. Yet he believes in *shari'a,* or Islamic law, as a basis for modern
legislation. And *shari'a,* too, can grow. "*Shari'a* is something expand-
able. You cannot imagine the extent of its flexibility," he has said, adding
that "in an Islamic democracy, you can actualize all its potential
flexibilities."

The next broad subject that Soroush addresses is the clergy. The rights
of the clergy are no greater than the privileges of anyone else, he argues. Thus in the ideal Islamic democracy, the clergy also have no *a
priori* right to rule. The state should be run by whoever is popularly
elected on the basis of equal rights under law.

Soroush advocates an even more fundamental change in the relationship between religion and both the people and the state. Religious leaders
have traditionally received financial support from either the state (in
most Sunni countries) or the people (in Shi'ite communities). In both
cases, Soroush argues, the clergy should be "freed" so that they are not
"captives" forced to propagate official or popular views rather than the
faith of the Koran.

A religious calling is only for authentic lovers of religion and those
who will work for it, Soroush says. No one should be able to be guaranteed a living, gain social status, or claim political power on the basis of
religion. Clerics should work like everyone else, he says, making independent incomes through scholarship, teaching, or other jobs. Only such
independence can prevent them—and Islam—from becoming compromised.

Finally, Soroush deals with the subject of secularism. Arabic, the
language of Islam, does not have a literal translation for this word. But
the nineteenth-century Arabic word *elmaniyya*—meaning "that which
is rational or scientific"—comes close. In this context, Soroush views
secularism not as the enemy or rival of religion, but as its complement:
"It means to look at things scientifically and behave scientifically—
which has nothing to do with hostility to religion. Secularism is nothing
more than that."

Modernism, according to Soroush, represented a successful attempt to challenge the "dictatorship of religion" by increasing the emphasis placed upon unaided reason in the conduct of human affairs. He maintains that the tension between reason and religion since the sixteenth century has been "welcome and beneficial for both" and has opened the way for an eventual *postmodern* reconciliation between the two.

Soroush's thought has wide-ranging implications. His work often echoes themes that lay behind the Christian Reformation. He shows how to empower Muslims by establishing a role for the individual—as a believer and as a citizen. Soroush refines, even downgrades, the role of the clergy—a particularly sensitive topic in Iran, for Shi'ite Islam stresses the doctrinal and interpretive authority of clerics far more than does Sunni Islam. Soroush also redefines, and to some degree separates, the relative roles and powers of the mosque—religious jurisprudence—and the state. The adoption of his ideas would signify a stunning shift for the only major monotheistic religion that provides a highly specific set of rules by which to govern society as well as a set of spiritual beliefs.

In a spirit similar to the one that characterized the Christian Reformation, he argues against rigid thinking and elitism. Soroush is a believing Muslim and has no wish to abandon the values of his faith; rather, he wants to convince his fellow Muslims of the need to face modernity with what he calls a spirit of "active accommodation . . . imbued or informed with criticism." By pointing the way to innovative interpretations of the Koran and the *shari'a,* he provides a foundation for a pluralist and tolerant society.

## Rachid al-Ghannouchi

While Soroush prefers the cosmic overview, Rachid al-Ghannouchi's thinking is rooted in his experiences in Tunisia, and then applied to other Muslim societies. He has also been heavily influenced by Third World nationalism and the views of intellectuals from the global South who see their region as locked in a struggle against Northern "neocolonialism." A popular philosophy teacher and speaker educated in Damascus and Paris, Ghannouchi founded the Mouvement de la Tendance Islamique (MTI) in 1981 during a brief interlude of Tunisian political liberalization. Tunisia's government refused to legalize the MTI, however, citing laws that excluded religious parties from politics. Ghannouchi persisted in calls on the regime to share power by introducing political pluralism and economic justice. He was jailed from 1981 to 1984; after his release, the authorities forbade him to teach, speak in public, publish, or travel.

In 1987, Ghannouchi was again arrested and charged with plotting to overthrow the government. He was released after a bloodless coup in November 1987, which led to another brief political thaw. The MTI,

### Excerpts from a Lecture by Sheikh Rachid al-Ghannouchi
### Chatham House, London, 9 May 1995

The Koran acknowledges the fact that conflict and competition are natural features of development and of the balance of power within each individual, within each society, and at the global level. However, while the Koran calls for jihad as well as the use of peaceful means to establish justice and equality, it condemns aggression and oppression and warns against falling captive to selfishness and lust. Furthermore, the Koran recognizes the legitimate right of an oppressed to resist and even fight in order to deter oppression, but it warns against the perpetration of injustice.

Koranic teachings encourage humans to seek justice and to cooperate . . . in serving the interests of humanity, which is perceived as a single family that . . . is created by One Creator. . . . Thus Islam recognizes as a fact of life the diversity and pluralism of peoples and cultures, and calls for mutual recognition and co-existence. . . .

Contrary to the claims of Huntington and his colonial ancestors, such differences do not justify war but provide a good ground for richness, plurality, and cooperation through complementarity rather than incongruity. . . . [D]iversity is a challenge that provokes and awakens the powers of creation and innovation in nations, ridding them of laziness and flaccidity. . . .

While on the one hand Islam guarantees the right of its adherents to ijtihad in interpreting the Koranic text, it does not recognize a church or an institution or a person as a sole authority speaking in its name or claiming to represent it. Decision making, through the process of shura, belongs to the community as a whole. Thus the democratic values of political pluralism and tolerance are perfectly compatible with Islam.

Outside its own society, Islam recognizes civilizational and religious pluralism and opposes the use of force to transfer a civilization or impose a religion. It condemns the use of religion for material or hegemonic purposes. . . .

Once the Islamists are given a chance to comprehend the values of Western modernity, such as democracy and human rights, they will search within Islam for a place . . . [to] implant them, nurse them, and cherish them just as the Westerners did before, when they implanted such values in a much less fertile soil.

renamed Al-Nahda in early 1989 to remove religious overtones, was promised a place at the political table. But by the time of the April 1989 legislative elections, the thaw was over. Reforms were stalled and confrontations mounted. Ghannouchi went into voluntary exile. The government charged Al-Nahda with plotting a coup; the party was outlawed and Ghannouchi was sentenced *in absentia* to life imprisonment. Britain granted him political asylum in 1993, and he is now the most prominent Islamist leader living in the West.

Ghannouchi is controversial. In speeches and interviews, he often declares himself to be "against fundamentalism that believes it is the only truth and must be imposed on all others," yet he has visited Tehran, has traveled briefly on a Sudanese passport when he went into exile, and has condemned Zionism and Westernization. His 1993 book *Civil Liberties in the Islamic State* is dedicated to dozens of people, including "the forerunners of Islamic liberalism in the women's movement" and prisoners of conscience of every creed. But it is also dedicated to an imprisoned Hamas leader, to the late Ayatollah Khomeini, and to Malcolm X.

Of all the major Islamist leaders, however, Ghannouchi seems to have expanded his thinking the most in recent years. In Tunisia, his understanding of democracy was a matter of theory only. He used to say that, as an Islamist, he was not afraid of ideas and wanted a free dialogue with believers in different faiths and political systems. Since the beginning of his exile in 1989, he has traveled in Europe and the United States, come into contact with a wide range of policy makers and opinion leaders, and experienced the workings of different democratic systems firsthand. His years of exile have tempered some of the well-worn jingo common in Islamist parlance. Although the field of comparison is small, Ghannouchi now ranks among Islamism's most accessible and mature thinkers on the issue of democracy. Whatever happens in Tunisia or to Al-Nahda, his contributions will remain important to Islamic thought.

Ghannouchi advocates an Islamic system that features majority rule, free elections, a free press, protection of minorities, equality of all secular and religious parties, and full women's rights in everything from polling booths, dress codes, and divorce courts to the top job at the presidential palace. Islam's role is to provide the system with moral values.

Islamic democracy is first the product of scriptural interpretation. "Islam did not come with a specific program concerning our life," Ghannouchi said in one of several interviews between 1990 and 1995. "It brought general principles. It is our duty to formulate this program through interaction between Islamic principles and modernity." Believers are guaranteed the right of *ijtihad* in interpreting the Koranic text. Their empowerment is complete since Islam does not have an institution or person as a sole authority to represent the faith—or contradict their interpretations. The process of *shura,* moreover, means that decision making belongs to the community as a whole. "The democratic values of political pluralism and tolerance are perfectly compatible with Islam," he maintains.

Second, Islamic democracy is also a product of recent human experience. The legitimacy of contemporary Muslim states is based on liberation from modern European colonialism, a liberation in which religious and secular, Muslim and Christian, participated together. "There is no room to make distinctions between citizens, and complete equality is the base of any new Muslim society. The only legitimacy is the legitimacy of elections," he said. "Freedom comes before Islam and is the step leading to Islam."

Ghannouchi concedes that Islam's record in the areas of equality and participation has blemishes. Previous Muslim societies were built on conquest. But he contends that the faith has also traditionally recognized pluralism internally, noting the lack of religious wars among Muslims as proof of Islam's accommodation of the Muslim world's wide diversity. Citing the Koran, he explains that Islam condemns the use of religion for material or hegemonic purposes: "O mankind! We created you from a single [pair] of a male and a female, and made you into nations and tribes, that ye may know each other, not that ye may despise [each other]" (Sura 49:13).

Ghannouchi calls the act of striking a balance between holy texts and human reality *aqlanah,* which translates as "realism" or "logical reasoning." *Aqlanah* is dynamic and constantly evolving. As a result Ghannouchi, like Soroush, believes that Islam and democracy are an inevitable mix. In a wide-ranging address given in May 1995 at the Royal Institute of International Affairs in London, he said: "Once the Islamists are given a chance to comprehend the values of Western modernity, such as democracy and human rights, they will search within Islam for a place for these values where they will implant them, nurse them, and cherish them just as the Westerners did before, when they implanted such values in a much less fertile soil." He pledged Al-Nahda's adherence to democracy and the alternation of power through the ballot box, and called on all other Islamist movements to follow suit in unequivocal language and even in formal pacts signed with other parties.

Ghannouchi's acceptance of pluralism is not limited to the Islamic world. Responding to Samuel P. Huntington's widely discussed essay on the "clash of civilizations,"[3] Ghannouchi contends that cultural or religious differences do not justify conflict, but instead can provide ground for cooperation rooted in a mutual recognition of complementarity. "We appeal for and work to establish dialogue between Islam and the West, for the world now is but a small village and there is no reason to deny the other's existence. Otherwise we are all doomed to annihilation and the destruction of the world," he said in a 1994 interview.[4] In his 1995 London address, he added: "Islam recognizes as a fact of life the diversity and pluralism of peoples and cultures, and calls for mutual recognition and coexistence. . . . Outside its own society, Islam recognizes civilizational and religious pluralism and opposes the use of force to transfer a civilization or impose a religion."

## A Long Way To Go

Christianity's Reformation took at least two centuries to work itself out. The Islamic Reformation is probably only somewhere in early midcourse. And the two movements offer only the roughest of parallels. The Christian Reformation, for example, was launched in reaction to the papacy and specific practices of the Catholic Church. In contrast, Islam has no central authority; even the chief ayatollah in the Islamic Republic of Iran is the supreme religious authority in one country only.

But the motives and goals of both reformations are similar. The Islamic reformers want to strip the faith of corrupt, irrelevant, or unjust practices that have been tacked on over the centuries. They are looking to make the faith relevant to changing times and conditions. They want to make the faith more accessible to the faithful, so that believers utilize the faith rather than have it used against them. And they want to draw on Islam as both a justification and a tool for political, social, and economic empowerment.

The Islamic reformist movement has a very long way to go. Although there are a handful of others besides Soroush and Ghannouchi making serious or original contributions to the debate, they still represent a distinct minority. The changes that they seek to promote will experience bumps, false starts, and failures, and may take a long time. Yet the Islamic Reformation represents the best hope for reconciliation both within Islam and between Islam and the outside world.

## NOTES

1. Olivier Roy, *The Failure of Political Islam,* Carol Volk, trans. (Cambridge: Harvard University Press, 1994), esp. 1–27.

2. See John Voll, *Islam: Continuity and Change in the Modern World* (Syracuse: Syracuse University Press, 1995).

3. Samuel P. Huntington, "The Clash of Civilizations?" *Foreign Affairs* 72 (Summer 1993): 22–49.

4. "Dr. Rachid Gannouchi: Tunisia's Islamists Are Different from Those in Algeria," interview by Zainab Farran in *Ash-Shiraa* (Beirut), October 1994, 28–32.

# 23

# THE CHALLENGE OF SECULARIZATION

*Abdou Filali-Ansary*

**Abdou Filali-Ansary,** *editor of the Morocco-based journal* Prologues: revue maghrébine du livre, *is author of* L'Islam: Est-il hostile à la laïcité? *(1997). He has served as general secretary of Université Mohammed V in Rabat, and write frequently on cultural topics. The present essay originally appeared in the April 1996 issue of the* Journal of Democracy.

Robin Wright and Bernard Lewis both seem to address the question of whether there is an "Islamic Reformation" going on now, and if there is, what content, direction, and influence it is likely to have. The raising of this question betokens an important shift in the way that Western observers view the Islamic world. Wright and Lewis implicitly acknowledge that behind the confrontations and violence that we witness today in many Muslim societies, there lies a situation marked by some kind of pluralism and opposition of ideas. In other words, there is not merely a fight, but a debate. To recognize this is already to take a giant step away from the familiar Western academic and journalistic stereotypes of Muslim societies as places overwhelmed by religious fanaticism, rejection of "the other," and crises of identity.

The dramatic importance of the question under discussion should need no emphasis: Islam, one of the major world religions, may be living through a turning point in its history, one that will bring it face-to-face with the challenges of the human condition at the beginning of the twenty-first century.

Bernard Lewis proceeds according to his well-known "macro-historical" approach. He casts his gaze across large spans of history, constitutive elements of Islamic faith, and some features of Middle Eastern languages in order to construct a grand schema that explains what is happening now and illuminates its links with the mainstream of Islamic (and also Middle Eastern) history. He draws on a larger arsenal of disciplines (history, theology, linguistics) than does Wright, and discusses a greater variety of subjects (religious beliefs, historical facts, linguistic usages and concepts) in order to create a highly seductive synthesis of his own.

While Lewis acknowledges that the term "Islam" can be confusing, he himself is not always sufficiently careful in his use of it. He goes back and forth from Islam as a religion to Islam as a historical civilization, from detailed observations to general remarks. He seems to be guided by the "inner logics" that he sees lurking behind the observed data, molding attitudes, behaviors, and ways of understanding. His conclusions about the present situation point to a clash of such logics, one that pits Muslim communities against their Western counterparts. These inner logics are what he considers to be the true core of observed reality; facts, which appear on the surface, manifest the core imperfectly, much as the shadows that flicker on the wall of Plato's cave provide only a crude representation of the realities that give them shape.

Robin Wright, in contrast, adopts an approach at loggerheads with the one prevailing in specialized academic circles. She prefers to try to understand the debate by "listening" to two of its key participants: Iranian philosopher Abdul Karim Soroush and Tunisian political leader Sheikh Rachid al-Ghannouchi. Wright assumes that ideas, not conscious or unconscious determinisms, rule human societies, which simply cannot be understood through external observation or historical reconstruction alone. This, it would seem, is why she has chosen, among living Muslim thinkers, to discuss two prominent and highly controversial figures, each of whom is thought to exert a large (and in all likelihood growing) influence on thoughtful people in the Muslim world.

## Strange Companions

This approach, much simpler than Lewis's and apparently without major risks, nonetheless raises a troubling question: How and why did Wright choose her two subjects? In posing this question I intend much more than the usual perfunctory observation, to be completed by remarks about the complexity of the situation, the availability of a large set of potential subjects, and the unavoidable arbitrariness of choice. In no way can one say that the two thinkers presented are minor, ordinary, or random specimens of contemporary Islamic thought. Indeed, they are generally considered to represent something close to opposite extremes on a spectrum: Ghannouchi is a main representative of Islamist attitudes and thought (and faces persecution from his government for that); Soroush is a formidable intellectual opponent of Islamism (for which he, too, faces persecution from his government). These considerations are by no means peripheral; they must be taken into account in any analysis that groups these two men together as workers in a single project. In fact, Wright's surprising decision to group them together is not devoid of logic, but it is a logic that she does not elaborate.

In what way can we consider *both* Ghannouchi and Soroush—the Islamist and the critic of Islamism—to be representatives of an ongoing "Islamic Reformation"? Is the opposition between the tendencies that they represent merely apparent, or do we face two opposite ways of reforming Islam?

*Soroush wants to make the followers of Islam more inwardly Muslim by enabling them to adopt a piety based on free adherence and personal commitment rather than custom, habit, and conformism.*

It should be observed beforehand that many controversies surrounding Islamic thought focus so heavily on semantics, on names for ideas and persons, that the real issues often disappear from sight. Many thinkers who are called or who call themselves "Islamists" make such large concessions to the power of unaided human reason that one may wonder what is left to render their thought Islamic. On the other hand, many secularists, especially nationalists, pay such reverence to Islamic dogmas that one may wonder if reason has any role left to play in their thought. The whole confrontation sometimes seems like so much posturing, where the real choices are never clarified or faced.

Does this apply to Soroush and Ghannouchi? Both, it is true, seem to accept Islam as a point of reference and to concentrate their efforts in an attempt, as Wright says, "to reconcile Islam and modernity by creating a worldview that is compatible with both." There is, however, an important difference masked by their apparent allegiance to the same flag. For Ghannouchi, the principal question is always how to free the community from backwardness and dependence on "the other." However significant his concessions in favor of democracy and freedom of thought, the community—not the individual—remains for him the ultimate reality and objective. Democracy and freedom of thought are instruments that Muslims should use to achieve their community's goals and defend its interests. They are tools for raising the community of Muslims to the level of power and efficiency that Western nations currently enjoy. Muslims can use these tools, argues Ghannouchi, because they work and because they are not opposed to Islamic principles, which remain the ultimate standard.

Soroush is not interested in showing Muslims how to achieve a more advantageous competitive position in the struggle with "the other." For him, the main adversary dwells within Muslims themselves, or rather within a complex of traditions that has long barred Muslims from the free implementation of reason and from direct contact with the sources of their faith. The urgent task is therefore to free Muslims from Islam understood as a social and historical heritage, as a set of overwhelming external conventions defining views and behavior, or, to use Henri

Bergson's expression, as a "closed religion."[1] Soroush wants to make followers of Islam more inwardly Muslim by enabling them to adopt a piety based on free adherence and personal commitment rather than custom, habit, and conformism. He argues further that this turn toward Islam understood as an "open religion" represents not a radical innovation, but rather a return to the original essence of the faith in its purity. For him, the basic reality and objective is the person, the individual believer. In this, Soroush is closer to modern humanism and is a true reformer. Ghannouchi, by contrast, is not.

## Responses to Secularization

Taken together, Soroush and Ghannouchi illustrate the broad alternatives offered by the situation in which Muslim societies now find themselves as they face the inescapable challenges of secularization in the modern world. It should be stressed that secularization is a comparatively recent phenomenon. It began in Western Europe and has spread throughout the world. Its pace and exact form have varied a great deal from place to place, depending on a host of political, sociological, economic, and other variables. The world's religions have adopted varying responses to it, usually featuring some mixture of adaptation and self-defense designed to meet the new conditions. In short, societies have shown different ways of responding to the secularizing tendency.

Muslim societies have not experienced secularization as an internal or autonomous move. (Some scholars believe that such a move did begin within Islamic societies in the eighteenth century, but was never allowed to unfold autonomously.) External influences either started the secularization process or disrupted it (another point on which historians disagree). But secularization is already a reality in the Muslim world. No Muslim society today is governed solely with reference to religious law; religious traditions no longer possess absolute or near-absolute predominance (except perhaps in some remote rural areas); and newly emerging leadership classes are almost everywhere displacing or marginalizing the clerisy of theologico-legal experts who used to control meaning and organization in these societies. Yet even while all this has been happening, Islamic reformation has not yet been accomplished. In the Muslim world, secularization is preceding religious reformation—a reversal of the European experience in which secularization was more or less a consequence of such reformation.

Wright's examination of Soroush and Ghannouchi offers us excellent examples of the responses that this evolution has elicited. These responses point in two opposite directions. There are voices, like Ghannouchi's, calling for a return to the "implicit constitution"[2] that Islam is supposed to have provided (and which may not be opposed to democracy, or may even find in it a good expression of some of Islam's requirements). These are typically calls to resist "Westernization" and to return to the original (and never fully implemented) Islamic constitution via a course of general reform that usually involves the moralization of public affairs and of political and social relationships. Appeals like these are reminiscent of the "natural and cyclical reflex" to seek a purified and more forceful version of Islam that the fourteenth-century Arab historian Ibn Khaldun observed in Muslim societies whenever rulers exceeded the limits of the tolerable. For all their sincerity and effectiveness in terms of influence on the masses, such appeals grow out of attitudes that are trapped in the past. They can in no way lead to a real democratization of society.

By refusing to make religion the only means of reforming society, the other and opposed response tries to free Muslims from the "Khaldunian" cycle of rigorous reform enforced by an energetic outgroup, followed by the corruption and enervation of the reformers. This view recommends the reform of religious feeling and belief as the best means of making men free and responsible, and of placing them on the surest path to ordered and enduring liberty.

Soroush surely belongs to what Wright describes as "a growing group of Islamic reformers" who "are shaping thought about long-term issues," and whom she contrasts to "reactive and proactive groups [that] address the immediate problems of Islam's diverse and disparate communities." Ghannouchi, clearly, belongs with these latter groups. If we adopt the comparison with what happened in Christendom, the dividing line between Soroush and Ghannouchi is more or less equivalent to the one that separated the Reformation from the Counterreformation.

## NOTES

1. Henri Bergson, *The Two Sources of Morality and Religion,* R. Ashley Audra, trans. (Notre Dame: University of Notre Dame Press, 1977; orig. publ. 1932).

2. See Ernest Gellner's comments on Islam as an "entrenched constitution" in his *Postmodernism, Reason, and Religion* (London: Routledge, 1992), 12, 16.

# 24

# THE SOURCES OF ENLIGHTENED MUSLIM THOUGHT

*Abdou Filali-Ansary*

*Abdou Filali-Ansary* is editor of the journal Prologues: revue maghrébine du livre. *His many publications include* L'Islam et les fondements du pouvoir, *a French translation (with an introduction) of the seminal essay by Ali Abderraziq. This essay originally appeared in the April 2003 issue of the* Journal of Democracy.

To begin, how appropriate is the term "liberal Islam" for the current of thought to which we are referring? There has in fact been a great deal of general hesitation on this question. To mention but a few of the alternatives proposed lately, there are: "reformed Islam," "modern Islam," "protestant Islam," "positive Islam," "the Islam of modernity," "enlightened Islam," and on they go. But "liberal Islam" is the one that seems to be the most widely accepted nowadays.

How adequate is it? "Liberal" in the strict political sense, is the opposite of "totalitarian" or "authoritarian" and, as an adjective, refers in principle to an ideology or set of overlapping ideologies. Applying it to a world religion presupposes the assimilation of that religion to a common framework with a secular ideology. Is this semantically adequate, intellectually accurate, or morally appropriate? There are grounds for skepticism on all three counts. Can we consider a world religion as being commensurable with an ideology? If so, are we aware of all the assumptions we make in doing so and the consequences that they entail? World religions have been with us for centuries, having shaped common understandings for many generations. Indeed, the ethical views that prevail in our societies are directly linked to the teachings of these religions, even if many around us no longer accept religious traditions as vessels of the truth. Modern ideologies, on the other hand, have tended to be either short-lived frameworks for political action or conceptual platforms that remain objects of debate and, so, subject to constant redefinition.

The second word in the expression "liberal Islam" raises another series of concerns. "Islam" has been in use, among Muslims and non-Muslims, to refer to many different conceptions and phenomena at once. It is used—and this is important to note—to designate both the equivalent of what Christians call "Christianity" *and* that of what they call "Christendom." On the one hand, there are the beliefs, rites, and narratives associated with religion; and, on the other, there are the events and facts—including the various "layers" of interpretation proposed down through the generations—associated with its history. The use of the same term for these two sets of "objects" has led to a habitual blurring of any categorical distinction between them (broadly put, the distinction between "religion" and "history"), often implicitly or at best half-consciously, leaving people little aware of the intellectual consequences involved. It thus creates misunderstandings between interlocutors and imprints a stamp of confusion on most debates. Marshall G.S. Hodgson, in his highly influential book *The Venture of Islam,*[1] coined the terms *Islamdom* and *Islamicate* in order duly to distinguish these objects from Islam itself.[2]

The problem is not, again, merely one of semantics or formal linguistic accuracy. It is a source of major confusions that, as we can see around us every day, lead many people to conflate norms and facts, and to combine beliefs and historical phenomena, in trite and damaging ways. Among those usually called "fundamentalists," it has become common to raise historical contingencies about Islam to the status of authoritatively normative models. Among social scientists, meanwhile, it has become almost as common to attempt to explain contemporary phenomena by recourse to religious precepts. An "ethos" specific to Muslims is often invoked as the "real" or "underlying" or "inside" explanation for this or that action or event, even where local and contingent causes (political, economic, or social) are clearly at work. There is today a widespread, almost Platonic, assumption of essentialism when it comes to Islam, which in turn reinforces the confusions created by its multiple and overlapping meanings.

The choice of terms here can have surprisingly far-reaching effects. For example, the very expression "liberal Islam" would, within Muslim societies, greatly handicap the acceptance of the very trends and approaches to which the phrase is meant to refer. "Liberal Islam" seems to set up a new strain of "Islam" alongside the existing ones—introducing new divisions or creating new partisan attitudes—and links it to what are perceived, accurately enough, as largely secular attitudes, Western in origin. The values associated with liberalism in Europe and North America are not expressed in the same terms as the religious and cultural values traditionally held by Muslims. Here, one thinks of the observation by Rifaa Tahtawi, a Muslim intellectual who traveled to Europe in the nineteenth century, that what Europeans called "liberty" referred to what Muslims called "justice." The use of the adjective "liberal" would not convey to Muslim publics the same positive connotation that it has in English and other European languages.

All right then, one might ask, what alternative do we have? Should we choose among the other proposed labels? Most of them, as mentioned earlier, use the name of Islam in a way that conflates religion and history, norm and fact. But there may be a salubrious alternative in the expression "enlightened Muslim thought." This phrase seems to convey an appropriate description of the turn that is now happening around us, since "enlightenment" points to the ideas of understanding and of openness to a tradition of critical thinking that is shared by European and Middle Eastern societies.

## The Challenge of Modernity

The call for a "liberalization" or reformation of Islam has been heard regularly for more than a century. And among Muslims, the need for radical reform has been deeply felt since the eighteenth century. The term initially proposed by Muslim thinkers and political leaders was *Islah,* which means redress or reform.[3] Initially, and until the 1920s, it referred to the need for redressing the then-current state of affairs among Muslims, an idea that had more to do with curing social ills or reforming society than with reformulating religious dogmas. What it meant was reform of the popular *religiosity* and its related social behaviors, not the reexamination of orthodox *religious beliefs* by the protectors of orthodoxy. These protectors continued to hold their beliefs to be valid for all eternity and beyond the ambit of human criticism. In these views, a premodern idea of absolute truth prevailed, one taken to be fully transparent to the human mind. Any ills, dysfunctions, or negative tendencies in human life were considered matters of human frailty, ultimately traceable to ignorance, misunderstanding, or vice. Problems were never linked to the ways in which religious views were transmitted to and received in public consciousness. In other words, the reformist movement of the nineteenth and early-twentieth centuries never broached the question of the *historicity* of the established orthodoxy. This attitude still remains predominant among Muslims and within their societies, where the dominant conceptions of truth are linked to a premodern epistemology in which the external world is understood to be directly and passively accessible to the human mind.

Today, many Muslim scholars, who are in a way the heirs of the reformists, feel the need to fight this naive and untenable attitude by stressing the inherent relativity of human interpretations. Thus is born the divide between fundamentalism or Islamism on the one hand (which is not so much literalist as it is simply premodern in an epistemological sense), and on the other hand those scholars (some of whom may be called modern and others of whom lean toward traditionalism) who agree on the intrinsic limitations of the human mind, the inaccessibility of absolute truth, and the need for more historically accurate readings of textual traditions. The reform or liberalization of Islam, even if called for from within different currents of thought, does not have the same meaning for these groups—traditionalists, fundamentalists, and modernists—since they are embedded in different epistemological views.

The call for reform and liberalization comes also, and insistently, from outside Muslim societies. It has seemingly taken the place of the assertions of Islamic backwardness that used to be widely heard in European intellectual and political circles in the nineteenth and early-twentieth centuries. Many non-Muslim scholars, journalists, and political leaders proclaim the need for the *aggiornamento* (updating), reform, or modernization (again, the exact terms vary) of Islam. The most striking thing about these calls is the dominant influence on them of a model drawn from Christian history, that of the Protestant Reformation. This model is taken to represent a turn in the history of Western religious communities during which views once held to be orthodox were thrown out and replaced by new ones more appropriate to the spirit of the time. Reformation necessarily meant revolution, with traditional religious doctrines being discarded and novel ones adopted. The model envisions a break or rupture that occurs at a particular moment and is propagated within the community at large. And this break is, in turn, a kind of "big bang" that leads to profound changes in prevailing attitudes. Such is clearly indicated by the numerous calls for the emergence (or appointment) of a "Muslim Luther" or the convening of a "Muslim Vatican II," to mention the religious event with which the term *aggiornamento* is most famously associated.

The truth of the matter is that there has been a great effervescence of thought among Muslim intellectuals since the late nineteenth century. One cannot help but be struck by the breadth, intensity, and sustained character of the debates that have been going on within the Muslim world for over a hundred years, a phenomenon for which there is no contemporary equivalent in any other religious or cultural community. One has to go back to sixteenth-century Western Europe—the age of the Reformation and its attendant wars of religion—in order to find a phenomenon of comparable nature and intensity. In the history of Muslims, one would have to go back to the Great Discord *(Fitna Kubra)* that followed the assassination in 656 C.E. of Uthman ibn Affan, the third caliph, in order to find such intense debates on basic issues.[4]

Since the nineteenth century, the main questions have been: How should Muslims face the challenges of modernity? What role should traditions play in the social and political order? And in what ways should ethical principles be conveyed and religious traditions implemented under contemporary conditions?

The quality and diversity of the answers that these questions have elicited vary so widely that it seems almost impossible to subject them to any kind of orderly or accurate classification. Some observers, such as Ernest Gellner, have gone back to Ibn Khaldun (1332–95) and tried to adapt his theory of historical cycles to contemporary phenomena.[5] Muslim societies, says Gellner, display a pattern in which moments of tension and the search for purification alternate with moments of relaxation and moral "realism." Contemporary calls for return to the pure forms of the faith and the strict implementation of all prescriptions show that we are now in a "tense" Gellnerian moment, while a "relaxed" moment tends to be characterized by fascination with Western, secular, modern forms of social and political life. The tokens of secularism and modernity have come to replace such traditional signs of "relaxation" as immorality or the lack of will—accounting for why the main opposition is now between fundamentalism and Western-inspired secularism. As Gellner correctly argues, what reshaped the cycle was modern mass education, which in widening access to the written cultural traditions, ended up strengthening the hand of fundamentalism. For the policies upon which this education was implemented were such that, instead of opening minds to critical inquiry and rational approaches, they favored a return to premodern views and attitudes. In this neo-Khaldunian view, the chances of a liberal, secularized Islam are, therefore, very limited. And, indeed, taking Ibn Khaldun's theory as a starting point is a path to reestablishing classical essentialism; it is another way of asserting that Islam always leads to similar patterns of behavior, as it did in the past, and as it must do in the present.

Similar classifications are normal in contemporary literature. Their common feature is to view contemporary debates among Muslims as a continuation of old confrontations, and to consider present-day realities as being determined by a remote history, on the assumption that earlier moments have imprinted rigid, stagnant, repetitive patterns.

One fairly refined variant of such classifications, however, is offered by Charles Kurzman. In the introduction to his widely read anthology *Liberal Islam,* he contrasts "liberal" Islam with "customary" and "revivalist" Islam, respectively. Customary Islam, "which represents the great majority of Muslims in most places and times," includes the diverse expressions of popular religiosity that prevail in premodern contexts: "The customary tradition is not a unitary phenomenon, since each region of the Islamic world has forged its own version of customary practice."[6] This seems to refer to what anthropologists describe as "popular" religiosity or "low Islam," in contrast to "high Islam," which is defined by the *ulama*—that is, by learned elites with access to written sources. The main opponent of this customary tradition is the "revivalist" tradition, "known variously as Islamism, fundamentalism, or Wahabism," which also seems to be modern expressions of what anthropologists called "high Islam."[7] Here, Kurzman is in line with anthropologists such Gellner: While Kurzman avoids using their termi-

nology, he does, as they do, implicitly assume a direct continuity between premodern and modern Muslim societies. The customary and
revivalist traditions are considered to be two rival forms engaged in
constant competition, alternating between open hostility and mutual
acceptance. But are the contemporary versions of these two traditions
really reproductions of the high and popular Islam of old times? Or are
they rather modern, "ideologized" forms of religious discourse? Experts have debated this question intensely for decades. The stakes are
more than academic, too, for the debate's outcome has the potential
decisively to shape how decision makers understand the basic issues
and trends within contemporary Muslim societies.

The third, or "liberal," strain can be understood as the only one that
genuinely accommodates the "fruits of modernity." In this sense, the
liberal strain is something like a "branch" of traditionalism that is ready
to make partial, and more or less consistent, concessions to modern ideas
and ways of doing things. Liberal Islam is similar to revivalist Islam in
its opposition to the notion that the merely customary has great authority. Yet liberalism distinguishes itself from revivalism by taking a far
more positive attitude toward modernity. Or as Kurzman puts it, the
liberal tradition's main feature is its

> critique of both the customary and revivalist traditions for what liberals
> sometimes term "backwardness," which in their view has prevented the
> Islamic world from enjoying the fruits of modernity: economic progress,
> democracy, legal rights, and so on. Instead, the liberal tradition argues
> that Islam, properly understood, is compatible with—or even a precursor
> to—Western liberalism.[8]

After expressing some perfunctory caveats—by observing, for example,
that the three traditions "overlap and intervene and should not be considered mutually exclusive or internally homogeneous"—Kurzman
claims that "as heuristic devices, the three labels provide significant
insight into the recent history of Islamic discourses."

This is where Kurzman overlooks the essential point. On the one
hand, the two first traditions (customary and revivalist) are *not* adequate
as "heuristic devices" for understanding the present situation, since they
imply a continuation of premodern attitudes and ignore or minimize the
processes at work in modern contexts. The third category, the "liberal"
one—to which his work wants to direct attention—becomes, by the same
token, a mixture of extremely contrasting attitudes, assembled in one
category based on the sole reason that they show some readiness to
accommodate the "fruits of modernity."

This is clearly shown first by the history of the liberal trend that Kurzman
outlines. He goes back to the eighteenth century to identify the birth of
liberal Islam, naming Shah Wali-Allah (1703–62) as the initiator of the
liberal tradition—yet acknowledges a little later that Wali-Allah "did

not place any great stock in 'modern' forms of knowledge and deemed traditional Islamic scholarship to be sufficient to meet the demands of the contemporary world."

Kurzman then carries on with this "genealogy" by turning to the most renowned reformists of the nineteenth century: Jamal al-Din al-Afghani (1838–97), Sayyid Ahmed Khan (1817–98), and Muhammed Abduh (1849–1905). These "liberals," Kurzman ultimately concedes, "sought to impose themselves as tutelary authorities." They show "respect for modernity" by their willingness to introduce "Western subjects" into the traditional curriculum, but they still consider that the practice of *ijtihad* (or "rational inquiry")—which is supposed to open the way to modernization—is not open to anyone but should be restricted to competent religious scholars. One can only express skepticism at the idea of calling thought like this "liberal."

Kurzman's discussion of the "modes of liberal Islam" clearly implies the adoption of a category encompassing virtually anyone who shows any readiness to accommodate the fruits of modernity, including those who do no more than pay lip service to modern attitudes and practices. Here he proposes another triad, based on differing relationships to the primary sources of Islam: "the divinely revealed book (Qur'an) and the divinely inspired practice of the Prophet Mohammad (Sunna), which together constitute the basis for Islamic law *(shari'a)*." Not only does Kurzman reduce all debate over the category of liberal Islam to the issue of religious law and its relevance to contemporary conditions; he also arbitrarily defines the "modes" that he posits: "The first mode takes liberal positions as being explicitly sanctioned by the *shari'a*; the second argues that Muslims are free to adopt liberal positions on subjects that the *shari'a* leaves open to human ingenuity; the third mode suggests that the *shari'a*, while divinely inspired, is subject to multiple human interpretations. I call these modes *liberal, silent* and *interpreted*."

In fact, the first of these "modes," the one which alleges that orthodox traditions contain all of the positive "fruits of modernity," is clearly the apologetic mode. This can be described more adequately as advocating what Said Amin Arjomand describes as a form of *Islamic modernism:*

> It can be said generally that the advocates of Islamic modernism through-
> out the twentieth century and the Muslim world maintained that Islam
> was the most perfect religion and therefore had the best answers to all
> problems of modern social and political organisation, purporting apolo-
> getically to deduce democracy, equality of women, and principles of social
> justice and human rights from its sources. To them Islam was the Straight
> Path and could generate the perfect modern social and political system
> by re-examining its fundamentals.[9]

Defined in such terms, this mode is anything but liberal. It is simply a set of formal (mostly verbal) concessions, the main idea being, as

Kurzman puts it, that "Islam is timeless and unchanging, and that Muslims must interpret the world of God as literally as possible." It is, in other words, a modernized formulation of the idea that Islam is the archetype of the world, or that it provides a "blueprint" for the social order—a notion that is clearly dear to "fundamentalists" and other radical opponents of liberalism. To insist on calling this a "mode" of liberal Islam only clouds the picture. It leads us to miss one of the basic dividing lines in the ongoing debates between Muslims, and it leads Kurzman to make mistakes such as calling the clear-cut conservative A. Alaoui M'daghri—a former Moroccan minister of Islamic affairs and prominent apologist for traditional Islam—part of the liberal trend.

This same problem is further confirmed by the two other modes that Kurzman discusses. *Silent* and *interpretive* are in fact two complementary and indivisible formulations of one and the same attitude, as better contemporary research reveals: The sacred texts do not provide a comprehensive and systematic body of laws. The rules they propose are a collection of moral injunctions, including some prescriptions, and convey an ethical outlook that defines the Islamic approach to life and its meaning. It befell later generations of Muslims to build legal systems, or rather methodologies, that enabled them to extract or develop new rulings from the original "scriptural" prescriptions. As they are based on empirical observations, both the silent and the interpretive "modes" in fact express a historicist approach to Muslim traditions. By calling these modes "historicist," I mean that they recognize basic historical facts and keep their distance from any ideological attitude in which the development of systematic Muslim legal thought is understood as a simple explication of an "archetype" or "blueprint" itself deemed to be coeternal with the last message from God.

I would propose, then, to redraw Kurzman's categories: The first group, on my view, consists of traditional religious scholars, whose expertise covers mainly the late written works of Islamic law, and who remain faithful to the traditional worldview (combining premodern epistemological outlooks with traditional contents); the second group, radical Islamists, who combine traditional contents and premodern epistemological views with modern ideological attitudes; and the third, which I consider the most enlightened, those scholars who seek ways of reconciling modern epistemological views with a classical cultural and religious heritage.

## Faith and Scholarship

In the 1920s—in 1924–25, to be precise—a very important divide opened up within the reformist movements that had been sweeping Muslim societies since the middle of the nineteenth century. The precipitating event was Kemal Atatürk's abrogation of the Islamic caliphate in Turkey; and the divide was in itself a major turn in the history of most Muslim societies, setting off developments that went in two different directions. One of these led to what we now call revivalism, fundamentalism, or Islamism, while the other gave birth to an enlightened approach to religious traditions. Traditional scholars "survived" in this context, and were attracted by one or the other of the two trends. After the abrogation of the caliphate—when the institution which symbolized the continuity and permanence of historical Islam was eliminated—a number of scholars turned away from those who called for its restoration, rejecting apologetic attitudes while remaining faithful to the fundamental ethical teachings that they drew from Muslim traditions. This was the beginning of a crucial evolution within Muslim intellectual life.

Thus while revivalism (or fundamentalism) was hardening and systematizing its ideology, some thinkers moved in the opposite direction and began—for the first time in a dozen centuries—to raise the basic, essential questions that had divided early Muslim communities, hoping to tackle these issues from fresh angles, or to propose new views based on a critical rethinking of the prevailing conceptions. Ali Abderraziq's 1925 essay asking "Was the Prophet a King?"[10] was path-breaking in more than one respect. It raised the issue of the relationship between religious and political authority and challenged Muslims to come up with new answers. The return of such a question, posed as it was in such a direct way, profoundly shook traditional learned elites throughout Muslim societies. Ali Abderraziq's question is still with us; indeed it is *the* question that most Muslim intellectuals take it upon themselves to attempt to answer.

So what has happened since the divide of the 1920s? The two tendencies coming out of it have crystallized even further: One claims that there is an essence of Islam, a single Islamic pattern that we can contemplate and study, and from which we can deduce the answer to any question that we may meet in the course of our lives. This is the prevailing idea of Islam among revivalists, fundamentalists, and Islamists, and also, in slightly different forms, within some scholarly circles in North American and European universities.[11] One can find many publications in which the claim is put forward that Islam is this or that discrete and homogenous thing, ignoring the diversity and the richness that have characterized the history of Muslims. The idea of *shari'a* as a system of eternal prescriptions, drawn directly from sacred texts, is an illustration of this attitude. According to the rival point of view, which has been well documented by historical research, Islamic law is instead the outcome of processes that have unfolded over the course of Muslim history, and indeed often relatively late in that history. It belongs therefore to the realm of facts that can be "situated," *not* to the realm of principles and norms as such. It is the recognition of this distinction that defines the other great post-1925 tendency, the new attitude and approach that I refer to as "enlightened" Muslim thought.

This second tendency, which is enlightened and liberal in the sense given to these words in the West, is thus founded on modern epistemological premises that abandon ahistorical essentialism. It accepts the methods and suppositions of modern scholarship, and rejects the idea of Islam as an archetype of truth that can serve as a blueprint for social and political order. Enlightened Islamic thought accepts the legitimacy of attempting to link expressions of the sacred to the historical settings in which these expressions were formulated, and thus recognizes the historicity of these expressions. Yet it remains faithful to the idea of an "external" origin of the norms and views expressed by the Prophet, and it affirms their sacred character and universal validity. In other words, it accepts a principle of heterogeneity that makes room for both the universal and the particular; it sees prophetic prescriptions as being *universal* in that they are sacred in origin, conveying ethical principles which are intended for all humans and which converge with principles taught by other religious and philosophical traditions, and *particular* in that they express one historically bounded vision of such principles.

Since the 1920s, thinkers who work along these lines have emerged in many contexts. The most renowned are those whose writings have been composed in or translated into European languages, such as Ali Abderraziq, Fazlur Rahman, Mohamed Mahmoud Taha, Abdullahi An-Na'im, Mohamed Talbi, Mojtahed Shabestari, Abdelmajid Charfi, and Abdul Karim Soroush. It is striking how many corners of the Muslim world these thinkers hail from, including communities of new emigrants in Europe and North America. They do not form a "school" in any sense, for there is no direct or indirect affiliation among them. They speak different languages, pursue different disciplines, and reside in different countries. But they do share a strong "family resemblance." The avenue opened by this trend is commending itself to many, across cultures and disciplines, not as an eternal idea uncovered, or a potentiality unfolded at a moment in history, but as a "reading" that emerges out of the application of rigorous scholarship and hermeneutic insight to Muslim traditions. Enlightened Muslim thought is represented by a great diversity of thinkers and has emerged out of varying contexts, but it shares in common a tendency toward subtler views about truth and its relationship to reality than those dominant in antiquity.

Three Muslim thinkers exemplify key aspects of this enlightened turn of mind (though this does not necessarily mean that they should be considered the leading lights in this relatively large intellectual family). Ali Abderraziq opened the way to the new approaches; Fazlur Rahman offered an in-depth theoretical articulation of them; and Abdelmajid Charfi and Abdul Karim Soroush initiated the process of building around them an institutionalized school of thought.

Ali Abderraziq (1888–1966) was the first who broke with the "re-formist" trend and its mixture of premodern epistemological views of religious traditions and apologetic leanings. His famous question "Was the prophet a king?" signaled a fundamental break with classical or essentialist ideas and a turn toward critical reasoning. He challenged established views and submitted them to rational inquiry, raising the issues of their coherence and adequacy in light of the available textual and historical sources. His departure from the search for the eternal Islam was a reaction against traditionalist intellectual efforts to demonstrate the *precedence* of Islam over such modern values such as rationality, democracy, and human rights.

He also attempted to test the validity of orthodox views by examining their internal logic. Traditional Muslims think that Mohammad founded a state by leading the first community of believers in Medina, even though the Koran famously denies that he could be a king or temporal ruler of any kind. Abderraziq examined the Koranic verses most often used to back up the claim that a particular form of state is prescribed by Islam and found that what these verses expressed were basic principles of consultation and obedience to "those in charge" (not necessarily to be understood as kings or political rulers of any kind). To corroborate his claims, he adduced extra-Koranic historical evidence showing that the first *ummah* (community) of believers whom Mohammad led from Mecca to Medina in 622 C.E. had none of the features of a polity.

Abderraziq's break with traditional notions stirred huge waves of protest, accusation, and attempted refutation. It is noteworthy that most of these hostile reactions came both from traditional clerics and from reformists (such as Rachid Rida) associated with what would later become known as Islamism. General readers, who for the first time in Muslim history could follow such a controversy through the press, showed not the slightest sign of hostility to Abderraziq's ideas. Their "silence" could not be understood as anything other than approval for what amounted to a systematic critique, by a Muslim intellectual writing for fellow Muslims, of longstanding attempts to rationalize tyranny and theocracy with the stolen mantle of sacred tradition.

The second figure who illustrates the enlightened turn is Fazlur Rahman (1919–86). Like Abderraziq, he had a solid training in traditional Muslim disciplines, but he also had a modern university education. As a scholar who possessed both traditional religious learning and a knowledge of modern textual analysis, he was superbly equipped to widen the scope of rational inquiry into the elaborations and systems that Muslim scholars had built upon the basis of the early Islamic texts. His specialty was a systematic scrutiny of the historical processes that produced some of the basic conceptions prevailing among Muslims. And his appraisal of the ways in which orthodoxy was constructed was severely critical, and left no room for the assertion that there is a venerable "Islamic system" that somehow "pre-includes" modern norms.

Instead, Rahman perceived a specific moral "ethos" that emanated from Islamic scriptures and the Prophet's example. He questioned traditional explanations of revelation that minimized Mohammad's role and set the stage for the emergence of the doctrine that the Koran is eternal. These ideas about the role of the Prophet in the transmission of revelation[12] stirred protests comparable to the ones that greeted Abderraziq in 1925. In an essay entitled *Islam and Modernity,* Rahman offered one of the most radical reexaminations of the learned Muslim traditions and their reproduction, showing how they were shaped by a mindset sharply opposed to the ethos of the initial *ummah.*[13] And he pointed to the negative consequences of sacralizing such traditions and allowing them to appear as the sole valid expressions of Islamic religious tenets.

Supporting the movement of enlightened thought is a trend that looks at Muslim traditions as "layers" of narratives or forms of social organization, each referring to a common source, which can be studied as objects of knowledge without necessarily assuming the validity of religious claims. Here, religious traditions are considered to be accumulations of social institutions, written traditions, different myths, and different forms of expression, which claim to refer to a common core, and present themselves as expressions of something far beyond ordinary human experience. Spokespersons for this trend include such renowned scholars as Mohammed Arkoun or Ridwan Assayyid. One can say that hundreds of scholars—Muslim and non-Muslim alike, and belonging to different disciplines and schools—are engaged in this endeavor in universities and research institutions around the world. In fact, we are now living through a period in which the history of Muslims is being rewritten on a vast scale. New knowledge and new understandings are offering support to enlightened Muslims and giving radicals more reasons for fear. The new learning does tend to favor the emergence of religious, moral, and sometimes intellectual relativism within the circles of its adepts and those influenced by them. However, its greatest impact has been its support for enlightened thinkers interested in exploring implications for religious consciousness. In a way, one can describe this tendency as one in which scholarship is being put in the service of religious enlightenment.

At the edge of this current, Abdelmajid Charfi (b. 1944) is an example of the enlightened Muslim intellectual as scholarly institution-builder. Through his writing, his instruction of important young scholars, and his work in organizing a department of religious studies within the University of Tunis, he has inaugurated one of the first new systematic analyses of traditional Islamic dogmas, taking into account the views and methods of contemporary social science, comparative religion, and ethical reasoning. His *Islam Between Message and History* proposes a comprehensive alternative to the views held by Islamists and ultraconservatives. He draws a sharp distinction between the religious and ethical message of Islam and its reception within Muslim communities separated by time, space, and culture. He offers a new reading of one of the basic dogmas held by Muslims—namely, that of the end (or "sealing") of revelation. The traditional interpretation strengthens the finality of the scriptural prescriptions as the last and most accomplished expression of divine will. Charfi, building on both early traditional sources and modern scholarship, stresses that this new reading marks not merely the close of one period but also the opening of new horizons for the human venture, built on new knowledge, ethical experimentation, and the liberation of mind and will.

Finally, Abdul Karim Soroush emerges as a representative of a rich and powerful Iranian movement, which has attracted active thinkers from within both religious institutions and secular circles, and which benefits from a large following within Iranian society as a whole. This movement displays the clear influence of the Shi'ite learned traditions, where philosophy and rational theology have been cultivated without disruption for centuries. It firmly upholds the distinction between religious truths (absolute but inaccessible by themselves) from human knowledge (necessarily situated and thus relative). At the same time, it resists the reduction of religious principles to legalistic, external prescriptions by in-depth explorations of the ontological, eschatological, and ethical dimensions of religious experience, drawing clearly from the mystical heritage of Persia and the Middle East.

## Belief and Identity

One of the most important consequences of the enlightened tendency—and one that further distinguishes it from the radical and traditionalist alternatives—is its capacity to distinguish between religious faith and assertions of collective identity. In the enlightened view, religion is a historically situated expression of spiritual visions and ethical ideals. Historical-critical analyses and other forms of scientific inquiry need not provoke fears of loss, whether of belief, social cohesion, or identity. These fears, which seem to have played an important role in the radicalization of Islamism, are defused within enlightened thought. Expressions of identity should be local, geographical, and cultural. The realization that Islam, properly understood, is *not* a system of social and political regulation frees up space for cultures and nations—in the modern sense of those words—to lay the foundations of collective identity. This opens the way, in turn, to the acceptance of a convergence with other religious traditions and universalistic moralities, beyond political and cultural boundaries and in more than formal terms. It also opens the way to a full respect for civic spheres in which Muslims can coexist as equal citizens with non-Muslims. Moreover, both this acceptance and this respect are to enlightened Muslim minds matters of principle and not merely grudging tactical concessions (of the sort some Islamists make) to a prevailing but illegitimate balance of forces or a fashion of the day.

What is more, the enlightened turn recognizes that Islam's axial texts breathe a spirit of social justice, equality, and solidarity with the poor. Islam gave birth to a community based on the ideal of adherence to a common creed, and not to some tribal or ethnic sense of belonging. It remained throughout history a framework vindicating equality and generated repeated attempts to enact those principles in the sociopolitical order. Today, however, most of these aspirations can be channeled through established political institutions and forms of expression. Muslims are no longer obliged to "practice politics within religion"—that is, to adopt religious formulations in order to express political agendas, as was the case in premodern times.[14] The creation of political arenas where citizens have the benefit of freedom of expression and political action opens the way to modern types of collective behavior.

We may ask whether progress in modern scholarship, and the reduction of some conceptions held to be sacred to the status of historical expressions, would lead to relativism or "disenchantment"—a dissociation from faith in the spiritual and from those moral attitudes associated with it. The answer is "not necessarily." The idea behind enlightened Muslim thought is that even if we accept the historicity of traditions, even if we accept the point of view of modern scholarship, there is behind these traditions an "Otherness" that provides an insight into the meaning of existence and the basis of ethical principles. We have to accept what modern scholarship has brought to us, in particular the critical attitude to all religious traditions, ours as well as others'. But we have to assume that these traditions, despite their historicity, point to the divine and capture its inspiration and ethical guidance. This is, in a way, a reassertion of the "Rushdian" creed, the conception that Ibn Rushd (or Averroës, 1126–98) originally proposed, which was later misrepresented and rejected in Muslim societies as the theory of the "double truth." The "Rushdian" creed asserts the idea that reason understands its own incapacity to provide ethical guidance, and thus refers us to religion, but that religion itself points back to reason as the way to develop adequate ways and means of enacting ethical principles in historical settings. The truth is one, but it is apprehended at different levels and in different modes. Mohamed Abed Jabri identifies this aspect of the nature of truth as the postulate that lies at the foundation of modernity.[15] Ibn Rushd came from Spain, and his ideas were well known among the learned of Western Europe during the High and Late Middle

Ages. It was indeed an acceptance of his insight among European Christians that helped to open the way to new understandings of the possible relationships between religion and sociopolitical order in Europe. There is no inherent reason why it cannot provide a foundation for such new understandings among Muslims as well.

## NOTES

1. Marshall G.S. Hodgson, *The Venture of Islam: Conscience and History in a World Civilization,* 3 vols. (Chicago: University of Chicago Press), 1961–74.

2. Marshall G.S. Hodgson, *Rethinking World History: Essays on Europe, Islam and World History* (Cambridge: Cambridge University Press, 1993).

3. "Islah," in *Encyclopedia of Islam* (Leiden: Brill, 2001).

4. Hichem Djaït, *La grande discorde: Religion et politique dans l'Islam des origines* (Paris: Gallimard, 1989).

5. Ernest Gellner, "Flux and Reflux in the Faith of Men," *Muslim Society* (Cambridge: Cambridge University Press, 1981).

6. Charles Kurzman, *Liberal Islam: A Sourcebook* (New York: Oxford University Press, 1998), 3–14, passim. The discussion of and quotes from Kurzman in the present essay all refer to these pages, which form his introduction to this volume.

7. Ernest Gellner, *Postmodernism, Reason and Religion* (London: Routledge, 1992).

8. Charles Kurzman, *Liberal Islam,* 6.

9. Said Amir Arjomand, "The Reform Movement and the Debate on Modernity and Tradition in Contemporary Iran," *International Journal of Middle Eastern Studies* (November 2002): 723.

10. See Ali Abderraziq, *L'Islam et les fondements du pouvoir,* trans. Abdou Filali-Ansary (Paris: La Découverte, 1994).

11. Again, Gellner gives one of its best formulations at the opening of one of his most important works, *Muslim Society* (Cambridge: Cambridge University Press, 1981), 1: "Islam is the blueprint of a social order. It holds that a set of rules exists, eternal, divinely ordained, and independent of the will of men, which defines the proper ordering of society. . . . In traditional Islam, no distinction is made between lawyer and common lawyer, and the roles of theologian and lawyer are conflated. Expertise on proper social arrangements, and on matters pertaining to God, are one and the same thing."

12. See Fazlur Rahman, *Islam,* 2nd ed. (Chicago: University of Chicago Press, 1979).

13. Fazlur Rahman, *Islam and Modernity* (Chicago: University of Chicago Press, 1984).

14. Mohamed Abed Jabri, *Al-'aql al-siyâsi al arabi: muhaddidâtuh wa tajalliyâtuh* (Arab political reason: Determinants and manifestations) (Casablanca: Al-Markaz Ath-Thaqafi al-Arabi, 1990).

15. Mohamed Abed Jabri, *Naqd al-'Aql al-'Arabi: Takwin al-'Aql al-'Arabi* (Critique of Arab reason, vol. I: The formation of Arab reason) (Casablanca: Al-Markaz Ath-Thaqafi al-Arabi, 1991).

# 25

# THE ELUSIVE REFORMATION

*Abdelwahab El-Affendi*

***Abdelwahab El-Affendi*** *is a senior research fellow at the Centre for the Study of Democracy, University of Westminster, and coordinator of the Centre's Project on Democracy in the Muslim World. His books include* Who Needs an Islamic State? *(1991) and* Rethinking Islam and Modernity *(2001). This essay originally appeared in the April 2003 issue of the* Journal of Democracy.

The overriding political problem with modern Islam is not just the embarrassing absence of democracy in most Muslim countries, but the more basic failure to provide any form of stable, and even minimally consensual governance at all. This problem is so glaring and of such long standing that it is difficult to dismiss out of hand the role of such "prepolitical" factors as culture and, in particular, religion in explaining it.

The more weight we ascribe to these "prepolitical" factors, the greater the need appears to be for a radical intellectual and ethical reorientation of Islam. But the argument that such a reorientation should take the form of an "Islamic Reformation" is nevertheless a precarious one. Despite the achievements of scholars who have followed the *sunna* (tradition) of Max Weber in using religion to explain social phenomena, it remains risky for social scientists to double as amateur theologians, especially when they want to speak in a prescriptive mode. This need not discourage us from dabbling in theology, as long as we remember that theology and political sociology are profoundly different enterprises. The greater risk is not that theology will corrupt social science, but the reverse. Social scientists have a dangerous tendency to take such theological concepts as "the rule of God" at face value and then run away with them—projecting, for example, simplistic contrasts with the political concept of "the rule of man."

The question of whether liberal democracy can be given a "truly" Islamic basis is unanswerable, since there cannot conceivably be any Islamic democratic movement which is untouched by the influences and challenges of Western liberal-democratic thought and practice. Meanwhile, any modern Islamic reform movement trumpeting its liberal-democratic potential begs the question of whether religious-cum-cultural reform is a precondition for democratization, since to cite favorably the presumed liberal-democratic potential of a particular interpretation of Islam is to assume that there is already a broad Muslim constituency for liberalism and democracy as things desirable in and of themselves.

Not all those classified as "Muslim liberals" base their liberalism on theological assumptions; in fact the majority do not. But the conceptual amalgam that travels under the "Muslim liberal" label is more problematic than the easy combination of adjectives suggests—and not only because the term "liberal" is as hotly contested as it is. Islamic liberalism is often defined as a tendency that "share[s] common concerns with Western liberalism,"[1] in particular the privileging of "rational discourse" that aims primarily at "agreement based on goodwill" among participants in public life.[2] This appears to be a circular definition, tautologically generating the conclusion that "liberal Islam" is more congenial to democracy than other modes of Islam. If Muslim liberals are by definition those who share Western liberal democratic ideals, and if non-liberals are those who do not, then it goes without saying that "Muslim liberalism" is the intra-Islamic tendency that would promote liberal democracy within Islam.

It is significant, though, that reality does not accord with this "tautology." Those groups and thinkers who have gone the furthest in promoting "liberal" theologies within Islam (like the Ahmadis in Pakistan, the Bahais in Iran, or the Republican Brothers in Sudan) have been less inclined toward modern liberal democracy than toward positions of the sort taken by such early-modern Western liberals as John Locke, Jeremy Bentham, or James Madison, all of whom were at best "reluctant democrats."[3] Nor is it difficult to see why, since most of these reformist schools of Islam were often marginalized and even persecuted.

Liberalism—understood broadly as support for individual autonomy and the political and civil liberties that underpin it—has not always been democracy-friendly.[4] Liberals have often worried that empowered but misguided masses can threaten fundamental rights and liberties, especially property rights. In spite of the intimate relationship that is now thought to hold between liberalism and democracy, significant tensions persist between them—with certain tenets of classical liberalism even being arguably "profoundly hostile to democracy."[5]

## Governance and Belief

It goes without saying that Islamic teachings, traditionally understood, certainly conflict with aspects of Western liberalism, but that does not in itself mean that they are an obstacle to democracy. Any set of religious beliefs, even beliefs based on caste stratification, could be compatible with democracy (understood as consensual popular rule) if they are shared by all members of the community. On the other hand, differing and incompatible versions of beliefs would make democratic consensus difficult, regardless of their content.

One could, at this point, venture the counterintuitive thesis that not only Islam, but all religion is essentially "democratic," in the sense that religion as a matter of individual conscience can only be espoused freely. Religious communities—from the early Hebrews to early Christians, and down to the Pilgrims, Mormons, and Nation of Islam—depended for their existence on the continuous promotion of consensus. Otherwise they tended to fragment very quickly. Like any source of moral or spiritual values, religion can be deployed as an element of intimidation and coercion against dissidents (actual and potential), but that can only happen once the values in question have been widely accepted and have become constitutive of the community itself. The central problem that religion poses for democracy (or any form of government) is that strongly held beliefs or loyalties can also make consensus hard to secure.

Muslim communities have responded positively both to democracy and to most aspects of liberalism. Limits on state authority, the separation of powers, and constitutionalism in general, have traditionally found strong support in Muslim circles. For evidence one could point to the constitutionalist movements that emerged in Iran, Egypt, and the Ottoman Empire during the nineteenth century. And upon gaining independence from colonial rule, almost all Muslim countries adopted some form of proto-democratic rule. Many leading reformers put forth theological-political arguments for the compatibility of democracy and Islam. For the most part, however, these countries were run by instinctive liberals who did not bother to offer religious arguments for their political beliefs. The "founding fathers" in countries like Pakistan and Malaysia fit this mould, as did the monarchies of post-independence Iraq, Morocco, Egypt, Jordan, and Libya. The subsequent collapse of proto-democracy from one Muslim country to the next coincided with general trends in the wider Third World, and had more to do with secular ideologies such as socialism and nationalism rather than shifts in religious thought.

All dictatorships in the Muslim world in fact remain secular—as they must, since dictatorships are by definition political systems that subordinate all values and considerations, including religious ones, to regime survival. Even where dictatorships venture a theological justification, they do not lose this secular character. Ayatollah Khomeini's doctrine of the "absolute jurisdiction of the jurist" *(Mutlaq Velayat-e-Faqih)*, enunciated in 1988, demonstrates as much, based as it is on the argument that the survival of the Islamic state is the supreme value to which all other religious obligations must be subordinated. But unless the theological principle in question has real majority support, the regime's continuing survival cannot be ascribed to its theological credentials, but more to its secret police or petrodollars.

## The Islamist Challenge

In the twentieth century, a rising number of Muslim thinkers *did* attempt to produce religious arguments against democracy and in favor of more "authentic" Islamic models, such as that of *shura* (consultative system) or various kinds of guardianship by religious scholars. Sayyid Abu'l-A'la Mawdudi (1903–79) from the Indian subcontinent, Sayyid Qutb (1906–66) from Egypt, and Ayatollah Ruhollah Khomeini (1900–89) from Iran argued that the democratic idea of popular sovereignty directly contradicted the sovereignty of God.[6] Yet all these authors advocated some form of modern constitutional practice—albeit always with the proviso that some (variously defined) religious authority should have a final veto on the decisions of elected bodies. But these thinkers, like those theologians who serve as apologists for existing autocracies today, have enjoyed little popular support.

The rising popularity of Islamist trends has posed a dual challenge for democratization. On one hand, it has created a fear among liberals that democratic forms may hand power to illiberal Islamists. On the other, despots have used the Islamist threat to resist pressures to democratize—often with support from some local liberals and major foreign powers. Moreover, disillusionment among many Muslims with contemporary experiments in Islamization (in Iran, Pakistan, Afghanistan, Sudan, and Saudi Arabia) has given rise to new liberal tendencies that claim the Islamic mantle and marshal religious arguments. Some commentators see these new tendencies as sure signs of a shift toward liberalism in the Muslim world, especially in Iran, where disillusionment with the Islamic "republic of virtue" is at its most acute:

> If, as the Christian West has shown, widespread disenchantment with attempts to create a "City of God" on Earth ultimately fuels the rise of a democratic "City of Man," then Islamic civilization is on the verge of a decisive, and familiar, breakthrough.[7]

Charles Kurzman distinguishes three strands of Islamic liberalism. One argues that Islamic teachings are essentially liberal; another argues that Islamic teachings are neutral toward liberalism; a third accepts that there is a conflict between liberalism and traditional Islam but argues that they can be reconciled through a process of mutual reinterpretation.[8] The new trends belong to this third or "revisionist" strand—a category represented by important movements such as Nahdatul Ulama in Indonesia and the reformism behind President Mohammad Khatami in Iran, as well as by individuals such as Iran's Abdul Karim Soroush. For our purposes, the first two categories can be referred to as modes of "traditional" Islamic liberalism and the third, as "critical" Islamic liberalism.

Yet one can point beyond these to a fourth category, one exemplified by emerging parties such as Justice and Development in Turkey and Morocco or Ennahada in Tunisia, movements such as the Muslim Youth Movement of Malaysia or certain splinters from the Muslim Brotherhood in Egypt and Syria, and personalities such as Tarek al-Bichri in Egypt. These groups combine traditional with critical liberalism in that they show a full awareness of, and sympathy with, the revisionist trends, but they do not themselves explicitly make revisionist arguments. Instead, they self-consciously (if often tacitly) prefer to postpone or bypass the thorny issues implied by a commitment to both liberalism and Islam.

The positive aspect of these new trends is that they have helped to create prodemocracy coalitions by deliberately removing some of Islam's most contentious theological-political issues from the table, at least for the short to medium term. But unlike most traditional Islamic liberals, who were often unaware of or unconcerned with divisive issues, the new Islamic liberals are acutely aware of them and know that at some point they will need to defend their own stance on these hard questions, even if it is wise to get them off the front burner of politics for now. In places like Iran, the new liberalism has managed to generate broad coalitions that encompass critical Islamic liberalism, traditional liberalism, and even plain secular liberalism. As a result, it has managed to secure wide popular support for its programs of reform, as indicated by the landslide victory Khatami secured in the last presidential and parliamentary elections in Iran.

The rise of such a coalition does not, of course, prevent rivals from raising the issues that the new movements have wanted to keep off the agenda, and thus from reopening the battles anew. But these critics are less likely to mobilize significant popular support, and so less likely to destabilize the system. Recent elections in Turkey, Egypt, Indonesia, Morocco, Pakistan, and Malaysia have shown that radical parties, such as the Islamic Party of Malaysia or Fazilet in Turkey, do not enjoy significant popular support. Violent Islamist organizations, such as Egypt's Islamic Group, are even more isolated. The resulting stability may make it possible to debate these issues in a calmer atmosphere and maybe even to resolve them.

It can, in conclusion, be said that an "Islamic Reformation" is neither necessary nor sufficient for enabling Muslims to build stable and consensual political institutions. A reformation may be a desirable thing; that is a matter for Muslim believers to decide. But its prospect is unlikely to improve the outlook for political stability in the short term.

Like the Christian Reformation before it, it would more likely be a dauntingly divisive and bloody affair.

## NOTES

1. Charles Kurzman, "Liberal Islam: Prospects and Challenges," *MERIA Journal* 3, No. 3 (September 1999), available online at *http://meria.idc.ac.il/journal/1999/issue3/jv3n3a2.html*.

2. Leonard Binder, *Islamic Liberalism: A Critique of Development Ideologies* (Chicago: University of Chicago Press, 1998), 1–5, 358–59.

3. David Held, *Models of Democracy,* 2nd ed. (Stanford: Stanford University Press, 1996), 100.

4. Marc F. Plattner, "From Liberalism to Liberal Democracy," *Journal of Democracy* 10 (July 1999); David Beetham, "Liberal Democracy and the Limits of Democratization," in David Held, ed., *Prospects for Democracy: North, South, East, West* (Cambridge: Polity Press, 1993).

5. David Beetham, "Liberal Democracy and the Limits of Democratization," 58.

6. Abdelwahab El-Affendi, *Who Needs an Islamic State?* (London: Grey Seal Books, 1991), 49–56.

7. See the editors' introduction in Mahmoud Sadri and Ahmed Sadri, eds., *Reason, Freedom and Democracy in Islam: Essential Writings of Abdolkarim Soroush* (Oxford: Oxford University Press, 2000).

8. Charles Kurzman, "Liberal Islam."

# 26

# THE SILENCED MAJORITY

## Radwan A. Masmoudi

***Radwan A. Masmoudi*** *is founding president of the Washington, D.C.–based Center for the Study of Islam and Democracy* (www.islam-democracy.org.) *He is also editor-in-chief of the Center's quarterly publication,* Muslim Democrat, *and the author of numerous articles on democracy, diversity, and human rights in Islam. This essay originally appeared in the April 2003 issue of the* Journal of Democracy.

Liberal Islam is a branch, or school, of Islam that emphasizes human liberty and freedom within Islam. Liberal Muslims believe that human beings are created free—a concept that is so important to highlight in the Muslim world today—and that if you take away or diminish freedom, you are in fact contradicting human nature as well as divine will. While some people want to impose their views on others, liberal Muslims insist that people—both men and women—must be free to choose how to practice their faith. This is in accordance with the basic teaching of the Koran that "there can be no compulsion in religion." Forcing religion on people contradicts a basic requirement of religion: that human beings are supposed to come to God of their own free will.

Unlike the rather starkly opposed "liberalisms" of the United States and Europe, respectively, Islamic liberalism emphasizes *both* the liberty of the community *(ummah)* from occupation and oppression, and at the same time the liberty of the individual within the community. Nor does it conflate the latter with the former: Like classical libertarians such as Frédéric Bastiat, Ludwig von Mises, or Friedrich von Hayek, Islamic liberalism places explicit emphasis on limited government, individual liberty, human dignity, and human rights. "Moderate Islam" is another description often used for the ideas and representative figures that I have in mind. But "moderate" does not precisely capture the pervasive ideological orientation suggested here. The main pillars of Islamic liberalism are:

Liberty *(hurriya)*—Human beings are created free and must remain free; freedom of thought, freedom of religion, and freedom of movement are essential to life as envisaged by our creator. Without freedom, life and religion have no meaning and no flavor. God, in his unlimited wisdom, intended human beings to be free; free to believe or disbelieve and free to practice or not practice. It is wrong and counterproductive to impose religion on people, and it is also against the will of God.

Justice *(adl)*—Equality before God must translate into equality on earth. Only God can be the judge of who is best among us. Justice must be upheld for everyone—man or woman, Muslim or non-Muslim, friend or foe, Arab or non-Arab. Justice means that every human being is treated fairly and equally by society and by the government. Injustice toward a single human being is an injustice toward all and an affront to the Almighty God.

Consultation *(shura)*—God is against oppression and dislikes oppressors. The affairs of the community and the society must be decided through mutual consultation and consent. Consultation must include all members of the community and must be binding on the rulers or officeholders. Prophet Mohammad, who died without designating a ruler, indicated to his companions that they must elect the ruler themselves and that the ruler must be held accountable to them.

Rational interpretation *(ijtihad)*—God has prescribed important goals for believers to achieve on earth (such as *shura,* justice, freedom, dignity, and peace). However, the way to achieve these objectives is mostly left up to Muslims themselves, who must decide using reason, knowledge, and faith what is best for them and for their community. Islam has no clergy and no hierarchy, and therefore all Muslims must voice their opinion, in light of the teachings of Islam and the changing needs and priorities of society. It is vital for the Muslim *ummah* today that the doors of *ijtihad*—closed for some 500 years—be reopened.

There are *many* scholars and leaders for this growing movement in the Muslim world, although they are not well known in the West. They include Tarek al-Bichri and Saleem al-Awwa (Egypt), Mohamed Talbi (Tunisia), Anwar Ibrahim (Malaysia), Fathi Osman, Aziza al-Hibri, and Abdulaziz Sachedina (United States), Shafeeq Ghabra (Kuwait), Abdelwahab El-Affendi (Sudan), Nurcholish Madjid (Indonesia), Ibrahim al-Wazir (Yemen), and Abdul Karim Soroush (Iran).

## Why Is It Silent?

The good news is that liberal Islam represents the overwhelming majority within the Muslim world today. The bad news is that it is a silent majority—or perhaps more accurately, a *silenced* one. There are two minority groups in the Muslim world that are fighting, literally, over political control: secular extremists and religious extremists. For the most part, secular extremists are in power, as they have been for the last 50 years, but they have lost legitimacy largely because of their unabashed and relentless efforts to impose their views on society. The religious extremists also want to impose their views, but many of them are in jail, or in hiding. They are not in power, except in two or three countries. They have also lost legitimacy because they advocate violence. Between these two extremes, we find the majority of the people, who want to practice their religion faithfully, but who also want to live in the modern age; that is, they want a modern, moderate, and appropriate interpretation of Islam.

## Is Liberal Islam Likely to Grow?

In the long run, yes, because it is the only alternative that combines faith and reason. In the short run, it depends: Liberal Muslims are caught between a rock and a hard place. The rock is the state (and its internal police forces, or *mukhabarat*) in the oppressive form it predominantly takes in the Muslim world, which is constantly pounding society in general. These states do not like liberal Islam because it threatens the corrupt status quo that they sustain. Because these states often do not distinguish between liberal and fundamentalist Islam, they tend to perceive religion itself as a threat. In the Muslim world, the state has often taken the stand that you are "with us or against us," and if you try to criticize it in any way, you are automatically seen as a threat and silenced. The hard place is the aggregation of fundamentalist groups who want to monopolize Islam. These groups accuse anyone talking of moderation, patience, legitimacy, reason, and pragmatic thinking of being un-Islamic or anti-Islam. The religious authorities in most Muslim countries have little credibility because they so often accede to the enormous pressure they are under either to side with the state or to side with the fundamentalists.

The key to the success of liberal Islam is more freedom. Lack of freedom in Muslim countries is stifling society, preventing any debate on what is wrong with the Muslim world today. You add to the lack of freedom a loss of dignity, a sense of hopelessness and despair, and you have a fertile ground for all kinds of extremism and violence. Hence, the solution is to allow liberal Islam to grow, which means radically expanding freedom of the press, freedom of religion, freedom of thought, and freedom to form independent organizations. This is, of course, the essence of democracy.

Some claim that the Muslim world needs the rule of law, but not necessarily democracy. It is impossible to separate the two; ultimately, you cannot have rule of law without democracy. When the law comes from an illegitimate government, it is illegitimate, and its enforcement—in the absence of independent branches of government—leads to dictatorship.

The transition to democracy may take a few years. But it must be real, it must be sustained, and it must be irreversible. Governments in the Muslim world have become adept at promising democratic reforms while delivering more oppression. And this has created an environment of great disappointment and frustration.

The international community needs to exert sustained pressure on the existing governments to allow more freedom, because it is in their own interest and in that of their societies, as well as in the interest of peace and stability in the world. Of course, they will scream and complain of interference and demand that their "sovereignty" be respected. But we must insist, because this is the only way out of the terrible situation that we all find ourselves in.

Moderate and liberal Muslims should be allowed to have a voice. Repressive regimes must not be allowed to use the war on terrorism to silence all opposition or to lump all Islamists together. Those who advocate extremism and violence are the enemies of mankind and of Islam and must be stopped before they bring havoc and mayhem to their own countries and to the world. Real and genuine reforms are needed, and liberal and moderate voices cannot be heard in an environment of fear and repression.

The international community should make democratic reforms in the Muslim world a priority. As a start, the United States and European countries must stop supporting dictators in the name of stability. We all know that the stability provided by dictators is an illusion that only breeds violence and extremism. To promote peace and strengthen the voices of liberal Islam, Muslim countries must gain experience with democratic institutions and practices. Experience with democracy will allow Islamic movements to become more moderate and adapt their visions, thoughts, and strategies to the needs of their societies and the requirements of the twenty-first century. The contrasting examples of Turkey and Algeria are very telling in this regard. Staunchly secular Turkey allowed Islamists to participate in the political process and thus is on the road to becoming a model democratic state in the Muslim world. Algeria, however, chose to crack down harshly on its Islamist party in 1992 and is still recovering from a ten-year-old civil war, which has resulted in the deaths of more than 150,000 people and the radicalization of Islamist groups around the world.

## A Glimmer of Hope

Liberal Islam is thriving and well in the United States and in Europe. Many free-thinking Muslims who could not tolerate the repressive environments of their own countries have escaped to the West, where they now live in freedom. They represent significant groups that can, and I believe will, play a major role in modernizing Islam and in promoting liberal and moderate views of Islam in the Muslim world. The reformation of Islam will require freedom and democracy, and right now, the only place where we have them is in the West. It is for this reason that I believe reformation will begin in the West. Muslims who live in the West are an important asset for liberal Islam, for all those who share its goals of peace, freedom, and democracy, and ultimately for the Muslim world itself.

It is imperative that U.S. Muslims play a leading role in reforming the Islamic world, principally by spreading understanding among Muslims generally, and their leaders in particular, of the values and merits of democracy. Friends of Islam and, indeed, everyone who hopes for peace and interfaith harmony should do all they can to support liberal Islam, the nascent voice of the Muslim world's silenced majority.

# 27

# FAITH AND MODERNITY

### Laith Kubba

*Laith Kubba is senior program officer for the Middle East at the Na-
tional Endowment for Democracy. He was the director of the
international program of the Al-Khoei Foundation in London and the
founder of the Islam 21 project. He has been an active participant in a
number of Iraqi democratic organizations and has served on the boards
of such regional institutions as the Arab Organization for Human Rights
and the International Forum for Islamic Dialogue. This essay originally appeared in the April 2003 issue of the* Journal of Democracy.

In assessing the nature of "liberal Islam" and its political prospects, we
must of course devote careful scrutiny to the adjective that we are attaching to "Islam," for the term "liberal" has many meanings. Moreover,
as Abdou Filali-Ansary indicates in his essay, there is an even more
fundamental question that must be defined when we examine the idea
of "liberal Islam"—namely, what is "Islam"? The importance of this
question can scarcely be understated. All too often, it is answered on
the basis of seriously misleading assumptions about what is "naturally"
the case that liberal Muslims must challenge or, as it were, "denatural-
ize" if they are to win the hearts and minds of their coreligionists around
the world.

There is an unfortunate tendency among certain critics as well as
certain supporters of the Muslim religion to conflate Islam as such with
all sorts of attributes, practices, and institutions that are in fact quite
exogenous to it. It is common, for example, to hear Islam equated with
*shari'a* law, or *shari'a* with Islam. In this way, "Islam" has become a
code word for such a wide range of ideas and things that its true meaning—within the Muslim world no less than outside it—has become
almost completely obscured, suppressed, or lost. Among the sad results
of this loss is the ease with which those who would naysay any new
turn within the religion can do so simply by calling such a path "inau-
thentic." This is so whether the naysayers see themselves as critics or as

supporters of Islam. In the face of this situation, we must clarify what authenticity truly means. A good way to start is to distinguish between the *core message* of Islam on the one hand, and on the other the often-problematic *baggage* that has come, over the course of centuries, to cluster around that message.

In trying to identify liberal, modernist, or—to use Filali-Ansary's term—enlightened Muslims, it is essential to ask: How should one define Islam? Does one look to the whole of the historical heritage and body of traditions that Muslims have inherited, or does one look to the revelation upon which all Muslims agree? To speak of Muslims is to speak of a vast number of people—almost a billion or more these days, and growing—from many countries, often with distinct heritages and traditions. To speak of the Koran is to speak of the one single book upon which the unity of the Muslim faith depends. The relationship between these diverse heritages and traditions, on one hand, and the revelation that unites all Muslims, on the other, is far from straightforward. To sort it out, one must know: What are the defining sources of Islam? This is a highly controversial issue among Muslims, and yet it is also a question that any serious defender (or any serious student, for that matter) of the liberal or modernist Muslim position cannot avoid asking.

A second and no less essential question is how Muslims deal with the sources that they take to be definitive of Islam. When we Muslims look to the revelation of the Koran and seek, as it were, to "translate" or "mediate" its message for the modern world—not just as it touches on our personal lives but as it relates to our social and political arrangements as well—how do we think about this translation or mediation? Do we accept all the historical baggage, all the interpretations that have been built up over the centuries in reference to the revelation of the Koran, as somehow authoritative over it? Given that at least some of these interpretations conflict with each other, do we have a way of fully and nonarbitrarily identifying any *one* of them with the authority of the Koran itself? Or do we, alternatively, understand these interpretations and narratives of Muslim history in a genuinely *historical* way—that is, relative to the circumstances in which they are written? This is a second key question, the answer to which profoundly determines our understanding of what it means to implement Islam in the modern world, and which is essential in defining who is a liberal or modernist Muslim and who is not.

My own view—and that of many others, including those involved in a very laudable project called Islam 21 *(www.islam21.net)*—is that the defining source of Islam is revelation itself. While there are profound sources of Islamic *inspiration* beyond the Koran and down through history—and while these sources must be taken seriously by anyone interested in the *meaning* of Islam—Islamic *authority* is the Koran's alone. The world's Muslim traditions have been formed under the deep influence of scripture; and it is certainly important to come to terms with the different messages and claims that have been variously derived from that influence. Scripture has *influenced* these traditions, even *formed* them, if you like. But it has not *sanctified* them, and it is a mistake to think that it has done so. Unless we diverge from what has for too long been taught among the *ulama*—unless we get beyond the outdated epistemology that underlies this teaching and the rationalizations for theological authority that derive from it—we risk not only retarding the political momentum of liberal Islam, but also impeding access to the true meaning of Islam itself.

## The Clash of Attitudes

Given these points of divergence, how do they relate to the sort of nascent liberal evolution that is now taking place in the understanding and practice of Islam in public life in some quarters of the Muslim world? This question may turn partly on the prospects for liberal interpretations of scripture, but I think that it is more accurate to say that it turns on the prospects for *modern* interpretation of scripture; indeed, I think it turns on Muslim attitudes about modernity as such.

In this respect, we can identify two contemporary tendencies among Muslims: First, there is a *secularist* persuasion. Advocates of this view see the modern world in a positive light but also see modernity and Islam as inimical, and typically promote the former over the latter. This school of thought is famously prominent in Turkey, of course, but it also influences many other Muslim countries, and it has shown its advantages and limitations. But it is not the modernist tendency with the greater momentum. That momentum belongs to a second tendency: Muslims who insist that if we are to come to terms with the modern world, we must not abandon ourselves to a point of view that is wholly external to Islam in doing so.

If we look more closely at this second tendency, we can see within it a further division between two approaches. The first—which now predominates on the ground but is in fact the more intellectually and politically problematic—sees the modern world and what it offers negatively. It claims to embrace modernity but on distinctly "Islamic" terms. This is an implicit contradiction that cannot be resolved without addressing it at the core: In order to modernize our institutions, we Muslims must do more than grudgingly resign ourselves to modernity. Rather, we must embrace modernity's contributions to the common heritage of humanity and try to make the best of what modernity has to offer. As it happens, the trail that leads to the modern world has been blazed by Western countries. Yet modernity's benefits ought to be accepted not because they are Western, but because they are good and relevant.

A great many Muslims have a problem with this because 1) modernity's terms of reference have not evolved from within our own heritage, and 2) because there is a perception of political conflict with the West, a perception that has grown largely out of a recent history of colonization. There is an ongoing bundle of issues associated with that history which exacerbates this anti-Western attitude and generates the well-known incoherence of wanting modernity's benefits (regardless of their original historical provenance) while at the same time condemning modernity itself as a "Western import" or a "foreign imposition."

The second approach—still nascent, but full of possibility—tries to address these issues more subtly and from a standpoint that rises above the grievances issuing from colonialism. In this view, tracing exactly where and how modern modes and orders evolved is less important than weighing their intrinsic merits. Aware of Islamic civilization's great and many contributions to the world, this approach seeks to take advantage of the best that humanity has to offer, precisely for the sake of pursuing such high Islamic ideals and virtues as truth, justice, charity, brotherhood, and peace.

A final point of divergence in trying to define who is a liberal or a modernist among Muslims lies in their attitudes regarding relations between tradition on the one hand, and politics or public life on the other. Here as elsewhere, we Muslims have too often conflated regional or local custom with Islam itself. A fundamental distinction needs to be made between the message of Islam and all the historical traditions that have accumulated around it over the years, not only in Arabia but throughout the world. All of these traditions have been conditioned by their times, by their human limitations, and they should not be confused with Islam itself.

As it is with respect to specific manifestations of religion, so it is with respect to the relationship between religion and public life. Here too, the traditions of interpretation that have grown up around Islam are not themselves sanctified by Islam. Muslims accordingly can and should approach these traditions in a spirit of liberty, modernizing them, adapting them, stretching them. And they can do so from within an authentically Muslim framework, while at the same time taking their lead from the West in some respects, because there is nothing in the origins and nature of Islam itself that precludes doing so.

Take, for example, the role of women—or to be more precise the segregation of men and women that has been practiced so ubiquitously throughout Muslim history. There is no justification at all for this in our religion's original message. It has come from extra-Islamic cultural sources, been transposed into an Islamic idiom, and labeled with the name of Islam. Again, if we refer to the Koran, I can have one copy and nobody worldwide will disagree with what that copy says. But if we refer to *shari'a* law there is no holy book called *Shari'a*. And if we refer to Muslim traditions, there is no specific collection of Muslim traditions. There are only collections. They have a flavor of Islam, and they have certainly come to relate themselves to, and often define themselves in terms of, Islam; but they need not be dealt with by faithful Muslims as coextensive with Islam or as sharing in its sanctity.

This is no less true when it comes to questions of government and politics. For many Muslims, the model of the first Islamic community that came into being after the *hajj* to Medina in 622 C.E. provides the conceptual framework for any Islamic political order. Indeed, the very name Medina is symbolic of an ideal: The town's pre-Islamic name was Yathrib, and it became known by its current name of al-Medina (which means "the city" in Arabic) as a token of its importance in Islamic history. For this reason, it is quite poignant, I think, to consider what *modern* Medina is, how this city has evolved over time, what it has become. Thus considered, Medina makes an excellent reference point for thinking about liberal Islam. It has been 28 years since I first visited Medina in 1975, but when I think of what I saw there even then, I wonder about what civic life must have been like during the early Muslim centuries, and what it is like now in that complex, cosmopolitan metropolis that remains one of the holiest places in the Islamic world.

Thinking about the Medina of old helps us to grasp the political concepts and principles that were at work during the seedtime of Islam, but in no way can that bygone city provide—nor was it ever meant to—a method of running the complex cities, states, and societies in which we live today. There is nothing in specifically Muslim history—not even the Ottoman Empire, which was multinational, religiously very tolerant by the standards of its time, and also the most recent Muslim society to rank as what we today would call a superpower—that can fully prepare us for the political and social challenges and opportunities that we Muslims face in the contemporary world.

Yet there is much in our faith and its legacy of ethical reflection and action that can guide us, even if our history hands us no ready-made recipes. Liberal, modernist Muslims look at modernity and see an opportunity as well as a challenge. To take advantage of the former, they know that they must confront the latter. Buoyed by their faith and ready to give their best in thought, word, and deed, they accept these twin historic tasks, the challenge no less than the opportunity, with confidence born out of a desire to secure for the nearly one-fifth of the world's population that is Muslim full access to all that is worthy in the common heritage of humankind.

# 28

# ISLAMISTS AND THE POLITICS OF CONSENSUS

*Daniel Brumberg*

**Daniel Brumberg** *is associate professor of government at Georgetown University and a visiting scholar at the Carnegie Endowment for International Peace during the 2002–2003 academic year. He has been a visiting fellow at both the U.S. Institute of Peace and the International Forum for Democratic Studies. This essay originally appeared in the July 2002 issue of the* Journal of Democracy.

One of the greatest barriers to illuminating political Islam is the belief that Islam demands a specific form of politics. Although some might think this idea no longer holds sway, it has lately reappeared in the guise of cultural relativism. Thus two scholars of Islam argue, "In Islamic history, there are a number of very important concepts and images. . . . These are the foundations for the Islamic perception of democracy . . . [based on] core concepts . . . central to the political position of virtually all Muslims."[1] While "the definition" of these concepts "varies" and thus is not fixed, most Muslims are said to aspire to a culturally authentic "Islamic democracy" whose core trait is a consensual rather than a win-or-lose vision of democratic politics.[2]

This is a dubious thesis. To say that someone is Muslim tells us little about that person's concept of democracy. Moreover, the supposition that Muslim identity trumps all others is erroneous. Muslims may be secular, traditional, or orthodox; they may also think of themselves as belonging to ethnic groups—Kurds in Iraq, Turkey, Iran, and Syria; or Berbers in Morocco and Algeria—whose customs and values can take precedence over Islamic identity. In short, political identity is not necessarily shaped by religion. Indeed, while Islamists invariably speak in the language of "authenticity," their Islam is a *political construct* that borrows from both Western and Islamic political thought. Because the resulting amalgam of ideas and symbols points in many and even contradictory directions, in no sense can it be said that the Islamic faith itself requires consensual politics.

This does not mean that some form of consensual politics would be inappropriate. Indeed, democracy in the Islamic world might well fare best where political institutions, rules, and procedures allow all (or most) voices to be represented. But this has little to do with Islam. Indeed, if Islam guaranteed a high level of consensus, it would in fact provide an ideal basis for majoritarian democracy, that is, one in which those who lose elections sit in opposition while those who win exercise legitimate political power. It is precisely the *absence* of unity that requires political institutions emphasizing agreement and cooperation. Power-sharing is necessary not only because Muslims differ as to the most beneficial relationship of mosque and state but also because such divisions often provoke concerns that election victors will impose their particular vision of Islam on others. By promising inclusion, power-sharing could allay such fears in ways that promote accommodation. Hence the key questions: Will Islamists share power with groups that espouse alternative notions of political community? What conditions will help or hinder consensus-based politics?

## Autocracy with Democrats

Writing in 1972, when Arab nationalism still overshadowed Islamism, Iliya Harik remarked that the central problem in the Arab world is "the imposition of uniformity on a pluralistic social reality, with nationalism as the mold and reality as the mosaic."[3] In their efforts to press the cause of unity, Islamists have a clear advantage over Arab nationalists: Islamists speak for a monotheistic faith that inspires the loyalty of most Muslims. Inasmuch as Islam evokes the ideal of one *ummah* or community, it offers an array of symbols that Islamists can use to legitimate unitary—or what I call *harmonic*—ideologies and programs.

Some hold that this quest for unity is so intrinsic to Islamism that it virtually precludes the forging of pluralistic power-sharing pacts. Thus John Waterbury writes that Algeria's Islamic Salvation Front (FIS) "in no way resembles [Poland's] Solidarity." The latter struck an agreement with General Jaruzelski because Solidarity's aims focused on the pragmatics of economic and political power rather than existential issues such as religious identity. But unlike Solidarity, Islamists "do not oppose, or wish to replace, incumbent power blocs because they are undemocratic but because they have no sense of mission."[4] This crusade to ensure that the state's primary mission is to guarantee one overarching ideology has invariably alarmed women's organizations, ethnic minorities such as Berbers and Kurds, secular intellectuals and professionals, and of course military officers, who have gladly invoked such fears to justify autocracy. The resulting alliance between potential democrats and police states offers an inverted image of political reform in Eastern Europe and the Third World. In the latter cases, none-too-

democratic elites nonetheless found democratic institutions and procedures useful for dealing with regime-versus-opposition conflicts, thereby
paving the way for "democracy without democrats." In the Middle East,
by contrast, fear of Islamist victories has produced "autocracy *with* democrats," as key groups that might choose democracy absent an Islamist
threat now actively support or at least tolerate autocrats. As one secular
Algerian said of his country's 1992 coup, "when faced by a choice between FIS's Ali Belhadj and General Khaled Nezzar, I chose the
general."[5]

Even a brief look at Arab states suggests how pervasive this logic is.
In Iraq, Syria, and Bahrain, ethnoreligious minorities have enforced
autocracies in part because they fear the consequences of democratization. This anxiety has grown in direct proportion to the length of their
incumbency. The longer they have used repression to survive, the more
autocrats rightly fear that reform will lead to their being toppled or even
killed. The military-based regimes in Egypt and until recently Algeria
(though that could change again) are stuck in the same trap. While their
rulers are, for the most part, Sunni Muslims and thus do not represent
ethnoreligious minorities, their efforts to narrow the scope of democratic participation have sometimes received tacit support from key
groups that fear the consequences of full-fledged democratization. Yet
by quarantining both Islamist and secular voices, these regimes have
fettered potential democrats while alienating Islamists who might favor
accommodation. Even rulers who might accept reform are stymied amid
the increasing political isolation that results from this strategy, and are
finding it harder and harder to climb out of the very hole into which
they have helped to dig themselves.

Although the picture seems bleak, it is not without some brighter
spots. In Kuwait, both Islamist and secular members of parliament have
maintained an uneasy détente with the royal family since 1992. In Turkey, the moderate Islamist Justice and Development (Adl wal Tanmiya)
party won 363 seats in the 550-member Grand National Assembly in
November 2002. In Algeria, a multiparty coalition dominated by the
two government-oriented parties includes two Islamist parties that together won 27 percent of the seats in the 1997 National People's
Assembly elections. Further afield, in Indonesia, several Islamist parties have shared power in a succession of fractious cabinets since the
June 1999 elections. And in Morocco and Bahrain, Islamists made gains
in parliamentary elections in the fall of 2002. There may be a trend
toward inclusion, even if most of the regimes that have made room for
Islamists are unlikely to allow a leap from hobbled pluralism to competitive democracy.[6]

Which states are more likely to dig themselves out of autocracy rather
than get buried by it? Those scholars who argue that Islam is intrinsically illiberal, or who define away the problem by offering relativist

concepts of "Islamic democracy," offer little in the way of explanation, and of prediction still less. Yet instrumentalist accounts that reduce Islamism to little more than a source of rationalizing ideologies are equally limiting. Islamist ideologies may be "constructed," but they are shaped by and encapsulated within a *multitude* of ideal social, political, and cultural identities and interests that can contradict as well as complement one another. Thus the challenge is not to figure out whether Islamism is "essentially" democratic versus autocratic, or liberal versus illiberal. Instead, it is to see whether this or that Islamist group is acting within a hegemonic political arena where the game is to shut out alternative approaches, or else within a competitive—let's call it *dissonant*—arena where Islamists, like other players, find themselves pushed to accommodate the logic of power-sharing.

What do I mean by "dissonant"? Consider Lebanon: There the ideological, cultural, and political divisions between and within the Islamic and Christian communities have been institutionalized in a consociational system that not only offers all key groups representation but, just as important, creates constraints that make it unlikely that any one Islamist group will have either the means or the inclination to impose a single ideological vision on the state. Thus while Lebanon's Hezbollah is not, philosophically speaking, a champion of pluralism, in practice its leaders do not and *cannot* favor the imposition of an Islamic state. While one might argue that the decisive constraint on Hezbollah is the presence of Syrian troops, even absent this check it is difficult to imagine Hezbollah pursuing a hegemonic project, since doing so would surely spark another civil war (a war that Hezbollah's leaders know they cannot win, and which could draw Syrian or Israeli involvement). In short, a dissonant political field has this paradoxical quality: It invites competition and conflict, but can also create incentives for sharing power.

Lebanon is not the only example of dissonance in the Islamic world. The tendency to treat it as an exceptional case is a consequence of many factors, not least of which is the culturalist account of Islamism critiqued above. But the failure to grasp fully the political significance of dissonance also reflects a poverty of sociological imagination. For as Arend Lijphart argues, identity cleavages come in many forms: religious, ethnic, linguistic, social, and even ideological.[7] Viewed through this expansive prism, we can see dissonance even in countries whose leaders have denied its existence. Consider Algeria, where despite decades of rule by a single party that spoke in the name of *le peuple,* society is a mosaic of crosscutting and overlapping cleavages based on clans, ideology (Islamism versus secularism, state socialism versus the market), and ethnicity (Berbers versus Arabs). The effort to repress these differences led to autocracy (1962–88), to a failed experiment in pluralistic politics (1989–91), to the bloody civil war that exploded after the army pulled the plug on elections in 1992, and finally to a regime which,

since 1997, has tried to institutionalize dissonance by selectively incor-
porating Islamist, Berber, secular-democratic, and military-bureaucratic
groups through a controlled system of party representation.

Algeria's urgent attempt to create a more competitive playing field
reminds us that the mere existence of social, cultural, or ideological
differences is insufficient to create ideological and political dissonance.
Instead, a dissonant political arena is a product of a lengthy state-building dynamic that institutionalizes competing visions of community in
different organizations, associations, or political parties. However autocratic, such *dissonant states* create a multipolar arena that abets
competition and negotiation. By contrast, *harmonic states*—meaning
those which attempt to create unity or its appearance through repression, cooptation, or distraction—create a unipolar field that can easily
become a place for deadly games of "winner takes all" between rulers
and their opponents.[8]

We can readily trace the implications of these contrasting dynamics
for politics in predominantly Muslim countries. By distancing themselves from the cultural, religious, or ideological project of any one
group, dissonant states not only serve as arbiters of competing identities; more decisively, they leave institutional and ideological legacies
that make it difficult for any one Islamist party to impose its views on
the state itself. This competitive field opens up the space for negotiating power-sharing arrangements. By contrast, harmonic states not only
coopt or repress rival Islamist voices and institutions; through schools,
media, and government-controlled mosques, such states spread an image of themselves as the supreme representative of a united cultural
community that by its very nature lives in peace. The more successfully
they spread this utopian vision, the more likely it is that harmonic states
will spawn the very Islamist radicals who then bitterly damn such states
for shirking their duty to champion "the Arab nation" or "the Islamic
*ummah*." And once radicals fill the ideological and institutional vacuum,
the space for accommodation can get fatally narrow. Algeria learned
this lesson the hard way. Saudi Arabia—the harmonic Islamic autocracy *par excellence*—must constantly suffer allegations from its clergy
that it has failed to carry out its holy mission.

## Contrasting Indonesia and Algeria

While dissonant states create incentives for power-sharing and harmonic states produce the opposite, statecraft can play a vital role in
determining whether leaders will reap the benefits of dissonance or minimize the liabilities of hegemony. To appreciate the interplay of
state-building legacies and statecraft, we can briefly consider the cases
of Indonesia and Algeria.

Indonesia is the Islamic world's best example of dissonant state building. While 90 percent of its 228 million people are Muslims, since roughly 1900 its society has been marked by two overlapping ideological and institutional divides: between nationalists and Muslims, and between Muslims and other Muslims. The latter cleavage emerged in the 1920s as a reaction to the creation of Muhammadiyah, a movement inspired by Arab reformists that sought—much to the chagrin of rural Javanese Muslims—to rid Islam in Indonesia of pre-Islamic or Sufi-mystical practices. Rural Muslims responded to this illiberal project by creating the Awakening of Traditional Religious Leaders (Nahdatul Ulama or NU). NU's leaders held that the only way to defend their 40 million members from the "modernizing" impulse of Muhammadiyah was to embrace the principle that the state could never serve as a vehicle of Islamization. Although some Islamists sought to transform Indonesia into a hegemonic state, by the 1970s a dissonant political field was the firm reality.

So long as President Suharto (1967–98) enforced this ban, NU backed him. But when he began flirting with Islamist autocrats in the early 1990s, NU began pushing for democracy. Abdurrahman Wahid was one of several Islamic leaders who moved NU toward pluralism, winning support from younger people in both NU and Muhammadiyah. By the late 1990s, the political arena featured Islamist autocrats and Islamist pluralists, secular nationalists, and the military, a secular if illiberal force in Indonesian politics. When Suharto fell in 1998 and reform got underway, the new party system reflected the three-way split of nationalists, Islamist pluralists, and Islamist autocrats. Wahid and his party steered between the first and the second of these three groups, thus emerging as a key power broker. But after Wahid was elected president in October 1999, he failed to capitalize on the legacy of dissonance he had inherited. Although a democrat, he responded to the efforts of other Islamist and secular leaders to influence (or manipulate) his policies by dismissing potential rivals from the cabinet. His erratic statecraft led to his resignation in July 2001.

On becoming president, Vice-President Megawati Sukarnoputri formed a cabinet with leaders from all the major parties. Yet this effort to sustain power-sharing faces obstacles, not least of which is a severe economic crisis that is eroding support for moderate Islamic parties. Moreover, Wahid's resignation has undercut his party's capacity to serve as a balancer between Megawati's secular-nationalist base and the more autocratic Islamist parties. Hamzah Haz, a former leader of one of the latter groups, is now vice-president. He is currently supporting the call of several small Islamist parties to insert language in the 1945 Constitution that effectively favors the application of Islamic law *(shari'a)*. This effort will probably fail because most Indonesians, including many pious Muslims, oppose it. Yet many doubt that Megawati has the leadership skills to ensure that Indonesia's experiment in pluralistic power-sharing will survive.

Algeria offers a telling contrast to Indonesia. I have already alluded to the recent Algerian civil war as the paradoxical and tragic fruit of a longstanding harmonic state. Some argue that had the FIS taken power in 1992, the Islamists' political and economic incompetence would have cured Algeria of its lingering taste for utopia. After all, a significant part of the FIS support was a protest vote, not an endorsement of Islamism. Yet the same could be said about Iran in 1979. In both cases, Islamist elites and their well-organized backers sought a hegemonic state. Had the FIS prevailed, it might have followed in the footsteps of the Islamic Republic of Iran by building control mechanisms strong enough to survive the inevitable discrediting of its utopian ideology. As Iran's more recent experience demonstrates, even the most profound legitimacy crisis may fail to undermine a state's autocratic institutions.

Algeria's current leaders have concluded that they cannot rule without a modicum of legitimacy, or in total defiance of their country's multivocal social and ideological fabric. Since the 1997 parliamentary elections, they have tried to invent a dissonant political order by promoting a multiparty government that includes two Islamist parties, the Renaissance Movement and the Movement for a Peaceful Society. While both benefit from government patronage, the latter has garnered a measure of credibility as an advocate for an Islamic alternative that repudiates violence and the notion of an Islamic state. Yet embedding dissonance at this late date is not easy: Recent polls show that 48 percent of voters attribute little credibility to the party system.[9] State-controlled inclusion of Islamists is certainly preferable to total exclusion, but unless rulers have the ingenuity and guts to give opposition parties real power, this tactic may invite frustration rather than enhance legitimacy. Forward-looking statecraft is thus essential, a point that Algeria's leaders will want to keep in mind as they struggle to transcend a legacy of conflict whose final chapter is not yet written.


## NOTES

1. John L. Esposito and John O. Voll, *Islam and Democracy* (Oxford: Oxford University Press, 1996), 23. Esposito repeats this argument, albeit more equivocally, in *Unholy War: Terror in the Name of Islam* (Oxford: Oxford University Press, 2002), 145.

2. John L. Esposito and John O. Voll, *Islam and Democracy,* 18–19, 28–29. The authors would like to have it both ways by arguing that the definition of Islamic concepts varies, but that an Islamic notion of democracy proceeds from a perception of politics intrinsic to Islam and thus *distinct* from Western notions of democracy. For example, on page 26 they write that the Muslim "perception of the 'caliph' becomes a foundation for concepts of human responsibility…" (that provides) "a basis for distinguishing between democracy in Western and Islamic terms." Elsewhere they discuss "local democratic traditions" there are "often consensual rather than majoritarian," (22), or to be more precisely, a concept of *ijma* or "consensus" which "can become both the legitimation and the procedure for an Islamic democracy" (29). These assertions clearly

favor a culturalist view of Islam. Indeed, if the definition of the core Islamic concepts they identity were infinitely malleable then the concept of an "Islamic democracy" would be meaningless.

3. Iliya F. Harik, "The Ethnic Revolution and Political Integration in the Middle East," *International Journal of Middle East Studies* 3 (July 1972): 310.

4. John Waterbury, "Democracy Without Democrats? The Potential for Political Liberalization in the Middle East," in Ghassan Salamé, ed., *Democracy Without Democrats? The Renewal of Politics in the Muslim World* (London: I.B. Tauris, 1994), 39.

5. Interview, Algiers, 18 February 2002.

6. Thomas Carothers, "The End of the Transition Paradigm," *Journal of Democracy* 13 (January 2002): 5–21.

7. Arend Lijphart, *Democracy in Plural Societies: A Comparative Exploration* (New Haven: Yale University Press, 1977).

8. For an elaboration of this argument, see Daniel Brumberg, "Dissonant Politics in Iran and Indonesia," *Political Science Quarterly* 116 (Fall 2001): 381–411.

9. "Près de la moitié des Algériens désespèrent des parties politiques," *www.algeria-interface.com/new/article.php?rub=2* (access date 29 April 2002).

# 29

# AN EXIT FROM
# ARAB AUTOCRACY

*Vickie Langohr*

**Vickie Langohr** *is assistant professor of political science at the College of the Holy Cross in Worcester, Massachusetts. She has published essays in the on-line version of the* Middle East Report *as well as in the* International Journal of Middle East Studies *and* Comparative Studies of South Asia, Africa, and the Middle East. *This essay originally appeared in the July 2002 issue of the* Journal of Democracy.

In the aftermath of September 11, Arab politics have come under unprecedented scrutiny in the West. As the unremittingly authoritarian nature of Arab regimes has come into ever sharper focus, this lack of democracy is decried as a cause of anti-regime and anti-Western violence at the same time that it is depicted as the only reliable short-term shield against the exact same phenomena. Arab autocracies, it is argued, encourage violence domestically by blocking peaceful change, and export violence by using state-controlled media to deflect demands for accountability with propaganda against the United States, Jews, or the West. These same autocracies, however, must be supported because they are all that blocks the rise to power of even more viciously authoritarian and illiberal groups. Since the Arab world lacks popular ultranationalist movements, the most likely candidates for the category of illiberal challengers are Islamist parties, whose presumed commitment to Islamic law *(shari'a)* renders them debatable defenders of democracy at best.

Scholars unwilling to write the Arab world off as congenitally inhospitable to democracy generally advocate one of two gradual paths for the exit from autocracy. Both start from the same assumption—that if free elections were held today, Islamist parties would win, either because many Arab voters support them or because opponents would be inadequately mobilized to defeat them. The first proposed exit from this situation is an economic one—delay meaningful democratization until economic development creates middle classes, widely thought to foster liberal democracy and hinder extremism. The second approach focuses on politics. Instead of opening the floodgates of political competition all at once, the offer of gradual inclusion in the political system should be used to induce Islamists to moderate their more objectionable, illiberal goals—or at least to secure a commitment that their goals will not be implemented extraconstitutionally. Inclusion breeds moderation, we are told, and Islamists who reject undemocratic behavior in exchange for inclusion will be transformed, like Western Europe's postwar communists, from destabilizing antisystem parties into accepted representatives of a legitimate ideological trend.

The suggestion that substantive democratization be put off until middle classes develop is of limited usefulness. On the one hand, its assumption that middle classes do not support Islamists is belied by Islamist successes in the elections within middle-class professional syndicates; on the other, the growth of strong middle classes in several Arab countries has not made regimes any more willing to devolve power democratically. Western pressure is needed to push Arab autocracies toward a phased-in democratic opening designed to strengthen opposition parties.

## The Current State of Arab Islamist Politics

Islamist parties have been allowed to organize and compete openly in Jordan, Kuwait, Lebanon, Morocco, the Palestinian Authority, and Yemen. Their participation has been much more heavily restricted in North Africa. In Algeria, the military staged a coup in January 1992 to forestall the all-but-certain victory of the Islamic Salvation Front (FIS) in the second round of legislative elections. The FIS remains banned, though two other Islamist parties have been permitted to contest elections. In Tunisia, when the Mouvement de la Tendance Islamique (MTI) announced plans to form a political party in 1981, its leaders were summarily imprisoned. A brief 1986 amnesty was followed by further repression, and after members running as independents captured 14 percent of the vote in the 1989 parliamentary elections, the MTI's leader went into exile and hundreds of members were tried before military tribunals.[1] Repression of the MTI continues apace, with Human Rights Watch reporting in 2002 that MTI members, convicted almost exclusively for participation in "unauthorized" peaceful activities and not for violence, account for most of Tunisia's political prisoners.[2] The Egyptian government has been somewhat more lenient with the Muslim Brotherhood, allowing Brothers to run for parliament as independents while doing all it can to undermine their chances, often through police repression.

The histories and social origins of the Islamist parties that have been allowed to compete are quite diverse. Jordan's Muslim Brotherhood and Yemen's Islah party have always been firmly part of "the system." The Jordanian Brotherhood competed in parliamentary elections in the 1950s and 1960s and again after parliament's reinstatement in 1989, while Islah's leader heads the most powerful tribal confederation in the country. The two other large Islamist parties permitted to compete—Hezbollah in Lebanon and Hamas in Palestine—have quite different origins. Hezbollah grew out of the severely impoverished Shi'ite community in Lebanon. While neither Islah nor the Jordanian Brotherhood has been associated with violence, Hamas and Hezbollah mount attacks against Israel, and in their early years both used force against fellow citizens to enforce their conception of Islamic norms, with Hamas supporters attacking unveiled women in Gaza, and Hezbollah destroying bars. For the past few years, however, neither group has used force against its domestic foes. Hezbollah says that it has foresworn civil strife in favor of peaceful politicking. Skeptics have their doubts, but after the May 2000 Israeli withdrawal from South Lebanon left Hezbollah fighters in total control of the area, they made no move to impose their will on southern Christians and others. Instead, the party has won praise for its emphasis on reconciliation across religious lines in the war-ravaged area.

The Islamist parties that have been allowed open participation therefore run the gamut from those that have always been part of "the system" to parties that have much more aggressively challenged the status quo. It is interesting to note that, in contrast to the case of more peaceful movements like the Muslim Brotherhood in Egypt and the Tunisian MTI, which have worked valiantly to be included, the possibility that Hamas and Hezbollah would *not* be allowed to participate does not appear even to have been considered. Sectors of Lebanese society strongly opposed to Hezbollah's Islamist agenda respect its resistance to Israeli occupation in the South, and both groups' commitment to helping their societies through extensive networks of social services seems, even to many of their detractors, to have won them a place at the political table. Despite their widely varying origins and histories, Islamist parties across the region, whether legal or excluded from formal politics, generally seek to 1) expose official corruption and 2) rid the public sphere of practices deemed incompatible with Islam, such as the drinking of alcohol or the intermixing of boys and girls in school. Contrary to popular perception, activism regarding the Arab-Israeli conflict is not a priority for many Islamist parties, especially those in countries that share no border with Israel. Even in Egypt, the most high-profile anti-Israeli campaigns are waged by the secular left. Other than Hamas and Hezbollah, only the Jordanian Brothers make it a priority to oppose various Israeli or American actions, but in this they differ little from secular Jordanian politicians.

## Is the Middle Class the Answer?

It is far from clear that rising middle classes will, in and of themselves, lead to voter moderation and political openings. Several Arab societies already have substantial middle classes, and they often vote in large numbers for conservative Islamist parties like the Muslim Brotherhood to represent them in their professional syndicates. The Muslim Brothers, for example, dominated the most prestigious syndicates in Egypt, including those of the lawyers and doctors, for much of the late 1980s and the 1990s. Still more importantly, we know from Latin America and other regions that even a preponderant middle class is not enough by itself to trigger democratization. Tunisia, for instance, is the most literate (almost 70 percent can read) and arguably the most solidly middle-class country in the Arab world,[3] but still has a markedly authoritarian political system in which meaningful opposition is banned, critical media are silenced, and torture is widespread. Authoritarian regimes can suppress middle classes just as successfully as poorer ones, but middle classes inexperienced in organizing and mobilization can be much more easily marginalized than more radical groups if these regimes are overthrown. While the mere existence of middle classes is no guarantee of democracy, a gradual opening of the political system is the most reliable path to successful democratization, in part because it improves the chances that non-Islamists from the middle *and other* classes will compete successfully against Islamists.

It is worth mentioning here that, even if free elections were held immediately, it is still far from certain that Islamists would win. Those who doubt this proposition typically cite the case of Algeria, where in the early 1990s the regime allowed, within the space of one year, free competition for municipal and national legislative elections. The Islamic Salvation Front (FIS) then took 54 percent of the vote for local and regional assemblies and won 188 of 232 seats on the first ballot for the legislature before the military preempted the second round.[4] The argument that the coup was the lesser of two evils is belied by the horrific civil war that followed and has killed as many as 100,000 people. While the coup is often justified by the need to protect Algerian women from the FIS's regressive gender-related policies, it is not clear that these policies, had they been enacted, would have created a worse climate for women than that fostered by the ensuing war, during which as many as 2,600 women have been raped or sexually assaulted.[5]

As disastrous as the Algerian situation has been, however, evidence from other Arab countries suggests that it may be unique. Islamists elsewhere have never won more than 30 percent of the seats in the legislative elections that they have been allowed to contest—a feat achieved by Jordan's Islamic Action Front (IAF) in 1989. In Yemen, where elections are freer and Islah wins support not only because of its Islamist program but also because its leader heads the country's most powerful tribe, the party won only 20.6 percent of the seats in the 1993 Consultative Assembly and 17.6 percent in 1997. In Lebanon, where a consociational formula allots Shi'ite Muslims 27 out of 128 parliamentary seats, Hezbollah supporters won just a dozen seats in 1992 and ten in 1996.

The possibility of Islamist victories in free elections would probably drop further were non-Islamist parties freer to organize and mobilize. Across much of the Arab world, the vast majority of the non-Islamist opposition contests elections as independents. In Jordan in 1989, independents won 57 percent of the seats while no opposition party other than the IAF won more than 4 percent. In Yemen in 1997, independents won 54 seats, Islah won 53, and the next largest party won three. This trend toward independent candidacies saps the opposition's potential, preventing the formation of programmatic agendas behind which parties can build consistent support and encouraging candidates to make ethnic or tribal appeals that fragment the electorate. Authoritarian rule promotes the independent-candidacy trend by blocking the formation of new parties with potentially broad appeal. The Egyptian Political Parties Commission has approved only one new party in the last 20 years. Autocracy also encourages centrifugal tendencies in already-weak secular opposition parties that, with little influence and few spoils, have little reason to stick together. Finally, it is important to note that while Arab authoritarian regimes repress Islamists with particular venom, the restrictions they place on political life hurt secular parties much more than Islamist ones. Secular parties prevented from public mobilization and denied television time have few other channels to connect with potential supporters, whereas Islamists can always use the much-harder-to-control mosque to get their message across.

## A Plan for Gradual Democratization

Any gradual democratization, then, should be structured to increase the strength of parties, which will redound to the relative advantage of currently weak secular parties. An obvious place to start would be by increasing the power of Arab legislatures. Except in Lebanon, Arab parliaments do not rule, and executives are not chosen through free and fair elections. The most logical way to begin democratizing these systems would be to lower the stakes of the transition by increasing the competitiveness of the parliament while initially maintaining executive dominance. While this could be done through the adoption of proportional representation—almost all Arab regimes have some version of winner-take-all systems—the more important step would be to allow opposition parties freedom of movement and mobilization and guaranteed access to television during campaigns. Although a parliament with strong opposition parties would naturally present a more effective challenge to the executive, institutional changes are also needed. A good first step would be to make prime ministers, now almost always made and unmade by executives, elected by and responsible to their parliaments. Finally, after parties have had an opportunity to develop their strength in the newly less-restricted parliaments for two or three election cycles, free and fair competition for executive office should be allowed.

How would this come about? The West and the United States do not dictate the course of Arab domestic politics, but they do have enormous leverage. To the extent, moreover, that Western governments fund repressive Arab regimes, they are complicit in the maintenance of authoritarian rule and the human rights violations it entails. Access to coveted preferential trade agreements and eligibility for foreign aid should be leveraged to ensure Arab regimes' implementation of gradual plans for democratization. Western governments first need to declare their understanding that regimes which defend autocracy by crying "The Islamists are coming!" are in fact crying wolf. Every regime that has invoked the Islamic threat in hopes of forestalling Western pressure for democratization has subsequently revealed its true intentions by brutally repressing opposition of all stripes.

Three years ago, U.S.-based scholars and a former U.S. ambassador to Tunisia praised the regime's crackdowns on Islamists as essential to its "emerging democracy."[6] They failed to note that after outlawing the MTI in the early 1990s, the regime quickly moved to stifle all protest. A prominent politician from the opposition Socialist Democratic Movement was returned to prison in mid-1991 after publicly opposing the president's attempts to change the constitution in order to seek a fourth term. A civil court judge disgusted by regime control of the judiciary wrote an open letter claiming that Tunisian judges "render verdicts dictated to them by political authorities,"[7] and Tunisia's president has been singled out by the Committee to Protect Journalists as one of the ten worst enemies of the press worldwide in three of its last four annual contests, a ranking bested only by China's Jiang Zemin.[8] The Egyptian government has headed in the same direction—after winning a pass from the United States on democratization by waving the Islamist card, it attacked human rights groups and NGOs and used repression and fraud to increase the government-controlled share of parliamentary seats from 68 percent in 1987 to 88 percent currently.

What is needed is Western pressure on Arab autocracies to adopt phased-in democratic openings that are designed to strengthen opposition parties and that have clearly specified stages and a plan for completion of full democratization within three electoral cycles. If Arab autocrats are not pressured to democratize now, they may, having blocked all channels for peaceful protest, fall violently later. This is by no means a given, but what is certain is that when such takeovers do occur, the most radical elements win, and Western supporters of past autocracies pay a high price. It is worth remembering that Iran in the 1970s had a large middle class which produced some of the first opponents of the shah's regime. The shah's brutal rule, however, had barred the middle class from organizing, and attempts to set up a liberal democratic successor regime were crushed by the onslaught of more radical groups, who repaid decades of U.S. support for the shah with attacks on Americans around the globe. Pressure now on Arab autocracies to move toward democratization is the best way to avert a repeat of this pattern.

## NOTES

1. Susan Waltz, *Human Rights and Reform: Changing the Face of North African Politics* (Berkeley: University of California Press, 1995), 71–72.

2. *Human Rights Watch World Report 2002: Tunisia (www.hrw.org/wr2k2/mena9.html).*

3. *U.S. Department of State Country Report on Human Rights Practies, Tunisia,* 2001 *(www.state.gov/g/drl/rls/hrrpt/2001/nea/8303.htm).* The State Department report notes that more than 60 percent of Tunisians can be said to be middle-class and enjoy a comfortable standard of living. *The United Nations Human Development Report, 2001,* reports Tunisia's adult literacy rate as 69.9 percent, well above those of other regional leaders *(www.undp.org/hdr2001/indicator/cty_f_TUN.html).*

4. Hugh Roberts, "From Radical Mission to Equivocal Ambition: The Expansion and Manipulation of Algerian Islamism, 1979–1992," in Martin E. Marty and R. Scott Appleby, eds., *Accounting for Fundamentalisms: The Dynamic Character of Movements* (Chicago: University of Chicago Press, 1991), 428–29.

5. For the toll of Algerians killed, "disappeared," and raped in the civil strife, see the U.S. State Department's Human Rights Report 2001 *(www.state.gov/g/drl/rls/hrrpt/ 2001/nea/8244.htm)* and the Human Rights Watch Country Report on Algeria for 2001 *(www.hrw.org/wr2k1/mideast/algeria.html).*

6. Mamoun Fandy, Moncef Cheikhrouhou, and Robert Pelletreau, "Tunisia's First Contested Presidential Elections," *Middle East Policy* 7 (October 1999).

7. This and the rest of this paragraph are based on the *Human Rights Watch World Report 2002: Tunisia (www.hrw.org/wr2k2/mena9.html).*

8. Only two other Arab leaders have made it onto the CPJ "enemies" list, and each of them only once: Egypt's Hosni Mubarak in 1999 and then-Jordanian prime minister Abd el-Salam al-Majali in 1998 *(www.cpj.org/enemies/enemies1998.html; www.cpj.org/ enemies/enemies_99.html; www.cpj.org/enemies/enemies_00.html; www.cpj.org/en- emies/enemies_01.html).*

# 30

# TERROR, ISLAM, AND DEMOCRACY

## Ladan Boroumand and Roya Boroumand

*Ladan Boroumand, a former visiting fellow at the International Forum for Democratic Studies, is a historian from Iran with a doctorate from the Ecole des Hautes Etudes en Sciences Sociales in Paris. She is the author of* La Guerre des principes *(1999), an extensive study of the tensions throughout the French Revolution between the rights of man and the sovereignty of the nation. Her sister Roya Boroumand, a historian from Iran with a doctorate from the Sorbonne, is a specialist in Iran's contemporary history and has been a consultant for Human Rights Watch. They are working on a study of the Iranian Revolution.*

"Why?" That is the question that people in the West have been asking ever since the terrible events of September 11. What are the attitudes, beliefs, and motives of the terrorists and the movement from which they sprang? What makes young men from Muslim countries willing, even eager, to turn themselves into suicide bombers? How did these men come to harbor such violent hatred of the West, and especially of the United States? What are the roots—moral, intellectual, political, and spiritual—of the murderous fanaticism we witnessed that day?

As Western experts and commentators have wrestled with these questions, their intellectual disarray and bafflement in the face of radical Islamist (notice we do not say "Islamic") terrorism have become painfully clear. This is worrisome, for however necessary an armed response might seem in the near term, it is undeniable that a successful long-term strategy for battling Islamism and its terrorists will require a clearer understanding of who these foes are, what they think, and how they understand their own motives. For terrorism is first and foremost an ideological and moral challenge to liberal democracy. The sooner the defenders of democracy realize this and grasp its implications, the sooner democracy can prepare itself to win the long-simmering war of ideas and values that exploded into full fury last September 11.

The puzzlement of liberal democracies in the face of Islamist terrorism seems odd. After all, since 1793, when the word "terror" first came into use in its modern political sense with the so-called Terror of the French Revolution, nearly every country in the West has had some experience with a terrorist movement or regime. Why then does such a phenomenon, which no less than liberal democracy itself is a product of the modern age, appear in this instance so opaque to Western analysts?

Islamist terror first burst onto the world scene with the 1979 Iranian Revolution and the seizure of the U.S. embassy in Tehran in November of that year. Since then, Islamism has spread, and the ideological and political tools that have helped to curb terrorism throughout much of the West have proven mostly ineffective at stopping it. Its presence is global, and its influence is felt not only in the lands of the vast Islamic crescent that extends from Morocco and Nigeria in the west to Malaysia and Mindanao in the east but also in many corners of Europe, India, the former Soviet world, the Americas, and even parts of western China.

Before the Iranian Revolution, terrorism was typically seen as a straightforward outgrowth of modern ideologies. Islamist terrorists, however, claim to fight on theological grounds: A few verses from the Koran and a few references to the *sunna* ("deeds of the Prophet") put an Islamic seal on each operation. The whole ideological fabric appears to be woven from appeals to tradition, ethnicity, and historical grievances both old and new, along with a powerful set of religious-sounding references to "infidels," "idolaters," "crusaders," "martyrs," "holy wars," "sacred soil," "enemies of Islam," "the party of God," and "the great Satan."

But this religious vocabulary hides violent Islamism's true nature as a modern totalitarian challenge to both traditional Islam and modern democracy. If terrorism is truly as close to the core of Islamic belief as both the Islamists and many of their enemies claim, why does international Islamist terrorism date only to 1979? This question finds a powerful echo in the statements of the many eminent Islamic scholars and theologians who have consistently condemned the actions of the Islamist networks.

This is not to say that Islamic jurisprudence and philosophy propound a democratic vision of society or easily accommodate the principles of democracy and human rights. But it does expose the fraudulence of the terrorists' references to Islamic precepts. There is in the history of Islam no precedent for the utterly unrestrained violence of al-Qaeda or the Hezbollah. Even the Shi'ite Ismaili sect known as the Assassins, though it used men who were ready to die to murder its enemies, never descended to anything like the random mass slaughter in which the Hezbollah, Osama bin Laden, and his minions glory.[1] To kill oneself while wantonly murdering women, children, and people of all religions and descriptions—let us not forget that Muslims too worked at the World Trade Center—has nothing to do with Islam, and one does not have to be a learned theologian to see this. The truth is that contemporary Islamist terror is an eminently modern practice thoroughly at odds with Islamic traditions and ethics.[2]

A striking illustration of the tension between Islam and terrorism was offered by an exchange that took place between two Muslims in the French courtroom where Fouad Ali Saleh was being tried for his role in a wave of bombings that shook Paris in 1985–86. One of his victims, a man badly burned in one of these attacks, said to Saleh: "I am a practicing Muslim. . . . Did God tell you to bomb babies and pregnant women?" Saleh responded, "You are an Algerian. Remember what [the French] did to your fathers."[3] Challenged regarding the religious grounds of his actions, the terrorist replied not with Koranic verses but with secular nationalist grievances.

The record of Saleh's trial makes fascinating reading. He was a Sunni Muslim, originally from Tunisia, who spent the early 1980s "studying" at Qom, the Shi'ite theological center in Iran. He received weapons training in Libya and Algeria, and got his explosives from the pro-Iranian militants of Hezbollah. In his defense, he invoked not only the Koran and the Ayatollah Khomeini but also Joan of Arc—who is, among other things, a heroine of the French far right—as an example of someone who "defended her country against the aggressor." After this he read out long passages from *Revolt Against the Modern World* by Julius Evola (1898–1974), an Italian author often cited by European extreme rightists. This strange ideological brew suggests the importance of exploring the intellectual roots of Islamist terrorism.[4]

## The Genealogy of Islamism

The idea of a "pan-Islamic"[5] movement appeared in the late nineteenth and early twentieth centuries concomitantly with the rapid transformation of traditional Muslim polities into nation-states. The man who did more than any other to lend an Islamic cast to totalitarian ideology was an Egyptian schoolteacher named Hassan al-Banna (1906–49). Banna was not a theologian by training. Deeply influenced by Egyptian nationalism, he founded the Muslim Brotherhood in 1928 with the express goal of counteracting Western influences.[6]

By the late 1930s, Nazi Germany had established contacts with revolutionary junior officers in the Egyptian army, including many who were close to the Muslim Brothers. Before long the Brothers, who had begun by pursuing charitable, associational, and cultural activities, also had a youth wing, a creed of unconditional loyalty to the leader, and a paramilitary organization whose slogan "action, obedience, silence" echoed the "believe, obey, fight" motto of the Italian Fascists. Banna's ideas were at odds with those of the traditional *ulema* (theologians), and he warned his followers as early as 1943 to expect "the severest opposition" from the traditional religious establishment.[7]

From the Fascists—and behind them, from the European tradition of putatively "transformative" or "purifying" revolutionary violence that began with the Jacobins—Banna also borrowed the idea of heroic death as a political art form. Although few in the West may remember it to-day, it is difficult to overstate the degree to which the aestheticization of death, the glorification of armed force, the worship of martyrdom, and faith in "the propaganda of the deed" shaped the antiliberal ethos of both the far right and elements of the far left earlier in the twentieth century. Following Banna, today's Islamist militants embrace a terrorist cult of martyrdom that has more to do with Georges Sorel's *Réflexions sur la violence* than with anything in either Sunni or Shi'ite Islam.[8]

After the Allied victory in World War II, Banna's assassination in early 1949, and the Egyptian Revolution of 1952–54, the Muslim Brothers found themselves facing the hostility of a secularizing military government and sharp ideological competition from Egyptian communists. Sayyid Qutb (1906–66), the Brothers' chief spokesman and also their liaison with the communists, framed an ideological response that would lay the groundwork for the Islamism of today.

Qutb was a follower not only of Banna but of the Pakistani writer and activist Sayyid Abu'l-A'la Mawdudi (1903–79), who in 1941 founded the Jamaat-e-Islami-e-Pakistan (Pakistan Islamic Assembly), which remains an important political force in Pakistan, though it cannot claim notable electoral support.[9] Mawdudi's rejection of nationalism, which he had earlier embraced, led to his interest in the political role of Islam. He denounced all nationalism, labeling it as *kufr* (unbelief). Using Marxist terminology, he advocated a struggle by an Islamic "revolutionary vanguard" against both the West and traditional Islam, attaching the adjectives "Islamic" to such distinctively Western terms as "revolution," "state," and "ideology." Though strongly opposed by the Muslim religious authorities, his ideas influenced a whole generation of "modern" Islamists.

Like both of his preceptors, Qutb lacked traditional theological training. A graduate of the state teacher's college, in 1948 he went to study education in the United States. Once an Egyptian nationalist, he joined the Muslim Brothers soon after returning home in 1950. Qutb's brand of Islamism was informed by his knowledge of both the Marxist and fascist critiques of modern capitalism and representative democracy.[10] He called for a monolithic state ruled by a single party of Islamic rebirth. Like Mawdudi and various Western totalitarians, he identified his own society (in his case, contemporary Muslim polities) as among the enemies that a virtuous, ideologically self-conscious, vanguard minority would have to fight by any means necessary, including violent revolution, so that a new and perfectly just society might arise. His ideal society was a classless one where the "selfish individual" of liberal democracies would be banished and the "exploitation of man by man" would be abolished. God alone would govern it through the implementation of Islamic law *(shari'a)*. This was Leninism in Islamist dress.

When the authoritarian regime of President Gamal Abdel Nasser suppressed the Muslim Brothers in 1954 (it would eventually get around to hanging Qutb in 1966), many went into exile in Algeria, Saudi Arabia,[11] Iraq, Syria, and Morocco. From there, they spread their revolutionary Islamist ideas—including the organizational and ideological tools borrowed from European totalitarianism—by means of a network that reached into numerous religious schools and universities. Most young Islamist cadres today are the direct intellectual and spiritual heirs of the Qutbist wing of the Muslim Brotherhood.

## The Iranian Connection

Banna and the Brotherhood advocated the creation of a solidarity network that would reach across the various schools of Islam.[12] Perhaps in part because of this ecumenism, we can detect the Brothers' influence as early as 1945 in Iran, the homeland of most of the world's Shi'ites.

Returning home from Iraq that year, a young Iranian cleric named Navab Safavi started a terrorist group that assassinated a number of secular Iranian intellectuals and politicians. In 1953, Safavi visited Egypt at the Brothers' invitation and presumably met with Qutb. Although Safavi's group was crushed and he was executed after a failed attempt on the life of the prime minister in 1955, several of its former members would become prominent among those who lined up with the Ayatollah Khomeini (1900–89) to mastermind the Islamic Revolution of 1979.

Khomeini himself first took a political stand in 1962, joining other ayatollahs to oppose the shah's plans for land reform and female suffrage. At this point, Khomeini was not a revolutionary but a traditionalist alarmed by modernization and anxious to defend the privileges of his clerical caste. When his followers staged an urban uprising in June 1963, he was arrested and subsequently exiled, first to Turkey, then to Iraq. The turning point came in 1970, when Khomeini, still in Iraq, became one of the very few Shi'ite religious authorities to switch from traditionalism to totalitarianism. Much like Mawdudi,[13] he called for a revolution to create an Islamic state, and inspired by Qutb, he condemned all nontheocratic regimes as idolatrous. His followers in Iran were active in Islamist cultural associations that spread, among others, the ideas of Qutb and Mawdudi. Qutb's ideology was used by Khomeini's students to recapture for the Islamist movement a whole generation influenced by the world's predominant revolutionary culture—Marxism-Leninism.

Khomeini became a major figure in the history of Islamist terrorism because he was the first truly eminent religious figure to lend it his authority. For despite all its influence on the young, Islamism before the Iranian Revolution was a marginal heterodoxy. Qutb and Mawdudi were theological dabblers whom Sunni scholars had refuted and dismissed. Even the Muslim Brothers had officially rejected Qutb's ideas. As an established clerical scholar, Khomeini gave modern Islamist totalitarianism a religious respectability that it had sorely lacked.

Once in power, the onetime opponent of land reform and women's suffrage became a "progressivist," launching a massive program of nationalization and expropriation and recruiting women for campaigns of revolutionary propaganda and mobilization. The Leninist characteristics of his rule—his policy of terror, his revolutionary tribunals and militias, his administrative purges, his cultural revolution, and his accommodating attitude toward the USSR—alienated the majority of his fellow clerics but also gained him the active support of the Moscow-aligned Iranian Communist Party, which from 1979 to 1983 put itself at the service of the new theocracy.

Khomeini's revolution was not an exclusively Shi'ite phenomenon. Not accidentally, one of the first foreign visitors who showed up to congratulate him was the Sunni Islamist Mawdudi; before long, Qutb's face was on an Iranian postage stamp. Khomeini's successor, Ali Khamenei, translated Qutb into Persian.[14] Khomeini's own interest in creating an "Islamist International"—it would later be known by the hijacked Koranic term Hezbollah ("party of God")—was apparent as early as August 1979.

## The Islamist "Comintern"

As these ties suggest, Islamism is a self-consciously pan-Muslim phenomenon. It is a waste of time and effort to try to distinguish Islamist terror groups from one another according to their alleged differences along a series of traditional religious, ethnic, or political divides (Shi'ite versus Sunni, Persian versus Arab, and so on). The reason is simple: *In the eyes of the Islamist groups themselves, their common effort to strike at the West while seizing control of the Muslim world is immeasurably more important than whatever might be seen as "dividing" them from one another.*

The Lebanese-based, Iranian-supported Hezbollah is a case in point. Its Iranian founder was a hardcore Khomeini aide who drew his inspiration from a young Egyptian Islamist—an engineer by training, not a theologian—who was the first to politicize what had been a purely religious term. A closer look at the organization reveals the strong influence of Marxism-Leninism on the ideology of its founders and leadership. The group's current leader, Mohammad Hosein Fadlallah, influenced by Marx's and Nietzsche's theories on violence,[15] has openly advocated terrorist methods and tactical alliances with leftist organizations.[16] Hezbollah is a successful creation of the Islamist "Comintern." "We must," says Sheikh Fadlallah, "swear allegiance to the leader of the [Iranian] revolution and to the revolutionaries as to God himself," because "this revolution is the will of God."[17] One indication of the extent of this allegiance is the fact that all the negotiations over the fate of the hostages held in Lebanon ended up being carried out by Tehran. Similarly, the head of Iran's Revolutionary Guards boasted about having sponsored the attack against French and American peacekeeping forces in Lebanon.[18] Hezbollah's chief military planner, Imad Mughaniyyah, is an Arab who operates from Iran. Western intelligence agencies suspect that Hezbollah has been working with bin Laden on international operations since the early 1990s.[19] Hezbollah's terrorist network in Lebanon contains both Shi'ite and Sunni groups, and there is also a Saudi Arabian wing that was involved in the Khobar Towers bombing, which killed 19 U.S. troops in 1996.

Also inspired by the Iranian Revolution was the independent Sunni terrorist network that later became the basis of al-Qaeda. The Tehran regime began forming propaganda organs to sway opinion among Sunni religious authorities as early as 1982.[20] Among the supranational institutions created was the World Congress of Friday Sermons Imams, which at one time had a presence in no fewer than 40 countries. The overarching goal of these efforts has been to mobilize the "Islam of the people" against the "reactionary Islam of the establishment."[21] For a variety of reasons this network has remained loosely organized, but all of its branches spring from and are fed by the same ideological taproot.

The influence of Iran's Islamist revolution was also cited by the members of Egyptian Islamic Jihad who gunned down President Anwar Sadat in October 1981. Their theoretician was an engineer, Abdessalam Faraj, who was also fond of quoting Qutb to justify terror.[22] The conspirators—including the junior army officers who did the actual shooting—were inspired by the Iranian model, and expected the death of Sadat to trigger a mass uprising that would replay in Cairo the same sort of events which had taken place two years earlier in Tehran[23] (where the Iranian authorities would subsequently name a street after Sadat's killer). Among those imprisoned in connection with the plot was a Cairo physician named Ayman al-Zawahiri. He became Egyptian Islamic Jihad's leader after serving his three-year prison term, met bin Laden in 1985, and then joined him in Sudan in the early 1990s. Zawahiri, who would become al-Qaeda's top operational planner, is reported to have said publicly that Osama is "the new Che Guevara."[24]

The Islamization of the Palestinian question is also partly due to Khomeini's influence on the Palestinian branch of Islamic Jihad. Its founder was another physician, this one named Fathi Shqaqi. His 1979 encomium *Khomeini: The Islamic Alternative* was dedicated to both the Iranian ruler and Hassan al-Banna ("the two men of this century"). The first press run of 10,000 sold out in a few days.[25] Shqaqi, who was of course a Sunni, had nonetheless traveled to Tehran to share the Friday sermon podium with Ali Khamenei, denouncing the Mideast peace process and accusing Yasser Arafat of treason.[26]

## Distorting Islam's History and Teachings

As these examples show, such distinctions as may exist among these terrorist groups are overshadowed by their readiness to coalesce and collaborate according to a common set of ideological beliefs. These beliefs are properly called "Islamist" rather than "Islamic" because they are actually in conflict with Islam—a conflict that we must not allow to be obscured by the terrorists' habit of commandeering Islamic religious terminology and injecting it with their own distorted content. One illustration is the Islamists' interpretation of the *hijra*—Mohammad's journey, in September 622 C.E., from Mecca to Medina to found the first fully realized and autonomous Islamic community *(ummah)*. Despite a wealth of historical and doctrinal evidence to the contrary, half-educated Islamists insist on portraying this journey as a revolutionary rupture with existing society that licenses their desire to excommunicate contemporary Muslim societies in favor of their own radically utopian vision.

The Islamic Republic of Iran also rests on heterodoxy, in this case Khomeini's novel and even idiosyncratic theory of the absolute power of the single, supreme Islamic jurisprudent *(faqih)*. It was not a coincidence that one of the first uprisings against Khomeini's regime took place under the inspiration of a leading ayatollah, Shariat Madari.[27] Officials of the regime have admitted that most Iranian clerics have always taken a wary view of Khomeinism. It is important to realize that the religious references which Khomeini used to justify his rule were literally the same as those invoked a century earlier by an eminent ayatollah who was arguing for the legitimacy of parliamentarism and popular sovereignty on Islamic grounds.[28] Koranic verses lend themselves to many different and even contradictory interpretations. It is thus to something other than Islamic religious sources that we must look if we want to understand Islamism and the war that it wages on its own society, a war in which international terrorism is only one front.

In a brief article on bin Laden's 1998 declaration of *jihad* against the United States, Bernard Lewis showed brilliantly how bin Laden travestied matters not only of fact (for instance, by labeling the invited U.S. military presence in Saudi Arabia a "crusader" invasion) but also of Islamic doctrine, by calling for the indiscriminate butchery of any and all U.S. citizens, wherever they can be found in the world. Reminding his readers that Islamic law *(shari'a)* holds *jihad* to be nothing but a regular war and subject to the rules that limit such conflicts, Lewis concluded, "At no point do the basic texts of Islam enjoin terrorism and murder. At no point do they even consider the random slaughter of uninvolved bystanders."[29]

What gives force to the terrorist notion of *jihad* invented by the Iranians and later embraced by bin Laden is not its Koranic roots—there are none—but rather the brute success of terrorist acts. Bin Laden has spoken with particular admiration of the Iranian-sponsored suicide truck bombing that killed 241 U.S. Marines and others in Beirut on 23 October 1983, precipitating the U.S. withdrawal from Lebanon.[30] Bin Laden was also not the first to think of setting up training camps for international terrorists—the Tehran authorities were there before him.[31]

A Friday sermon given in 1989 by one of these authorities, Ali Akbar Hashemi Rafsanjani, then president of the Islamic Parliament, reveals better than any other the logic of Islamist terrorism. Attacking the existence of Israel as another front in the pervasive war of unbelief *(kufr)* against Islam, Rafsanjani added:

> If for each Palestinian killed today in Palestine five Americans, English, or French were executed, they would not commit such acts anymore. . . . [T]here are Americans everywhere in the world. . . . [They] protect Israel. Does their blood have any value? Scare them outside Palestine, so that they don't feel safe. . . . There are a hundred thousand Palestinians in a country. They are educated, and they work. . . . [T]he factories that serve the enemies of Palestine function thanks to the work of the Palestinians. Blow up the factory. Where you work, you can take action. . . . Let them call you terrorists. . . . They [the "imperialism of information and propaganda"] commit crimes and call it human rights. We call it the defense of rights and of an oppressed people. . . . They will say the president of the Parliament officially incites to terror. . . . [L]et them say it.[32]

There is no reference here to religion; Rafsanjani's appeal is purely political. The West's offense he calls human rights; against it he urges Muslims to wield terror as the best weapon for defending the rights of an oppressed people. Rafsanjani, moreover, proudly commends "terror" by name, using the English word and not a Persian or Arabic equivalent. Thus he employs the very term that Lenin had borrowed from *la Terreur* of the French Revolution. The line from the guillotine and the Cheka to the suicide bomber is clear.

With this in mind, let us look for a moment at the French Revolution, where the modern concept of political terror was invented, to find the explanation that the Islamic tradition cannot give. When it announced its policy of terror in September 1793, the "virtuous minority" which then ran the revolutionary government of France was declaring war on its own society. At the heart of this war was a clash between two understandings of "the people" in whose name this government claimed to rule. One was a group of 25 million actually existing individuals, each endowed with inherent rights. The other was an essentially ideological construct, an abstraction, an indivisible and mystical body, its power absolute. The Terror of the French Revolution was neither a mistake nor an unfortunate accident; it was meant to purify this mystical body of what the terrorist elite regarded as corrupting influences, among which they numbered the notion that individual human beings had unalienable rights.[33]

The spokesmen of the Islamist revolution echo the terrorists of Jacobin France. The denigration of human rights marks the spot where the internal war on Muslim society meets the terrorist war against the West. Suffice it to hear bin Laden's comments on the destruction of the World Trade Center: "Those awesome symbolic towers that speak of liberty, human rights, and humanity have been destroyed. They have gone up in smoke."[34] Every Islamist terror campaign against Westerners during the last 20 years has had as its cognate an Islamist effort to tyrannize over a Muslim population somewhere in the world. Think of the ordeal to which the Taliban and al-Qaeda subjected the people of Afghanistan, or of what ordinary Algerians suffered during the savage Islamist civil wars of the 1990s. Or think of the state terror that daily labors to strangle any hope for recognition of human rights in Iran. To explore fully this correlation between terror against the West and tyranny against Muslims would take a separate essay. Yet we can get an idea of its nature by considering the first instance of Islamist terrorism against the United States, the 1979 hostage-taking in Tehran.

## Holding Democracy Hostage to Terror

As they released the hostages in January 1981, the Tehran authorities crowed over their victory, which Prime Minster Mohammad Ali Rajai called "the greatest political gain in the social history of the world" and an act that "had forced the greatest Satanic power to its knees." At first glance this claim might seem foolish, for the United States had said no to the revolutionary government's demands to hand over the shah and unfreeze Iranian assets. But a closer look shows that the Iranian Islamists had in fact scored a big political and ideological victory over both the United States and their domestic opponents, and thus had ample cause for jubilation.

The seizure of the U.S. embassy took place at a time when Khomeini and his allies had not yet consolidated their tyrannical regime. An Assembly of Experts was drafting the constitution of the Islamic Republic. Opposition was gaining strength daily in religious as well as in moderate secular circles. The Marxist-Leninist left, angered by a ban on its press, was growing restive. Open rebellions were breaking out in sensitive border regions populated by ethnic Kurds and Azeris. By sending in its cadres of radical students to take over the U.S. embassy and hold its staff hostage, the regime cut through the Gordian knot of these challenges at a single blow and even put itself in a position to ram through its widely criticized Constitution. Rafsanjani's assessment of what the act meant is instructive:

> In the first months of the revolution, the Washington White House decided in favor of a coup d'état in Iran. The idea was to infiltrate Iranian groups and launch a movement to annihilate the revolution. But the occupation of the embassy and the people's assault against the U.S.A. neutralized this plan, pushing the U.S. into a defensive stand.[35]

One could describe this version of the facts as a parody: The U.S. government in 1979 clearly had neither the will nor the ability to stage a coup against the Islamic Republic. But totalitarians typically speak an esoteric language of their own devising. Those who administered the Terror in revolutionary France painted some of their country's best-known republicans with the label "monarchist" before sending them off to be guillotined. The Bolsheviks called striking workers and the sailors of Kronstadt "bandits" and "counterrevolutionaries" before slaughtering them. In 1979, promoting human rights was a prominent aspect of how the United States described its foreign policy. By Rafsanjani's logic, therefore, any Iranian group that spoke of human rights was thereby revealing itself as a tool of the United States.

And indeed, as muddled negotiations over the hostages dragged on, the administration of President Jimmy Carter dropped any talk of supporting democracy in Iran[36]—the very cause for which Carter had taken the risk of ending U.S. support for the shah. Meanwhile, the revolutionary regime began using the Stalinist tactic of claiming that anyone who spoke in favor of a more representative government was really a U.S. agent.[37] With the hostage crisis, the Islamist regime was able to make anti-Americanism such a leading theme that Iranian Marxists rallied to its support, while Moscow extended its tacit protection to the new theocracy.

After the failure of the U.S. military's "Desert One" rescue attempt on 25 April 1980 and eight more months of negotiations, the United States at last succeeded in obtaining the release of the hostages. To do so, it had to agree to recognize the legitimacy of the Iranian revolutionary regime, and it had to promise not to file any complaints against Iran before international authorities, despite the gross violations of human rights and international law that had occurred. Though these concessions may have appeared necessary at the time, in retrospect we can see that they emboldened the Islamists to sink to new levels of hatred and contempt for the West and its talk of human rights. For had not the revolutionary students and clerics in Tehran forced the Great Satan to abandon its principles and brought it to its knees?

The terrorists accurately assessed the extent of their victory and drew conclusions from it. They used terror to achieve their goal, and upon the continued use of terror their survival depends. "[America] is on the defensive. If tomorrow it feels safe, then it will think to implement its imperialistic projects."[38] Among these projects are human rights, which a representative of the Islamic Republic denounced before the UN Human Rights Committee as an "imperialist myth."[39]

From the taking of the hostages in Tehran in 1979 until the terrorist attacks of last September, Western policy makers too often implicitly downgraded the claims of justice and shirked their duty both to their own citizens and to the cause of human rights by refusing to pursue the terrorists with any real determination. Considerations of "pragmatism" and "prudence" were put forward to justify a sellout of justice which, in one of the cruelest ironies revealed by the harsh light of September 11, proved not to have been prudent at all.

Since the impunity granted to the hostage-takers of Tehran, terrorist outrages have increased both in frequency and in scale. In addition to all the questions raised about security measures, intelligence failures, accountability in foreign-policy decision making, and the like, the atrocity of September 11 also forces citizens of democratic countries to ask themselves how strongly they are committed to democratic values. Their enemies may believe in a chimera, but it is one for which they have shown themselves all too ready to die. In the mirror of the terrorists' sacrifice, the citizens of the free world are called to examine their consciences; they must reevaluate the nature of their loyalty to fragile and imperfect democracy. In particular, the strongly solidaristic networks that the Islamist totalitarians have created should make citizens in democratic societies ask how much they and their governments have done to help prodemocracy activists who have been persecuted for years in Iran, in Algeria, in Afghanistan, in Sudan, and elsewhere. Unarmed, they stand on the front lines of the struggle against terror and tyranny, and they deserve support. Here is a moral, political, and even philosophical challenge upon which the minds and hearts of the West should focus.

## Whither the Muslim World?

Islamist terror poses a different but no less grave problem for those of us (including the authors of this essay) who come from Islamic countries, and it carries a special challenge for Muslim intellectuals. Public opinion in the Muslim world has largely—if perhaps too quietly—condemned the massacres of September 11. In Iran, young people poured spontaneously into the streets, braving arrest and police violence in order to hold candlelight vigils for the victims. But there were also outbursts of celebration in some Muslim countries, and sizeable anti-American demonstrations in Pakistan. Perhaps more disturbing still have been the persistent and widespread rumors going around Muslim societies that somehow an Israeli conspiracy was behind the attack. The force and pervasiveness of this rumor are symptoms of a collective flight from an uncontrollable reality. It is true that the Palestinian question is a painful and complicated one that requires an equitable solution. But it is equally true that reaching for foreign conspiracies has become an easy way of evading responsibility for too many of us from Muslim countries.

For the last several centuries, the Islamic world has been undergoing a traumatizing encounter with the West. Since this encounter began, our history has been a story of irreversible modernization, but also of utter domination on the one side, and humiliation and resentment on the other. To Muslim minds the West and its ways have become a powerful myth—evil, impenetrable, and incomprehensible. Whatever the Western world's unfairness toward Muslims, it remains true that Western scholars have at least made the effort to learn about and understand the Islamic world. But sadly, the great and brilliant works of the West's "Orientalists" have found no echo in a Muslim school of "Occidentalism."

We have been lacking the ability or the will to open up to others. We have opted for an easy solution, that of disguising in the clothes of Islam imported Western intellectual categories and concepts. In doing so we have not only failed to grasp the opportunity to understand the West, we have also lost the keys to our own culture. Otherwise, how could a degenerate Leninism aspire today to pass itself off as the true expression of a great monotheistic religion? The Islamists see themselves as bold warriors against modernity and the West, but in fact it is they who have imported.and then dressed up in Islamic-sounding verbiage some of the most dubious ideas that ever came out of the modern West, ideas which now—after much death and suffering—the West itself has generally rejected. Had we not become so alien to our own cultural heritage, our theologians and intellectuals might have done a better job of exposing the antinomy between what the Islamists say and what Islam actually teaches. They might have more effectively undercut the terrorists' claim to be the exclusive and immediate representatives of God on earth, even while they preach a doctrine that does nothing but restore human sacrifice, as if God had never sent the angel to stop Abraham from slaying his son.

Our incapacity to apprehend reality lies at the root of our paranoia. If we were to take a clear and careful look at the West, we would see that it draws its strength from its capacity for introspection and its intransigent self-criticism. We would know that Western culture has never stopped calling on us, on the figure of the stranger, to help it understand itself and fight its vices. When it could not find the other, it invented it: Thomas More imagined a faraway island called Utopia to mirror the social problems of his time; Michel de Montaigne couched his criticisms of French politics in the form of a conversation with an Indian chief from Brazil; and Montesquieu invented letters from a Persian tourist to denounce the vices of Europe.

Had we had our own eminent experts on Western civilization, we might know that the West is a diverse, plural, and complex entity. Its political culture has produced horrors but also institutions that protect human dignity. One of these horrors was the imperialism imposed on Muslim and other lands, but even that did as much harm to the Europeans themselves as it did to us, as anyone familiar with the casualty figures from the First World War will know. Our experts might have helped us understand that Qutb and Khomeini's denunciations of human rights were remarkably similar to Pope Pius VI's denunciation of the French Declaration of the Rights of Man of 1789. We might have grasped that, not long ago, Westerners faced the same obstacles that we face today on the road to democracy. Citizens in the West fought for their freedoms; in this fight they lost neither their souls nor their religion. We too must roll up our sleeves to fight for freedom, remembering that we are first and foremost free and responsible human beings whom God has endowed with dignity.

## NOTES

We would like to thank Hormoz Hekmat for his useful comments and critiques and Laith Kubba for providing some useful information.

1. Bernard Lewis, *The Assassins: A Radical Sect in Islam* (New York: Oxford University Press, 1987), 133–34.

2. On the heterodoxy of the Islamists' references to Muslim jurisprudent Ibn Taymiyya (1263–1328), see Olivier Carré, *Mystique et politique: Lecture révolutionnaire du Coran par Sayyid Qutb, Frère musulman radical* (Paris: Cerf, 1984), 16–17. On Ibn Taymiyya's theology and life, see Henri Laoust, *Pluralisme dans l'Islam* (Paris: Librairie Orientaliste Paul Geuthner, 1983).

3. This account of the Saleh case is based on reports in *Le Monde* (Paris), 8 and 10 April 1992.

4. For an overview of the career of Islamist terror networks, see Xavier Raufer, *La Nebuleuse: Le terrorisme du Moyen-Orient* (Paris: Fayard, 1987); Roland Jacquard, *Au nom d'Oussama Ben Laden: Dossier secret sur le terroriste le plus recherché du monde* (Paris: Jean Picollec, 2001); Yossef Bodansky, *Bin Laden: The Man Who Declared War on America* (Rocklin, Calif.: Prima, 1999); Gilles Kepel, *Jihad: Expansion et déclin de l'islamisme* (Paris: Gallimard, 2000); and Yonah Alexander and Michael S. Swetnam, *Usama Bin Laden's al-Qaida: Profile of a Terrorist Network* (New York: Transnational Publishers, 2001).

5. To confront Western colonialism, Muslim intellectuals and religious scholars such as Sayyid Jamal al-Din 'al-Afghani of Iran and Muhammad Abduh of Egypt concluded that a reformation and a new interpretation of Islam were needed in Muslim societies. The reforms that they advocated were aimed at reconciling Islam and modernity. They sought to promote individual freedom, social justice, and political liberalism. After the First World War, however, this movement was succeeded by one that was hostile to political liberalism. On Afghani, see Nikki K. Keddie, *An Islamic Response to Imperialism: Political and Religious Writings of Sayyid Jamal al-Din 'al-Afghani* (Berkeley: University of California Press, 1983). On Abduh, see Yvonne Haddad, "Muhammad Abduh: Pioneer of Islamic Reform," in Ali Rahnema, ed., *Pioneers of Islamic Revival* (London: Zed, 1994), 31–63.

6. This section draws on David Dean Commins, "Hassan al-Banna (1906–49)," in Ali Rahnema, ed., *Pioneers of Islamic Revival*, 146–47; as well as Richard P. Mitchell, *The Society of the Muslim Brothers* (London: Oxford University Press, 1969). See also Gilles Kepel, *Muslim Extremism in Egypt* (Berkeley: University of California Press, 1993).

7. Richard P. Mitchell, *The Society of the Muslim Brothers,* 29.

8. The widespread but mistaken impression that a Shi'ite cult of martyrdom serves as a religious inspiration for suicide attacks is one of the illusions about themselves that the terrorists skillfully cultivate. It is true that Shi'ites revere Hussein (d. 680 C.E.), the third Imam and a grandson of the Prophet, as a holy martyr. Yet Shi'ite teaching also enjoins the avoidance of martyrdom, even recommending *taqieh* ("hiding one's faith") as a way of saving one's life from murderous persecutors. Moreover, Sunnis are not noted for devotion to Hussein, and yet when it comes to suicide attacks, there is little difference between the Sunnis of al-Qaeda and the mostly Shi'ite cadres of Hezbollah. There are striking similarities between the Islamist justification for violence and martyrdom

and the discourse of German and Italian Marxist terrorists from the 1970s. On this subject see Philippe Raynaud, "Les origines intellectuelles du terrorisme," in François Furet et al., eds., *Terrorisme et démocratie* (Paris: Fayard, 1985), 65ff.

9. On Sayyid Abu'l-A'la Mawdudi, see Seyyed Vali Reza Nasr, *The Vanguard of the Islamic Revolution: The Jama'at-i Islami of Pakistan* (Berkeley: University of California Press, 1994); and Seyyed Vali Reza Nasr, *Mawdudi and the Making of Islamic Revivalism* (New York: Oxford University Press, 1996).

10. Olivier Carré, *Mystique et politique*, 206–7.

11. Muhammad Qutb, Sayyid Qutb's brother, was among the Muslim Brothers who were welcomed in Saudi Arabia. He was allowed to supervise the publication and distribution of his brother's works, and became ideologically influential in his own right: The official justification for the Saudi penal code uses his definition of secular and liberal societies as a "new era of ignorance." Exiled Muslim Brothers became influential in Saudi Arabia. Wahabism, the intolerant and fanatical brand of Islam that prevails in Saudi Arabia, was not in its origins a modern totalitarian ideology, but it provides fertile ground for the dissemination of terrorist ideology and facilitates the attraction of young Saudis to terrorist groups. See Olivier Carré, *L'utopie islamique dans l'Orient arabe* (Paris: Presses de la Fondation Nationale des Sciences politiques, 1991), 112–14; and Gilles Kepel, *Jihad*, 72–75.

12. Banna's followers recalled that he often said, "Each of the four schools [of Islam] is respectable," and urged, "Let us cooperate in those things on which we can agree and be lenient in those on which we cannot." Richard P. Mitchell, *The Society of the Muslim Brothers*, 217.

13. Sayyid Abu'l-A'la Mawdudi, *The Process of Islamic Revolution* (Lahore, 1955).

14. See Baqer Moin, *Khomeini: Life of the Ayatollah* (London: I.B. Tauris, 1999), 246.

15. Cited in Olivier Carré, *L'utopie islamique dans l'Orient arabe*, 197.

16. Cited in Olivier Carré, *L'utopie islamique dans l'Orient arabe*, 231–32.

17. Olivier Carré, *L'utopie islamique dans l'Orient arabe*, 232.

18. The then-head of the Iranian Revolutionary Guards, Mohsen Rafiqdoust, said that "both the TNT and the ideology which in one blast sent to hell 400 officers, NCOs, and soldiers at the Marine headquarters have been provided by Iran." *Resalat* (Tehran), 20 July 1987.

19. On 22 March 1998, the *Times of London* reported that bin Laden and the Iranian Revolutionary Guards had signed a pact the previous February 16 to consolidate their operations in Albania and Kosovo. Roland Jacquard adds that in September 1999, the Turkish intelligence services learned of an Islamist group financed by bin Laden in the Iranian city of Tabriz. See Roland Jacquard, *Au nom d'Oussama Ben Laden*, 287–88.

20. The first conference on the unification of Islamist movements was organized under Iranian auspices in January 1982. See the speeches of Khamenei and Mohammad Khatami (who is now the elected president of the Islamic Republic) in *Etela'at* (Tehran), 9 January 1982.

21. Xavier Rauffer, *La Nebuleuse*, 175.

22. Charles Tripp, "Sayyid Qutb: The Political Vision," in Ali Rahnema, ed., *Pioneers of Islamic Revival*, 178–79.

23. Gilles Kepel, *Jihad*, 122–23.

24. Roland Jacquard, *Au nom d'Oussama Ben Laden,* 76.

25. Gilles Kepel, *Jihad,* 187 and 579.

26. As reported in *Jomhouri-e Islami* (Tehran), 5 March 1994 (14 esfand 1372), 14 and 2.

27. Reported in the daily *Khalq-e Mosalman,* 4 and 9 December 1979.

28. M.H. Nad'ni, *Tanbih al-Omma va Tanzih al-mella* 5th ed. (Tehran, 1979), 75–85.

29. Bernard Lewis, "License to Kill: Usama bin Ladin's Declaration of Jihad," *Foreign Affairs* 77 (November–December 1998): 19. Bin Laden's declaration of *jihad* mentions Ibn Taymiyya's authority and yet clearly contradicts the latter's ideas on *jihad.* Ibn Taymiyya explicitly forbids the murder of civilians and submits *jihad* to strict rules and regulations. See Henri Laoust, *Le traité de droit public d'Ibn Taimiya* (annotated translation of *Siyasa shar'iya*) (Beirut, 1948), 122–35.

30. See "Declaration of war against the Americans occupying the land of the two holy places: A Message from Usama Bin Muhammad bin Laden unto his Muslim Brethren all over the world generally and in the Arab Peninsula specifically" (23 August 1996), in Yonah Alexander and Michael S. Swetnam, *Usama Bin Laden's al-Qaida,* 13.

31. In 1989, the vice-president of Parliament, Hojatol-Eslam Karoubi, proposed the creation of training camps for the "anti-imperialist struggle in the region." Quoted in the daily *Jomhouri-e Eslami* (Tehran), 7 May 1989, 9.

32. *Jomhouri-e Eslami* (Tehran), 7 May 1989, 11.

33. In this connection, it is worth noting that after the end of the Terror, the Declaration of the Rights of Man and the Citizen was not officially restored to constitutional status in France until 1946.

34. Howard Kurtz, "Interview Sheds Light on Bin Laden's Views," *Washington Post,* 7 February 2002, A12. Bin Laden gave this interview to Tayseer Alouni of the Arabic-language satellite television network al-Jazeera in October 2001.

35. Ali Akbar Hashemi Rafsanjani, *Enqelabe va defa'e Moqadass* (Revolution and its sacred defense) (Tehran: Press of the Foundation of 15 Khordad, 1989), 63–64.

36. Russell Leigh Moses, *Freeing the Hostages: Reexamining U.S.-Iranian Negotiations and Soviet Policy, 1979–1981* (Pittsburgh: University of Pittsburgh Press, 1996), 174–75.

37. In an interview that ran in the Tehran daily *Jomhouri-e Eslami* on 4 November 1981 to mark the second anniversary of the embassy seizure, student-radical leader Musavi Khoeiniha remarked that the neutralization of Iranian liberals and democrats was the hostage-taking's most important result.

38. Ali Akbar Hashemi Rafsanjani, *Enqelabe va defa'e Moqadass,* 64.

39. *Amnesty International Newsletter,* September 1982. The representative was Hadi Khosroshahi, another translator of Sayyid Qutb.

# INDEX